World without End

World without End

Economics, Environment, and Sustainable Development

David W. Pearce and Jeremy J. Warford

PUBLISHED FOR THE WORLD BANK
OXFORD UNIVERSITY PRESS

Oxford University Press

OXFORD   NEW YORK   TORONTO
DELHI   BOMBAY   CALCUTTA   MADRAS   KARACHI
KUALA LUMPUR   SINGAPORE   HONG KONG   TOKYO
NAIROBI   DAR ES SALAAM   CAPE TOWN
MELBOURNE   AUCKLAND
and associated companies in
BERLIN   IBADAN

© 1993 The International Bank for Reconstruction
and Development / THE WORLD BANK
1818 H Street, N.W.
Washington, D.C. 20433 U.S.A.

Published by Oxford University Press, Inc.
200 Madison Avenue, New York, N.Y. 10016

Manufactured in the United States of America

First printing January 1993

The findings, interpretations, and conclusions expressed in this study are entirely those of the authors and should not be attributed in any manner to the World Bank, to its affiliated organizations, or to members of its Board of Executive Directors or the countries they represent.

Library of Congress Cataloging-in-Publication Data

Pearce, David (David William) and Jeremy J. Warford
   World without end : economics, environment, and sustainable
development / David W. Pearce and Jeremy J. Warford
      p.   cm.
   Includes bibliographical references and index.
   ISBN 0-19-520881-1
      1. Sustainable development. 2. Economic development—
—Environmental aspects. 3. Environmental policy—Economic aspects.
I. Warford, Jeremy J. II. Title.
HD75.6.P433   1993
338.9—dc20   92-39551

CIP

Contents

Preface

THIS VOLUME IS THE OUTCOME of several years of research, fieldwork, and policy advice concerned with the rapidly growing subject of environmental economics in developing countries. We make no claim to originality of research and have borrowed freely from the existing literature. In at least two respects, however, this volume is unique.

First, it uses a great deal of material, such as background papers and research conducted for the World Bank, that is not readily available to the wider public. Indeed, most of the literature on the environment and economic development has not been published to date.

Second, we have synthesized the literature relevant to policy. No other book has attempted this to the extent we have done (see, however, Bojo, Mäler, and Unemo 1990). Our emphasis is on policy. The pure theory of environmental policy is similar in industrial and developing economies, and several good texts deal with it (for example, Pearce and Turner 1989; Tietenberg 1988).

We have tried to make the style and presentation accessible to a wide audience. To this end we have adopted an approach familiar to readers of the World Bank's *World Development Report*, perhaps the most indispensable annual guide to problems in developing countries—and which in 1992 had environment as its theme—and the World Resources Institute's *World Resources Report*, which contains the most powerful compilation of resource and environmental statistics (see World Bank 1992; World Resources Institute 1990).

Some of the chapters overlap. This is deliberate and, in fact, unavoidable. Since many readers may only want to read about a specific subject, such as population, poverty, market-based incentives, or tropical forests, we have attempted to make each chapter self-contained. We experimented with several sequences for the chapters and found that, regardless of the overall structure, we frequently had to share information among chapters to make each story coherent.

Environmental economics as a consolidated body of thought is perhaps twenty-five years old. Its application to developing countries is more recent. In both manifestations it is unfamiliar to many people, including professional economists. We have therefore tried to outline the basic theoretical underpinnings of the ideas being brought to bear on policy analysis in the environment and development nexus. Of necessity, the description of the theory is brief and superficial.

The approach throughout is that of the economist. This inevitably emphasizes certain types of solutions to environmental problems in the developing world. Although many other disciplines in the physical and behavorial sciences must be involved, we are convinced that solutions that neglect economics are not solutions at all and risk making problems worse, not better. We are also aware that our extensive use of World Bank material will not appeal to those who see the Bank as an agent of the wrong kind of development. We hope those who espouse different approaches will nonetheless read this book and subject their own views to the ultimate test: can they be implemented in practice?

Finally, many individuals have contributed to this volume by supplying material, commenting on drafts, and, over the years, by discussion and debate of the issues. We particularly wish to thank Richard Ackermann, Edward Barbier, Jean-Philippe Barde, Scott Barrett, Joanne Burgess, Herman Daly, John Dixon, Mohamed El-Ashry, Salah El Serafy, Robert Goodland, Stein Hansen, Vijay Jagannathan, Bindu Lohani, Bill Magrath, Karl-Goran Maler, Anil Markandya, Afsaneh Mashayekhi, Mohan Munasinghe, Raymond Noronha, Hans Opschoor, Zeinab Partow, Ken Piddington, Michel Potier, Visvanathan Rajagopalan, Robert Repetto, Julie Richardson, Robert Saunders, Emil Salim, Gunter Schramm, Walter Spofford, Andrew Steer, Tim Swanson, Kerry Turner, Herman van der Tak, five anonymous reviewers, and many, many others. We would also like to express our sincere gratitude to several people who assisted us in the arduous task of processing this manuscript, notably Valerie Edmundson, Elizabeth Forsyth, Rose Marie Fructuoso, Steven Georgiou, Virginia Hitchcock, and Nimalka Moonesinghe. Sue Pearce and Mercedes Warford bore with us throughout and provided moral support, without which this work could not have been completed. We are forever grateful.

PART ONE
Sustainable Development

1

Environment and Development:
An Overview

If poverty is to be reduced and the standard of living of the average person improved, economic growth must remain a legitimate objective of national governments and the world community. But most people are now painfully aware that pursuing economic growth without paying adequate attention to the environment—both built and natural—is unlikely to be sustainable: it cannot last. The issue, which is also the premise of this book, is how, not whether, to grow. Many disagree with us even at this level. They argue that limits to growth are set by the carrying capacity of the earth, particularly its capacity to receive more and more waste from the world's economic system. According to this analysis, sustainable growth is an illusion and sustainable economies are feasible only if growth is reduced, perhaps to zero or less, until an optimum level of economic output is achieved.

We share their belief in potential limits, even if humanity continues to discover new technologies. Rapid population growth, for example, can quickly negate the benefits of technology. We differ from the antigrowth school, however, in our belief that the limits can be avoided—that the world will not necessarily come to an end—if imaginative policies are devised and implemented. The basic idea is simple. The world economy is inextricably linked to the environment because societies must extract, process, and consume natural resources. All those resources must end up

3

as waste through the principles of mass and energy conservation. The quantitative link, the coefficient of environmental intensity, can, however, be reduced substantially. Because of this, the environmental impact of economic activity can be reduced even as the economy is allowed to grow.

Environmental intensity can be changed if we reappraise how we pursue economic growth. We must examine how we conserve energy and materials (ensure that materials and energy inputs are not wasted) and how we use technologies that lower the environmental intensity per unit of economic activity. Such technologies need to aim at source reduction; that is, they must avoid damage and economize on the amount of energy and materials used to produce the same amount of output over and above any reductions in wasteful use (conservation). Whatever the coefficient linking economic activity to environmental impact, damage can be avoided by preventing waste from entering the environment. Recycling materials is an example of damage avoidance, as is using flue gas desulfurization plants to remove sulfur oxides from burning fossil fuel.

Conservation and technology are the technical means to secure sustainable economic growth. The policy issue is, however, how to introduce them without having unacceptable effects on the process of using real income. Cleaner technologies, for example, are not free. The major theme running throughout this book is that there have to be incentives to conserve resources and incentives to change technology. Of course, a major incentive is to obey the law if failure to do so results in a major penalty. This is the so-called command-and-control solution. Command and control has been the main instrument for improving environmental quality and will continue to be of major importance in the future. The causes of much environmental degradation lie, however, in the workings of the economy and particularly in economic distortions that are part of government policies. Since the economy and the environment are so closely linked, policies aimed at achieving one social or economic objective inevitably affect the environment, even if this is not the intention of the policymaker. If the causes of environmental degradation lie in the workings of the economy, then so does the solution. Command-and-control measures may therefore only disguise the underlying causes. Throughout the book, we stress the need to investigate economic distortions and correct them on environmental grounds.

This book focuses on the problems facing developing countries. We argue that environmental quality is important in all nations, but especially in the poorest countries. We underscore this contention by showing that environmental degradation results in lost economic output, that is, lost gross national product (GNP), and that maintaining environmental quality and the supply of natural resources is fundamental for the health and well-being of all people. Thus poor water quality results in disease. Land degradation means less biomass for fuel and fodder and lost food output as soil quality declines (see below and chapter 2).

The sequence of the arguments may be summarized as follows.

- First, the environment is important to the economy and the well-being of all persons.
- Second, the causes of environmental degradation frequently lie in the workings, especially the mismanagement, of the economy.
- Third, solving environmental problems will involve correcting economic distortions and providing incentives for resource conservation and source reduction.

Economic incentives play an important role in resource conservation. Incentives can be enabling by, for example, defining property rights so that those who use a resource have an interest in conserving it for the future. Property rights thus replace uncertain ownership, which deters conservation. Incentives may take the form of price signals. Market prices may replace controlled or subsidized prices and reflect more clearly the private costs of production. As economies develop, the scope for social cost pricing can take the form of environmental taxes, tradable pollution permits, tradable resource quotas, and so on (see chapter 8). Incentive systems use the market or create markets in environmental assets. As such they wield the power of the marketplace without surrendering environmental quality to free market forces, which alone do not reflect environmental values.

For both the developing and industrial worlds, then, a sequence of policy actions emerges. The first is to create property rights in the environment if none exist or to define them more clearly if they are vague or incomplete. The second is to remove disincentives to resource conservation by scrutinizing existing subsidy regimes. Subsidies may be overt—price controls, for example—or disguised—the failure of governments to extract resource rents through taxation (see chapter 7). The third policy action is to move prices closer to the social costs of production. The full panoply of policy measures is of course larger and richer than these basic prescriptions, and other measures are illustrated throughout the book.

At the international and global level a further issue arises. All countries of the world share the so-called global commons—that is, the protection afforded by the ozone layer, the role that the atmosphere plays as a carbon sink, and the services provided by the world's oceans. Only collective action can conserve these resources, yet many countries contribute relatively little to global pollution or have few resources to devote to environmental protection. Still others contribute significantly to global pollution but lack the resources to control that contribution (China's production of carbon dioxide, for example). The poor, small contributors will become richer and more significant contributors as they develop. Hence a near-universal agreement must be reached to control the grazing of the global commons (see chapter 14).

The challenge here is to devise systems of incentives for securing cooperation. This is perhaps the major challenge if collective solutions are to be found to the threats posed by global warming, deforestation, and ocean pollution. Cooperation may take many forms. Wealthy nations that care about environmental problems in poor countries can, for example, engage in debt reduction measures, such as the well-known debt-for-nature swaps (see chapter 13). Other potential trades exist as well. For example, country A sets a target for reducing pollution (say, carbon dioxide) but finds that it is cheaper to do so in country B than in country A. An opportunity for mutual benefit exists: country A could transfer its pollution control technology to country B because it does not matter where carbon dioxide pollution originates. If country A wishes to slow deforestation in country B, then A could transfer resources to help B with forest conservation. Country A benefits by protecting the forest, and country B secures a resource transfer whose value is greater than the returns from deforestation. If the world in general benefits from country B's conservation policy, then it should pay country B for the benefits it receives over and above what country B receives. This is the principle underlying the Global Environment Facility (see chapter 14). Ultimately, if the developing world is to help design and implement major cooperative solutions to global problems, further resource and technology transfers will be needed. The scope for mutually beneficial trades is significant.

Environmental degradation is popularly explained by poverty, population growth, indebtedness, the international trading structure, misguided multilateral aid policies, and environmentally insensitive private foreign investment. All these factors are relevant, but focusing exclusively on any one of them is simplistic and misleading. Poverty cannot be an exclusive cause of environmental degradation since many poor countries practice successful resource conservation and rich countries use more resources and emit more waste than poor ones. Rapid population growth undoubtedly depletes resources and threatens sustainable development, but it is often accompanied by misdirected policy measures or other factors that degrade resources. Foreign indebtedness may well be associated with pressures to export timber from tropical forests or to produce export crops that displace subsistence crops, which are subsequently grown on marginal lands. But indebtedness may itself be a symptom of misdirected economic policy. Structural adjustment lending by aid agencies has a mixed record of environmental impact, but no unitary evils can explain environmental degradation.

The interactions among exogenous driving forces, such as population growth, the status quo, and economic and social policy, are therefore complex. The theme of this book is that action needs to be targeted toward economic policies that have, as their incidental effect, environmental loss. Such policies can be changed and can have dramatically beneficial environmental and economic effects. Alleviating poverty, reducing debt, and slowing population growth are all important but take a long time to be effected and longer still to benefit the environment. Moreover, where structural adjustment policies are shown to have a negative environmental impact, the policy response should not be to abandon structural adjustment, which has, after all, many benefits. Rather, the response should be to redesign structural adjustment policies or to ensure that the policies to offset the adverse environmental impact are in place.

We have tried to explore these and other major issues in this volume. Since the subject of the environment and development is changing rapidly, we are aware that many of our illustrations will be superseded quickly by better, more up-to-date material. In the meantime, we hope this book will guide readers and practitioners of development to the salient issues.

Two Environmental Revolutions

The first revolution in attitudes toward the environment occurred in the late 1960s and early 1970s and was characterized by the debate over environmental quality versus economic growth. The late 1980s and early 1990s witnessed a second revolution, which is revisiting and broadening many of the original concepts and arguments in the context of sustainable development. In part, the change of focus since the 1960s and 1970s reflects the impossibility of persuading the rich nations that they should not get even richer. It also reflects changing perceptions about the traditional models of economic growth. Much of the debate in the 1970s was over whether traditional economic policies aimed at raising real incomes could be pursued in the face of limits to growth. In the 1980s the focus of the debate shifted to how growth could be achieved in an environmentally benign way. Clearly, good environmental policies will help growth, and economic growth, if sensibly managed, will help the environment.

The earlier models of economic growth were, by and large, oriented toward capital and stressed that investment in machines, factories, and infrastructure was needed if incomes were to increase. These models were later supplemented by others in which technological progress played a major part. The experience of the newly industrial countries seemed to bear out the feasibility of growth through capital investment and technological change alone.

The persistence of poverty in most of the developing world seemed to refute these models as much as the experience of the newly industrial countries seemed to support them. Reexamining the capital-led model suggested that it might continue to be adequate where environments are fairly robust, but that in the more fragile environments of many developing countries agriculture in particular seems not to respond to the traditional approach. The green revolution—the application of high technology to agriculture—brought substantial gains in food output but reduced the resilience of agriculture to shocks such as pests, diseases, and climatic variation. The direct relationship that exists between agriculture and the natural resources on which it depends suggested a different approach, in which technology and capital matter a great deal, but so do the free inputs of nature. In short, the awareness of the environment as central to the functioning of economic systems began to change how economists perceived the role that natural environments play in the development of poorer nations.

The 1980s showed that limits to economic change do exist if economies are not managed in an environmentally sensitive way. It is important, however, to distinguish these limits from absolute limits to economic growth and development, which apply if economies are managed as if environments do not matter. If economies are suitably managed, economic growth can occur within a set of bounds established by the need to maintain biological resources at a minimum critical level. Moreover, maintaining those resources at levels much higher than the minimum standards can frequently advance, rather than retard, economic development.

This change has perhaps best been captured by the term "sustainable development," which quickly became the catchphrase for the second environmental revolution of the 1980s. Sustainable development describes a process in which the natural resource base is not allowed to deteriorate. It emphasizes the hitherto unappreciated role of environmental quality and environmental inputs in the process of raising real income and the quality of life.

Appreciation of the central position that environment holds in the economy continues to expand. Natural habitats that have in the past appeared to have no obvious economic function are gradually being recognized as valuable resources. Tropical forests protect watersheds, act as habitat for potentially valuable species, and regulate climate. Wetlands purify water, protect inland areas from storm surges, and provide a major source of biodiversity. In these cases natural environments act as life-support systems and as parts of the major biological, geological, and chemical cycles that regulate the conditions in which we all live. Many of these ecologically important environments are located in the developing world, yet their functions are critical to all nations, both rich and poor.

Indeed, the internationalization of environmental problems is perhaps the most significant characteristic of the modern debate. The depletion of the ozone layer and the greenhouse effect do not respect national boundaries; they are global evils that cannot be avoided by any one nation. The developing world is as much at risk, and in many cases more so, as the industrial nations even though they have done relatively little to create these threats. Indeed, the disparity between the responsibility that rich and poor bear for the environmental problems emerging at the close of the twentieth century has prompted the recent search for better ways of pursuing solutions in common and of encouraging richer nations to help poorer ones avoid and bear the consequences of those problems.

Environmental Economics

By linking environment to economic development, the philosophy of sustainable development would inevitably need to embrace the economics of environment. As a subject, environmental economics emerged mainly in the 1950s and 1960s and was propounded largely in North America. Stimulated by new environmental regulations, efforts to assess the economic costs and benefits of environmental projects and policies as well as the comparison of market-based interventions such as effluent charges and regulations were led by Allen Kneese and his colleagues at Resources for the Future (see, for example, Kneese 1964; Herfindahl and Kneese 1965; Krutilla and Eckstein 1958). Major advances were made in techniques to assess the value of environmental impact, particularly in the areas of air and water pollution, which were the subject of extensive regulations. The questioning of economic growth from a limits-to-growth standpoint also spawned an extensive literature, written largely by economists outside the United States, that looked at the implications of absolute resource limits for traditional models of economic growth (see, for example, Dasgupta and Heal 1979; Mäler 1974).

The science of economics has always had something to say about the relation between economic welfare and the stock of natural assets, and the emerging literature on environmental economics found many important historical contributions.[1] The idea of looking at pollution as an externality—a cost imposed by one agent on another party without any compensation being paid—had already been developed by Arthur Pigou in the 1920s (Pigou 1932). The analysis of how fast to deplete an exhaustible resource such as coal or a metal ore had already been advanced by Gray (1914) and Hotelling (1931). Even the economic analysis of limits to growth owed something to the concept of the steady state developed by John Stuart Mill more than a century before (Mill 1900).

Only in the past twenty years, however, did the building blocks for a comprehensive theory of environment and economic development emerge. It is hardly surprising therefore to find the theory imperfectly developed. In particular, although the theory was consolidated and applied extensively to empirical issues in the industrial world in the 1970s, the empirical analysis of conditions in developing countries has not until recently progressed rapidly. Nonetheless, much has been learned from the experience in the industrial countries, and many of the original concepts were broadened in the 1980s as the emphasis shifted to sustainable development. At their most basic, the differences between the two periods can be summarized in five sets of issues, which are expanded in other chapters: tradeoff or complementarity, valuation, focus on the industrial or developing world, exhaustible or renewable resources, and localized or global concern.

Tradeoff or Complementarity?

Many of the participants in the 1970s viewed growth and environment as inevitably in conflict, whereas in the 1980s the pendulum moved toward the view that growth and environment are potentially compatible. The environmentalists' prescription for policy in the 1970s was that growth of the economy and the population had to be constrained if environmental quality was to be preserved. The most famous publication advocating this view was *Limits to Growth* (Meadows and others 1972). The rationale for preserving environments was that even a stationary level of economic activity could not be sustained unless the environment was conserved. In addition, conservation was morally right, an attitude based on a concern for other living species. This study received considerable criticism from economists, primarily with regard to its failure to appreciate the extent to which scarcity would, through the price mechanism, stimulate technological innovation and the search for substitutes.

The limits-to-growth approach in general was extensively analyzed by economists in the 1970s. The main body of the professional literature on environmental economics was devoted to models of economic growth in which resources were an extra factor of production, along with labor and capital, and sometimes also a source of direct welfare from amenity, which is simply something, like a beautiful landscape, that enhances the quality of life. This literature was generally concerned with finding the best or optimal path of economic growth in the context of assumed fixed stocks of exhaustible resources and stocks of renewable resources (Pezzey 1989 presents an admirable survey of the literature). In this literature optimal growth is typically defined as growth that maximizes the present value of future streams of consumption (the discounted value of future flows of per capita consumption).[2] One important finding of this literature is that such optimality may be consistent with unsustainable paths of growth when the rates used to discount the future are sufficiently high. Put another way, if decisions regarding the use of resources are based on assumptions that minimize the importance of the welfare of future generations, the unsustainable use of resources may appear to be optimal.

The same growth models show that sustainability, which for the moment we interpret as per capita levels of welfare that remain constant or increase over time, could be achieved through suitable interventions that reduce the rate at which natural assets are depleted. The interventions should drive a wedge between economic activity and its effect on the environment (box 1-1). Put another way, efforts must be made to separate economic growth from environmental impact and to offset the negative effects of economic growth on the environment. The experience of the recent decades shows that this becomes increasingly possible as technological change occurs, as substitution between resources takes place,

Box 1-1. Sustainability, Optimality, and Government Intervention

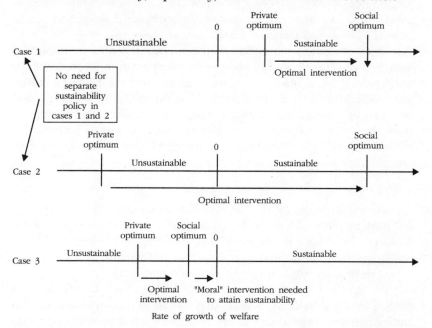

Sustainability means that per capita welfare increases (or is at least constant) over time. Optimality means that the growth path maximizes the present value of the future flows of welfare. The concept of present value takes into account the discounting of future welfare gains, which are regarded as less important the further into the future they occur. Private and social optima diverge: the most desirable rate at which to deplete resources from the standpoint of their owner is unlikely to be the best rate for society as a whole. In case 1 private and social optima are both sustainable. In case 2 the private optimum is unsustainable so that intervention is needed for both sustainability and social optimality. In case 3 both the private and social optima are unsustainable. Achieving the social optimum still does not secure sustainability.

Source: Adapted from Pezzey (1989).

and as higher real prices for goods that pollute lead to their conservation and substitution. This finding underscores the need to design incentives to switch from dirty to clean technologies and from polluting to non-polluting products.

The Valuation Issue

In the 1970s environmentalists assumed that environmental quality mattered and used scientific evidence to support their case. They did not, however, demonstrate the economic importance of environmental quality. Economic importance does not mean financial importance in this context. Something is economically important if it has a significant impact on human welfare. The 1980s saw the rapid development of techniques for, and practice in, measuring the economic damage and benefit derived from environmental change.

In both periods, environmental quality was regarded as important both as a direct source of human welfare and as an input to economic activity designed to raise human welfare. Recently the field of environmental economics has devoted more attention to demonstrating the importance of environment through valuation exercises that attempt to show that environmental degradation involves not just direct losses of welfare (through loss of amenity), but indirect losses through its effect on health and productivity.

The Focus on the Developing World

During most of the 1970s the debate about natural environments was confined to the problems of the industrial world. During the 1980s, however, the debate expanded to embrace the developing world and broadened from an emphasis on pollution and wildlife issues to a concern with broader issues of natural resource management.

Although the 1970s witnessed a major debate about the development process in the developing world, that debate tended to focus less on natural environments than on the traditional need to reduce poverty through alternative development paths (basic needs versus the rapid industrialization and export-led growth approaches; an early exception was Dasmann 1975).

In contrast, the 1980s extended the focus to embrace the issues facing developing countries. Much of the literature repeated the theoretical constructs of the literature on industrial economies, and the constructs and general directions were assumed, with good reason, to be the same, just as the concept of the rational economic man had been applied to development economics in general. The differences are of emphasis, not of concept.

First, many markets function extremely imperfectly in the developing world. Many informal markets, which Jagannathan (1987) defines as personalized exchanges without formal contracts, function beside formal markets. These are frequently designed to overcome the limited flow of information that results from communication difficulties and weak institutional structures. Second, the incentives to avoid regulation are also high in countries where monitoring, policing, and enforcing regulations are often difficult. Third, information in general is often very limited and of very poor quality in the developing world; even a population census may be of limited reliability. For example, the true forest area is frequently unknown, making a causal or policy analysis of deforestation immensely difficult.

These factors combine to make economic analysis of environmental problems and policy application in the developing world particularly difficult. Facts are not firm, and data are deficient. The market response may tell only a tiny part of the story. These observations will be borne out in the rest of this book. Despite the problems an extensive literature is emerging on the environmental economics of developing countries (see, for example, Bartelmus 1986; Bojo, Mäler, and Unemo 1990; Pearce, Barbier, and Markandya 1990; Schramm and Warford 1989). Much of the work results from the impact of the second environmental revolution on major aid-giving agencies such as multilateral development banks and bilateral agencies.

From Exhaustible to Renewable Resources

The 1970s stressed the rapid rate at which exhaustible resources were being depleted, and many of the arguments regarding limits to growth were presented in these terms. Fairly simple indicators of exhaustion were used, based on some measure of the consumption rate of the resource relative to its stock. Thus Meadows and others (1972) estimated that the supply of aluminum, given existing estimates of reserves, would run out in thirty-one years (that is, in 2003). World gold reserves would last only nine years (thus, gold production would have stopped in 1981). Lifetimes would have been longer if the estimates of reserves had been larger. The most notable exhaustible resource is, of course, fossil energy: coal, oil, and gas. The so-called energy crisis of the 1970s, brought on by the substantial hike in the price of oil from the Organization of Petroleum Exporting Countries, tended to give the discussion of resource exhaustion a politically relevant basis, even though the crisis was actually one of price, not physical availability. Indeed, known resource reserves have in many cases actually increased (table 1-1). The proven reserves of coal and lignite increased from 450 billion tons of oil equivalent in 1950 to 570 billion tons in 1990, while those of oil and gas increased more than eightfold during the same period.[3]

Table 1-1. Estimates of Global Reserves of Fossil Fuel, 1950–90
(billions of tons of oil equivalent)

Type of reserve	Proven c1950	Proven 1990	Ultimately recoverable 1955	Ultimately recoverable 1990	Actually consumed 1950–90	Actually consumed 1990
Coal and lignite	450	570	2,000	2,700	60	2.2
Oil and gas	30	250	200	500	100	4.8
Oil, shale, and tar sands	—	—	100	1,400	Small	Small
Total	480	820	2,300	4,600	160	7.0

— Not available.
Source: Based on estimates made at the Atoms-for-Peace conference (1955).

In the 1980s the emphasis shifted from exhaustible to renewable resources. First, it became apparent that resources that were in principle renewable may not in fact renew themselves. That depended critically on the actual management regime in place. The experience of ocean fishing and whaling was more than ample to show that renewable resources could be overexploited. The theoretical literature also drew attention to the conditions likely to exhaust a renewable resource: high discounting of the future, a high ratio of the price of the resource to the cost of harvesting it, and the extent to which the management regime limits access to the resource—the greatest risk being when access is not controlled at all.

Second, the professional literature tended to focus only on selected resources; fisheries and temperate zone forests were particularly well studied. Unfortunately, even now little of the literature on environmental economics theory demonstrates an understanding of ecological functions. As scientific knowledge grew, however, and as the ecologists' perspectives began to permeate environmental economics, it was recognized that the functions of the ecosystem in general behave as renewable resources. Thus the carbon cycle operates as a balanced system in which emitted carbon is absorbed by carbon sinks, notably oceans and forests. The rate at which fossil fuels are used may not threaten the scarcity of fossil fuels; such use does, however, generate carbon and methane emissions, which act as greenhouse gases, and sulfur and nitrogen oxide emissions, which cause acid rain. This is cause for concern. What matters is the constraint that bites first; for fossil fuels, the limited capacity of the waste-receiving environments is likely to be the most significant constraint.

Third, as the perspective of the developing countries emerged, it became quickly apparent that renewable resources are the most critical for the immediate livelihood of the world's poor. Overexploiting water, biomass (trees, crop residues, and grass cover), and soil (a mix of exhaustible and renewable characteristics) has formidable implications for human welfare.

From Localized to Global Concern

Although the 1970s exhibited a marked concern for global environmental threats, the global focus expanded even more in the 1980s. Publications such as Meadows and others (1972) were concerned with threats to the well-being, even the survival, of the world. In the 1980s, global concerns became still more important as increased evidence confirmed the internationalization of environmental issues. The major development was the recognition that many resources are shared, either directly in a physical sense or indirectly as a shared value. Shared physical resources include the European-Scandinavian airshed, river systems that serve several countries (such as the Nile, which serves Egypt, Ethiopia, and Sudan), the oceans beyond exclusive economic zones, and the carbon cycle. Shared value means that a resource may be located wholly within one country, but that its economic value benefits other countries as well. Indeed, the value to other countries may be greater than the value to the host country, as many argue is the case with tropical forests and many endangered species.

To pave the way for discussions in subsequent chapters and to highlight some of the themes of this book, the following sections address the present approach to environment and development. They consider the possibilities that exist for reconciling environment and sustained growth, look at the costs of resource degradation in both industrial and developing countries, and introduce incentives for encouraging sustainable development.

Reconciling Growth and Environmental Impact

Simple intuition suggests that sustained growth is possible without damaging the environment if consideration of environmental impact can be systematically integrated into economic decisions; put another way, the ties that lead from growth to negative environmental impact can be loosened. This is also suggested by the traditional economic growth models that take natural resources and environmental quality into account.

Pollutants and economic activity are linked by what is known as the principle of materials balance. The laws of thermodynamics tell us that the minerals and energy that are taken out of the environment must reappear somewhere else in the economic system; matter and energy cannot be destroyed. Their form may, however, be changed, so that they appear as waste products and gases. Moreover, waste energy cannot be recycled (although it may be used once, as in the case of combined heat and power systems), whereas waste materials can be, up to a point. This implies that any economic activity must always affect the environment, since some waste materials and energy must always be produced. Nevertheless, the amount of waste per unit of economic activity can be reduced. Moreover, if it can be reduced at a faster rate than the rate at which economic activity grows, the total amount of waste disposed of can be reduced over time.

The experience of the industrial world suggests that economic growth can be reconciled with environmental management. Trends in energy consumption are a good illustration. Figure 1-1 shows the relationship between gross domestic product (GDP) and total primary energy consumed in the countries of the Organisation for Economic Co-operation and Development (OECD) from 1970 to 1988. The trend moves systematically downward, meaning that one unit of economic activity used less energy in 1988 than it did in 1970. The rates of change were −33

Figure 1-1. Decline in Energy Requirements per Unit of GDP in OECD Countries, 1970-88

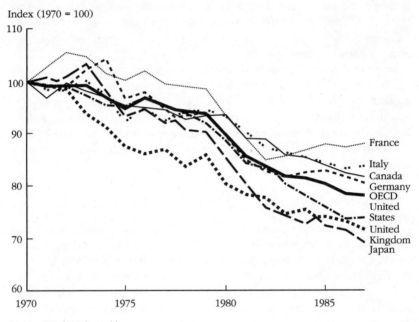

Index (1970 = 100)

France

Italy
Canada
Germany
OECD
United
States
United
Kingdom
Japan

Source: IEA (1987), p. 44.

percent in the United Kingdom, -27 percent in the United States, -23 percent in Italy, -22 percent in Germany, and -16 percent in France.

In part, these reductions have come about because of structural changes that have moved toward producing less energy-intensive outputs, but they have also occurred because of energy conservation induced by changes in the real price of energy. According to OECD (1988, p. 44), "increases in energy prices, especially from 1978 to 1982, have been the most important single factor behind the substantial improvements in energy efficiency over the past ten years, the corresponding reductions in energy intensity, and the slowing of energy demand growth."

Reduced energy consumption per unit of GDP is environmentally beneficial because energy consumption in the industrial world is linked to the emission of several air pollutants: sulfur oxides and nitrogen oxides (which contribute to acid rain), carbon dioxide (which contributes to global warming), and particulate matter (which is linked to respiratory illness). Figure 1-2 shows the relationship between GDP and sulfur oxide emissions in several countries of the OECD. Again the trend is downward, as would be expected due to changes in energy efficiency; sulfur oxide is produced mainly by power stations and industrial boilers. The change in the ratio also reflects regulatory policies within OECD countries, notably

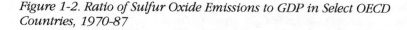

Figure 1-2. Ratio of Sulfur Oxide Emissions to GDP in Select OECD Countries, 1970-87

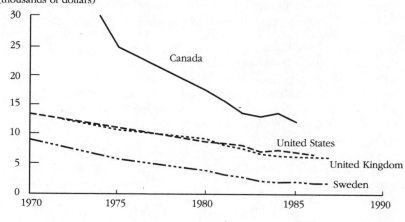

Kilograms of sulfur oxide produced per GDP (thousands of dollars)

Source: OECD (1991).

the United Nation's Economic Commission for Europe's Convention on Long-Range Transboundary Air Pollution and the European Community's Large Combustion Plants Directive. These measures seek to reduce the amount of sulfur and nitrogen oxides emitted into the atmosphere.

The data from industrial countries on energy consumption and sulfur oxide emissions suggest that economic growth can be separated from its effect on the environment. Of course, the picture is far more complicated than can be ascertained by analyzing the ratios of single pollutants to GDP. If GDP grows faster than the ratio declines, total emissions will increase. Reductions in one pollutant may also be secured by increasing emissions from another. Thus reducing the amount of sewage sludge dumped at sea may, for example, increase the amount of pollution on the land where the sludge is tipped or in the air if it is incinerated. Nonetheless, the evidence suggests that technological change can substantially alter the coefficients between real income and environmental impact. This is the technological change that holds out the greatest promise for sustainable development.

How far is this finding relevant to the developing world? Pursuing the energy example, changes in the consumption of commercial energy (petroleum products, coal, and gas) per unit of GNP over time show marked variability among countries (table 1-2). The changes cannot be explained in any simple fashion. In some cases, such as the Sudan, commercial energy supplies have been constrained by foreign exchange shortages.

Table 1-2. Change in the Commercial Consumption of Energy per Unit of GNP in Select Developing Countries, 1970–86

Country	Percentage change, 1970–86
Bolivia	+83
Cameroon	+118
Chile	−14
China	−14
Costa Rica	+10
Ecuador	+45
Kenya	−43
Nepal	+69
Nigeria	+252
Philippines	−23
Senegal	+23
Somalia	+229
Sudan	−47
Tanzania	−19
Thailand	+39
Trinidad	+59
Tunisia	+46
Turkey	+32
Uruguay	−38
Zaire	+30

Source: World Resources Institute (1988), table 20.1.

Other countries have launched fairly successful energy conservation campaigns: the Philippines and Thailand are examples (Gamba, Caplin, and Mulckhuyse 1986). In China, energy conservation has been advanced through schemes that set quotas on energy use. Usage in excess of quotas can only be secured at higher prices.

Nevertheless in many developing countries growth in the demand for energy is inevitable if incomes are to be increased and standards of living improved. Reducing the ratio of energy consumption to GNP is, however, feasible. Thus Gamba, Caplin, and Mulckhuyse (1986, p. 3) stress that "economically, increasing the efficiency of energy use is normally more attractive than investing additional resources to increase the domestic supply. In addition, energy conservation and demand management can produce results faster than can measures to increase supply."

Determining the Costs of Resource Degradation

In recent years, environmental economists have improved their ability to measure the economic cost of environmental and resource degradation. By and large, however, environmental analysis does not require economic tools and methods that are new and distinct from those used in

Table 1-3. Costs of Damage from Pollution in the Netherlands, 1986
(billions of 1986 U.S. dollars, unless otherwise noted)

Type of pollution	Cumulative	Annual	Annual as a percentage of GNP
Air	1.2–3.0	0.5–0.8	
Water	—	0.1–0.3	
Noise	0.5	0.1	
Total	1.7–3.5	0.7–1.2	0.5–0.8

— Not available.
Source: Adapted from Opschoor (1986).

the past. Much progress has in fact been made simply by refashioning techniques to fit today's concerns.

The Industrial World

At the microeconomic level, various techniques have been developed for monetizing the environmental damage or gain that ensues from economic activity in the industrial world. These techniques tend to be of three kinds. The first set of approaches uses surrogate markets; for example, they value the impact of air pollution by examining its effect on property values, of health hazards by looking at risk premia in labor markets, and of recreational benefits by analyzing travel expenditures. The second set creates a market by using interviews and questionnaires to determine the willingness to pay for benefits. This direct questioning approach is especially useful for placing value on wilderness areas or endangered species. The third set estimates physical dose-response functions, for example, between air pollution and human health, and then values the impact using market prices or other unit values (for surveys of the various methodologies, see Pearce and Markandya 1989).

Macroeconomic valuations of resource degradation and environmental loss are few and far between. Despite the dearth of data, the costs of environmental degradation appear to be high. Allowing for the speculative nature of some of the damage estimated for the Netherlands and Germany (tables 1-3 and 1-4) and for the lack of comprehensiveness of the data (for example, the German data exclude water-based amenity affected by pollution), the analyses do suggest some policy conclusions.

First and foremost, if the German data, which are more comprehensive than the Dutch data, are approximately correct, significant net social benefits can be obtained by protecting the environment. On average, industrial countries spend around 1.5 to 2.0 percent of their GNP on pollution control. If the benefits are greater than this, the policy is more than justified. More detail on the cost-benefit comparison is considered below for the United States.

Second, damage from air pollution tends to dominate both the Dutch

Table 1-4. *Costs of Annual Damage from Pollution in Germany, 1983–85*

Type of damage	Cost (billions of 1983/85 U.S. dollars)	Cost as a percentage of GNP
Air pollution		
Health	0.8–1.9	
Materials	0.8	
Agriculture	0.1	
Forestry losses	0.8–1.0	
Forestry recreation	1.0–1.8	
Other forestry	0.1–0.2	
Disamenity	15.7	
Subtotal	19.3–21.5	2.6–2.9
Water pollution		
Fishing	0.1	
Groundwater	2.9	
Subtotal	3.0	0.4
Noise		
In the workplace	1.1	
Depreciation of the price of houses	9.8	
Other	0.7	
Subtotal	11.6	1.6
Total	33.9–36.1	4.6–4.9

Source: Schulz (1986); reprinted by permission.

and German estimates. This is as expected. As countries industrialize, they adopt polluting technologies. Agriculture contributes a diminishing share of the GNP, so the agricultural output that is lost from environmental degradation is expected to be small. The German data also suggest that noise nuisance is valued significantly, a finding in keeping with attitudinal surveys in which noise is frequently cited as a dominant source of environmental disamenity.

One study has considered the balance of costs and benefits to be gained from environmental policy. Freeman (1982) estimated the benefits to be derived from the U.S. Clean Air Act of 1970 and the Federal Water Pollution Control Act of 1972. The study evaluated the benefits as being the reduction and mitigation of air pollution from 1970 to 1978 and the control of water pollution from 1972 to their expected level in 1985. Table 1-5 shows the results for a single year, 1978. Of the total estimated benefits of $26.5 billion (at 1978 prices) approximately 80 percent came from efforts to control air pollution and 20 percent from efforts to control water pollution.[4] Noise nuisance was not evaluated. This result is broadly consistent with the damage analysis for the Netherlands and Germany. Approximately $24.3 billion of the $26.5 billion aggregate damage was utility increasing (it appeared as a benefit in the valuations

Table 1-5. *Benefits of Pollution Control in the United States, 1978*

Type of pollution	Amount (billions of 1978 U.S. dollars)	Percentage of GNP
Air pollution		
Health	17.0	
Soil	3.0	
Vegetation	0.3	
Materials	0.7	
Property values	0.7	
Subtotal	21.7	1.0
Water pollution		
Recreational fishing	1.0	
Boating	0.8	
Swimming	0.5	
Waterfowl hunting	0.1	
Nonuser benefits	0.6	
Commercial fishing	0.4	
Diversionary uses	1.4	
Subtotal	4.8	0.2
Total	26.5	1.2

Source: Freeman (1982).

of individuals) but was not measured as a share of GNP. This finding is significant for the debate over the extent to which measures of GNP capture environmental losses and gains. The data for the United States suggest that those measures do not capture them. Only 8 percent of the environmental benefits reduced market costs or increased marketed output. Finally, government policies to control stationary-source air pollution showed net benefits. Expenditures of some $9 billion a year produced benefits of perhaps $21 billion. For mobile-source air pollution, however, expenditures of $7.6 billion a year achieved benefits of some $0.3 billion, which is remarkably cost inefficient.

The environmental cost and benefit analyses for industrial countries suggest that estimating national damage and benefits is feasible despite significant margins of uncertainty. Moreover, the real damages clearly lie, as one would expect, in the pollution, notably air pollution, associated with industrialization. The importance of noise pollution reflects the rapid growth of road and air travel, both of which are very much a function of income growth. The data do not suggest figures associated with the loss of habitat, nor do they adequately capture the costs to nonusers (the loss of welfare associated with the loss of species and habitat that is unrelated to direct use of the assets in question).

The Developing World

Assessing the costs of resource degradation and environmental pollution in the developing world is in its infancy. Yet, if the theme of the

Brundtland Commission and others—that environment matters even in the narrow terms of measured economic growth—is to be substantiated, damage assessment must be afforded high priority. Such damage assessment has been carried out in developing countries and tends to address the immediate problems of soil erosion, deforestation, and the like, while studies on the industrial countries tend to focus on pollution.

AFRICA. Where a detailed assessment of the costs of resource degradation is not possible, as is true in many African countries, a best-guess calculation should be made to see whether the issue is worth pursuing. Such an exercise was carried out for Burkina Faso, where the total amount of biomass lost each year in the form of fuelwood and vegetation was calculated (table 1-6). The resulting losses included household energy (fuelwood) forgone, which was valued at market prices; millet and sorghum crops forgone, which were also valued at market prices; and reduced livestock yield (lost fodder). According to these calculations, loss of biomass, arising from both man-made and climatic factors, could be costing Burkina Faso as much as 9 percent of its GNP, with crop productivity losses alone standing at almost 2 percent of GNP. A similar exercise was performed for Mali (box 1-2). The effects of soil erosion on agricultural crops are estimated to cost perhaps 0.2 percent of Mali's GNP a year and more if allowance is made for losses in subsequent years.

Box 1-3 presents estimates of the costs of deforestation in Ethiopia. Although the analysis is fairly crude, it is based on a detailed assessment of the forestry and energy sectors in Ethiopia in 1984 (Newcombe 1989). That analysis suggests that deforestation costs appear in the form of forgone agricultural output. Here the link is the diversion of livestock dung from use as a fertilizer to use as a fuel that substitutes for scarce fuelwood. The resulting cost is perhaps 6 percent of total GNP and 12

Table 1-6. *Losses of Crops, Livestock, and Fuelwood in Burkina Faso, 1988*

Region	Fuelwood (cubic meters)	Livestock (UGB)[a]	Cereal (tons)
Sahel	0	175,000	19,000
Plateau Central	900,000	26,000	260,000
Sudano-Guinean	1,200,000	0	27,360
Total	2,100,000	201,000	306,360
Price per unit (CFAFS)[b]	22,258	50,000	50,000
Total losses (billions of CFAFS)	46.7	10.0	15.3

Note: The total cost of damage equaled CFAF 72 billion, or 8.8 percent of GNP.
a. UGB, Unités de Gros Bétail, are a standardized unit for measuring livestock.
b. CFAFS are a currency union of several countries linked to the French franc.
Source: Adapted with corrections from Lallement (1990).

Box 1-2. On-site Costs of Soil Erosion in Mali, 1988

A standard approach to determining the costs of soil erosion is to estimate soil loss using the universal soil loss equation (USLE). The USLE relates soil loss to rainfall erosivity, R; the erodibility of soils, K; the slope of the land, SL; a crop factor, C, which measures the ratio of soil loss under a given crop to that from bare soil; and conservation practice, P (so that no conservation is measured as unity). The USLE is then calculated as

$$\text{(B-1)} \qquad \text{Soil loss} = R \cdot K \cdot SL \cdot C \cdot P.$$

The next step is to link soil loss to crop productivity. In a study of soil loss effects in southern Mali, Bishop and Allen (1989) applied the following equation to estimate the impact of soil loss on crop productivity.

$$\text{(B-2)} \qquad \text{Yield} = C^{-bx}$$

where C is the yield on newly cleared and hence uneroded land, b is a coefficient varying with crop and slope, and x is cumulative soil loss.

Finally, the resulting yield reductions were valued. A crude approach is simply to multiply the estimated crop loss by its market price, in the case of cash crops. The impact that changes in yield have on farm incomes is generally more complex than this. For example, yield reductions would reduce the requirement for weeding and harvesting. The Mali study allowed for these effects by looking at the total impact on farm budgets with and without erosion.

The procedure described is an example of a dose-response or production-function approach to valuation. The dose is soil erosion, the response is crop loss. Another approach is to look at the costs of replacing the nutrients that are lost with soil erosion. Nutrient losses can be replaced with chemical fertilizers, which have explicit market values. The replacement cost approach is helpful but assumes that all soil loss is undesirable. Since we do not know if correcting for all soil loss is worth attempting (indeed, it is unlikely to be worthwhile), replacement cost approaches need to be used with caution. (Using the replacement cost approach, Stocking [1986] estimates the following annual losses of nutrients from soil erosion in Zimbabwe: nitrogen, 1.6 million tonnes; organic carbon, 15.6 million tonnes; and phosphorus, 0.24 million tonnes. In 1985 prices the total cost for all Zimbabwe lands, using the price of commercial fertilizer to value the replacement nutrients, was $1.5 billion, or a startling 26 percent of GDP in 1985.)

Table B1-2 shows the results for Mali using the two approaches. The effects of soil erosion on agricultural crops in Mali are estimated to cost perhaps 0.2 percent of GNP a year and more if allowance is made for losses in subsequent years. Because soil loss in any one year has effects in subsequent years, the data show both an annual loss and a present value loss expressed as a loss in a single year. Bishop and Allen (1989) draw several conclusions from their study:

- Economic losses from soil erosion in Mali are high enough to warrant conservation investments in some areas in the south of the country
- Investing in additional agricultural output may be less profitable than a

(continued on next page)

simple financial appraisal would suggest, and an estimate of expected soil erosion must be built into the analysis, which will lower rates of return
• Most important, it is necessary to ask why soil erosion occurs.

The authors cite restrictions on access to informal credit and insecure land tenure as important factors in Mali. High risks also contribute to high farmer discount rates, and measures can be taken to reduce risks.

Table B1-2. Costs of Soil Erosion in Mali, by Measure Used

Type of loss and measure used	Millions of U.S. dollars	Percentage of GDP	Percentage of Agricultural GDP
Based on USLE and farm budgets			
National annual loss of income	4.6	0.2	0.6
Discounted present value of income	31.0	1.5	4.0
Based on nutrient replacement	7.4	0.4	1.0

Source: Bishop and Allen (1989).

percent of agricultural GNP. This is the same proportion estimated for the direct costs of fuelwood loss in Mali.

What, then, do the damage cost estimates for Africa show? However imperfect the methodologies and the data bases, natural resource degradation clearly imposes severe costs on the economies of the poorest countries. There can be no pretence that the procedures are comprehensive, but they do suggest that land degradation in general is imposing costs on the order of 5 percent and more of GNP.[5]

ASIA. The most detailed studies of national environmental damage and resource depletion costs in developing countries have been carried out for Indonesia (Magrath and Arens 1989; Repetto and others 1989). Their analysis covers the depreciation of oil and forest assets and the costs of soil erosion. Although oil is a natural resource, these studies focus on forestry and soil erosion. A forest can be viewed as a natural capital asset similar to a man-made capital asset. The asset yields a service over time to which there is a corresponding income. An asset can depreciate for two reasons: changes in value and changes in physical condition. Value may change independently of any physical change; for example, its price can vary with demand. Obviously, value also changes if physical depreciation occurs. There is, in fact, a dispute in the national accounting literature over the correct way to account for the depletion of environmental assets.[6] The issue is further complicated because the relevant cost should be that of nonoptimal depletion: it cannot be assumed that all depletion is reprehensible.

Box 1-3. *Costs of Deforestation in Ethiopia*

The poorest countries rely heavily on fuelwood for energy. The only feasible substitutes are crop residues and animal dung, which also have value as sources of organic and nutrient inputs to the soil. Soil is, in turn, the critical factor in sustainable subsistence agriculture. Cycles of degradation can be observed. As population grows, the harvesting of fuelwood exceeds the rate at which forests and woodlands are regenerated. The forest is mined. The loss of trees that fix atmospheric nitrogen impairs the fertility of the soil. As fuelwood becomes scarce, crop residues and grass are used for fuel. The soil deteriorates even further as it loses these inputs. Finally, dung is diverted from being a manure to being a fuel. Soil depletion worsens still further.

One of the costs of deforestation, then, is the loss of crop productivity, which arises when dung is diverted from the soil for use as fuel. In a study of Ethiopia, Newcombe (1989) shows that approximately 90 percent of the cattle dung produced in Eritrea, and 60 percent in Tigrai and Gondar, is used for fuel. The damage cost of this diversionary use can be estimated in three ways. First, a crop-response function can be estimated, and the resulting fall in the yield of crops can be valued at market prices. This is analogous to the production-function approach for soil erosion. Second, the dung has an equivalent worth in terms of chemical fertilizers (although that value will be understated since dung contributes organic matter as well as nutrients). The replacement cost approach can be used to value the dung. Finally, dung is bought and sold on markets, so it can be directly valued at the ruling market price. The resulting valuations of dung were as follows: production-function approach (grain response): $47–$114 per tonne; replacement cost approach (fertilizer cost): $22 per tonne; and market price approach: $61–$91 per tonne. Newcombe (1989) estimated that Ethiopian households burned approximately 7.9 million tonnes of dung a year. At the average grain response value ($76), the dung is worth some $600 million annually.

Clearly, the whole $600 million cannot be debited to deforestation. Some dung would have been burned anyway. If half the dung burned was induced by deforestation, however, the annual cost would be $300 million, or 6 percent of Ethiopia's GNP in 1983. At the highest implicit value of dung, the cost would be 9 percent of GNP. As a percentage of agricultural GNP, these proportions would be roughly doubled.

Source: Adapted from information presented in Newcombe (1989).

Table 1-7 shows the results of an exercise to value deforestation and soil erosion in Indonesia. Estimates of the cost of deforestation are obtained by the depreciation approach (which is described in note 5 of this chapter). The soil erosion damage estimates are based on the production function approach.

EASTERN EUROPE. Political changes in Eastern Europe have brought to light the serious environmental degradation that has been one of the

Table 1-7. *Costs of Deforestation and Soil Erosion in Indonesia, 1975, 1980, and 1984*
(millions of dollars at current prices, unless otherwise noted)

Type and measure of loss	1975	1980	1984
Deforestation (physical depreciation of tree stocks)			
Total value	994	6,262	3,054
As a percentage of GNP	3.6	8.9	3.6
Soil erosion			
On-site	—	—	315
Siltation of irrigation systems	—	—	10
Harbor dredging	—	—	2
Reservoir sedimentation	—	—	46
Total value	—	—	373
As a percentage of GNP	—	—	0.4

— Not available.

Source: For forestry, Repetto and others (1989); for soil erosion, Magrath and Arens (1989).

by-products of the socialist nations' push for growth. The most detailed information available on the costs of this damage is from Poland, which has a history of costing environmental impact. Approximately 11 percent of the land in Poland, supporting 35 percent of the population, is classified by the government as areas of ecological hazard. Five regions—Upper Silesia, Kraków, Rybnik (all in the southwest of the country), Legnica-Glogów (west-central Poland), and Gdansk (on the Baltic)—are classified as areas of ecological disaster. All forms of pollution are serious, but air and water pollution and soil contamination generate the greatest economic costs. It is estimated that 30 percent of the economic costs of pollution damage arise from water pollution, 35 percent from air pollution, and a further 35 percent from soil contamination (Kabala 1989).

Table 1-8 shows estimates of the monetary value of the damage caused by all forms of pollution in Poland. The figures relate to damage existing in 1980, expressed in 1987 prices, and almost certainly understate the extent of the damage. The estimates also include figures for the cost of excessive use of resources. Table 1-9 tries to separate damage due to pollution from damage due to overuse of resources. The startling result is that the damage from pollution alone may amount to between 5 and 10 percent of Poland's GNP. These estimates are controversial, however, and a more detailed evaluation would likely show the costs of damage to be lower.

The Costs of Environmental Damage

Estimating the national costs of environmental damage is in its infancy, but the studies to date have some features in common. In the

Table 1-8. Costs of Pollution Damage and Excess Resource Use in Poland, 1987

Type of damage	Damage (billions of 1987 zlotys)	Percentage of GNP
Agriculture	150	
Forests	50	
Water resources	65	
Corrosion	215	
Excessive use of mineral resources	130	
Raw materials lost in discharges to air and water	50	
Health effects	115	
Total impact of pollution	595	7.7
Total environmental losses	775	10.0

Note: The 10 percent of GNP figure for total impact is widely quoted, but World Bank (1989) puts Poland's GNP at Zl12,700 billion in current 1987 prices. If the estimate of Kassenberg (1989) relates to 1987, the shares would be 6.1 percent for total environmental degradation and 4.7 percent for pollution damage. Note, however, that the damage relates to 1980 levels of pollution.

Source: Kabala (1989); Kassenberg (1989); World Bank (1989b).

industrial world, the German data suggest damage costs under 5 percent of GNP. Dutch estimates are lower (0.5–0.8 percent) but relate to partial effects only. Damage avoided in the United States because of environmental policy was some 1.2 percent of GNP, but the estimates omit noise nuisance and relate to 1978. A range of 1 to 5 percent of GNP thus seems to be a fairly reasonable estimate of the pollution damage caused by environmental degradation in the industrial world. The case of Poland, where pollution damage is at least 5 percent of GNP, may illustrate trends in what used to be the socialist economies.

Damage in the developing world could be expected to be higher than in the industrial world given the absence of environmental protection legislation and institutions. The estimates tend to support this. Soil erosion in Indonesia and Mali may cost some 0.4 percent of GNP. Deforestation in Ethiopia appears to cause a loss of at least 6 percent of GNP; in Indonesia, the costs of deforestation are 4 percent of GNP. Finally, total loss of biomass imposes a cost to the Burkina Faso economy of just under 9 percent of GNP. Estimates for other countries, not reported here, support the notion that environmental damage costs developing countries approximately 5 percent of their GNP. Moreover, this cost is in the form of lost productive potential; that is, real resource flows are associated with these losses. In the industrial economies the major part of the loss probably shows up in flows not connected to the GNP (changes in human welfare that are not captured by the conventional methods of national accounting). This indicates a need to adjust the national accounts.

Even if the quality of the data is uncertain—as seems likely—they confirm that environmental deterioration damages the economies of both

Table 1-9. Estimates of Environmental Damage in Select Countries, Various Years

Country and year	Form of environmental damage	Annual costs as a percentage of GNP
Burkina Faso, 1988	Crop, livestock, and fuelwood losses from land degradation	8.8
Costa Rica, 1989	Deforestation	7.7
Ethiopia, 1983	Effects of deforestation on the supply of fuelwood and crop output	6.0–9.0
Germany, 1990[a]	Pollution damage (air, water, soil pollution, loss of biodiversity)	1.7–4.2
Hungary, late 1980s	Pollution damage (mainly air pollution)	5.0
Indonesia, 1984	Soil erosion and deforestation	4.0
Madagascar, 1988	Land burning and erosion	5.0–15.0
Malawi, 1988	Lost crop production from soil erosion	1.6–10.9
	Costs of deforestation	1.2–4.3
Mali, 1988	On-site soil erosion losses	0.4
Netherlands, 1986	Some pollution damage	0.5–0.8
Nigeria, 1989	Soil degradation, deforestation, water pollution, other erosion	17.4
Poland, 1987	Pollution damage	4.4–7.7
United States,[b] 1981	Air pollution control	0.8–2.1
1985	Water pollution control	0.4

Note: Although the estimates use different techniques, relate to different years, and vary in the quality of the underlying research, they suggest some broad interpretations. In the industrial world total gross environmental damage may be around 2–4 percent of the gross national product; in the Eastern European countries, 5–10 percent; and in the poor developing nations, 10 percent and above.

a. Federal Republic of Germany before unification.

b. Measures the benefits of environmental policy (avoided rather than actual damages).

Source: For Burkina Faso, Lallement (1990); for Costa Rica, World Resources Institute (1991); for Ethiopia, Newcombe (1989); for Germany, Germany, Ministry of the Environment (1991); for Hungary, World Bank (1990c); for Indonesia, Repetto (1989) and Magrath and Arens (1989); for Madagascar, World Bank (1990c); for Malawi, World Bank (1991a); for Mali, Bishop and Allen (1989); for the Netherlands, Opschoor (1986); for Nigeria, World Bank (1990c); for Poland, Kassenberg (1986); and for the United States, Portney (1990) and Freeman (1982).

the rich and poor worlds alike and makes it particularly difficult and costly for a country to develop.

Offering Incentives for Sustainable Development

Sustainable development stresses the importance of permanent growth and development. Many past development policies have been based on the idea of a rush for growth, which was the result of beliefs about the lessons that history holds for the development process. Thus the achievements of the industrial world reflect a particular path of transition that moves from agriculture to industry to service-oriented economies. That transition was achieved at the cost of often-irreversible damage to the environment, such as the growing number of endangered species. The philosophy of sustainable development challenges the idea that this process can—or must—be replicated for the developing world. Clearly, securing gains in real income is a priority, but these gains are not, it is argued, sustainable if they impose the heavy costs of environmental damage.

Environmental destruction may simply be part of the price that must be paid to achieve a higher standard of living. All civilizations, for example, engage in deforestation to obtain fuel and building materials, yet they survive at high standards of living. Even if this view of ecological economic history is true, developing economies do not necessarily have to pursue the same development process pursued by the industrial countries. They do not necessarily have to destroy the environment. They may be better off developing with greater environmental protection. Some civilizations have not survived the deforestation process, environmental destruction does not guarantee sustained economic growth, and many industrial economies also had other resources to substitute for environmental resources, while many resource-poor economies today do not. Just because the industrial world sacrificed environmental quality for real income does not mean that the developing world must do the same. This is true for at least three reasons.

- Sacrifices of renewable resources in temperate zones are likely to cause less loss to human welfare than similar sacrifices in tropical zones, where the margin of fragility is much lower and where many developing countries are located. Simply put, small changes in environment may have large economic effects in most developing countries. The valuation studies discussed previously show the kinds of costs involved and suggest that the relative magnitude of environmental damage is high in the developing world.
- The industrial world is suffering the consequences of indifference to environmental quality and is now exerting great efforts to repair past damage, salvage what it can, and prevent further damage. A policy of reacting to damage once it has occurred—rather than trying to prevent it—is dangerous. The diminishing ozone layer and global warming are cases in point. Moreover, the industrial world is responsible for much of the existing global damage, which imposes costs on all nations.
- Countries do not need to engage in the same process of degradation. Growth in real income per capita can be achieved without major degradation if the ties that lead from economic growth to negative environmental impact are loosened. Sustainable development means precisely that process.

The last reason is the most important. To pursue growth without assessing whether the same goal can be achieved at less environmental cost is not rational. Disregarding environmental damage also threatens, as we have seen, the permanence of the development effort. But how can environmental concerns be integrated with economic growth? The clue lies in incentives and information. Two sets of incentives and information systems are critically important: those that reduce uncertainty about the future and those that send out the correct signals about price and quantity in the marketplace. Necessary elements include modifying the presentation of environmental and economic statistics so that the environmental impact of economic change can be discerned and the services of the environment highlighted and revising systems for appraising investments and policies to ensure that they adequately reflect and integrate the environmental impact.

Incentive Systems to Reduce Uncertainty

Most economic decisions are made in the context of uncertainty, yet uncertainty can be both beneficial and harmful for environmental quality. By choosing crops, crop mixes, or rotations that minimize the risk of failure in a drought, for example, a farmer is likely to adopt weather- and pest-resistant strains. Many problems with agricultural output arise from choosing the wrong technology or output mix in the face of uncertainty. This often occurs because farmers hold false beliefs about the potential to correct problems or because they discount the future heavily. The choice of technology and production method can be seen as a tradeoff among productivity, stability, equitability, and sustainability (figure 1-3).[7] Highly productive systems may not be sustainable (for example, the Mayan agricultural systems in the tropical forests of Central America). Equitable and sustainable systems may not be particularly productive (for example, the manorial system of agriculture in medieval Europe). Modern examples include large-scale irrigation systems in which high productivity appears to be incompatible with equitability and sustainability. Biological pest control is likely to be more sustainable but produces more fluctuating yields (instability) and lower productivity. Uncertainty about the future tends to bias the tradeoff toward productive but unsustainable systems.

Ensuring sustainability therefore requires efforts to reduce uncertainty. Some of the most important sources of uncertainty lie in the rights to resources (that is, the lack of secure tenure over land, the resources on the land, or both). Although the evidence is not conclusive, studies suggest that secure tenure over land improves long-run productivity and increases the value of the land (see, for example, Chalamwong and Feder 1986; Feder 1987; the picture is less clear for Africa than for other regions; see Feder and Noronha 1987). Granting tenure in and of itself may not improve the management of natural resources. The way in

Figure 1-3. Characteristics of Agricultural Performance

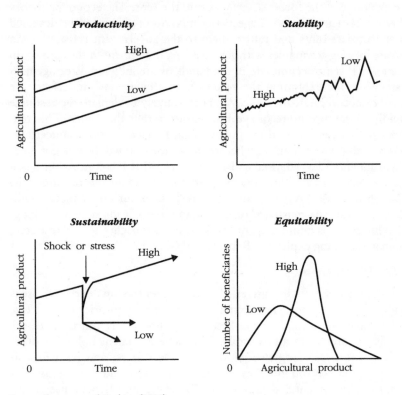

Source: Conway and Barbier (1990).

which tenure is granted also matters. In many parts of the developing world tenure is recognized de facto, and often de jure, only if land is cleared of vegetation. Southgate, Sierra, and Brown (1989) show quite clearly that deforestation in Ecuador is related not only to population pressure but also to the desire to establish land rights through land clearance.[8] The influence of uncertainty shows up clearly in this example. Since the rights to forested land are uncertain, while the rights to cleared land are certain (or nearly certain), the land is cleared.

Insecurity of tenure may also account for the destruction of resources being carried out by major corporations and government agencies. The theory of natural resource economics confirms that uncertainty can accelerate the rate of depletion of an exhaustible resource (Dasgupta and Heal 1979, chap. 13). An example arises in the context of the logging of tropical forests. The stumpage value (the value of the standing stock of timber) of tropical forests is very large. Governments, however, frequently fail to capture the rents because of policies that effectively enable the exploiter of the forest stock to secure the rent. The economic theory of resource-rent taxation suggests that taxation policies can be designed to appropriate rents and return them to the government rather than to private logging companies without deterring investment in the country in question. If rents accumulate in the hands of the individuals or agencies responsible for exploiting the resource, two environmental effects are likely to occur. First, the concessionaire is likely to deplete the resource rapidly to capture more of the rent earlier rather than later. This tendency will be reinforced if the policy toward the concession is uncertain, that is, if doubts exist about whether the concession will be renegotiated. Environmental degradation will be encouraged if the concession has a shorter time horizon than that needed to regenerate the resource (the rotation period). No new planting is likely to occur under these conditions. Second, the existence of exploitable rents leads to rent seeking, whereby other economic agents seek to acquire rights to the resource, again accelerating depletion (Repetto and Gillis 1988).

Prices as Incentives

Prices are powerful incentives. If prices are set too low, excessive use is made of the resource. The extreme example is zero-priced resources, which have no established market. The carbon-fixing functions of the oceans or forests are an example. The same argument holds for other resources such as energy, irrigation water, fertilizers, and pesticides. If their prices are set too low they tend to be overused, and overuse contributes to environmental degradation. To secure an efficient use of resources, outputs should be priced at their marginal social cost, which comprises the marginal costs of production and the external costs of the pollution or resource degradation caused by producing the good.

If markets functioned near perfectly, prices in the marketplace would probably reflect their marginal private costs of production. There are, however, at least two forms of market failure. First, many marketed goods have prices that reflect private costs of production but ignore social costs. Several means of intervening exist to ensure that social prices are charged, such as regulations that set standards, pollution taxes, and tradable permits. Second, many goods have no markets at all, and prices must be established for them. Assigning property rights to the free resource in question is one way to achieve this, although the resulting price may or may not reflect the full social cost.

In the developing world a considerable amount of environmental degradation is a result of the failure to price resources and goods at their marginal private cost, let alone their marginal social cost. To illustrate, table 1-10 shows the level of pesticide subsidies in eight countries. Subsidies range from 19 to 89 percent of the full cost of the pesticides, thus maintaining prices artificially low. Damage from excess use of pesticides

Table 1-10. Pesticide Subsidies in Eight Developing Countries, 1985

Country	Subsidy as a percentage of the full cost	Total value of the subsidy (millions of U.S. dollars)
China	19	285
Colombia	44	69
Ecuador	41	14
Egypt	83	207
Ghana	67	20
Honduras	29	12
Indonesia	82	128
Senegal	89	4

Source: World Resources Institute (1985).

shows up in several ways. For example, approximately 2 million cases of pesticide poisonings occur each year in the Asia and Pacific region, 40,000 of which probably result in death (Repetto 1988a). Exposure is highest among men, and death rates rise significantly in communities where insecticides have been introduced on an intensive scale. There is also evidence of health risks from fish caught in pesticide-contaminated ponds, paddies, and irrigation channels. New pest biotypes have emerged in response to large applications of some pesticides, thus decreasing the stability of crop production. Subsidies are not the only factor causing excessive use of pesticides; ignorance of the risks as well as use of pesticides that are not permitted in the industrial world also contribute to excessive use.

What is true of pesticides is also true of irrigation water, energy, fertilizers, lease values of land for mechanized agriculture, and other resources (Repetto 1988a). Irrigation charges tend to be a small proportion of the benefits that farmers receive from irrigation water: 8–21 percent in Indonesia and 11–26 percent in Mexico, but only 10 percent in the Philippines, 9 percent in Thailand, and 5 percent in Nepal. The resulting excessive use of irrigation water contributes to waterlogging, increases the salinization of soils, and wastes the water itself. Pricing reform thus has a major role to play in securing efficient development that takes into account the effects of use on the environment. The first priority is to relate the price charged to the costs of production (and to the border price if the resource is tradable). Later in the process of development, prices will need to be increasingly related to the full social costs of production.

Getting the price right is not a simple matter when it includes securing the right balance of environmental quality and short-term gains in output. This is readily illustrated in the context of the price of agricultural output. It is tempting to think that higher farmgate prices will stimulate an increase of the aggregate supply, thus making farmers better off and more able to make the long-term investments needed for sustainability, such as soil conservation, tree windbreaks, and water conservation. Evidence certainly suggests that practicing price discrimination against producers (keeping farmgate prices lower than border prices) is associated with lower rates of agricultural growth. One study for Africa suggests that between 1970 and 1981 countries with little or no discrimination had annual growth rates of 2.9 percent, those with medium price discrimination had annual growth rates of 1.8 percent, and those with high price discrimination produced annual growth rates of only 0.8 percent (Fones-Sundell 1987).

The effects of reducing discrimination are not, however, clear. First, price changes must be perceived as permanent if investment decisions are to favor conservation practices. Second, the nature of the response depends on security of tenure, resource rights generally, and access to credit. Third, if open-access resources are available—for example, virgin forest land—the supply response may extend rather than intensify use (farmers may clear new lands rather than subject existing lands to conservation investments). Fourth, and offsetting the incentive to extend use, higher farm incomes may lower personal discount rates and improve credit ratings, even within informal credit markets. These effects should assist conservation. Finally, although supply responses exist for single crops, price increases may cause farmers to switch between crops rather than increase output overall. The nature of the crop grown matters from the environmental standpoint. Tree crops and perennials, for example, are more likely to be good for soil conditions, whereas many root and grain crops (peanuts, cassava, sorghum, and millet) are erosive. Since nothing links price increases with the ecological status of the crop, supply responses are as likely to bring increases in erosive crops as not. As yet, then, the links between changes in output price and environmental quality in the long run have not been established. Remarkably, hardly any studies of agricultural supply responses mention the sustainability of the responses.

Fiscal Policies

Since price is instrumental in changing behavior, taxation policy also exerts an important influence on behavior that affects the environment. The scope for pollution taxes in developing countries is likely to grow in the future, although charges related to damage are still a rarity in the industrial world (Anderson 1990; Bernstein 1990; and Pearce 1990c). Other taxation policies are capable of adjustment, however, and existing policies frequently discriminate against the environment. As noted previously, governments frequently fail to capture rents from existing valuable resources such as forests. During the 1970s and early 1980s, for example, the governments of Ghana, Indonesia, and the Philippines captured rents at very low rates (table 1-11). The scale of the rents is worth noting:

Table 1-11. *Rent Capture in Tropical Forests in Four Developing*
Countries, Various Years
(billions of U.S. dollars, unless otherwise noted)

Country and time period	Actual rent	Government rent	Government rent as a percentage of actual rent
Ghana, 1971–74	0.08	0.03	38.0
Indonesia, 1979–82	4.40	1.60	37.3
Malaysia (Sabah), 1979–82	2.10	1.70	81.3
Philippines, 1979–82	1.00	0.17	16.5

Source: Repetto (1988c).

in Indonesia, for example, actual rents from 1979 to 1982 were $4.4 billion, or approximately $1.1 billion annually; of this amount, the government collected only $400 million a year. Scope exists, then, for revising fiscal policies even before paying attention to the potential for introducing taxes on pollution and other resource degradation. In much the same way, user charges, such as charges for water connections, have high potential for reducing water wastage. This, in turn, has an effect on pollution.

Information Systems

Information is a major input to sustainable development. At the most micro level, individual households need to be informed of the consequences of particular decisions about inputs and outputs. Looked at from the outside, there is also a need to use local knowledge and to observe and counteract the constraints that prevent sustainable practices from being used. Extension systems are clearly important in both these respects.

Governments also must be informed. The most important aspect of this need for information is the necessity to establish that economic policy affects the environment, which in turn affects economic welfare. Valuation studies are especially useful for establishing the link between environment and economic welfare and may be sufficiently formalized to warrant modified presentations of national accounts. Showing that economic decisions affect the environment is less easy, but analysis of incentive systems is a useful starting point. Since price policy tends to be fairly easily modified, subject to concerns about the social incidence of price changes and political implications, pricing should be given high priority in efforts to encourage sustainable development. Resource rights and land tenure offer another vital dimension of sustainable development policy.

Other information systems deserve far more emphasis too. Geographical information systems can mix satellite imagery with more standard ground-based information (ground truthing). This mix can then be used not only for the traditional purposes of mapping and assessing land capability, but also as a data base for interpreting environmental change over time. The systematic interaction of socioeconomic data bases and satellite imagery is still underdeveloped. (For interesting experiments that look at the interaction of poverty and environmental degradation, see Jagannathan 1989.)

Moving toward Sustainable Development

What can be learned from this brief overview of the issues connecting the environment with the economy? First, environmental damage matters not just because it affects psychic or noneconomic welfare, but also because it translates into lost production. These costs can be large, and existing evidence suggests that damage costs can amount to 5 percent and more of GNP.

Second, given the scale and nature of environmental damage, sufficient evidence exists to support the view forwarded by advocates of sustainable development that a greater priority must be given to environment if economic policies are to be sustainable.

Third, insofar as past development policy has been influenced by the theory of optimal growth—and it clearly has—there is a critical need to analyze the conditions under which optimal growth is also sustainable growth.

Fourth, since raising real income per capita must remain a major—but not the only—objective of development policy, growth with environmental quality can be achieved only by systematically considering and addressing the environmental effects of growth strategies. Where this cannot be achieved, it is essential to understand the nature of the tradeoffs between orthodox development goals and environmental deterioration. Better and more sophisticated attempts to value environmental functions are thus crucial.

Do priority areas emerge from the analysis? Because of the paucity and uncertainty of studies, hard and fast recommendations are difficult to make. The evidence on social cost does, however, suggest that for developing countries still at an early stage of development deforestation is likely to impose heavy losses on the economy. Even for rapidly industrializing countries forest resources are being mismanaged, and the costs of deforestation are significant. Soil erosion is important, but perhaps less important than might at first be thought. The impact of pollution is also important, and the experience of Eastern Europe and the industrial countries shows just how important the economic costs of pollution are. In the developing world water pollution and water management probably deserve the most attention primarily because water has such a large effect on the health of all the country's inhabitants. But costing that effect still seems very uncertain.[9]

Priority can be assigned to policies for action in the short, medium, and long terms: in the short term, the existing tax policy on private cost pricing; in the medium-long term, resource rights and land tenure; and in the long term, social cost pricing. A continuous theme has to be the provision of information for households, productive units, and government.

Although the debate about sustainable development has not convinced some economists that the nature of the development process must be changed, it has encouraged others to give natural resources an even higher status in policymaking than that suggested by valuation studies. These scholars stress several features of the workings of ecosystems: the extensive uncertainty surrounding the role of ecosystems in global and local life-support systems; the irreversibility of many of the effects in contrast to man-made capital, which can be increased or decreased at comparative will; and the values of environmental quality that are not related to use. The last feature explains much of the public concern over tropical deforestation and endangered species, which most people will never experience. Within traditional economic growth models, the amenity value of environmental assets acquires major significance, along with the environment as productive input. Combining these features of environmental assets with traditional concerns in order to secure optimal growth and intergenerational equity tends to support policies that conserve natural assets. Achieving sustainable development will continue to pose challenges for development economists and environmental economists alike in the future.

Notes

1. For an overview of the history of environmental economics theory, see Pearce (1991a), which highlights four major developments before the 1960s: the idea that ecological bounds exist to the scale of economic activity, which was presented in the works of Malthus (1820), Ricardo (1817), and Mill (1900) and popularized in Daly (1973); the perception of pollution as an external effect, which was first analyzed by Pigou (1932) and later by Kapp (1950) and Coase (1960); the theory of the optimal rate of depletion of an exhaustible resource, which was developed by Gray (1914) and formalized by Hotelling (1931); and the theory of optimal use of a renewable resource, which was included in studies ranging from Faustmann's work on forest rotations (Faustmann 1849) to Gordon's "Economic Theory of a Common Property Resource: The Fishery" (Gordon 1954).

2. For example, in the simplest cake-eating model, per capita consumption, c, depends on the rate of use of the per capita stock of a nonrenewable resource, s. Thus

(1-1)
$$c = (-ds / dt') \cdot e^{rt}$$

where r is the rate of technological progress and t is time. Utility, u, depends on c, such that

(1-2)
$$u(c) = c^v$$

where $0 < v < 1$. The aim, then, is to choose $s^*(t)$, that is, the optimal stock of the resource, to maximize

(1-3)
$$\int u(c) \cdot e^{-kt} \cdot dt$$

where k is the discount rate.

The solution to such a problem can exhibit both properties of optimality and sustainability (in the sense of nondeclining utility) provided the discount rate, k, is less than (or equal to) the rate of technological progress.

If the model is extended to allow for environmental productivity, then equation 1-1 could be rewritten:

$$(1\text{-}4) \qquad\qquad c = -S^{m/v} \cdot (-ds \,/\, dt) \cdot e^{rt}$$

where S is now the total stock of the resource, s is the stock per capita, and $m > 0$ measures the productivity effect of the total stock. Maximization of the present value of utility in this model yields several possible outcomes. If individuals do not behave cooperatively, that is, if they ignore the environmental value of the resource when planning their own optimal path, then sustainability is harder to achieve than in the simple cake-eating model. Significantly, higher discount rates tip the balance toward nonsustainability, and in some cases the optimal growth path is itself unsustainable (recall that optimality is defined as present value). See Pezzey (1989).

3. A billion is 1,000 million.

4. All dollar amounts are current U.S. dollars.

5. Fuelwood output arising from deforestation implies both a gain in GDP and, if the harvest is unsustainable, a loss as well. Thus the household production of fuelwood should be added to GDP if a value is not already imputed for it. The net depreciation of forest stocks needs to be deducted. In a study for Tanzania, Peskin (1989) estimated the following adjustments to conventional GDP. In Tanzania in 1980, 137 million person days were estimated to have been spent producing fuelwood. Valued at the then minimum wage of T Sh20 a day, this activity was worth T Sh2,740 million. The existing imputed value was T Sh207 million, so the adjustment led to a gain of T Sh2,533 million (2,740 − 207 = 2,533). Since around 69 percent of the wood cut was on an unsustainable basis, depreciation of T Sh1,891 million (0.69 x 2,740 = 1,891) constitutes depreciation that should be deducted from GDP if, as it should be, the interest is in net national product. The overall effect of the adjustments is to increase GDP 6 percent compared with the standard presentation and to increase the net national product 2 percent. Not all environmental adjustments therefore diminish GDP. The adjustments made relate only to the forests as sources of fuelwood and nothing else.

6. This dispute is between the depreciation approach and the user cost approach. The depreciation approach looks at the depreciation of natural assets in the same way that national accountants look at the depreciation of man-made capital. Net income equals gross income minus depreciation. So a given stock of a resource and the change in the stock during one year are estimated in physical terms. These physical changes are then valued at a price. For forests, for example, the price could be that of timber, although the true price may be much higher if nontimber values are also taken into account. The choice of prices is not straightforward. For the forest in Indonesia, for example, the valuation was at the rent of the timber, that is, the difference between the border price of timber and the costs of harvesting and transportation (the primary rent or stumpage value). Such valuations are not relevant to secondary forests, which are generated after the primary forest has been removed, because the best is taken first, and timber from secondary forests is simply not worth as much as timber from primary forests. In the Indonesian case this secondary rent was put at 0.5 of the primary rent. An example will illustrate how the analysis proceeds. In 1983 the opening physical stock was 24,239 million cubic meters. Natural growth was 51.9 million cubic meters. This growth was in secondary forest and hence was valued at the secondary rent of $17.72 per cubic meter and is an addition to value. Harvesting primary forest was 15.2 million cubic meters, so this is valued at the primary rent of $35.44, that is, $538.7 million is deducted from the value of the forest. Deforestation of secondary forest, 120 million cubic meters at $17.72, equals $2,126.4 million; logging damage of 30 million cubic meters at $17.72 equals $531.6 million; and fire damage of 153.8 million cubic meters (it was the year of a major fire), valued at an average of $25.10 to account for different mixes of primary and secondary timber, equals $3,860.4 million. The opening stock in 1983 was valued at $1,020,960 million. By adding the growth value and deducting the various losses, the closing stock is then $1,020,960 million plus $919.7 million minus $7,057.1 million equals $1,014,822.6 million. However, the rents changed during the year because world prices fell and the costs of harvesting rose slightly. At the end of 1983 the

stock had to be revalued. The stock was revalued by multiplying the end-of-year physical stock by the difference in the 1983 and 1982 rentals. Overall, then, the equation was the following:

End 1983 value = Opening 1983 value − (physical change × 1983 rentals) −
[end 1983 physical stock × (1982 rentals − 1983 rentals)].

The user cost approach is different. It looks at the revenue from the sale of the resource and splits that revenue into a capital element and a value-added element. The capital element is a user cost, that is, it is the benefit forgone in the future as a result of being without that part of the resource. The value-added component, however, is true income. To estimate user cost, one needs to estimate the discounted stream of future benefits forgone; this is the cost of resource depletion and should be deducted from GDP. The important point is that the depreciation approach does not affect GDP; whatever is depreciated is offset by the revenue generated by selling the resource. It does, however, affect the net domestic product, whereas the user cost approach affects GDP. How the share of true income to user cost is determined is still a matter of debate, but it has been suggested that the formula

(1-5) $$Y / R = 1 - [1 / (1 + r)^{n+1}]$$

gives the ratio of true income, Y, to royalties (R equals sales value minus costs), where r is the discount rate and n is the number of periods during which the resource is liquidated. $R - Y$ would then be the user cost. See El Serafy and Lutz (1989).

7. Although the diagrams in figure 1-3 were developed for agricultural systems, they contain implications for any economic system. All economic systems are ecosystems because they involve biological agents interacting with each other and with their environment. Systems can have low or high productivity; over time, output may fluctuate mildly or significantly or it may remain relatively stable. The manorial agricultural system, for example, involved hierarchical ownership and tenure of land, which was farmed in strips; its productivity was low. Systems may also be more or less equitable. Finally, systems may recover from shocks and stress, such as weather or intensive use, either quickly or slowly. The fundamental issue is whether ecosystems that are productive, stable, equitable, and sustainable are possible.

8. A statistical study of deforestation in Ecuador tested two hypotheses. First, using equation 1-6, it tested whether rural population pressure is determined by the local demand for agricultural products (measured by the size of the urban population in each area), the availability of soils suitable for agriculture, and accessibility (measured by the kilometers of roads in the area):

(1-6) $$\text{AGPOP} = b_0 + (b_1 \cdot \text{URBPOP}) + (b_2 \cdot \text{SOILS}) + (b_3 \cdot \text{ROADS}).$$

Second, using equation 1-7, it tested whether deforestation (DEFOR) arises from population pressure (AGPOP) and a measure of secure land tenure (TENSEC):

(1-7) $$\text{DEFOR} = b_4 + (b_5 \cdot \text{AGPOP}) + (b_6 \cdot \text{TENSEC}).$$

Using regression techniques, equation 1-6 was significant and confirmed that the pressure to deforest arises from opportunities to capture economic rents by colonizing new land. Similarly, equation 1-9 confirmed that both population pressure and the need to confirm land tenure (even a tenuous right to the land) are important factors explaining deforestation (Southgate, Sierra, and Brown 1989).

9. Some idea of the magnitude of these costs may be gauged, however. In 1979 an estimated 360 billion–400 billion working days were lost in Africa, Asia, and Latin America because of water-related diseases that kept individuals from work. At $0.50 a day, these continents lost some $180 billion–200 billion that year. Their GNP was around $370 billion, so output was below productive potential by perhaps 35 percent [200 / (200 + 370)]. On working days lost, see Walsh and Warren (1979).

2

The Concept of Sustainable Development

When the Brundtland Commission's *Our Common Future* was published in 1987, the concept of sustainable development took center stage in the debate over environment versus development. The concept had been embraced by the International Union for the Conservation of Nature in 1980 but remained, by and large, limited to the arena of conservationist dialog and thus had a limited impact on the thinking of governments and aid agencies.[1]

The concept emerged at a time when environmental issues were at the forefront of political debate. It was, however, a convenient phrase for rallying support rather than an agent for forcing environmental change. Moreover, as chapter 1 indicates, by holding out the promise that environment and economic development are potentially compatible or complementary objectives, sustainable development offered a welcome relief from the paradigm of conflict that had characterized the debate on limits to growth during the 1970s. One danger is that, insofar as pure complementarity is illusory, the concept of sustainable development could easily mislead policymakers. By asserting that complementarity exists, however, it at least forces policymakers to seek compatibility through more carefully designed projects and economic policy reforms.

Another danger is that sustainable development, as a political objective, could become diluted and ineffective. In large part this arises not because the concept focuses on sustainability—making things last—but because it uses the term development.

Economic Development and Economic Growth

Development implies change that leads to improvement or progress. Consequently, defining real development is a normative or value-laden issue, as is defining economic development. Not surprisingly, therefore, the definition of what constitutes economic development is disputed. It clearly involves change or transformation. An economy that raises its per capita level of real income over time without transforming its social and economic structure is unlikely to be viewed as developing.

Economic development is defined as achieving a set of social goals. Since these goals change over time, economic development is, to some extent, a process. A society in the process of economic development is likely to experience a combination of three sets of changes.

- An advance in the utility—which is simply satisfaction or well-being—experienced by individuals in society. A major factor contributing to advances in well-being is real income per capita. This is almost universally true in poor countries, although some would say it is not in rich countries. Another factor contributing to utility or well-being is the general quality of the environment. The well-being of the most disadvantaged sectors must be given greater weight in a developing society than that of society as a whole: if the well-being of society as a whole improves but that of the most disadvantaged sectors worsens, it seems reasonable to say that such a society is not developing.
- Advances, where needed, in the realms of education, health, and general quality of life (using the classification of Goulet 1971). Put positively, economic development involves advances in skills, knowledge, capability, and choice.
- Self-esteem and self-respect. A society is developing if it exhibits a growing sense of independence, which may be independence from domination by others or independence from the state.

Measuring the degree of change in a society and then reaching conclusions about the process of development are highly subjective tasks. For example, what would one call economic growth with equity, but without political freedom? Construed this way, economic development is a much wider concept than economic growth. Economic growth is generally defined as an increase over time in the level of real gross national product (GNP) per capita (or, sometimes, the real level of consumption per capita). The distinction between development and growth is important, for it means that prefixing sustainable to the term development separates sustainable economic development from sustainable economic growth. The two terms do not carry the same meaning.

Nonetheless, sustainable development and sustainable growth are linked. A society that does not maintain or improve its real income per capita is unlikely to be developing. If, however, it achieves growth at the expense of other social and political components, its development is being compromised.

Environment and Sustainable Development

At its most basic level, the philosophy of sustainable development asserts that environmental quality and the general services performed by natural environments are far more important than past development planning and economic management assumed. By raising the profile of the environment, sustainable development reflects a better understanding of the functions fulfilled by natural and built environments, which can be classified as follows.

- Direct contributions to the quality of life. Environments act as amenities. They are appreciated and enjoyed as a beautiful landscape, as an essential ingredient of recreational activity, and as the object of vicarious appreciation through television, film, and radio.
- Indirect contributions to the quality of life. Poor environments contribute to stress and ill health. Air and water pollution directly affect health, which, in turn, affects both the enjoyment of life and the ability of labor to support economic processes.
- Direct contributions to real income (GNP) through an environmental sector. The environmental sector—expenditures to protect the environment and provide amenity—creates income and employment. This fact is often overlooked when, as occurred during the 1970s, environment is viewed as a significant constraint on economic growth. Insofar as environmental expenditures are less productive (for GNP) than the expenditures they displace, economic growth is slower than otherwise would be the case. Generally, the impact of environmental expenditures is small (box 2-1).
- Direct contributions to economic activity as environmental inputs. Natural environments supply raw materials and energy in the form of oil, coal, gas, fuelwood, and minerals. The ability of the environmental media receiving these inputs to absorb and convert wastes (their assimilative capacity) is a further resource.
- Contributions to sustaining life-support systems generally. Although some ecological services are reasonably well defined, such as the watershed protection functions of tropical forests or the water purification functions of wetlands, they are frequently ignored in the economic analysis of environments. Other, broader services, which are often harder to characterize in economic terms, are of fundamental importance, since without them economies could not function in their current form, if at all. Stratospheric ozone, for

example, helps regulate the levels of radiation reaching the earth, while the natural carbon dioxide and other trace gases surrounding the earth help regulate climate. The oceans form part of the complex carbon and hydrological cycles essential for life, and ocean plankton is a critical component of the food chain and hence the productivity of the seas.

Broadly speaking, then, natural environments serve three major economic functions: they supply direct utility to individuals, they supply inputs to the economic process, and they supply services that support life. These three functions have direct relevance to how sustainable development is interpreted.

Sustainable Development and Equity

The philosophy of sustainable development seeks to elevate the importance of the environment in policymaking so that investments in enhanc-

---

Box 2-1. Expenditures on Environmental Protection and Economic Growth

In the 1970s the debate about environmental quality focused partly on whether economic growth was compatible with environmental quality. The antigrowth view argued that economic growth necessarily led to environmental degradation because growth meant that more and more raw materials and energy were being put into the economic system and hence more and more waste was being produced. Growth was expected to engender not only resource scarcity but also waste flows that would exceed the assimilative capacity of natural environments, thereby degrading or destroying essential life-support systems.

The progrowth view argued that growth was the only way to generate the funds for environmental protection, but that too much environmental expenditure would constrain growth, impair international competitiveness, and reduce employment.

Much the same set of arguments can be found in the modern environmental debate. Some empirical research has been done to test the validity of both views. In one such study, the OECD projected the effect that actual environmental expenditures would have on GNP or GDP in select countries. The results are shown in table B2-1, which compares GNP or GDP with and without environmental expenditures. The negative effect of environmental expenditures was generally less than 1 percent of GNP, and data from several countries indicated that environmental expenditures actually increased growth. That is, environmental programs produced either very small losses or actual gains in GNP. Furthermore, the effect is measured in conventional GNP, which does not take into account environmental damage as a reduction in income in the broader sense of well-being or utility. The results tend to support the argument that growth and the environment are complementary. Nevertheless, much more research is needed to establish a wider range of experience before firm conclusions can be reached.

Future trends may not be a linear extension of past or current experience. The effect on conventionally measured GNP could grow if environmental programs get more costly as expensive environmental problems loom large (the greenhouse effect, for example) and public pressure grows to increase environmental standards.

Table B2-1. Impact of Environmental Expenditures on GNP in Select OECD Countries, Various Years
(percentage gain or loss of absolute GNP)

Country, year, and nature of the program	First year	After several years	Final year	After the program ends
Austria, 1979–85				
Base program	—	—	−0.2	—
Increased program	—	—	−0.6/+0.5	—
Finland, 1976–82				
Water pollution	+0.3	+0.5	+0.6	—
France, 1966–74				
Actual program	—	—	+0.1	—
Increased program	—	—	+0.4	—
Netherlands, 1979–85	+0.1	—	−0.3/−0.6	−0.4/−0.7
Norway, 1974–83	—	—	+1.5	—
United States, 1970–87	+0.2	—	−0.6/−1.1	—

— Not available.

Note: Environmental programs do not have unambiguous effects on GNP. All the programs appear to increase GNP in the first year, but their effect in the final year may be positive in some cases and negative in others. Moreover, the effects on inflation were unfavorable, with maximum annual increases of 0.3–0.5 percentage points in the price index. The effects on employment were favorable.

Source: OECD (1985).

ing the environment, or preventing its degradation, are accorded a higher social rate of return than before. There is considerable evidence that this is indeed the case. Chapter 1 assembles national damage studies that provide initial evidence for this; chapter 5 looks at further evidence. But there are certainly other justifications for conserving environmental capital, including issues of equity within and among generations.

Intragenerational Equity

A constant or growing stock of natural capital is likely to serve the goal of achieving fairness within a generation, that is, achieving justice for the socially disadvantaged both within a country and between countries at a given point in time. This is especially true for poor developing economies that depend on their natural resources. Examples of intragenerational equity include reliance on biomass fuels such as fuelwood, crop residues, and animal waste; untreated water supplies; natural fertilizers (organic materials) to maintain soil quality; fodder from natural vegetation for livestock; and wildlife meat for protein (tables 2-1 and 2-2). Protecting

Table 2-1. Direct Dependence of Households on Biomass Fuels in Developing Countries, Various Years
(percentage of household energy met by biomass fuels)

Country and year	Fuelwood	Charcoal	Other biomass	Total
Benin, 1984	88	2	7	97
Botswana, 1982	96	..	..	96
Congo, 1985	84	3	..	87
Côte d'Ivoire, 1982	86	6	..	92
Ethiopia, 1982	40	1	58	99
Ghana, 1985	73	14	6	93
Kenya, 1985	83	12	..	95
Liberia, 1983	87	11	..	98
Malawi, 1980	99	..	..	99
Mauritania,1983	82	10	5	97
Niger, 1981	99	..	..	99
Nigeria, 1980	92	1	..	93
Senegal, 1981	86	11	..	97
Sierra Leone, 1984	91	4	..	95
Somalia, 1984	89	6	4	99
Sudan, 1981	54	35	9	98
Tanzania, 1981	96	3	..	99
Uganda, 1980	96	3	..	99
Zaire, 1983	93	6	..	99
Zimbabwe, 1980	85	..	..	85

.. Negligible.

Note: Households depend almost totally on biomass energy in most Sub-Saharan African countries. The picture is dominated by woodfuels—either fuelwood for direct burning or charcoal. Other biomass fuels—crop residues, tree litter, grass, and animal dung—are generally unimportant outside Ethiopia (within Ethiopia, however, most of the 58 percent of biomass fuel obtained from sources other than fuelwood and charcoal is dung).

Source: World Bank (1989a).

natural environments, by implication, safeguards this direct dependence and contributes to the health and welfare of the population. Of course, maintaining environmental capital also imposes costs on the poor by obliging them to pay for measures that conserve the needed asset. This is especially relevant when tax systems are regressive, a point we return to shortly.

Of course, resources can be and are substituted over time. In India, for example, some 42 percent of all households relied on fuelwood for energy in 1979, compared with only 27 percent in 1984. The principal substitutes were kerosene (18 percent of households used kerosene in 1979 compared with 36 percent in 1984) and liquid propane gas (7 and 11 percent, respectively; Leach 1988). Similarly, 50 percent of India's rural population now has access to safe drinking water compared with only 18 percent fifteen to twenty years ago (World Bank 1989).

Table 2-2. Access to Safe Drinking Water in Developing Countries
(percentage of the population)

Country	Urban	Rural	Total
Bangladesh	24	49	44
Benin	80	34	57
Bolivia	82	27	53
Brazil	89	71	84
China	81	—	—
Costa Rica	100	82	93
Dominican Republic	73	24	50
Egypt	88	44	62
Ethiopia	69	9	14
Haiti	59	30	38
India	76	50	57
Indonesia	43	36	39
Mexico	79	51	70
Nepal	70	25	28
Philippines	49	54	52

— Not available.
Note: Rural populations generally have less access to safe water than urban populations. It is not unusual for more than 50 percent of the total population to lack access to safe water, which underlines the health hazards posed by waterborne diseases that face much of the world's population.
Source: World Bank (1989a).

The importance that maintaining access to natural capital has for ensuring equity is less obvious for developed countries. Indeed, the contrary view—that the demand for environmental assets is biased toward the rich—tends to define the conventional wisdom (for this view, see Baumol and Oates 1988, chap. 15). However, supposing that the income elasticity of demand is high—that is, that the demand for environmental quality rises more than proportionately as income grows—is, as yet, unsupported by the evidence (Pearce 1980).

Before we can declare the environment to be a good that favors the rich—that is, a good that tends to be consumed proportionately more by the rich than by the poor—we need evidence that the amount of environmental goods consumed tends to rise more rapidly as income increases. Natural environments tend to be public goods, which means that, if available, they tend to be supplied to all groups because no group can be excluded from the benefits. Thus if air quality is improved because one group mounts a campaign for a better environment, persons who are indifferent to better air quality will also experience the improvement; they cannot be kept from enjoying the benefits of cleaner air. The supply of public goods, then, is shared and cannot exclude any one group. One implication is that since they wield more political power than the poor, the rich can force the poor to buy more environmental policy than they wish (this is, essentially, the argument presented by Baumol and Oates 1988).

Many environmental assets tend to be local rather than global. Air quality varies among areas, and the rich can buy better air quality than the poor by, for example, choosing where they work and live accordingly. If everyone were free to move in response to regional variations in environmental quality, each income group would be likely to consume the right amount of environmental goods to satisfy its preferences. In practice, even in industrial economies, mobility is often limited by income and social constraints: the poor cannot move to pleasant locations that are far from business districts, and business districts are, in turn, often congested, noisy, and polluted.

The gross benefits of environmental improvements in the industrial world do not seem to be systematically related to income. A review of the literature for the United States found that income elasticities for the benefits of the 1970 U.S. Clean Air Act were less than unity; this implies that, as income rose, the proportion of environmental benefit to income fell (D.W. Pearce 1980). However, the costs of meeting the U.S. standards for air quality were regressive: the poor paid a greater portion of their taxes to reduce pollution than did the rich, a reflection of the tax system at that time. In the United States, the net benefits of environmental quality appear to be regressive. Other studies, such as those of standards for water quality in the United States, offer no systematic pattern. Thus the evidence that the nature of localized environmental quality in the industrial world favors the rich is not compelling.

No systematic study has yet been conducted on the incidence of the environmental effects that have been hypothesized for, say, global warming, ozone depletion, or ocean pollution. By its very nature, global pollution does not respect wealth or persons, but its effects relative to actual income could, however, be most severe in poor countries, particularly low-lying countries that might experience flooding if the sea level were to rise.

As far as developing countries are concerned, environmental improvement is likely to be consistent with the goal of achieving equity within generations, especially in the poorest economies that depend on agriculture. In these economies, the trap of environmental degradation and poverty prevails: as poverty increases, natural environments are degraded to obtain immediate food supplies. As environments degenerate, the prospects for future livelihood decrease: environmental degradation generates more poverty, thus accelerating the cycle. The provision of natural capital offers one way to break the cycle. For wealthy countries, the evidence for the positive equity function of local environmental quality is inconclusive. For global pollution, the incidence of pollution has barely been studied.

Intergenerational Equity

The most widely quoted definition of sustainable development is development that "meets the needs of the present without compromising the ability of future generations to meet their own needs" (World Commission on Environment and Development 1987, p. 8). Although economists often have difficulty with the term "needs," this definition of sustainable development can also be expressed in the language of economics by replacing the concept of needs with that of well-being or welfare.[2] Needs, however, often imply that certain kinds of wants—nutrition, education, health—should be addressed first in any development plan. The definition of sustainable development can then be restated as development that secures increases in the welfare of the current generation provided that welfare in the future does not decrease.[3] This is known as intergenerational equity.

This definition is consistent with the idea of a Pareto improvement for society as a whole, where society is taken to embrace current and future generations.[4] This interpretation of sustainable development may be expressed as Pareto sustainability (a term coined by Mäler 1989b).

Chapter 1 distinguishes development that is sustainable from development that is optimal. Sustainable development is interpreted as a continuous increase in—or at least maintenance of—human welfare over time. This is consistent with the Brundtland definition. We might add to this the concept of survivability, which recognizes the existence of a minimum level of welfare below which societies cannot survive. Figure 2-1 illustrates the three ideas as paths of welfare over time. Optimal paths may be neither sustainable nor survivable, and sustainable paths may not be optimal.

Using the Pareto criterion to determine whether or not society will experience a welfare gain is of limited applicability. In too many situations, a given project or policy will make some people worse off and some better off. According to the Pareto improvement criterion, none of these projects or policies could be classified as a gain to society as a whole, and this is unduly restrictive. Economists have therefore modified the criterion so that it applies to situations in which some people gain and some lose. The revised criterion revolves around the idea of hypothetical compensation. Suppose a policy involves costs to society of $10, gains to group A of $20, and losses to group B of $8. If the gains and losses are comparable, we could say that the benefit to society is $20 − $8 = $12, and the cost to society is $10. The net gain is therefore $2. But since group B loses and group A gains, according to the strict Pareto criterion we could not sanction this policy. One way of seeing if a Pareto improvement is possible is to see what group B requires as compensation. A sum of $8 would be enough to offset their losses and leave them in the same

Figure 2-1. Optimality, Sustainability, and Survivability

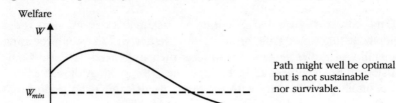

Note: Optimality is a path of development that maximizes the present value of future gains in human welfare. Sustainability is human welfare that rises, or at least does not fall, over time. Survivability is a path of development that lies above a minimum level of welfare; anything below it is not survivable. Being fair to the future could be interpreted as ensuring that the welfare path never falls over time.

Source: Pezzey (1989).

shape they were in before. If group A paid the compensation, their net gain would be $20 − $8 = $12. As a whole, there are also costs of $10 for the project. If we assume, for convenience, that these costs are met by group A, then A's final net gains would be $12 − $10 = $2.

The principle of hypothetical compensation does not involve actual compensation. That is, if the policy is adopted, group A really will gain $20 and group B really will lose $8. For this reason, the principle of hypothetical compensation deals in potential, not actual, welfare: potential welfare is increased if those who gain from a project or policy could compensate those who lose and still have something left over (this is the Kaldor-Hicks compensation principle).

The potential welfare criterion is much more than an academic construct. It underlies the philosophy of cost-benefit analysis, which compares the benefits and costs of a project. A project is sanctioned, at least in principle, if its benefits exceed its costs. Costs and benefits are recorded regardless of who bears the costs or receives the benefits. But to sanction a project or policy because its benefits exceed its costs is to engage in hypothetical compensation, which only asserts that the beneficiaries could compensate the losers and still receive net benefits.

Does this mean that we can identify sustainable development by simply subjecting all development proposals to cost-benefit appraisals? Although this is certainly one view of sustainable development, it is hardly adequate. It is also inconsistent with the Brundtland definition, which explicitly forbids actions that benefit the current generation but impose net costs on future generations. Under the principle of hypothetical compensation, a project that produces gains to the present but losses to the future can be justified if the current gains could be used to compensate future generations. The challenge, then, is to have the definition of sustainable development preclude the current generation from engaging in policies that actually make the future generation worse off. The obvious answer is to require intergenerational compensation.

Intergenerational Compensation

How might intergenerational compensation work? It might be brought about in two ways: the creation of an intergenerational fund and the preservation of nondeclining capital stocks.

An Intergenerational Fund

To ensure that future generations are not made worse off by the actions of the present generation requires a mechanism for transferring resources to the future. One transfer mechanism would involve actual cash. Imagine that the current generation engages in a policy that it knows will incur costs for future generations—say, the costs of disposing of long-lived radioactive waste or the costs of a rise in sea level due to global warming. Let the known costs in real terms be X. Assume also that the current generation knows when the costs will be incurred, and, to make the analysis simple, assume that this occurs at a specific time T years from now. Finally, assume that the real interest rate, r, is positive.[5] A sum of money, S, can then be set aside, which will cumulate to equal X in T years. The computation is simple compound-interest arithmetic:

$$S = X / (1 + r)^T.$$

The assumptions of this effort to determine the size of an intergenerational compensation fund are clearly simplistic. The values of both X and T are frequently unknown. In addition, the value of r will not necessarily stay the same.[6] If we are uncertain about the size of X, r, and T, the computation of S will be very hit-and-miss.

In some circumstances, where the parameters are well known and the interest rate is unlikely to change because of environmental factors, establishing an intergenerational compensation fund may be feasible. Such a fund could then be used to compensate future generations for losses incurred by the actions of current generations. The implication for current decisions, then, is that, at least where future generations are expected to be worse off, each project or policy that is likely to affect future generations negatively should be debited with the costs of future compensation, suitably discounted to the present. The concept of intergenerational compensation makes little difference to the cost-benefit appraisal of decisions, which would, in any event, compute the compensation required for future generations. Cost-benefit appraisal would show this compensation as a cost of the project and discount the cost to the present. The critical difference is that each and every project or policy involving this intergenerational externality must set aside actual sums of money for compensation.

Given the uncertainty surrounding many intergenerational externalities, the compensation fund has limited validity in practice. An alternative approach focuses on the idea of passing compensation on to future generations as assets, or capital.

Nondeclining Capital Stocks

Economists are used to thinking of several different types of capital. Machines, factories, and roads are examples of man-made capital, Km.[7] The stock of knowledge and skills is human capital, Kh. The stock of natural assets or environmental assets covers a wide spectrum. Soil fertility, forests, fisheries, the capacity to assimilate waste, oil, gas, coal, the ozone layer, and biogeochemical cycles are all natural capital, Kn. Therefore, the stock of all capital, K, can be written as

$$K = Km + Kh + Kn.$$

For convenience we shall incorporate Kh into Km. In addition, Kn is not a homogeneous category: some categories of natural capital support life and are thus more critical than others. That is, we may well want to distinguish oil from the ozone layer, gold from tropical forests, or bauxite from the carbon cycle. This diversity can be categorized by the degree of substitutability between types of capital. As a generalization, it might be much easier to substitute coal for oil (substitution within Kn) or capital equipment for mineral resources (Km for Kn) than to substitute Km for the ozone layer (some economists point to difficulties even with these forms of substitution since Km invariably contains Kn as an input; Perrings 1987). The degree of substitutability should thus be incorporated into the relative value given to different types of capital, taking into account that lack of substitutability, by itself, does not necessarily imply high value. That is, we would expect a tropical forest containing a rich store of biodiversity to have a higher value than, say, machinery. The problem, of course, is that these values are not readily observed because markets rarely exist for the life-support functions of natural environments. We also know little about how ecosystems function in the service of mankind.

We might therefore rewrite the simple identity above as

$$K = Km + Kn + Kn^*$$

where Kh is now included in Km, and Kn^* relates to critical capital for which substitution is difficult and perhaps impossible.

These definitions of capital are relevant because intergenerational compensation can be facilitated by passing on to the next generation an amount of capital, K, that is not less than the capital inherited by the present generation. The process of actual compensation is fair to future generations provided, of course, they do not mismanage their capital inheritance. It ensures that they will be no worse off than the current generation. This is the notion of intergenerational equity. The capital concepts enter into this intergenerational equity as follows. If the current generation leaves the next generation a stock of capital, K, that is not less than the stock currently possessed, the next generation can use that stock to generate the same level of welfare as this generation has.

This formulation represents a departure from some interpretations of the underlying principles of cost-benefit analysis, which some economists regard as dealing with efficiency considerations only. However, the idea of modifying cost-benefit analysis to allow for equity considerations within a generation is quite familiar, especially in the context of developing countries (for a discussion of equity weighing in industrial economies, see Pearce 1986; for developing economies, see Squire and van der Tak 1975). The approach adopted here takes intergenerational equity into account through actual compensation (the theoretical foundations for supposing that capital stocks must be held constant to achieve intergenerational fairness are set out in Solow 1986, pp. 141–49).

Substituting between Types of Capital

The previous section suggests that sustainable development is about conserving the overall capital stock since this is consistent with economic efficiency and intergenerational fairness. Focusing on the overall stock implies that substitution can take place between natural and man-made capital. The extent of this substitution depends on the comparative social rate of return. That is, whether or not we should allow deforestation or desertification depends on the social returns we can obtain by substituting man-made capital for the services of the natural environment.

This implicitly assumes that running down natural capital should be allowed only if the proceeds from doing so are invested to secure a higher rate of return in man-made capital. Some oil-rich countries carefully manage their portfolios to do exactly this. As their oil reserves are depleted, they reinvest a sizable proportion of the rents generated by exploiting those resources, sometimes in industry, sometimes in services such as banking, and often in property and financial assets elsewhere. But all too often the proceeds of environmental degradation or depreciation are consumed rather than reinvested. The issue of valuation is, once again, crucial to the analysis. It is not possible to rely on markets to determine the amount of substitution that should be made between natural and man-made capital. Very simply, markets fail to account for the unpriced services of the environment. To be accurate, valuations must trace the role and importance of natural capital, say, in the form of forests or ecological cycles, by way of economic functions.

When the natural capital in question becomes critical or essential, there may be little or no room for a tradeoff or substitution with other forms of capital. The idea that limited substitution possibilities exist for these forms of critical capital goes some way toward interpreting the concern that many environmental scientists have with preservation as a no-use option. In the language of sustainable development, they are concerned that future generations will inevitably be worse off if these critical systems are degraded now and that it may prove impossible, or at least very difficult, to compensate them by building other forms of capital. Such critical capital stocks need to be passed on intact. Identifying critical capital stock is difficult and only in part an economic issue. Human values and ecological analysis will have to show just how important such systems are.

Finally, the idea of maintaining or increasing total capital stock allows natural capital to decline if the valuation process warrants it. This permissible environmental depreciation contrasts with the idea of pure complementarity between environment and development, which is one interpretation of the Brundtland Commission's philosophy. Nevertheless, the proviso regarding proper valuation is consistent with the idea underlying all the literature on sustainable development: environmental conservation has a high social rate of return. We now turn to this idea.

Sustainable Development and Environmental Capital

In addition to its role in equity within and between generations, environmental conservation contributes to resilience and efficiency.

Natural Capital and Resilience

Both man-made and natural capital help economies recover from acute or chronic external shocks and stresses. At the starkest level, the likelihood that a poor agricultural country will be able to withstand external shocks, such as climatic variations, and stresses, such as international indebtedness, increases as its stock of natural capital—including working capital such as seed stocks and food security—grows. Man-made capital can also serve these functions, although it tends to lack an important feature of natural capital: diversity.

Some of the literature on sustainable development stresses that resilience requires the adoption of ecologically sensitive technologies adapted to local agroecological conditions. Animal draft power may therefore be better than tractors. Organic fertilizer supplies nutrients and body to the soil, unlike artificial fertilizers, which only provide a nutrient base and may increase the risk of runoff. Substituting man-made capital for depleted natural resources may, in any event, not be feasible in the poorest societies, which lack cash and foreign exchange. In this case, augmenting natural capital becomes the only route to sustainability. This explains the current focus on agroforestry, water harvesting techniques, and socially relevant technology.

Again, the rationale for conserving natural capital appears to be weaker for the industrial world. These countries have more flexible margins of risk than poorer countries, where rapid population growth and weak economic progress often produce very narrow risk margins in the face of external disturbances. When ecological systems come under stress, industrial nations are more capable than developing nations of substituting technology. But the comparative resilience of the industrial world to such shocks and stresses is mostly illusion. The technologies used to advance economic progress rely on the world's common property resources, notably the atmosphere and stratosphere for receiving air pollutants and the oceans for receiving liquid and solid effluents. The evidence of stress in those systems is not disputed; these include damage to the ozone, the greenhouse effect, acid rain, and major reductions in the biological diversity of oceans.

Citing resilience as a justification for conserving the natural capital stock is based on the idea that diverse ecological and economic systems are more resilient to shocks and stress than systems that are limited. In turn, to maintain diversity irreversible choices must be avoided as far as possible. Since knowledge is rarely lost forever—although tribal knowledge is lost if the tribe disappears—economic irreversibility is likely to be rare. A discontinued machine can be recreated, towns can be rebuilt, and so on. Nevertheless, ecological irreversibility is not unusual: natural species are lost every year, unique ecosystems are destroyed, and environmental functions are irreparably damaged. All this suggests that we should only destroy natural capital stock if the benefits of doing so are very large. Put another way, irreversible destruction of natural capital stock should be avoided unless the social costs of conservation are unacceptably large. This basic rule defines the safe minimum standards approach to environmental conservation (this approach was defined by Ciriancy-Wantrup 1952 and developed by Bishop 1978; box 2-2).

*Box 2-2. Illustrating the Safe Minimum Standards Approach
to Conservation*

Consider a piece of land faced with two options: development, D, and preservation, P. If D occurs, the benefits of P (B_p) are lost forever. The benefits of preservation are uncertain. We can characterize this uncertainty simply by saying that yes, Y, means that preservation benefits exist, while no, N, means that no preservation benefits exist. The benefits of D (B_d) are known with certainty. The possibilities are given in the matrix below, which shows the losses accompanying certain decisions.

For example, if we choose to develop the site, D, and the preservation benefits are positive, we lose B_p. If we develop and no preservation benefits exist, no losses occur. If we preserve, P, and positive preservation benefits exist, we lose the development benefits but gain the preservation benefits. Thus the choice combination P,Y produces a maximum loss of $B_d - B_p$. If we preserve and the preservation benefits turn out to be zero, we lose the development benefits.

The idea underlying the calculation of maximum losses, the last column in the matrix, is that we may wish to avoid these very large losses. More formally, an attractive option in the face of uncertainty and irreversibility is to minimize the maximum losses, or to minimax. The safe minimum standards approach pays particular attention to the fact that the lower B_d is, the more likely is it that the minimax solution will be preferred. That is, we should ensure that B_d really is large before committing ourselves to irreversible losses of natural capital.

Clearly, the degree of uniqueness of the asset in question is central to calculating the potential losses associated with irreversible development. For example, if the plot in question were unique, the benefits of preserving it would be much higher than if many similar plots existed.

*Table B2-2. Matrix for the Losses Produced by the Decision to Develop
or Preserve*

Option	Preservation benefits	No preservation benefits	Maximum loss
Develop (D)	B_p	0	B_p
Preserve (P)	$B_d - B_p$	B_d	B_d

Economic Efficiency

If important, natural capital should show up in higher rates of return to environmentally benign investments. Man-made capital, Km, tends to be a marketed product, whereas Kn tends to yield environmental services that have no market and hence no perceived price. Since the price of Kn appears to be lower than it should, more of Kn will be used than Km. Nor is there adequate incentive to augment natural capital since increments in it partly yield nonmarketed outputs and services with no price.

Revenues associated with an investment in Kn often considerably under-state the rate of return to augmenting Kn.

This bias reflects the primacy of markets (misplaced concreteness) as well as our ignorance of the multiple functions of natural systems. Reha-bilitating wetlands, for example, may yield both cash flows for fisheries and recreation and nonmarketed outputs such as hydrological protec-tion, water purification, and inland storm protection. Efforts to put economic value on these nonmarketed functions, and even to trace other disguised market functions of natural systems, demonstrate that the true rate of return to investments in Kn is significantly higher than the concen-tration of market outputs suggests (box 2-3).

The argument for economic efficiency does not, therefore, favor Km over Kn when they compete for investment funds. A more comprehensive valuation is needed of the economic services provided by natural capital systems.

Economic Implications of Sustainable Development

We have dwelled at length on the meaning of sustainable development in order to suggest several major steps that must be taken in practice. These steps are briefly surveyed here; later chapters deal with them in more detail.

Sustainability Indicators: Changing the National Accounting System

A significant amount of effort is already being directed toward modify-ing how economic progress is measured. The basic indicator of economic progress is GNP, which measures the aggregate value of the economy's output in a given year. GNP should be related to society's well-being—if it rises, well-being should have improved—but this is misleading. In addi-tion to other problems with using it as a measure of welfare, GNP does not record damage done to the environment, which may lower economic welfare. Just because environmental effects do not generally have mar-kets does not mean that they have no economic value. By measuring the value of marketed output, GNP essentially ignores the environment. Any environmental damage that occurs should be valued and deducted from GNP.

National account statisticians are accustomed to estimating the amount of depreciation of man-made capital. They deduct this deprecia-tion from GNP to get net national product (NNP). This is a better measure of well-being than GNP because it allows for the decay, or depreciation, of some of the wealth from which GNP flows. NNP ignores, however, natural wealth, which also depreciates. This occurs, for example, when oil reserves are depleted or the standing stock of forest is reduced. No logic can support including one form of depreciation and not the other.

Box 2-3. Ensuring That the Economic Rate of Return to Investment Reflects Environmental Benefits in Nigeria

Environmentalists often argue that tree-growing programs should be supported because they have many environmental benefits. Careful examination and measurement of the benefits of afforestation can greatly increase the economic rate of return to investments in forestry. One study in northern Nigeria shows how.

Afforestation in northern Nigeria has four benefits: (a) halting the decline of soil fertility (since trees typically reduce soil erosion); (b) raising the level of soil fertility; (c) producing tree products—fuelwood, poles, and fruits; and (d) producing fodder both from soil that is more productive and from forest fodder. Yet conventional analysis tends to concentrate only on tree products. In the arid zones of Nigeria, such analysis reveals rates of return of around 5 percent, which must be compared with the cut-off rate, which is usually much higher, of around 10 percent. In other words, afforestation does not pay. Once the other benefits are included, the increases in the rates of return can be dramatic.

Two investments were considered: shelterbelts, where trees are planted as windbreaks and thus protect land, and farm forestry, where farmers plant trees on the boundary of their farm, perhaps mixed with crops. Table B2-3 shows the rates of return for each investment.

The analysis shows that counting the benefits of wood alone produces negative net present value and correspondingly low internal rates of return. If allowance is made for the effects of trees on crop yields, and for expected rates of soil erosion in the absence of afforestation, the picture is transformed for both farm forestry and shelterbelts.

Source: D. Anderson (1987, 1989).

Table B2-3. Rates of Return to Shelterbelts and Farm Forestry

	Shelterbelts		Farm forestry	
Yield	*Net present value*	*Internal rate of return*	*Net present value*	*Internal rate of return*
Base case	170	14.9	129	19.1
Low yield, high cost	110	13.1	70	14.5
High yield	221	16.2	..	..
No erosion	108	13.5	75	16.6
More rapid erosion	109	13.6	60	15.5
Soil restored plus jump in yield	263	16.9	203	21.8
Wood benefits only[a]	−95	4.7	−14	7.4

.. Negligible.
a. Wood and fruit for farm forestry.

Accounting systems are beginning to be modified, but these changes are complex and costly. A feasible first step would be to publish a separate set of resource accounts that show, in nonmonetary units, just what is happening to the resources in a given country. Such accounts exist in France and Norway. More modest modifications can be made to sets of environmental statistics published in most countries, both industrial and developing. These accounts should show how changes in environmental variables are linked to changes in the economy. This at least avoids the error of managing the economy as if it were not related to environment. Chapter 4 looks at modifications to national income measures in more detail.

Correcting Prices

Ascribing the right economic value to natural resources is vital. Two ingredients are needed. First, the price of a natural resource should reflect its full value. That price is obviously linked to the cost of extracting or harvesting it. The market mechanism will ensure that these costs are reflected in the price, but extraction and harvesting can impose other costs as well. Removing timber indiscriminately from a tropical forest damages the watershed through river pollution and soil erosion. Those costs are not reflected in the price of timber, and the market has failed because the price of timber does not reflect the value of the natural environmental services effectively used. Prices should reflect not only the extraction and harvesting costs but also the environmental costs.

Another adjustment should be made to resource prices. If a resource is harvested sustainably, its stock will remain broadly constant over time. If it is used unsustainably, its stock will be reduced and what is lost will not be available to the next generation. This future benefit that is lost because of unsustainable management is called a user cost. Obviously, a user cost must be involved every time an exhaustible resource is extracted. A user cost is also attached to the unsustainable use of a renewable resource. The basic rule is that the proper pricing of natural resources should reflect the costs of extraction (or harvesting) plus environmental costs plus user costs (box 2-4).

The second adjustment is to the price of commodities. Because the production of goods and services uses environmental services and treats them as if they were free, the price of the goods and services produced are incorrect. The adjustment required is consistent with the principle of the polluter pays, in which the polluter must pay the costs of cleaning up the environment or the costs of the environmental damage done by producing the good in question. This can be done by imposing a charge on the good for its pollution content. Part of the cost will be passed on to the consumer in the form of higher prices. This may seem to make the consumer rather than the polluter pay, but it is exactly what should happen. The consumers are, after all, the ultimate polluter: they tell the

Box 2-4. Proper Pricing of Natural Resources

The underlying principle of natural resource pricing is that resource prices should reflect

- The cost of extraction or harvesting
- Any environmental costs involved in extraction, harvesting, and use
- The benefits forgone in the future from using a unit of the resource today.

The costs of extraction and harvesting are measured by their marginal cost (MC), which is the cost of taking one extra unit of the resource. Environmental costs should be estimated as the additional damage caused by the extra unit of resource harvested and used, which is the marginal external cost (MEC). The costs of future use forgone are also known as user costs or depletion premia. The user cost is usually estimated by looking at the costs of the replacement that future consumers will have to use—sometimes called the backstop technology. An estimate of the marginal user cost (MUC) is then MUC = $(Pb - C) / (1 + r)^T$, where Pb is the price of the replacement technology, C is the cost of extraction or harvesting, r is the discount rate, and T is the time period in which the replacement technology comes in.

Table B2-4 shows the cost, without the environmental costs, of supplying natural gas to various users in Bangladesh. The economic cost of supply is equal to MC + MUC, and this is compared with ruling prices. The price of sales to residential consumers is very close to the economic cost of supply, whereas it is higher for commercial users and much lower for small industrial consumers. The price also includes an excise duty collected by the government, so the price to the supplier of the gas (the utility) is well below the economic cost of the supply. This means that the suppliers operate at a loss and have no incentive to reinvest in further exploration.

Table B2-4. Economic Cost of Natural Gas in Bangladesh, by Type of User

Cost	Residential	Commercial	Small industry
Marginal cost	1.42	0.88	1.65
Marginal user cost	0.06	0.06	0.06
Economic cost	1.48	0.94	1.71
Sales price	1.49	1.77	1.47
Excise duty	0.45	0.61	0.55
Price to utility	1.04	1.16	0.92

Source: Julius and Mashayekhi (1990).

producer what they want and should therefore pay the full costs of its production. In practice, pollution charges are rare: the principle of the polluter pays is usually implemented by making the polluter pay the costs of regulations designed to achieve a given environmental standard. We need much more imaginative policies involving pollution charges. Chapters 7 and 8 look at pricing policy and environmental effects in more detail.

Project Appraisal

The third modification required to implement sustainable development is to alter how we appraise investments. When deciding on a development project, we all too often pay only lip service to the environment. This is especially true of the rules used by the bilateral and multilateral agencies that extend loans to the developing world. The practice is being changed slowly. We must change how we measure the environmental effects of projects and integrate environmental values into the economic appraisal. The techniques for doing this are widely available, although a large amount of work remains to be done. In the standard benefit-cost model, a project is potentially acceptable if benefits, b, minus costs, c, suitably discounted are greater than zero, that is, where r is the discount rate and t is time. The first modification ensures that costs include any environmental damage and benefits include any environmental gains arising because of the project. The rule is more explicitly written as

$$\Sigma_t (B_t - C_t \pm E_t)(1 - r)^{-t} > 0$$

where E is environmental loss $(-)$ or gain $(+)$. Chapter 5 looks in more detail at the valuation issue.

A second concern is r. If the discount rate is high, future environmental costs could appear unimportant when discounted. Some people believe the value of r should be lowered, perhaps even to zero in such circumstances. This view, which is not shared by the authors, is addressed in detail in chapter 3.

Notes

1. World Commission on Environment and Development (1987); International Union for the Conservation of Nature (1980). The intellectual heritage of the concept of sustainability is much older. For an overview, see O'Riordan (1988). Sustainability in the sense of sustainable yields from a constant optimal stock of renewable resources—which is fundamental to the broader concept of sustainability—was formally analyzed by economists studying forests in the nineteenth century and by economists studying fisheries in the twentieth.

2. Much of the economics literature prefers the term "utility," which can be translated as pleasure. We avoid the term here because well-being and welfare have a more acceptable, wider connotation. Development cannot be reduced strictly to advances in utility, as the earlier discussion of the meaning of development showed.

3. This definition is more limited than the criteria generally used for intragenerational and international policymaking. In international policymaking, most would argue that when costs are involved, compensation should go to the poor rather than to the wealthy. Extending this to arguments concerning equity among generations implies that if future generations are expected to be better off than the current generation or if they might benefit from other present policies, they should not be compensated for current policies. Future generations should only be compensated if they are expected to be poor.

4. A Pareto improvement is any situation in which at least one person can be made better

off (his or her welfare is increased) without anyone else being made worse off. When no further changes improve the welfare of some people without decreasing the welfare of others, we have a Pareto optimum. But no unique Pareto optimum exists; rather, there is a whole set of optima because the Pareto criterion is indifferent to the distribution of gains and losses. It tells us only that a move from an inefficient to an efficient point is worthwhile, not that a particular allocation of resources should be chosen from the many efficient allocations possible.

5. Economists are frequently ridiculed for assuming problems away. In this case, however, by making the assumptions explicit, we can identify the degree of realism in the proposal.

6. Indeed, in some contexts r will not be determined exogenously, that is, outside the confines of the compensation fund model. If the more serious scenarios relating to the greenhouse effect were to come about, environmental degradation would actually reduce the future growth of income, even though income growth is one of the factors determining the interest rate. In other words, the marginal productivity of capital will itself be affected by environmental change, but interest rates depend on the marginal productivity of capital. The interest rate is therefore endogenous. See Mäler (1989b).

7. Also termed reproducible capital; we avoid the term here because it can be confused with self-reproducing capital, such as a stock of trees.

3

Fairness and Time

Just as the concept exists of equity within a generation, so does that of equity between generations. Intergenerational equity has recently attracted a great deal of attention from philosophers, political scientists, and economists. This interest has undoubtedly been prompted by the nature of the environmental problems emerging as the twentieth century closes. The problems have become increasingly global in nature, and they cannot be reversed. Once primary tropical forests are destroyed, they cannot, generally, be recreated. Certainly, the species lost through their destruction cannot be recreated. Global warming also cannot be reversed once it occurs. This irreversibility confers a perpetual loss on all generations to come, and that loss will be greeted with varying degrees of regret that preceding generations did not act more wisely.

Views differ about how irreversibility should be built into the decisionmaking process and the advice given to decisionmakers. Keeping all options open could be enormously expensive and may not be justified if future generations are unlikely to regret the loss on a significant scale. Also few, if any, projects are evaluated by their costs and benefits in perpetuity. Practical considerations dictate that a finite period should be determined after which costs and benefits are cut off. Another feature of economic decisionmaking—the phenomenon of discounting—also cuts off future gains and losses.

As we shall see, discounting assigns diminishing weights to a given gain or loss as that gain or loss stretches into the future. In effect, discounting biases current decisions in favor of projects and policies that shift forward many of the costs. Ultimately, discounting discourages policymakers from undertaking measures whose benefits accrue far into the future because the benefits simply do not count. This is particularly relevant to investments with long gestation periods, such as afforestation with tropical hardwoods. Because discounting is unfair to the future, the economics of afforestation frequently look unattractive.

It is important, then, to investigate the underlying rationale for discounting, to look at the objections to using positive discounting procedures, and to investigate ways of escaping the tyranny of discounting (box 3-1).

The Rationale for Discounting

The process of discounting can best be understood by looking at the mechanism of compound interest. If $1 is invested at 5 percent compounded annually, that dollar will be worth $1.63 in ten years. Conversely, $0.61 invested now at the same rate of interest will be worth $1 in ten years. We would then refer to $0.61 as the present value factor for a ten-year period when the discount rate is 5 percent. Given this direct relationship between discounting and compound interest, it is evident that the higher the discount rate, the lower the discount factor will be and the faster it will fall as the time horizon is extended.

The practice of discounting arises because individuals attach less weight to a benefit or cost received in the future than they do to a benefit or cost received now. Impatience, or time preference, is one reason that individuals prefer the present to the future. The second reason is that since capital is productive, a dollar's worth of resources now will generate more than a dollar's worth of goods and services in the future. Hence an entrepreneur would be willing to pay more than one dollar in the future to acquire a dollar's worth of resources now. This is referred to as the marginal productivity of capital argument for discounting. Use of the word marginal indicates that the productivity of additional units of capital is the relevant factor.

The Choice of Discount Rate

The discount rate, a key instrument of economic policy, appears in various guises. As the underlying interest rate in the economy, it forms part of the mix of macroeconomic policy measures, such as monetary and public expenditure policies, designed to control inflation and influence savings rates. Private sector discount rates help determine the amount of private investment. In the extractive sectors, discount rates influence the rate at which natural resources such as oil are depleted.

Box 3-1. The Tyranny of Discounting

Concern about the effects of discounting arises for two main reasons: it appears to shift the burden of costs to future generations, and it precludes future generations from inheriting created natural wealth. For example, a radiation hazard occurring fifty years from now that was caused by, say, stored waste and costs £1 billion in environmental and health damage would have the following present value (assuming a 5 percent discount rate): £1,000,000,000 / (1.05)^{50} equals £87.2 million. The £1 billion has been reduced to one-tenth its cost at the time of occurrence. If, however, the discount rate is roughly equal to the prevailing interest rate, the £87.2 million could be set aside now to accumulate at 5 percent and thus provide a fund to compensate future generations for the damage done. This is the actual compensation of future generations, or the creation of a compensation fund. In this example, the fund would be difficult to determine since the occurrence of the event is uncertain (its probability is not known), its scale is uncertain, and its timing is uncertain (and this affects the size of the principal sum to be set aside). Some fund may, of course, be better than none at all, but determining intergenerational compensation is undoubtedly complex.

Where timing, scale, and probability are known, such funds make good sense. An example would be decommissioning a nuclear power station. Its life is known, the probability of decommissioning is one, and costs are now known with more certainty.

The other area of concern is the effect that discounting has on the inheritance of the future. The conspicuous example is forestry, but the analysis holds for any renewable resource with a long gestation period. In this case, the benefit of a tree that takes fifty years to grow appears to be comparatively insignificant in present values. The result is that unless special treatment is afforded to afforestation, the tree will not be grown and future generations will have forgone a benefit they cannot reproduce (because they would have to wait another fifty years, too).

Even here, the tyranny of discounting must not be exaggerated. Many critics of discounting feel that the tree, in this case, is undervalued. This is why we stress the importance of valuation, even though proper valuation is not sufficient because the idea of passing on inherited natural wealth would ensure more afforestation, not less (leaving aside the debate about the type of afforestation).

Source: Pearce, Markandya, and Barbier (1989).

Discounting thus plays a central role in economic policy, which explains why a long and wide-ranging debate has arisen about how the discount rate should be chosen (for an extensive survey of the issues, see Lind 1982). A parallel discussion debates how the discount rate should be chosen for developing countries (for an overview of the discussion, see Irvin 1978; Ray 1984).

Excluding questions of risk, which are discussed later, the two main contenders for the social discount rate are the social rate of time preference, based on the rate of time preference, and the opportunity cost of capital, based on the marginal productivity of capital. Although the two rates would be equal if markets were efficient and taxes nonexistent, in practice time preference rates tend to be lower than the opportunity cost of capital. The early debate on which rate to use focused on the source of the funds applied to the project and the eventual use of the benefits of the project. In particular, the extent to which the costs and benefits detracted from, or added to, consumption in relation to savings was seen to be of key importance in determining the choice of discount rate. In the context of developing countries additional difficulties arose because not only were benefits and costs valued differently at different points in time, but so was income to the government in relation to consumption and investment by the private sector. This debate has, to some extent, been resolved by two conventions: (a) defining one social group whose benefits or costs are declared to be the unit of account and multiplying the benefits or costs for other groups by a conversion factor to obtain comparable figures and (b) using a discount rate that is appropriate for the group whose costs and benefits have been declared the unit of account (the numeraire).

A commonly accepted convention is to declare uncommitted income in the hands of the government to be the unit of account. By doing so, the corresponding discount rate (referred to as the accounting rate of interest) can be approximated by a weighted average of the social rate of time preference and the opportunity cost of capital, with the weights being the proportions of the yields of the public project that are, on average, reinvested.

Although this approach has been accepted and the accounting rate of interest calculated for many countries, many scholars disagree about its validity in practice. Whereas accounting rates are frequently in the range of 4–7 percent, the actual rate used to determine projects funded by international agencies, such as the World Bank, is 10 percent or more. The complex reasons for these differences are not relevant here. It is worth noting, however, that even before environmental issues have been raised, economists do not agree on the choice of discount rate. In looking at the relationship between environmental considerations and discounting we need, therefore, to consider the arguments supporting the use of a range of different discount rates.

The Debate over Discounting from an Environmental Perspective

We take two approaches to analyzing the relation between environmental concerns and the social discount rate. The first reexamines the rationale for discounting and the methods of calculating discount rates, paying particular attention to the problem of the environment. The second approach analyzes the implications of particular environmental concerns. The objections to discounting can be presented under five headings: pure individual time preference, social rate of time preference, opportunity cost of capital, risk and uncertainty, and the interests of future generations.

Much of the environmental literature argues against discounting in general and high discount rates in particular (see, for example, Goodin 1982). In fact no unique relationship exists between high discount rates and environmental deterioration. Although high rates may shift the burden of cost to future generations, in principle the overall level of investment falls as the discount rate rises, thus slowing the pace of economic development in general. Since natural resources are required for investment, the demand for such resources is lower at higher discount rates. High discount rates may also discourage development projects that compete with existing uses that are environmentally benign—for example, the development of watersheds as opposed to the use of existing wilderness. Exactly how the choice of discount rate affects the overall use of natural resources and environment is thus ambiguous (for a discussion, see Markandya and Pearce 1988; for rigorous proof, see Krautkraemer 1985). This point invalidates the simplistic generalization that discount rates should always be lowered to accommodate environmental considerations.

Pure Individual Time Preference

In discussions of personal preferences, no one denies that the impatience principle exists and implies a positive individual discount rate. However, some argue against permitting pure time preference to influence social discount rates, which are the rates used to make collective decisions. Box 3-2 illustrates some of the problems associated with using time preference rates in the context of energy conservation measures.

The arguments against allowing observed time preference rates to influence social decisions can be summarized as follows. First, individual time preference is not consistent with maximizing welfare during an individual's lifetime (see Krutilla and Fisher 1985). This is a variant of a more general view that discounting time because of impatience is irrational. Second, what individuals want carries no necessary implications for public policy. Many countries force individuals to save, through state pensions, for example, which means that the state overrides private preferences concerning savings behavior. Third, the underlying value judgment is improperly expressed. A society that elevates the satisfaction of wants to a high status should recognize that what matters is the satisfaction of wants as they arise. This means that what matters is tomorrow's satisfaction, not today's assessment of tomorrow's satisfaction.

The validity of these objections to using pure time preference is clearly debatable. Overturning the basic value judgment underlying the liberal economic tradition—that individual preferences should count for social

Box 3-2. *Householder Discount Rates and Energy Conservation*

It is widely thought that substantial opportunities exist for implementing cost-effective energy conservation in dwellings in the industrial world (that is, investments in insulation, draft-proofing, water heating, and cooking would repay the householder handsomely). The presence of such large, profitable opportunities appears, however, to be inconsistent with rational decisionmaking. If the opportunities exist, why don't householders take advantage of them?

One explanation is that the costs of conservation are being understated. These include the costs of the appliances, materials, and labor used, but not the associated inconvenience, the cost of information, and so on. Another is that people are simply uninformed about profitable opportunities: the market has failed. Yet another is that the energy conservation market is in a state of disequilibrium (people are in the act of making the investments). This last view is perhaps inconsistent with reality: it was first expressed in the 1970s during OPEC-induced price increases for energy and is still being expressed nearly twenty years later.

Some studies explain the failure to invest by citing high householder discount rates. Hausman (1979) found that households in the United States with annual incomes of $6,000 had implied discount rates of 89 percent in the choice of energy-efficient, durable household goods such as refrigerators; at the same time, households with annual incomes of $50,000 had more rational discount rates of 5 percent. A study of the demand for new houses containing thermally efficient structures found that householder discount rates were nearly 8 percent, which reflected mortgage rates in the housing market. It is not clear, then, that households generally have very high discount rates for energy conservation. If they did, conservation would be less likely to be undertaken, and the environmental consequences of burning more fossil fuels would occur (Horowitz and Haeri 1990).

It is popularly thought that the potential for energy conservation in developing countries is small. However, since energy is expensive and must be used as efficiently as possible, the potential is, in fact, large. Various studies show that energy efficiency measures are frequently paid back within one year or even less. Perhaps 15–20 percent of energy could be saved in a cost-effective fashion. This has very important macroeconomic implications. If 20 percent of commercial energy was saved, developing countries would save $30 billion annually, or around 7.5 percent of the total value of their merchandise imports. Moreover, such measures would postpone large-scale measures governing the supply of energy, which would save on imports of capital and materials and allow donor funds to be used productively elsewhere.

Yet the same phenomenon occurs in the developing world as in the industrial world. Rational energy conservation measures are often not undertaken for many reasons: low energy prices that discourage conservation consciousness, lack of incentive, poor information, and government intervention. Poverty itself is a barrier. Even households using fuelwood could improve the efficiency of fires and stoves, however, and methods of improving the efficiency of charcoaling could make major contributions.

Source: Hausman (1979); Horowitz and Haeri (1990); World Bank and United Nations Development Programme (1989).

decisions—requires good reason. Philosophically, the third argument—that the basic value judgment needs to be expressed differently—is impressive. In practical terms, however, the immediacy of wants in the many developing countries with serious environmental problems might favor keeping the usual formulation of this basic judgment.

Social Rate of Time Preference

The social rate of time preference attempts to measure the rate at which social welfare or utility of consumption falls over time. Clearly, this rate depends on the rate of pure time preference, on how fast consumption grows, and, in turn, on how fast utility falls as consumption grows. The social rate of time preference is given by $i = ng + z$, where z is the rate of pure time preference, g is the rate of growth of real consumption per capita, and n is the elasticity of the marginal utility of consumption (n specifically refers to the percentage fall in the additional utility that is derived from each percentage increase in consumption). With no growth in consumption per capita, the social rate of time preference would be equal to the pure rate of time preference, z. If consumption is expected to grow, the social rate rises above the pure rate. The intuitive rationale is that the more one expects to have in the future, the less one is willing to sacrifice today. Moreover, this impact increases as marginal utility decreases rapidly with consumption.

Environmentalists point to the presumed positive value of g in the formula for figuring the social rate of time preference. First, they argue that underlying limits exist to the growth process. Positive growth rates of, say, 2–3 percent cannot be expected to continue far into the future because natural resource constraints limit the capacity of natural environments to act as sinks for waste products. This concern clearly must be taken seriously, as global warming from the emission of greenhouse gases and depletion of the ozone layer illustrate. The practical relevance that this argument has for economic planning is more controversial, although it may have more relevance for determining the way in which economies develop than for reconsidering the basic growth objective itself. A second concern highlights the problems of particular regions. In low-income Sub-Saharan Africa, for example, real consumption per capita fell 1.9 percent a year between 1973 and 1983. That is, g was negative. Does this mean that the social discount rate should be negative as well? Arguably it should, although past negative growth may not be relevant to a discount rate based on expected growth in the future. More significant, the pure component of time preference in the social discount rate could be very high. Real borrowing rates in poor economies are often between 10 and 15 percent and suggest what the personal time preference rates might be. These might justify the typical project appraisal rates of 10 percent or more used by lending agencies.

If using pure time preference rates is at all reasonable, are such rates acceptable? Many would argue that they are acceptable because the mere presence of poverty induces high discount rates as attention is focused on the immediate need for food rather than the longer-term need for food security. There is, however, a problem with inferring that rates of time preference are high because poverty exists in the context of environmental problems. High discount rates are one cause of environmental degradation because they encourage individuals to opt for short-term measures that satisfy immediate needs or wants and to ignore more environmentally appropriate practices such as planting trees. In turn, this environmental degradation leads to the poverty that causes high discount rates. Using these rates to evaluate investments oriented to the environment (such as soil conservation measures or afforestation) is erroneous.

Using a social rate of time preference based on these assumptions is only valid when sustainable changes can be expected in real consumption per capita. When environmental degradation is taking place and incomes are stagnant or falling, values of z should not be assumed to be relevant to the calculation of i. In these circumstances no clear rules govern which social rate of time preference should be chosen, although one could argue strongly that the value of i should be adjusted downward.

Opportunity Cost of Capital

The opportunity cost of capital is obtained by looking at the rate of return on the best investment of similar risk that is displaced because a particular project is undertaken. Thus, the investment undertaken must yield as high a return as that possible given the alternative use of funds. This is the basic justification for an opportunity cost discount rate. In developing countries with a shortage of capital, such rates tend to be very high and their use is often justified on the grounds of the allocation of scarce capital.

The environmental literature has attempted to discredit discounting on the grounds of opportunity cost. The first criticism is that opportunity cost discounting implies that benefits are reinvested at the opportunity cost rate, and this is often invalid. For example, at a 10 percent discount rate, $100 today is comparable to $121 in two years if the $100 is invested for the first year to yield $10 of return and then both the original capital and the return are invested for the second year. If the return is consumed but not reinvested, the critics argue, the consumption flows have no opportunity cost. What, they ask, is the relevance of a discount rate based on the assumption that profits are reinvested if they are consumed instead? The idea that the mix of consumed and reinvested benefits from an investment should modify the underlying discount rate is, in fact, familiar to economists. It provides one of the rationales for the weighted discount rate procedures advocated by many economists and, as such, has been widely discussed in the literature.

The second environmental critique of opportunity cost discounting relates to compensation across generations. Suppose that an investment today would cause environmental damages of x, T years from now. The argument for representing this damage in discounted terms by the amount $x / (i + r)^T$ is the following. If the amount of damage were invested at the opportunity cost of capital discount rate, r, it would amount to x in T years time. This amount could then be used to compensate those who suffer the damages in that year. Critics argue, however, that using the discounted value is only legitimate if the compensation is actually paid. Otherwise, they argue, those damages cannot be represented by a discounted cost.

The problem is that actual compensation is being confused with potential compensation. The project generates a sum that could be used to compensate the victim, and this is enough to ensure its efficiency. Whether the compensation will actually be carried out is a separate question and not relevant to the issue of how to choose a discount rate.

These two arguments against opportunity cost discounting are not particularly persuasive, although the first may be relevant to a weighted approach.

Risk and Uncertainty

It is widely accepted that a benefit or cost should fall in value as the uncertainty of its occurrence rises. Three types of uncertainty are generally regarded as relevant to discounting: (a) uncertainty about whether an individual will be alive at some future date (the risk of death argument), (b) uncertainty about the preferences of the individual in the future, and (c) uncertainty about the size of the benefit or cost.

First, the risk of death argument is often used as a rationale for the impatience principle itself, the argument being that a preference for consumption now rather than in the future is partly based on the uncertainty that one will be alive in the future to enjoy the benefits of one's restraint. The argument against this is that although an individual is mortal, society is not and thus should use other considerations to guide its decisions. This is a variant of the view that in calculating social rates of time preference, the pure time preference (element z) may be too high.

Second, uncertainty about preferences is relevant to certain goods and perhaps even certain aspects of environmental conservation. It is not relevant to projects or policies whose benefits include food, shelter, water, and energy. If anything, we can be more, not less, sure of future preferences for these goods. Moreover, economists generally accept that the way to allow for uncertainty about preferences is to include option value in an estimate of the benefit or cost. Option value is the value of reducing future uncertainty and is discussed in chapter 5.

Third, uncertainty about the size of the benefit or cost is relevant; the difficulty arises in adjusting the discount rate to allow for it. The effect of raising the discount rate to reflect risk is to impose a particular time profile on risk. If the chosen risk premium is 1 percent, the risk in ten years would be indicated by 1.01^{10} compared with, say, 1.01^{3} in three years. Risk cannot, however, be assumed to behave in this exponential fashion.

If uncertainty is not handled by adjusting the discount rate, how should it be treated? The alternative is to adjust the underlying stream of costs and benefits. This involves replacing each uncertain benefit or cost by its certainty equivalent. A certainty equivalent benefit can be defined as follows: if a benefit of B_1 accrues a level of uncertainty u_1, a benefit level of B_0, which is less than B_1, should exist and accrue with certainty so that the decisionmaker is indifferent to the choice between B_0 and the gamble of B_1, p_1. B_0 is the certainty equivalent value. This procedure seems to be correct, although the calculations involved are complex and the method is not clearly operational (see J. R. Anderson 1989; Dixit and Williamson 1989 for operationally relevant variations of this approach). This does not, however, imply that adding a risk premium to the discount rate is the solution since using such a premium implies the existence of arbitrary certainty equivalents for each of the costs and benefits (see, for example, Prince 1985, pp. 179–80).

The Interests of Future Generations

The extent to which using positive discount rates safeguards the interests of future generations is a matter of debate within the literature. With overlapping generations, borrowing and lending can arise as some individuals save for their retirement and others dissave to finance consumption. In such models, the discount rate that emerges is not necessarily efficient (it does not take the economy on a path that maximizes welfare in the long run). These models, however, have no altruism in them. Altruism is said to exist when the utility of the current generation is influenced not only by its own consumption, but also by the utility of future generations. This is modeled by assuming that the utility of the current generation, i, is also influenced by the utility of the second generation, j, and the third generation, k. This approach begins to address the question of future generations but does so in a specific way. What is being evaluated is the current generation's judgment about what future generations will think is important. It does not, therefore, yield a discount rate reflecting a broader principle of the rights of future generations. The essential distinction is between generation i judging what generations j and k want (selfish altruism) and generation i using resources in order to leave generations j and k with the maximum scope for choosing what they want (disinterested altruism; see Page 1977a).

Although disinterested altruism is important, its implications for the interest rate and the efficiency of that rate have yet to be established. The validity of this argument of overlapping generations has also been questioned on the grounds of the role that individuals play when looking at the interests of future generations. Individuals make decisions in two contexts: their private decisions reflect their own interests, and their public decisions take into account the interests of fellow beings and future generations. Market discount rates, it is argued, reflect the private context, whereas social discount rates reflect the public context. This is sometimes called the dual role rationale for why social discount rates are below market rates. It is also similar to the assurance argument, which states that individuals behave differently if they are sure that others will act the same way they do. Thus each person might be willing to make transfers to future generations if each is assured that others will do the same. The assured discount rate arising from collective action is lower than the unassured rate.

Other arguments are used to justify the idea that market rates are too high when placed in the context of the interests of future generations. The first is called the super responsibility argument (see Sen 1982). Market discount rates arise from the behavior of individuals, but the state is a separate entity responsible for guarding the collective welfare and the welfare of future generations. Thus the rate of discount relevant to state investments is different from the private rate, and since high rates discriminate against future generations, the state discount rate will probably be lower than the market rate.

The final argument used to justify the inequality of the market and social rates is the isolation paradox (Sen 1967). This is an n person extension of the two-person, nonzero-sum game of the prisoner's dilemma (see chapter 10). Individuals have a strictly dominant strategy, which produces an overall result that is Pareto inferior. A higher level of welfare could be achieved by collusion, but collusion must be enforced. The effect of the isolation paradox is similar to that of the assurance problem, although it arises from slightly different considerations. When individuals cannot capture the entire benefit of present investments for their own descendants, they do not make transfers even if assurance exists.

Demonstrating the difference between market and social discount rates in this context is not straightforward. The results are presented here, and proof is contained in Sen (1982). Individuals place some weight on the consumption of future generations, especially on that of their direct descendants. Assume that the following weights are placed on consumption: one's own consumption equals 1, the consumption of others in the current generation equals b, the consumption of descendants equals c, and the consumption of others in future generations equals a. If \$1 of savings today yields a return that is shared in the proportions h and $1 - h$ between descendants and others in future generations, the market rate of interest, π, equals $\{1 \;/\; [ch + (1 - h)a]\} - 1$.

Suppose that all n persons in the current generation agree to make a collective contract for saving an additional \$1 and that the return is enjoyed by descendants and others in the ratio of 1 to $n - 1$. The social rate of discount, p, is then equal to $\{[1 + (n - 1)b] / [c + (n - 1)a]\} - 1$. The possibility exists that π and p are the same, but as long as the current individual fails to capture the entire investment return for his or her descendants (h is greater than 1), or as long as the individual's selfishness toward others today is stronger than the concern for his or her descendants compared with concern for others in future generations (c is less than a divided by b), then p is less than π.

For a variety of reasons relating to the interests of future generations, the social discount rate may be lower than the market rate. The choice of the discount rate implies a need to look at an individual's public behavior, to leave the choice of the discount rate to the state, or to try and select a rate based on a collective savings contract. None of these options appears to offer a practical procedure for determining the discount rate in quantitative terms. What they do suggest is that market rates will not be proper guides to social discount rates once the interests of future generations are incorporated into the social decision rule. These arguments can be used to reject the use of a market-based rate if it is thought that the burden of accounting for the interests of future generations should fall on the discount rate. This is, however, a complex and untenable procedure. Perhaps the rights of future generations should be defined instead and then used to circumscribe the overall evaluation, leaving the choice of discount rate to the conventional considerations of the current generation. Such an approach is illustrated shortly.

Discount Rates and Specific Environmental Issues

In this section we look at specific environmental issues and see how they are affected by the discounting process. The issues considered are irreversible damage and the management of natural resources.

Irreversible Damage

Irreversibility is one special environmental consideration that might, at first sight, imply the adjustment of the discount rate. As the term implies, the concern is with decisions that cannot be reversed, such as the flooding of a valley, the destruction of an ancient monument, the disposal of radioactive waste, the loss of a tropical forest, and so on. The Krutilla-Fisher approach incorporates these considerations into a cost-benefit methodology (Krutilla and Fisher 1985; for a generalization, see Porter 1982).

Consider a valley containing a unique wilderness area, where a hydroelectric development is being proposed. The area, once flooded, would be lost forever, and the benefits forgone are clearly part of the costs of the project. The net development benefits can then be written as net benefit equals $B(D) - C(D) - B(P)$, where $B(D)$ is the benefits of development (the power generated, the irrigation gained, or both), $C(D)$ is the costs of development, and $B(P)$ is the net benefits of preservation (that is, net of any preservation costs). All the benefits and costs must be expressed in present values. The irreversible loss of the preservation benefits might suggest that the discount rate should be set very low: $B(P)$ would be relatively large because the preservation benefits would extend over an indefinite future. Since the development benefits cover a finite period (say, fifty years), the impact of lowering the discount rate would be to lower the net benefits of the project. In the Krutilla-Fisher approach, in contrast, the discount rate is not adjusted. Rather, it is treated conventionally, that is, set equal to some measure of the opportunity cost of capital.

The value of benefits from a wilderness area will grow over time. The reasons for this are that the supply of such areas is shrinking, the demand for their amenities is growing as income and population grow, and the demand is growing to have such areas preserved, even by persons who do not intend to use them (the so-called existence values are increasing). The net effect is to raise the price of the wilderness at a given annual rate of growth, say, g percent. If the price is growing at a rate of g percent and a discount rate of r percent is applied to it, the price is, in effect, held constant and the benefit is discounted at a rate of $r - g$ percent. The adjustment is similar to lowering the discount rate but does not distort the allocation of resources in the economy by using variable discount rates.

The Management of Natural Resources

The choice of discount rate is of particular importance for the management of natural resources, where the key decision is how much to consume now and how much to store for future consumption. It is intuitively clear that this decision will be influenced by the price of present versus future consumption (the discount rate). The full analysis of the relation between the discount rate and the pattern of natural resource exploitation is complex, but the main point is that the higher the discount rate, the faster is the rate at which an exhaustible resource is depleted and the more intense is the effort that goes into harvesting a renewable resource. This means that exhaustible resources will be depleted more quickly and smaller stocks of renewable resources will exist at higher discount rates. Moreover, the combination of high discount rates and high ratios of price to cost of harvesting can lead to optimal extinction of the resource (Clark 1990). The high price-to-cost ratio makes extracting the last unit of the resource profitable, and the high discount rate biases exploitation toward the present rather than the future.

These features of natural resource use have several implications for resource management policy. First, investments in the activity that exploits resources should pay special attention to how discount rates affect the time profile of benefits and costs. For example, if one project will exhaust a resource in ten years and another will do so in twenty-five years, the higher the discount rate, the more likely is it that the first project will be chosen over the second. High discount rates can exist for a number of reasons such as anti-inflationary monetary policy or capital rationing. They may be fully justified in those contexts but may have undesirable consequences for projects involving natural resources.

The exploitation of natural resources will also be excessive if the private discount rate is higher than the social rate and control of the resource is in private hands. Although discussed extensively, methods for correcting this overexploitation generally do not involve changing the private rate of discount. The reasons that this rate is too high pervade the whole economy, and the rate itself is not easily manipulated. Resources can be conserved if resource taxes are used that allow the government to capture more of the rent arising from resource development. Apart from slowing this development when desirable, taxes also mobilize funds for the government in a particularly efficient way.

For all these reasons, lowering the discount rates for particular natural resource projects is unlikely to be desirable. In addition, practical difficulties arise if some projects are treated as special and others are not. First, determining which projects are going to qualify for special treatment is complicated, and gray areas inevitably exist. Second, many decisions about resource exploitation are made privately, and changing discount rates for private individuals in one field of activity alone is not practicable. Third, even if discount rates were lowered, there is no guarantee that serious resource degradation will not occur.

A Sustainability Approach

The environmental debate has undoubtedly contributed valuable intellectual soul-searching to the discussion of discounting. It has not, however, demonstrated the need to reject discounting as such. We began this chapter by examining the concern over the use of discount rates that reflect pure time preference. We concluded that this concern does not support rejecting pure time preference completely. We also noted that an abnormally high rate of time preference can be generated when incomes are falling and environmental degradation is taking place. In these circumstances, it is inappropriate to evaluate policies, particularly policies relevant to the environment, using discount rates based on high rates of time preference.

The arguments that environmentalists voice against the use of the opportunity cost of capital discount rates are also, in general, not persuasive. To account for uncertainty in investment appraisal, it is better to adjust the cost and benefit streams for the uncertainty than to add a risk premium onto the discount rate. Finally, while analyzing the rationale for discounting, we examined the arguments for adjusting discount rates on various grounds of intergenerational justice. Although many of these arguments have merit, adjusting the discount rate to allow for them is generally not a practicable or efficient procedure. The need to protect the interests of future generations remains paramount in the environmental critique of discounting. Some alternative policy is therefore required if the discount rate is not going to be adjusted. One approach is to adopt a sustainability constraint.

Chapter 2 stresses that economic development requires a strong policy of protecting the natural resource base. The resource base—including all forms of capital—should perhaps be maintained intact or even enhanced. Some sustainability advocates go further and separate out natural capital for special attention. If conservation of natural environments is a condition of sustainability, and if sustainability addresses many of the valid criticisms of discounting, how might sustainability be built into project appraisal? Requiring that no project should contribute to environmental deterioration is absurd because it means rejecting all environmentally damaging projects, however small the damage. As chapter 1 shows, all economic activity contributes to environmental damage in one way or another. An alternative would be to require that actual compensation be paid for environmental damage, as opposed to the hypothetical compensation implicit in the benefit-cost rule. Actual compensation could take the form of a monetary payment or a requirement that actual damage be repaired or offset in some way. An investment that destroys a wetland, say, might offset the damage by recreating the wetland elsewhere. Such requirements are, in fact, increasingly common in rich, industrial economies. Carried to an extreme, however, offsetting all environmental damage could be stultifying.

The alternative would be to impose the sustainability constraint in a more general fashion so that overall capital stocks are not reduced. A policy or project would not be sustainable if, for example, the proceeds of environmental destruction were simply consumed. Similarly, sustainability would be breached if critical environmental capital were destroyed. Of course, if the investment in question substituted environmental capital with superior (higher rate of return) man-made capital, the orthodox benefit-cost rule would apply provided the value of the lost environmental capital were properly taken into account. In short, the sustainability approach stresses

- The importance of valuing environmental assets and their services
- The need to ensure that investments truly build up the stock of man-made capital
- The need to think about safe minimum standards when environmental capital is critical (see chapter 2).

The sustainability approach has some interesting implications for project appraisal (see Pearce, Markandya, and Barbier 1990). One of these is that the problem of choosing a discount rate largely disappears. The goal of adjusting discount rates to capture environmental effects is better served by the sustainability condition. Although it may have quite radical implications, a sustainability condition could avoid belaboring the tyranny of discounting and would remove the unrealistic requirement that all ethical and environmental concerns be accounted for by adjusting the discount rate. Nonetheless, the sustainability rule remains blurred and deserves more attention.

Note

This chapter relies heavily on a paper written by Markandya and Pearce (1991). We are indebted to Anil Markandya and to the editor of the *World Bank Research Observer* for permission to reproduce significant portions of that paper. The paper was also developed from a more extensive survey (Markandya and Pearce 1988), which was based on contract work for the Overseas Development Administration, United Kingdom.

4

Measuring Sustainable Development

The pursuit of sustainable development requires indicators of success, foremost among which is a definition of sustainability. According to the definition proposed in chapter 2, preserving the overall stock of capital is a prerequisite of sustainability. In other words, the depletion of natural resources may be associated with a buildup of other forms of capital. Environmental degradation alone is not, therefore, evidence of nonsustainability when sustainability is defined by the overall stock of capital. At the same time, the amount of substitutability between environmental and nonenvironmental assets has limits, and at least the critical environmental assets that support life should not be run down. This would allow other environmental assets to be reduced provided their loss was compensated for by a buildup of manufactured capital.

Nevertheless, a central problem remains. What would we say, for example, if the overall length of rivers with reasonable quality increased, but air pollution got worse? If we use physical indicators of environmental quality and resource degradation, we immediately face the problem of aggregating diverse indicators. That is, we need a price for water quality and a price for air quality. The overall value of environmental assets may then be computed, and this value should not decline according to this definition of sustainability.

This discussion can be summarized with the help of table 4-1, which

Table 4-1. Factors That Must Be Kept Constant or Rising to Maintain Sustainability

Type of indicator	Overall capital	Environmental capital	Critical environmental capital
Physical	Aggregation problem	Aggregation problem	Yes
Monetary	Yes	Yes	Not needed

Note: Efforts to calculate indicators of sustainability can be classified according to this matrix. Efforts to compute sustainable income tend to use the overall capital concept and seek to find a monetary indicator of sustainability. Environmental statistics such as river quality by the length of the river, sulfur oxide concentrations or emissions, and carbon dioxide emissions fit any definition of sustainability but face the aggregation problem when they relate to the first two definitions of sustainability.

presents a matrix of definitions of sustainability and two broad types of indicators. Because of aggregation problems, a monetary indicator must be found for measuring changes in the total capital stock over time. In the absence of such an indicator, we can only be sure that we are pursuing sustainable development if none of the environmental indicators declines. If a definition of sustainability is adopted in which at least the critical environmental assets do not decline, physical indicators can be used to identify nonsustainability. Basically, if each form of environmental capital is critical, each asset must be maintained. In such contexts placing a monetary value on the asset is not necessary: it is sufficient to identify and maintain the critical environmental assets. The next sections investigate the various attempts that have been made to find sustainability indicators.

Sustainable Income

The concept of sustainable development presented in chapter 2 suggests that a development path is sustainable if and only if the stock of overall capital assets remains constant or rises over time. The assets in question include manufactured capital (machines, roads, and factories), human capital (knowledge and skills), and environmental capital (forests, soil quality, and rangeland). To be on a sustainable development path, then, a nation must be living within its means, which, in this context, means not decreasing its overall capital assets. The proper measure of income corresponding to this idea of sustainability is widely accepted to be the amount that can be consumed without running the stock of capital down.[1]

Manufactured capital assets depreciate over time. If the value of these assets at the beginning of a year is X and the depreciation over the year is d, then the value of the assets at the end of the year is $X - d$. It follows that, to maintain capital, the amount d has to be set aside in a depreciation fund rather than be consumed. If consumption is C, depreciation is d, and gross output is Y, sustainable consumption is $Y - d$. An indicator of sustainability, then, is a measure of sustainable income, defined here as the level of income that can be secured without decreasing the overall level of assets.

Measuring sustainable income would mean significantly adjusting the system of national accounts. In many countries the net national product (NNP) is computed. This is defined as the gross national product (GNP) minus the depreciation on manufactured capital, Dm, and, occasionally, minus the depreciation of stocks of natural assets such as forests or energy reserves. Therefore, NNP = GNP − Dm.

Assuming that GNP is correctly measured, an issue we return to below, a measure of sustainable income is NNP* = GNP − Dm − Dn, where Dn is now depreciation on environmental capital, which is measured by the monetary value of environmental degradation during the year. This environmental damage will show up in two ways: as losses of unrecorded GNP (for example, a loss of wildlife species or loss of a fine view) and as losses of GNP that would otherwise be recorded (for example, crop output forgone because of air pollution). Expressed another way, the level of sustainable consumption is equal to GNP minus the investment required to sustain the overall capital stock.

Measuring this concept of sustainable income would require major changes in national accounting procedures because of the effort needed to compute Dn. It involves, however, no fundamental modifications to the conceptual basis of the United Nations System of National Accounts (see, for example, Daly 1989). A measure of sustainable income has been calculated for Indonesia (see Repetto and others 1989 and the discussion in chapter 1, especially note 4). Figure 4-1 shows the basic calculations for gross domestic product (GDP) rather than GNP. The difference is minor and relates to property income from abroad. GDP is then subjected to three adjustments: the depreciation of oil reserves, forest stocks, and soil.

The oil adjustment is made as follows. For any one year, it is possible to estimate the level of oil production, which represents the depletion of stocks. Stocks might also be reduced when estimated reserves are revised downward or oil spills occur. Stocks of nonrenewable resources might increase because reserve estimates are revised upward, new discoveries are made, and the skills used to recover known deposits are improved. In 1984, for example, Indonesia had an opening stock of 10,181 million barrels of oil. The net change over the year was a reduction of 450 million barrels. To find the value of each barrel it is necessary to compute the net price, rent, or royalty, defined as the market price at the point of export minus all the costs involved in bringing the resource to the point of sale. In 1984 this was $24.3 per barrel. Thus the value of the deprecia-

Figure 4-1. GDP and NDP as a Measure of Sustainable Income in Indonesia, 1971-84

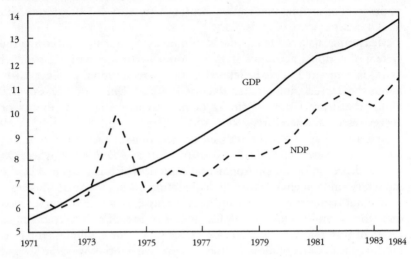

Billions of constant 1973 rupiah

Source: Repetto and others (1989).

tion of the oil reserves in 1984 was 450 million × $24.3 = $10,935 million. Converted to constant values, this adjustment is recorded in figure 4-1.

The adjustment for forest loss is made in a similar way (for more detail, see chapter 1, note 4). Additions to stock arise from the natural growth of forests and deliberate afforestation. Reductions arise from logging, damage to other trees from logging, clearance for agriculture, and fire. The net change is valued at the appropriate rental. For trees, this is the value of the standing stock before it is logged and processed, which reflects the maximum amount a concessionaire is willing to pay for that stock. This, in turn, reflects the flow of profits that the concessionaire expects to receive. In the Indonesian exercise, the same approach was adopted for stumpage values as was adopted for oil: the estimated costs of harvesting and delivering the stock to the point at which it is either exported or processed were deducted from the market price.

The costs of soil erosion were estimated by estimating the rate of soil loss and relating this loss to reductions in crop productivity. These reductions would, in turn, have an economic value determined by the market price of the crops. These calculations are complicated by the response of farmers to soil erosion. Farmers may, for example, switch to crops that are less sensitive to erosion but less profitable as well.

Figure 4-1 shows the overall result for the measure of GDP. The modified measure, net domestic product, does not measure sustainable income in the strict sense because it does not take into account the depreciation of manufactured capital. Few developing countries estimate this form of depreciation. While unadjusted GDP rose 7.1 percent a year between 1971 and 1984, the adjusted measure rose only 4 percent, a marked difference that clearly indicates the extent to which Indonesia has been living off its capital. Put another way, approximately 40 percent of the economic growth in Indonesia has not been sustainable.

The contrast between gross and net investment is perhaps more startling. The recorded gross investment in the economy is substantially higher than investment after the depreciation of environmental capital has been deducted. Indeed, the gross investment minus the depreciation of environmental capital was negative in 1979 and 1980.

Sustainable income can be measured, but only approximately. It is most readily calculated for resource-dependent economies, which are the economies most directly at risk from natural resource degradation.

A Wider Concept of Sustainable Income

The measure of sustainable income used in the Indonesian example assumes that GNP, or GDP, is correctly measured in the first place, with the only adjustment—significant though it is—being that the lost value of environmental assets is deducted to obtain a modified measure of net national product. A consideration of environmental damage reveals that GDP and GNP already contain distortions. This can be seen by considering what happens to GDP if a hypothetical supertanker carrying crude oil runs aground, causing massive ecological damage in the form of oil contamination of sea mammals and birds, loss of marine productivity in general, damage to tourist beaches, and so on (this example is taken from Potvin 1989).

The associated transportation activity and the oil spill itself produce the following effects:

- GNP increases because the transportation of oil results in value added.
- GNP is unaffected by the reduction in oil stocks represented by the tanker of oil, and so is NNP as conventionally measured.
- GNP increases because wages are paid and equipment is used to clean up the oil spill.
- Wildlife damage not associated with tourism, and the effects of the spill on marine productivity other than commercial species, are not reflected in GNP.
- GNP due to commercial fishing declines.
- GNP due to tourism is unaffected because tourists are likely simply

to go elsewhere: the area's loss is another area's gain. If tourists choose to go abroad, however, GNP declines.

* Even though the tanker may be damaged or lost, GNP does not decrease, but NNP might if the likelihood of such accidents is built into depreciation adjustments. GNP may actually increase as a result of the repairs carried out.

Clearly, different effects are working in different directions. It is perfectly possible, however, for the net effect of the oil spill to increase GNP, which seems counterintuitive if GNP is construed as an indicator of welfare. The reason for this is that the national income accounts do not take into account the environmental damage done (the depreciation of environmental assets). Also, the national accounts regard the costs of cleaning up the spill as gains to GNP, when they are actually offsetting costs arising from the damage done. Put another way, what is spent on the cleanup takes the country back to its original position. If the cleanup is successful, the country is no worse off than it was before the oil spill. It is certainly no better off, and any procedure that makes it seem better off is wrong. Cleanup expenditures are restorative expenditures.

Some analysts have suggested that the same argument applies to expenditures undertaken to prevent environmental damage. These expenditures offset damage that would otherwise occur. They themselves do not add to the true GNP of the country, but they do add to GNP as conventionally measured. These are defensive or aversive expenditures. Considerable doubt has been cast on the view that defensive expenditures must be deducted from GNP to arrive at a true measure of sustainable income.[2]

To get a more accurate measure of GNP as an indicator of welfare, it is widely suggested that at least the following adjustments must be made: sustainable income = $GNP - Dm - Dn - R - A$, where Dm is depreciation of man-made capital, Dn is depreciation of natural capital, R is restorative expenditure, and A is aversive expenditure. In this equation, GNP is measured conventionally, including A and R. The deduction of R and A is disputed.

Utility flows from the area of the oil spill, and the losses may not be captured by the measure of asset depreciation. This damage arises from the initial incident and may continue to occur over the long run if the mitigating expenditures do not wholly restore the environment. This form of environmental damage is not recorded in conventional GNP. In the case of the oil spill, this residual pollution—the damage that remains after mitigation—is expected to be picked up by Dn, the depreciation of natural assets, which should reflect the capitalized value of the loss of welfare over time. But consider the example of noise nuisance. Noise from aircraft and traffic is known to cause considerable loss of welfare for many people. Noise is not really associated with any form of asset depreciation, although it does affect the concentration and health of humans and could therefore result in the depreciation of human capital. It is, however, a cost associated with some of the gains in GNP (the movement of aircraft and vehicles). Hence residual pollution that affects the stock of environmental assets because it exceeds the absorptive capacity of the environment should be reflected in measures of GNP. Other environmental costs do not affect the stock of environmental assets but are current costs of production—for example, pollution that stays within the limits of the environment's absorptive capacity. They would be reflected in Dn and a lower NNP.

Finally, consider what happens if an exhaustible resource is used up too fast (that is, at a rate in excess of the optimal usage given the prevailing discount rates and demand and supply). In this case, current GNP will overstate true GNP. The same applies to renewable resources. If they are not used optimally, GNP as conventionally measured will overstate true GNP (these adjustments are quite complex; see Devarajan and Weiner 1988).

The concept of sustainable income requires two broad overall adjustments of GNP as conventionally measured.

First, GNP must itself be corrected by

- Deducting aversive and restorative expenditures (but doubts exist about this approach; see note 2)
- Deducting residual pollution damage
- Deducting overstatements due to nonoptimal use and depletion of natural resources.

Second, NNP must be calculated by

- Deducting depreciation of manufactured capital
- Deducting depreciation of environmental capital.

Thus, sustainable income equals GNP $- (R + A + N) - (Dm + Dn)$, where N is the overstatement due to nonoptimal use of natural resources.

The Physical Approach to Environmental Accounting

An alternative way to maintain a monitoring program designed to check on the sustainability of development is to keep track of changes in the physical measures of the stock and flow of resources. This method does not attempt to monetize those changes.

Resource Accounting in Norway

The Norwegian system of accounts defines two types of resources: materials and environmental. Materials resources are further divided into minerals, biotic resources, and inflowing resources, such as solar radiation and ocean currents. Energy accounts are also produced sepa-

Table 4-2. Structure of Material Resources Accounts for Norway

Type of account	Structure
Reserve accounts	
Beginning of the period	Resource base reserves (developed, undeveloped)
	Total gross extraction during the period
	Adjustments of resource base (new discoveries, reappraisal of old discoveries)
	Adjustment of reserves (new technology, cost of extraction, transportation, price of resource)
End of the period	Resource base reserves (developed and undeveloped)
Extraction, conversion, and trade accounts	
For export	Gross extraction by sector minus use of resource in extraction sectors equals net extraction by sector
	Import by sector minus export by sector equals net import by sector
	Changes in stocks
For domestic use	Net extraction plus net imports plus or minus changes in stock
Consumption accounts	Domestic use (category of final use, commodity)

Source: Alfsen, Bye, and Lorentsen (1987).

rately. Environmental resources are defined by their nonmarket nature; for example, water resources provide a waste-receiving and purifying function. In practice, the mineral and biotic resources included in the actual accounts are oil and some minerals, forestry, and fish; the only inflowing resource is hydropower. The environmental resource accounts cover the use of land, air pollutants, and two water pollutants (nitrogen and phosphorus). Table 4-2 presents the structure of the materials accounts, which aim to assist policymakers in their overall management of the economy. These are not, therefore, sustainable income accounts, nor do they pretend to be. They are used to forecast the use of natural resources and their implied environmental impact in the future. Energy accounts, for example, are used to forecast the demand for energy and air pollution emissions (table 4-3 illustrates the value of petroleum). Land use accounts are also helpful for planning the use of land. Less use is made of the fisheries and forestry accounts (see Lone 1988).

Resource Accounting in France

The French Comptes du Patrimoine Natural are extensive sets of accounts that describe and measure the economic, ecological, and social functions of environmental assets. Physical accounts resemble the Norwegian accounts but separate the stock from the use of the resource; these are illustrated, for forests, in table 4-4. Geographical accounts, which show the stock and flow of resources according to a predefined

Table 4-3. Value of Oil-in-Place in Norway, 1973–89
(billions of 1986 kroner)

Year	Wealth	Value of extraction	Expected return	Value of expected changes
1973	−47	−4	3	428
1974	482	−12	34	−130
1975	398	−12	28	60
1976	499	−7	35	13
1977	554	−3	39	−6
1978	590	10	41	504
1979	1,125	24	79	777
1980	1,955	55	137	239
1981	2,273	59	159	−233
1982	2,136	51	150	−88
1983	2,143	59	150	−441
1984	1,789	62	125	−460
1985	1,388	56	97	−731
1986	694	16	49	−219
1987	506	21	35	−106
1988	413	20	29	162
1989	582	29	41	—

— Not available.

Note: The value of extraction is deducted from the value of oil-in-place that year. An adjustment is then made for the expected return, and the value of the oil-in-place is revised because of expected changes in price. For any year, therefore, the value of wealth minus the costs of extraction plus the expected return plus or minus the value of expected changes gives the value for the next year.

Source: Norway, Central Bureau of Statistics (1990).

spatial unit, are complemented by agent accounts, which set out the stock and flow of resources according to who uses them. Agent accounts sometimes present solely physical units, but the ultimate objective is to combine monetary and physical units, resulting in complete monetization of environmental assets.

Once again, the accounts, which are rich in detail, are designed to aid planning and decisionmaking. They do not measure any concept such as sustainable income. Nonetheless, the accounts can trace the environmental effects of policy changes and general trends in the economy.

Environmental Indicators

The measurement of sustainable income holds promise for securing an indicator of sustainable economic growth, although even a measure of sustainable income may fail to pick up long-term sustainability because it

Table 4-4. Physical Account for Commercial Forests in France, 1969–79
(thousands of cubic meters)

Resource (asset) or use	Broadleaf	Coniferous	Total
Resource (asset)			
Volume of growing stock in 1969	980.1	6,526.5	7,506.6
Natural growth of initial stock	401.0	2,583.5	2,984.5
Natural growth by reproduction (recruitment)	41.1	258.4	299.5
Total	1,422.2	9,368.4	10,790.6
Use			
Natural reduction (mortality)	5.6	21.0	26.6
Accidental reduction (breakage and windfall)	9.7	481.2	490.9
Resource extraction (commercial felling)	92.0	1,474.0	1,566.0
Self-consumption	13.6	395.0	408.6
Adjustment	−29.4	+1,239.2	1,209.8
Volume of growing stock in 1979	1,330.7	5,758.0	7,088.7
Total	1,422.2	9,368.4	10,790.6

Source: Archambault and Bernard (n.d.); Theys (1989).

does not, for example, account for the effects of cumulative pollution. If growth and development are equivalent, sustainable income would be a measure of sustainable development. The proper measure of sustainable income would then be an estimate of net national product, making allowances of the kind discussed previously. Indeed, suitably defined and measured, net national product becomes a measure of the level of income that can be secured in the present without lowering real income in the future. This would be broadly consistent with the Brundtland Commission's definition of sustainable development (World Commission on Environment and Development 1987). As previously argued, however, income and development are not synonymous. Moreover, we are almost certainly a long way from being able to measure sustainable income, which requires an extensive effort to value the flow of services from environmental assets (see chapters 1 and 5). In the meantime, compromise solutions such as mixed physical and monetary accounts are welcome.

A final set of measures includes environmental indicators. These indicators do not attempt to measure sustainability as such, but rather to address some of the trends in the environment that can give rise to nonsustainability. Ideally, such measures should be associated with measures of pressure—the factors producing environmental change—and response—the ways in which societies react to changing environmental trends. Thus the pressure may be rising consumption of energy, which, in turn, is the result of rising population and income, perhaps encouraged by energy subsidies. The environmental effect could be sulfur oxide emis-

*Table 4-5. Estimated Air Pollution in Norway in 1987 Using
Input-Output Tables*
(gross production in millions of 1987 kroner)

Production sector and commodity group	Direct emissions			Total emissions		
	Carbon dioxide[a]	Nitrogen oxides[b]	Sulfur dioxide[b]	Carbon dioxide[a]	Nitrogen oxides[b]	Sulfur dioxide[b]
Agriculture	23	22	44	51	341	161
Food	12	36	78	27	152	153
Textiles	13	33	62	25	166	107
Pulp and paper products	60	149	645	97	338	942
Printing and publishing	1	9	2	29	292	126
Nonindustrial chemical and mineral products	119	190	215	171	427	350
Basic metals	172	227	1,352	235	423	1,779
Fabricated metals, ships, and oil platforms	4	13	10	17	180	78
Construction	8	97	10	40	286	114
Wholesale and retail trade	14	5	1	34	227	47
Private services	5	105	12	20	210	42
Domestic transportation, excluding coastal transportation	70	522	51	88	741	94
Coastal transportation	570	12,561	2,705	617	13,413	2,887
Private health and veterinary services	5	35	3	21	200	48

Note: Input-output tables show how each sector of the economy draws on the output of other sectors. Suppose sector A contributes X tons of carbon dioxide directly, and sector B contributes Y tons per dollar of output. If A uses z dollars of B's output, then A's total direct and indirect emissions are $X + (z \cdot Y)$.
a. Tons.
b. Kilograms.
Source: Norway, Central Bureau of Statistics (1990).

sions. The response could be increased expenditure on pollution abatement.

Numerous sources of environmental statistics have been compiled, but comparatively few link pressure and effect (for excellent collections of environmental data covering the industrial and some of the developing countries, see World Resources Institute's *World Resources,* which is published annually; OECD 1989; United Nations Environment Programme 1990). A sophisticated example of how the sectoral composition

Table 4-6. Annual Rates of Soil Erosion in Select Countries
(tons of soil eroded per hectare)

Country	Amount of soil eroded
Developing countries	
Burkina Faso	5–35
Burma	139
China	11–251
El Salvador	19–190
Ethiopia	42
Indonesia	43
Kenya	72–138
Madagascar	25–250
Nepal	25–70
Industrial countries	
Belgium	10–25
Canada	
British Columbia	30
New Brunswick	40
Nova Scotia	2–26
United States	18

Note: Soil erosion affects industrial and developing economies alike. Although extremely crude, the data suggest that developing countries are likely to suffer higher rates of erosion than richer countries.

Source: World Resources Institute (1988), table 17.6.

of GNP affects air quality is presented in table 4-6. Here, in the case of Norway, the emissions of carbon dioxide (a major greenhouse gas), nitrogen oxides, and sulfur dioxide are related to various sectors of the economy using an input-output table. The relevance of the input-output framework is that the indirect emissions of pollutants from a product may be more important than the direct emissions. Thus printing a book may contribute little directly to emissions, but if the manufacture of the paper and the transportation associated with distribution are taken into account, the emissions arising because the book is produced are significantly greater. Determining coefficients of this kind is important for forecasting emissions. Projecting GNP is not enough. A breakdown of GNP by sector must be projected as well since different sectors contribute substantially different amounts of pollution, as table 4-5 shows.

This level of sophistication is not yet readily available for the developing world. Tables 4-6 and 4-7 show some very rough data on rates of soil erosion and salinization of irrigated areas in both the industrial and developing worlds. Soil erosion and salinity of soils affect industrial and developing countries alike. The ability of each to combat these forms of environmental degradation is, however, very different. The output for-

Table 4-7. Rates of Salinity and Waterlogging in Select Countries
(millions of hectares, unless otherwise noted)

Country	Area irrigated	Area affected by salinity	Percentage affected
Egypt	2.9	0.8	28
India	50.0	12.0	24
Pakistan	12.4	3.2	26
United States	21.5	4.0	19

Note: Salinization of irrigation water affects industrial and developing economies alike. Developing countries are likely to suffer higher rates of salinity and waterlogging than richer countries, although the differences are not as great as the differences for erosion. The final column is approximate since the year for the area irrigated may be different from the year for the area affected by salinization.

Source: Chilton (1989).

gone because of soil erosion, for example, matters a great deal more to the developing world than to the industrial world. As chapter 1 notes, refining and extending these kinds of data bases is vital if natural resources are to be managed properly in the developing world.

Notes

1. The basic idea of sustainable income was established by J. R. Hicks (1946, p. 172): "We ought to define a man's income as the maximum value that he can consume during a week, and still expect to be as well off at the end of the week as he was at the beginning. Thus, when a person saves he plans to be better off in the future; when he lives beyond his income, he plans to be worse off."

2. Thus Dasgupta and Mäler (1991) demonstrate that a true measure of net national product (NNP) would comprise the following:

$$\text{NNP} = (W_c \cdot C) + (W_x \cdot X) + [W_z \cdot J(R,P)] + (W_{k2} \cdot K_2)$$
$$+ (W_L \cdot L) + [p_1 \cdot (dK_1 / dt)] + [p_2 \cdot (dK_2 / dt)]$$
$$+ [p_3 \cdot (dK_3 / dt)] + [p_4 \cdot (dK_4 / dt)]$$

for an economy in which W = welfare, C = aggregate consumption, X = fuelwood, L = labor effort, K_1 = man-made capital, K_2 = clean air, K_3 = forest stocks, K_4 = defensive capital, W_c = change in welfare arising from a small change in aggregate consumption C, p_1 = shadow price of K_1 and others, P = emission of pollutants, and R = rate of expending a portion of final output to mitigate damages to the flow of amenities.

NNP includes defensive expenditures (the last item in the equation), so they should not be deducted from GNP.

5

Evaluating Environmental Damage and Benefits

As outlined in chapter 1, it is possible to demonstrate that economic decisions affect the environment through the intermediary role played by the flow of materials and energy. This carries the critical implication that the state of the environment can be affected by economic policy that alters economic variables. In short, if economic events have environmental impact, then so does their management. Economic policy can therefore be used as an instrument of environmental policy.

It is just as important, however, to understand that the term "environment" is an abstraction. In reality, natural environments are many, diffuse, and above all, linked to one another. Consider the example of soil erosion discussed in chapter 1. The economic impact of soil erosion is not confined to crop losses at the site of the erosion (on-site losses). The eroded soil must go somewhere. It may be picked up by high winds and cause air pollution. It may enter rivers and add to sedimentation in other parts of the watershed (which may be beneficial, as with agricultural systems that flourish on silt from rivers, or costly, as when turbidity causes fish populations to decline). Sediment in hydropower reservoirs can be very costly if it reduces the live capacity of a dam.

Tracing the environmental impact of an economic event, then, requires an understanding of the system of ecological and physical links in the environments likely to be affected. Figure 5-1 illustrates one set of links

Figure 5-1. Ecological Effects of Deforestation

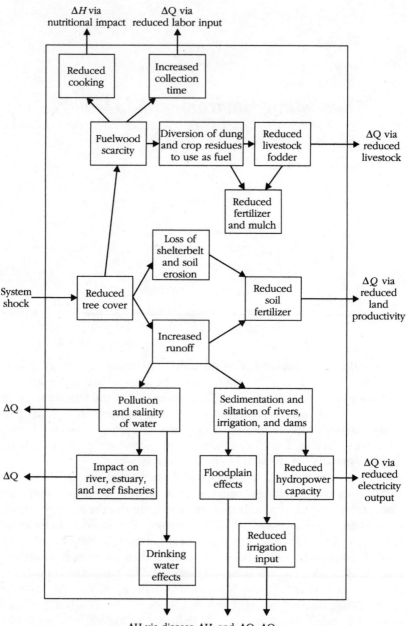

Note: ΔQ refers to effects that show up in measured or measurable indicators of development. ΔH refers to effects on health.
Source: Markandya and Pearce (1989).

related to the effects of an initial event giving rise to deforestation. Removing the tree cover affects the watershed and reduces the protective function of the forest. Sediment loads may change, affecting rivers and lakes, including hydropower reservoirs. Figure 5-1 merely scratches the surface of the complex, dynamic processes that may occur. The effects of an economic event in one location may not be replicated in another. Much depends on the nature of the ecosystems and the social responses to environmental change. Moreover, the nature of the change may not be smooth. Economics tends to assume that change takes place in a fairly continuous fashion, but change of an ecosystem may be a discontinuous response to critical loads of pollutants rather than a process of graduated change. As Myers (1988, p. 40) notes,

> Ecosystems may work in a nonlinear fashion, and across a broad expanse of space and time. The long-term and cumulative consequences of stress will be impaired functioning of the entire ecosystem and destabilization of its structures. Stress responses will appear in the form of a decline in the "natural" efficiency of resource use (nutrient losses expand as ecosystems become "leaky"), changes in energetics, an increase in parasitism, and a decrease in mutualism and other positive interactions. As human communities and their technologies continue to expand, they will exert increasing pressures on natural resource stocks and ecosystems, and ecological discontinuities will become more common.

This point is important. Predicting the environmental response to economic change can be difficult in the presence of discontinuity. Prediction is more difficult still because the various links within and between ecosystems are often unknown. Nonetheless, it is vitally important to investigate the links and likely outcomes as far as possible.

Economic Valuation

Several times in the preceding chapters the issue of valuation has arisen. Chapter 1 reveals how important the economic cost of pollution damage and resource degradation can be when expressed as a percentage of gross national product (GNP). Such national damage estimates are obviously very crude but nonetheless show that environmental quality matters at the macroeconomic or sectoral level. Chapter 3 illustrates procedures for adjusting the national accounts to reflect such damage and the depreciation of natural resource stocks. Once again, these adjustments demonstrate the importance of environmental quality and resource conservation. Adjusting the national income accounts also shows that conventional indicators of economic progress can be very misleading. Making these adjustments is an exercise in monetary valuation.

Valuation is also important at the microeconomic and sectoral level.

Understanding the full costs and benefits of a project is essential to making investment decisions. Box 2-3 shows how important this understanding could be in afforestation projects. The same message holds for any investment that seeks to rehabilitate or protect natural resources and for any investment that has either positive or negative externalities.

Thus we have two broad reasons for engaging in valuation exercises: first, to show that environment matters for planning at the macroeconomic level and, second, to show how it matters for making efficient allocative decisions at the microeconomic level. The remainder of this chapter investigates more closely the underlying theory of valuation, the techniques for valuation, and the ways in which valuation has been used in practice. Before launching into the topic, however, it is important to understand how economists determine value. Misconceptions about the purpose and nature of economic valuation account for most of the dispute between economists and other scholars.

Value can be broadly categorized as either instrumental or intrinsic. Instrumental value refers to the capacity of something, when used, to satisfy a want or preference. Intrinsic value is regarded by ecological philosophers as being inherent to something. Opinions vary widely as to what possesses intrinsic value, in particular whether value can reside in both conscious and unconscious objects or whether only conscious objects can possess intrinsic value (see Naess 1973; Regan 1981).

Instrumental, or use value, can be divided into direct value, indirect value, and option value. Intrinsic, or nonuse, value is also referred to as existence value. An illustration using values arising in the tropical forest context is presented in table 5-1.

Direct use values are fairly straightforward in concept but not necessarily easy to measure in economic terms. Thus the output of minor forest products can be measured using market and survey data, but the value of medicinal plants is extremely difficult to measure. Indirect values correspond to the ecologists' concept of ecological functions or services and are discussed in detail below.

Option values relate to the amount that individuals are willing to pay to conserve a tropical forest for future use. That is, the forest is not used now but may be used in the future. Option value resembles an insurance premium to ensure the supply of a resource or service whose availability would otherwise be uncertain. Although option value is not necessarily positive, it is likely to be positive for tropical forests.[1]

Quasi-option value has also been identified in the literature (see Fisher and Hanemann 1987; Henry 1974). It is the value of information that arises after the choice has been made to conserve or develop now. For example, the choice may be either to conserve or to develop the tropical forest now. If conservation is chosen, the choice in the next period can also be either to conserve or to develop. If development is chosen now and irreversible change occurs, however, only development can be cho-

Table 5-1. Total Economic Value of Tropical Forests

	Use value			Nonuse value	
Direct	Indirect	Option	Quasi-option	Existence
Sustainable timber	None	None	None	None
Products other than timber	Nutrient cycling	Future uses according to direct + indirect value	None	Forests as an object of intrinsic value, a bequest, a gift to others, a responsibility (stewardship); includes cultural and heritage values
Recreation	Watershed protection	None	None	None
Medicine	Reduction of air pollution	None	None	None
Plant genetics	Microclimate	None	None	None
Education	None	None	None	None
Human habitat	None	None	None	None

Note: Total economic value = use value, which is (direct value + indirect value + option value) (quasi-option value + existence value).

sen in the next period. In between the two periods information may arise that enhances the value of preservation, such as a scientific discovery about the flora and fauna. Quasi-option value is the value of learning about the future benefits that would be precluded if development were chosen now. It is positive if the information depends on the passage of time, which it probably would for tropical forests. Quasi-option value cannot be added to option value, which measures a different concept.

Existence value relates to valuations of the environmental asset that are unrelated either to current or to optional use. Its intuitive basis is easy to understand because a great many people are willing to pay for the existence of environmental assets through wildlife and other environmental charities. Empirical measures of existence value, obtained through questionnaires (the contingent valuation method), suggest that existence value can be a substantial component of total economic value. This finding is even more pronounced when the asset is unique, suggesting that the potential existence values are high for tropical forests and especially for luxuriant, moist forests (see Brookshire, Eubanks, and Randall 1983; Brookshire, Schulze, and Thayer 1985; Schulze and others 1983).

Typically, debates between advocates of instrumental and intrinsic value tend to assume that pursuing instrumental value is inconsistent with protecting intrinsic value. Thus using land for development is inconsistent with using it for wilderness. As we shall argue later, the inconsistency is only partial; it rests on a narrow interpretation of use values and ignores the ways in which nonuse values arise.

The pursuit of economic values as a goal is in itself a value judgment requiring a metaethical decision. It clearly implies that economic values rather than intrinsic values should be pursued.

Total Economic Value

Total economic value, or TEV, equals direct use value plus indirect use value plus option value plus existence value. The components of TEV cannot, however, simply be aggregated: that is, before being added to the equation, components must be shown not to be mutually exclusive (for example, the benefits of clear-felling and the benefits of watershed protection). Tradeoffs exist between different types of use value and between direct and indirect use values. In practice, then, the TEV approach must be used with care. Nevertheless, exploring total economic value helps us investigate economic value.

The cost-benefit rule for adopting a policy or project is as follows:

$$(5\text{-}1) \qquad \sum (B_t - C_t - E_t)\,[1\,/\,(1 + r)^t] > 0$$

where B_t = benefits in time t, C_t = costs in time t, E_t = net environmental costs in time t, and r = the discount rate.

The terms C and E are separated in order to focus on environmental costs and benefits. The net value of E is construed to be a cost (a positive value subtracted from other net benefits), but in a number of cases E may well be a benefit. Considering the specific case of land use, and the alternative of leaving land as wilderness, the constituent parts of E can be partitioned as benefits forgone because of the land use sacrificed by the project and as externalities (costs and benefits) associated with a given land use.

A development that takes up land previously used for recreation, wilderness, and so forth imposes a cost in the form of benefits from the previous land use that are lost. Such costs would typically encompass aesthetic externalities such as damage to buildings or unsightly development near a historic monument or wilderness area. The principles underlying the valuation of positive and negative E are no different.

A Deterministic Model for Land Use Benefits Forgone

Consider first a deterministic world in which no uncertainty exists. We are interested in environmental damage (benefits) and consider first the category of land use benefits forgone. Then we can write

(5-2)   TEV = TUV + TEXV

where TEV = total economic value, TUV = total use value, and TEXV = total existence value.

If TEV is sacrificed because of a development, then equation 5-2 is substituted into equation 5-1, and we can accept a project if

(5-3) $\Sigma_t [B_t - C_t - (\text{TUV} + \text{TEXV})] [1 / (1 + r)^t] > 0.$

Similarly, TUV + TEXV is added to net benefits if the policy or project improves the environment.[2] Since the impact of pollution has been omitted so far, equation 5-3 is an incomplete model for choice.

Imagining a hypothetical project will help us probe the TUV and TEXV components further. Imagine that a new road is scheduled to pass through an environmentally valuable area. Environmentally valuable means either that it has been officially scheduled as valuable or that its potential damage excites significant protest. The damage to the environmentally valuable site is thus a component of E in equation 5-1 and is subject to being decomposed according to equation 5-2 (as yet, no uncertainty exists). Use values for the site tend to be confined to two classes of people: residents and visitors. The use value in question might be for recreation, for example. Persons who are neither residents nor visitors do not have use values since they neither live in nor visit the area.

Each of the three classes of people may have existence values for the site. Residents and visitors may value it whether they use it or not. Persons who are neither residents nor visitors may also have existence values if they learn about the asset and wish to conserve it even though, by definition, they neither visit nor reside near it. In order, therefore, to uncover TEV in the deterministic context, we must identify the three mutually exclusive categories of individuals who value the resource and, if possible, uncover both their existence and their use values.

An Uncertainty Model for Land Use Benefits Forgone

We now need to relax the assumption of a certain world and introduce uncertainty. If relevant, uncertainty affects all components of TEV by turning them into ex ante concepts. An ex ante valuation involves judgments about expectations for the future based on what is known now, at the time of valuation. The literature on environmental economics tends to distinguish two kinds of uncertainty with regard to environmental assets.

Supply uncertainty concerns the continued availability of the environmental asset in question. Supply tends to be the most relevant source of uncertainty in the environmental context because the stock of environmental assets is perceived to be diminishing rather than increasing over time. In industrial countries, the disappearance of species and the reduction of wildlife habitat tend to support this presumption. Improvements in air quality tend to point in the other direction. Supply uncertainty thus appears to be somewhat important for evaluating projects and policies with environmental consequences. The implications of supply uncertainty for valuation are addressed shortly.

Demand uncertainty relates to uncertainty that an individual expressing a valuation will, in fact, demand the commodity at the time of use in the future. Demand uncertainty can arise because either future incomes or preferences are uncertain.

The two types of uncertainty are relevant because they modify equation 5-2 and therefore equation 5-3. The literature has yet to agree on the most desirable procedure. Some authors retain equation 5-2 but alter the meaning of the terms so that they become ex ante concepts that depend on probabilities about the state of the world (independent of policy) and on the way policy alters the environment (this procedure is used by Randall 1987, 1990). More popular has been the concept of option value, which was introduced by Weisbrod (1964) and followed by an extensive literature (for important material on option value, see R. Bishop 1982; Freeman 1985; Plummer and Hartman 1986; V. K. Smith 1987). Option value (OV) is the difference between the amount someone is willing to pay in order to retain the option of using an environmental asset in the future (the option price, OP) and the expected value of the ex post consumer surplus, $E(CS)$.[3] That is, we can write

$$(5\text{-}4) \qquad\qquad \text{OP} = E(CS) + \text{OV}.$$

Since $E(CS)$ is the equivalent of TUV in equation 5-2, the component OV has been added to the deterministic model to reflect uncertainty. In other words, equation 5-3—the deterministic cost-benefit model with land use forgone—now must be modified to become

$$(5\text{-}5) \quad \Sigma_t \{B_t - C_t - [E(CS) + \text{ov} + \text{texv}]\} [1 / (1 + r)^t] > 0.$$

A great deal of the literature is occupied with the sign of ov. Although the sign of ov is generally indeterminate, an important case is when demand is certain, but supply is uncertain. In this case, the valuer knows what he or she wants in the future but cannot be sure that the object of value will be available, and ov tends to be positive. When future demand is uncertain because future income is uncertain and future supply is certain, ov is negative for individuals who are averse to risks. If the uncertainty of future demand is a result of uncertain future preferences (state-dependent preferences), the sign of ov is ambiguous. This implies that normal cost-benefit analysis, which simply computes $E(CS)$, over-states the benefits of conservation if ov is, in reality, negative.

Few empirical studies claim to have separated option value from the overall willingness-to-pay concept of option price. That is, most studies tend to estimate option price itself without further decomposition. A number of studies in the United Kingdom and United States (see the section of this chapter on recent valuation experience) have found that option and nonuse values can be very significant indeed in relation to use values, particularly when unique assets are concerned (endangered species, unique habitats, heritage).

Total Economic Value and Pollution

We can now complete the cost-benefit model by incorporating the various effects of pollution. These effects may be negative or positive, depending on the project or policy in question. The cost-benefit model is simply extended to account for pollution as follows:

$$(5\text{-}6) \quad \Sigma_t \{B_t - C_t [E(CS) + \text{ov} + \text{texv}] - \text{tec}\} [1 / (1 + r)^t] > 0$$

where TEC refers to damage costs from pollution. Such damage would normally be estimated using techniques such as hedonic property prices, contingent valuation, and indirect procedures involving dose-response functions (see appendix). Land-use benefits forgone can be estimated using the same techniques, but existence and option values can only be derived using contingent valuation approaches.

Recent Valuation Experience

Table 5-2 shows some of the recent estimates of environmental values secured in the United Kingdom. The use of different measures of willing-ness to pay (WTP; per visit, per household, per hectare) makes any de-

Table 5-2. Valuation Studies in the United Kingdom
(British pounds per household or person a year, unless otherwise stated)

Study and source	Valuation	Method
Button and Pearce (1989)		
Canal amenity	517,000	HPM, aggregate value
Green and Tunstall (1991)		
Green and others (1988, 1989, 1990)		
River quality, 1987–88	9.6	CVM, user values
Beach amenity, 1988–89	14.0–18.0	CVM, user values
Coastal sites, 1989	21–25	CVM, nonuse values
Hanley (1988)		
Straw burning	WTP, 5.2	CVM, user values
	WTA, 9.6	
Hanley (1989)		
Forest recreation	0.34–15.1 per trip	TCM, user values
	1.2 per trip	CVM, user values
Harley and Hanley (1989)		
Nature reserves	1.2–2.5 per visit	CVM, user values
	2.0–3.5	TCM, user values
Turner and Brooke (1988)		
Coastal amenity	15	CVM, local users
	18	CVM, nonlocal users
Willis and Benson (1988)		
Nature reserves	46–251 hectares a year	TCM, all users
	6–34 hectares	TCM, wildlife visitors only
	25 hectares a year	CVM, nonuse values
Forest recreation	1.9 per visit	TCM

Note: WTP, willingness to pay; CVM, contingent valuation method; WTA, willingness to accept; TCM, travel cost method; HPM, hedonic price method.

tailed comparison difficult. The broad impression is that values cluster in the range of £10 to £25 per household a year for river quality, beach erosion, and coastal recreation; £25 corresponds to approximately 0.2 percent of the average income. For forest recreation, trip values appear to range widely, although the extent of the range depends on one study (Willis and Benson 1988). Other environmental services have been the subject of too little study to discern any possible tendency for clustering.

Table 5-3 presents some nonuse values in the United States. Insofar as they have actually been estimated, they appear to be significant.

Environmental Valuation in the Developing World

Chapter 1 provides examples of broadbrush attempts to value environmental damage at the national level in developing countries as well as several more sophisticated attempts to value resource depreciation. A

Table 5-3. Estimates of Nonuse Value in the United States
(U.S. dollars per household a year)

Study	Total	Preservation	Use	Option[a]	Existence
Bishop, Boyle, and Walsh (1987)					
Striped shiners	—	—	—	—	1–6
Bowker and Stoll (1988)					
Whooping cranes	5–149	—	—	—	—
Boyle and Bishop (1987)					
Bald eagles	6–75	—	—	—	5–28
Brookshire, Eubanks, and Randall (1983)					
Grizzly bears					
Hunters	—	—	—	10–21[b]	—
Observers	—	—	—	21–22[b]	—
Nonusers	—	—	—	—	15–24
Bighorn sheep					
Hunters	—	—	—	11–23[b]	—
Observers	—	—	—	18–23[b]	—
Nonusers	—	—	—	—	7
Desvousges, Smith, and Fisher (1987)					
Water quality	—	—	—	54–118[b]	—
Edwards (1988)					
Groundwater quality	—	—	—	285–1,436[b], 3–14[c]	—
Schulze and others (1983)					
Visibility					
Grand Canyon only	—	45–62	—	—	—
Southwest parklands	—	79–116	—	—	—
Plume removal	—	34–51	—	—	—
Stoll and Johnson (1984)					
Whooping cranes	—	2–3	—	29–42[c]	0–39
Sutherland and Walsh (1985)					
Water preservation	—	8	—	3[b]	5
Walsh, Loomis, and Gillman (1984)					
Wilderness	107	32	76	9[c]	11

— Not available.

Note: Option prices are reported in present values and converted to annual values. Preservation values are use plus existence values, but use values are smaller than existence values. User values per recreation day have been converted to values per household a year using average trips a year.

a. Some studies estimate option price, some estimate option value.

b. Option price.

c. Option value.

review of the valuation techniques might give the impression that they have limited relevance in the developing world (see the appendix to this chapter). Hedonic property price approaches rely on housing markets that function fairly well. Wage premia models require labor markets that

function equally well. Contingent valuation models require reasonably
sophisticated interview techniques that collect willingness-to-pay responses from individuals. Production function approaches are less problematic since, as we have seen, the costs of soil erosion, for example,
should show up in market responses through reduced crop yields. Although applying all valuation techniques to developing countries is in its
infancy, enough evidence exists to show that the techniques can be applied. The following section illustrates various approaches through case
studies.

Production Function Approaches

Production function approaches have perhaps the greatest potential
for valuation in the context of developing countries. Numerous studies
underline this. Table 5-4 looks at the issue of logging versus fishing and
tourism in an area of the Philippines. Logging operations commenced in
1985 in Bacuit Bay, Palawan. The bay supports two other industries that
earn foreign exchange: tourism and marine fishing. The logging produced high rates of sedimentation in the bay, damaging coral reefs and
the fishery. A valuation study was undertaken principally to evaluate
gross revenues with and without a hypothesized ban on logging. The
study concluded that a logging ban was clearly preferable to no ban, and
this finding was not greatly affected by either raising the discount rate or
assuming different sedimentation-damage rates.

Table 5-5 looks at another study in the Philippines (Briones 1986). In
this case, a multipurpose dam was to be built on the Lower Agno River
to supply hydroelectricity, irrigation water, and flood control as well as
improve water quality. At the same time, however, the reservoir was
expected to trap tailings from gold and copper mines in the watershed,
despite the existence of tailing dams for trapping the mine waste. The
study evaluated a watershed management plan designed to reduce reser-

Table 5-4. *Revenues Generated by Fishing and Tourism with
and without a Ban on Logging, Bacuit Bay, Philippines, 1987–96*
(millions of 1987 U.S. dollars at present value given a 10 percent discount rate)

Activity	Option 1: ban on logging	Option 2: no ban on logging	Option 1 minus option 2
Fisheries	17.2	9.1	8.1
Logging	0.0	9.8	−9.8
Tourism	25.5	6.3	19.2
Total	42.7	25.2	17.5

Note: If logging is banned, gross revenues from tourism and fishing would be $43
million. If logging is not banned, tourism and fishing would continue, but at reduced rates
because of damage from sedimentation. Gross revenues from logging, tourism, and fishing
would then be $25 million. Clearly, it pays to ban logging and maintain the fishery.
Source: Hodgson and Dixon (1988).

Table 5-5. Benefits of Watershed Management in the Context of a Multipurpose Dam, the Philippines
(billions of U.S. dollars in present value given a 10 percent discount rate)

Cost or benefit of management scheme	Low erosion	High erosion
Cost	5.33	7.34
Benefit	14.50	30.36
Net benefit	9.17	23.02

Note: Introducing a watershed management scheme that involves afforestation, controls soil erosion, and protects the forest reduces by $14 million to $30 million the costs of sedimentation damage caused by mine tailings in the dam reservoir. Because its costs are much lower, the scheme shows net benefits.
Source: Briones (1986).

voir sedimentation. Sedimentation was shown to reduce the originally forecast net benefits of $2.97 billion to $2.60 billion–$2.67 billion over a fifty-year period. The issue, then, was whether the $0.30 billion–$0.37 billion loss could be reduced, at a net gain, by investing in watershed management. Watershed management was found to have positive net benefits: the costs of introducing a management scheme were less than the expected costs of sediment damage (other studies on production function valuation can be found in Bojo, Mäler, and Unemo 1990; Dixon and others 1988).

Table 5-6 looks at a forest development project in Nepal (Dixon and others 1986). The production function approach was used, but this time several alternative market values were adopted to value the effects of the project. The project was concerned with improving the use of land, the quality of 7,000 hectares of timber stand, and the management of 16,000 hectares of scrubland; with building additional fencing to stop livestock damage; and with establishing 4,000 hectares of forest for fodder, fuelwood, and fencing timber. Its goals, or outputs, were to increase the amount of fuelwood and fodder, raise productivity of the land, and reduce soil erosion. To find the incremental productivity arising from the management program, it was necessary first to estimate what the value of output from the land would be without the project.[4] As an example, grazing land produces two products, milk and animal dung, which is used as fertilizer. Each animal produces 15 kilograms of nitrogen equivalent and 2 kilograms of phosphorus equivalent a year. Nitrogen is valued at NRs6 per kilogram and phosphorus at NRs18 per kilogram, so that one animal produces (15 kilograms x NRs6) + (2 kilograms x NRs18) of fertilizer a year, or NRs126. Each hectare supports 0.0857 of an animal, so fertilizer production per hectare is 0.0857 x NRs126 = NRs11 per hectare.

Scrubland and unmanaged forest produce fertilizer, milk, and fuelwood. Fuelwood is valued three ways. First, it is sold on the market, and

Table 5-6. Valuing the Benefits of a Hill Forest Development Project in Nepal
(millions of rupees of output for total land area)

Year of the project	Output with project	Output without project	Output with project minus output without it
1	12.5	7.5	5.0
2	5.3	7.2	−1.9
3	10.8	6.9	3.9
4	5.8	6.6	−0.8
5	9.9	6.4	3.5
40	21.7	1.6	20.1

Note: The forest management project involved changes in land use, so the output from each type of land use had to be valued and then the changes arising from differences in value due to differences in land use and increased productivity on a given land use had to be examined. The discounted value of the net benefits was then compared with the discounted value of the costs. The result was expressed as an internal rate of return of 8.5 percent.

Source: Dixon and others (1988).

the market price net of collection costs was NRs280 per cubic meter. Second, animal dung is a substitute for fuelwood. Dung could, in turn, be valued several ways, but the method chosen was to look at crop responses. Thus, 1 cubic meter of wood equals 0.6 tons of dried manure, which equals 2.4 tons of fresh manure. Maize yields were estimated to rise 15 percent because 6 tons of fresh manure are applied to a 0.5-hectare plot each year. Thus a hectare that currently produces 1.53 tons of maize would produce 1.8 tons. Since maize output is worth NRs1,200 per ton, the productivity gain would be NRs1,200 x (1.80 tons − 1.53 tons) = NRs324. Hence the value of a cubic meter of wood is (324 rupees x 0.5 hectares) / 6 tons = NRs27 per hectare for fresh manure = NRs27 x 2.4 tons = NRs65 per cubic meter. Third, fuelwood can be valued by the time taken to collect it. Each family spends 132 days a year collecting 7.92 cubic meters. Since NRs5 per day is the alternative income that could be earned from other activity, each cubic meter of wood costs (132 days x NRs5) / 7.92 cubic meters = NRs83.

Thus output can be calculated by looking at each type of land. When project interventions are envisaged, output should be estimated for the new use of land under the project and compared with output without the project.

Valuation of environmental effects is not only relevant to investment decisions, but also to social cost pricing (see chapter 8). The basic idea is that the price of a product should reflect not just the private costs of production, but also any environmental costs attributed to its production. This basic principle can also be applied to a resource. Oil products, for example, should be priced to reflect the costs of extraction, transportation, and processing and the impact of any pollution that can be attributed to their production. Box 5-1 outlines a study that analyzes fuelwood pricing in Haiti in this context (Hosier and Bernstein 1989). The basic rule used is marginal opportunity costs = marginal costs of harvesting + marginal external costs + marginal user costs, or MOC = MC + MEC + MUC.

MEC is the value of any environmental damage arising from the use of the resource. MUC is the value of future benefits forgone as a result of using one unit of the resource today. If a resource is genuinely renewable, its use today should not involve a cost in the future because the resource can regenerate. Many renewable resources are not used this way, however, so it may be legitimate to speak of a user cost component of the overall true cost (the MOC) of the resource (for more on the concept of MOC, see Markandya and Pearce 1989). Hosier and Bernstein's study found that actual prices for fuelwood in Haiti are too low. MOC is from 1.5 to 10.0 times greater than MC, which, in this study, is approximated by the actual market price. Effectively, fuelwood is underpriced in the marketplace. The low price partly explains the overuse of fuelwood in Haiti and its associated environmental impact.

Discrete Choice Valuation

Discrete choice valuations are derived by comparing actual choices to see what they imply for the value of the good chosen and its attributes. For example, consider how households choose their source of water in developing countries. A study was conducted of the choices facing households in a village in Kenya. In that village, water can be obtained from vendors who deliver it to the house, from kiosks where it is sold to members of the household, who then must carry it to the dwelling, or from wells, where it is collected directly by the household (Mu, Whittington, and Briscoe 1991; Whittington, Mu, and Roche 1990; Whittington and others 1989).[5] Each option presents a different set of prices, from zero for the open well to the market price for the kiosk and the vendor. Each also presents a different amount of time needed to collect the water, from none for the vendor to significant amounts for the open well and the kiosk. The results of the analysis indicated that households buying water from vendors placed a particularly high value on the time that would otherwise be spent in collecting water. Overall, the implied value of time for those who purchased from water vendors or kiosks was roughly equal to the average wage rate. This kind of valuation procedure has evident uses for planning investments in a water supply. Connecting villages to a water supply will save the households' time spent collecting the water, and a value of the time saved should appear as a benefit of the connection scheme. The procedure shows how such benefits might be estimated.

Discrete choice approaches can estimate the willingness of all consumers to pay for a supply of water. On the assumption that consumers

---

Box 5-1. Determining the True Price of Fuelwood in Haiti

Fuelwood is bought and sold in markets in Haiti, but the market price does not reflect the true cost of harvesting it. At least three external costs are associated with the use of fuelwood. First, trees contribute to soil nutrients. One ton of dry firewood in Haiti produces some 760 kilograms of dry foliage, which, in turn, is equivalent to 17 kilograms of nitrogen. The market price for nitrogen fertilizer is some G150–G250 a ton. Converted to tons of oil equivalent, the value of fuelwood in relation to its contribution to fertilizer is G12.0–G19.8 a ton. This value is lost by harvesting, so it appears as a fertilizer externality in the estimates below. Second, trees reduce soil erosion. In Haiti soil erosion is associated with a 2 percent reduction in farm income. Allowing for the number of trees per farm, their weight, and the amount used as fuelwood, the soil erosion externality is G45 a ton. Third, soil erosion is associated with reservoir sedimentation. Reservoir sedimentation reduces the generation of electricity, which has a direct market cost. On this basis, around G$10 per ton of oil equivalent of fuelwood must be debited as the sedimentation externality.

In addition to external costs, user costs exist if the resource is thought of as depletable rather than renewable. A formula for estimating the marginal user cost is $\mathrm{MUC} = (P_b - C) / (1 + r)^T$, where P_b is the price of the substitute technology (kerosene, say), C is the cost of harvesting fuelwood, r is the discount rate, and T is the time at which fuelwood is exhausted (see D. W. Pearce and Turner 1989, chap. 18). This, then, is the basis for obtaining values of G10–G290 per ton of fuelwood.

Table B5-1. *True Price of Fuelwood in Haiti, by User, 1985*
(value in gourdes)

Marginal opportunity cost	Rural household	Rural industry	Urban industry
Market price	18.5	37.3	129.0
Externality			
Fertilizer	20.0	20.0	20.0
Soil erosion	45.0	45.0	45.0
Sedimentation	10.0	10.0	10.0
User costs	69.5	66.2	50.0
Total	163.0	178.5	254.0

Source: Hosier and Bernstein (1989).

If marginal external costs alone are allowed for, the ratio of marginal opportunity cost to marginal cost of harvesting is 1.6 to 5.0. Allowing for marginal user cost, which is debatable, the ratios are much greater. All the estimates are subject to considerable uncertainty, but the analysis illustrates a further role for valuation procedures.

perceive the benefits of supply as not just time savings but also health and convenience, such a measure would indicate the overall benefit of a given water supply. This could then be compared with the costs of supplying the water. Such a procedure would contrast with current rules of thumb used to develop water supply projects, which frequently assume that willingness to pay is equal to between 3 and 5 percent of household income. This assumption has no firm empirical basis. Box 5-2 shows the results of a discrete choice model for supplying connections to public water systems in the Punjab, Pakistan. The procedure used to estimate willingness to pay was based on observations in five villages, all of which had a system of piped water. Some households chose to connect to the piped system, others did not. In general, households who did not connect to the system used indoor hand or electric pumps to collect groundwater. The benefits of a piped system are that it generally improves the quality of water, allows indoor plumbing to be installed, and makes the water supply more reliable.

The decision to connect is influenced by three prices: a one-time connection fee, a monthly tariff unrelated to consumption, and the costs of connecting the specific household, which tend to vary with distance from the water line. Other factors influencing the decision to connect were assumed to be income, socioeconomic characteristics of the household, the availability of women and children to collect water from other sources, and household attitudes to water quality. The relation that exists between these factors and the decision to connect or not allows us to construct a demand function for being connected to the piped system. A demand function is, in fact, a willingness-to-pay function. The area under the demand curve is the total or gross willingness to pay, and the area under the curve but net of the actual payment made is the net willingness to pay, or consumer surplus (see figure B5-2). This example demonstrates that determining the value of the benefits of water supply is feasible in developing countries. Given the enormous magnitude of the investments in water supply, and the rules of thumb used to justify many of them, valuation procedures should be developed.

Contingent Valuation

Contingent valuation methods (CVM) ask people whether they are willing to pay for a benefit. Applied to developing countries CVM could be an important component of project appraisal since, frequently, the output of a project is not marketed. This is the case, for example, with water supply investments, which absorb a substantial amount of donor funds. The presumption has been that people will pay up to approximately 5 percent of their income for piped water. In practice, however, this is not always the case. People often retain their old sources of supply even when

---

Box 5-2. Willingness to Pay for Piped Water in the Punjab, Pakistan

The benefits of an improved supply of water tend to be assumed rather than demonstrated. A study in the Punjab (Altaf and others 1990) showed how a demand function for piped water could be estimated by looking at the relation of past decisions to connect or not connect with various factors: connection prices, income, socioeconomic factors such as education, and attitudes to water quality. The study estimated a simplistic demand function of the kind presented in figure B5-2 and showed that the gross willingness to pay was always positive but that the consumer surplus for some households was negative (they were willing to pay less than the ruling effective tariff). For others the consumer surplus was positive. If aggregated, the benefits could be compared with the costs of providing the connections for piped water, greatly improving the basis on which decisions about water supply are made.

Figure B5-2. Willingness to Pay

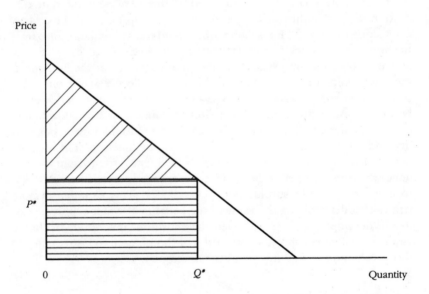

At price P^* the quantity Q^* of water is purchased. The crosshatched area is the consumer surplus, the lightly shaded area is the actual payment made. Con-
(continued on next page)

the new supply is provided. For this reason, it is important to find the value of supplying water to a specific village or town.

A contingent valuation study of water supply was conducted in Haiti (see MacRea and Whittington 1988; Whittington and others 1990). Tests for strategic and starting point bias were conducted by varying the questions given to different respondents. By and large, no evidence of sumers with valuations less than P^* have a negative consumer surplus. Those with valuations above P^* have a positive consumer surplus.

Table B5-2 shows the estimates of consumer surplus per household (for one of the models used by the authors). The actual prices were PRs102 in the sweet water area and PRs119 in the brackish water area. The consumer surplus must be added to these prices to estimate gross willingness to pay. For many households, willingness to pay is less than the tariff, which explains why they do not connect. Others do not connect for reasons other than price.

Table B5-2. Consumer Surplus per Household in Punjab, Pakistan, by Type of Area, 1985
(consumer surplus per household in 1985 rupees)

Consumer surplus per household	Sweet water		Brackish water	
	Connected	Not connected	Connected	Not connected
Mean	78	26	43	19
Minimum	−1	−38	−21	−94
Maximum	282	107	133	54

Source: Altaf and others (1990).

these biases was found. The mean bid—the average willingness to pay— for public standpipes was Gs5.7 (about $1) a month, or about 1.7 percent of household income. This is significantly lower than the 5 percent rule referred to above. The mean WTP for private connections was Gs7.1, or around 2.1 percent of average income. Whittington and others (1990) concluded that it was possible to obtain reasonable consistent answers from a contingent valuation survey among a very poor, illiterate population.

Ecosystem Valuation of Tropical Forests

The idea of total economic value (TEV) has already been introduced for valuing both resources and pollution damage. The subsequent case studies looked at the costs of pollution damage and other externalities arising from the misuse of natural resources. TEV can also be applied to the choice of land use. This section takes an extended look at one major, controversial issue of land use: the use of tropical forest land.

Various options exist for using the land in tropical forests. It could be left alone. If humans are not allowed to use forest land at all, this option might be seen as preservation. Maintaining the forest stock in broadly its original state, but allowing humans to use it, could be defined as conservation. There is also a broad spectrum of conservation options. Limited, selective logging might be permitted if it is followed by natural or managed regeneration of the removed timber. The harvesting of forest products, such as the production of latex or the gathering of rattan, might be accomplished without removing timber stock. Agricultural clearance using shifting cultivation might be practiced with the forest being allowed to regenerate fully as a new plot is exploited. Some experts do not regard shifting cultivation as a conservation option, and the terminology is not universally accepted. The basic idea remains that conservation involves use without significant destruction of the forest ecosystem. Above all, any option for use that produces irreversible effects is not a conservation use of the land. Development options would then include clearing land for agricultural use without any intent to secure regeneration, clear-felling timber without regeneration, or removing the forest to use the land for infrastructure, such as a road or a mining or industrial development. By and large, development options preclude the regeneration of the forest because development programs damage forest soils. This is not inevitable, but it is very likely.

The issue, then, is how the framework of total economic value can help policymakers and others choose between land use options.

The Rate of Deforestation

Global concern about the rate of tropical deforestation accelerated in the 1980s. Data for all types of forests are approximate, and different sources use different definitions of tropical forest and deforestation. However, annual rates of deforestation at the end of the 1980s were apparently somewhere between 14 million and 17 million hectares (table 5-7). Depending on how forest area is defined, this rate of deforestation may equal 1.8 to 2.1 percent of the remaining area of tropical forest (taken to be some 8 million square kilometers, or 800 million hectares). Although comparisons are difficult because of changing definitions, deforestation rates may have been much lower, around 0.6 percent a year, in the late 1970s.

Attention has focused on tropical forests because they serve so many diverse functions, the primary forest has unique evolutionary and ecological characteristics, and the threat to their existence is accelerating. In the briefest of terms, tropical forests

- Are the homeland of many indigenous peoples, some of whom practice shifting cultivation
- Provide the habitat for extensive fauna and flora (biodiversity), which are considered to have inherent value, educational value, value for breeding crops, and medicinal value
- Supply hardwood timber
- Supply other forest products such as fruit, nuts, latex, rattan, meat, honey, resins, and oils
- Provide recreation (ecotourism)
- Protect watersheds by retaining and regulating the flow of water and cleansing water pollution and organic nutrients

Table 5-7. Preliminary Estimates of Tropical Forest Area and Rate of Deforestation for Eighty-Seven Tropical Countries, 1981–90

(thousands of hectares)

Regions or subregions	Number of countries studied	Total land area	Forest area, 1980	Forest area, 1990	Area deforested annually, 1981–90	Annual rate of change, 1981–90 (percent)
Latin America	32	1,675,700	923,000	839,900	8,300	−0.9
Central America and Mexico	7	245,300	77,000	63,500	1,400	−1.8
Caribbean subregion	18	69,500	48,800	47,100	200	−0.4
Tropical South America	7	1,360,800	797,100	729,300	6,800	−0.8
Asia	15	896,600	310,800	274,900	3,600	−1.2
South Asia	6	445,600	70,600	66,200	400	−0.6
Continental Southeast Asia	5	192,900	83,200	69,700	1,300	−1.6
Insular Southeast Asia	4	258,100	157,000	138,900	1,800	−1.2
Africa	40	2,243,400	650,300	600,100	5,000	−0.8
West Sahelian Africa	8	528,000	41,900	38,000	400	−0.9
East Sahelian Africa	6	489,600	92,300	85,300	700	−0.8
West Africa	8	203,200	55,200	43,400	1,200	−2.1
Central Africa	7	406,400	230,100	215,400	1,500	−0.6
Tropical Southern Africa	10	557,900	217,700	206,300	1,100	−0.5
Insular Africa	1	58,200	13,200	11,700	200	−1.2
Total	87	4,815,700	1,884,100	1,714,800	16,900	−0.9

Source: World Resources Institute (1992).

- Act as a store of carbon dioxide
- Fix carbon in secondary forests and reforested areas
- Serve a possible regional microclimatic function.

These are economic functions because they contribute to human welfare either directly or indirectly.[6] How should the total economic value of a tropical forest be determined? The issue is important because decisions about the use of tropical forest land are made all too often with an imperfect understanding of the total functions of the forest. Even when they are broadly understood, only some of the functions enter into the economic calculus that determines land use. In particular, the direct use values (for timber or agriculture) dominate decisions about land use, and the wider environmental values are neglected. The resulting asymmetry of values explains much deforestation, and analyzing it can indicate policy instruments for improving the management of forests.

Calculating Total Economic Value

One approach to making decisions about the use of tropical forests is the cost-benefit approach. Under this, decisions to develop a tropical forest must demonstrate that the net benefits from development exceed the net benefits from conservation. Development is taken to mean a use that is inconsistent with keeping the forest close to its natural state.

Conservation could have two dimensions: preservation, which would be formally equivalent to outright nonuse of the resource, and sustainable conservation, which would allow limited uses of the forest that are consistent with retaining the natural forest. The definitions are necessarily ambiguous. Some people would argue, for example, that ecotourism is not consistent with sustainable conservation; others would argue that it may be. Accepting the lack of precise lines of differentiation, the rule of the cost-benefit approach would be to develop the forest if and only if DEVBEN − DEVCOST > CONSBEN − CONSCOST. That is, the development benefits minus the development costs must be greater than the benefits of conservation minus the costs of conservation. Rearranging this inequality, we have DEVBEN − DEVCOST − Net CONSBEN > 0. It is not sufficient, therefore, for the net benefits of development to be positive. The forgone net benefits of conservation must also be subtracted from the net benefits of development (Pearce 1989; Pearce and Turner 1989, chap. 20).

Typically, the benefits and costs of development can be fairly readily calculated because of the attendant cash flows. Timber production, for example, tends to be undertaken for commercial markets and thus is associated with market prices. Conservation benefits, however, are associated with a mix of cash flows and nonmarket benefits, and this association imparts two biases. The first bias is that the components of the first inequality that are associated with cash flows appear more real than those not associated with such flows. Concreteness is misplaced, and decisions are likely to be biased in favor of the development option because the benefits of conservation cannot be calculated easily. The second bias follows from the first. Unless incentives are devised so that the nonmarket benefits are internalized into the mechanism for choice of land use, conservation benefits will automatically be downgraded. Very simply, those who stand to gain from, say, timber extraction or agricultural clearance cannot consume the nonmarketed benefits. This asymmetry of values imparts a considerable bias in favor of the development option.

In both inequalities, CONSBEN is measured by the total economic value of the tropical forest, which is explained in table 5-1.

Direct Use Values in the Tropical Forest

Direct use values may be classified broadly as timber and nontimber uses. Nontimber products include fruits, nuts, rattan, latex, resins, honey, and wild meat.

TIMBER. Logging for timber can be consistent with conservation if the regime for managing timber practices sustainable forestry. Sustainable forestry, which leaves the original ecosystem broadly intact, effectively requires the management of natural forests: selective cutting combined with natural regeneration. Traditionally, natural management regimes have been regarded as producing losses unless

- Biological growth rates are very high
- Stumpage prices (log prices) are high
- Management is effective and at minimum cost
- The discount rate is low compared with typical commercial and even official government levels (Leslie 1987).

This bias explains the general absence of sustainable natural management systems in tropical forestry.[7] Inefficiency arising from government interference is of considerable importance for high-cost, unsustainable management.

Table 5-8 presents estimates of the financial profitability of six forestry systems in Indonesia. TPI is a selective cutting system that takes only the largest commercial trees (over 50 centimeters in diameter at breast height). The management of TPI is crucial since careless selective cutting can damage the residual stock, reducing future harvests. In its ideal form, however, it is a sustainable system. Complete harvesting and regeneration (CHR) is a system where all merchantable trees are harvested, followed by natural or enriched regeneration. INTD is an intensive dipterocarp system in which heavily managed plantations are located on clear-felled land. PULP refers to plantations of fast-growing species for pulp. SAW refers to sawtimber plantations at rotations of ten and twenty years. Environmentally, TPI should be ranked above CHR.[8] INTD is an untried system that may or may not be environmentally better than CHR. At first view, SAW and PULP seem to be environmentally undesirable since they typically involve uniform plantings of nonindigenous species on cleared land. Locating such plantations on currently unforested land could, however, be important for carbon-fixing purposes.

Table 5-8 suggests that rapid-growth plantations for producing pulp are most financially desirable at an interest rate of 6 percent but are also desirable at a rate of 10 percent. Of the systems involving the least management, the selective cutting system is not favored except at the low discount rate of 5 percent. Typically, the discount rates used to appraise projects in developing countries are 10 percent and above. Table 5-8 therefore bears out the general presumption that natural management systems based on selective cutting are less profitable than managed intensive systems and, perhaps, clear cutting systems with some natural regeneration.

Many caveats must, however, be attached to this conclusion. First, the results are likely to be specific to the location. Second, they relate to financial profitability, not economic worth. An economic assessment would allow for shadow pricing, or a valuation procedure that reflects the worth of the investment to the economy as a whole rather than to a forest concessionaire.[9] Third, the discount rate is crucial. Shadow pricing may dictate a lower rate depending on the nature of the rationale used for discounting (Markandya and Pearce 1988). Nonetheless, appealing directly to timber benefits is clearly a risky defense for the sustainable use of tropical forests.

PRODUCTS OTHER THAN TIMBER. Products other than timber can be important sources of revenue. In Indonesia, for example, exports of

Table 5-8. *Financial Profitability of Forest Management Systems in Indonesia, by Discount Rate, 1986*
(net present value in 1986 U.S. dollars per hectare)

Regime	5 percent	6 percent	10 percent
TPI	2,705	2,409	2,177
CHR	2,690	2,593	2,553
INTD	—	2,746	2,203
PULP	—	2,926	2,562
SAW10	—	2,165	2,130
SAW20	—	2,419	2,278

— Not available.

Note: TPI, selective cutting; CHR, complete harvesting and regeneration; INTD, intensive dipterocarp system; PULP, plantations of fast-growing species for pulp; SAW10, sawtimber plantations at ten-year rotations; SAW20, sawtimber plantations at twenty-year rotations. Net present value includes revenues from the initial harvest of standing stock.

Source: Pearce (1987). The base data come from Sedjo (1987a, 1987b).

nontimber forest products rose from $17 million in 1973 to $154 million in 1985, comprising 12 percent of the export earnings of forest products (D. W. Pearce, Barbier, and Markandya 1990, chap. 5). They rose to $238 million in 1987 (de Beer and McDermott 1989). Exports of rattan alone earned $80 million in 1985. Tropical forests also supply essential oils such as camphor, cinnamon, clove, and nutmeg, a trade worth some $1 billion a year (Myers 1983). It cannot be assumed that the exploitation of nontimber products is itself free of environmental damage. The management record for many nontimber products is hardly better than that for tropical timber.[10] Analysis of fruit and latex yields on a 1-hectare plot of rain forest in the Peruvian Amazonia suggests that revenues generated by nontimber products may actually exceed those generated by timber (Peters, Gentry, and Mendelsohn 1989; table 5-9).

The implication of table 5-9 is that tropical forest conservation might be achieved simply by appealing to financial profitability. Much forest may be damaged unnecessarily because alternative management regimes are not investigated for alternative crops. Several dangers are, however, inherent in extrapolating from a 1-hectare plot to an entire forest. First, markets for nontimber products are very unlikely to be that large. As production of nontimber products expands, their price is likely to fall. Second, the Peruvian case considers a plot of land located near to markets, whereas most tropical forest areas are located far from the marketplace, which increases the cost of transportation. The analysis also raises an important question: if exploiting forests for nontimber products is privately profitable, why are so few forests used for this purpose? Put another way, why does the exercise of market forces fail to produce this result?

The answer to this question reveals some of the most important policies for conserving tropical forests. A great deal of deforestation would be avoided if markets were allowed to function more efficiently. Direct government interference distorts price signals, making the extraction and, more important, the clearance (usually by fire) of timber for agriculture profitable. This interference takes well-established forms. In the case of Brazil, for example,

Table 5-9. Timber and Nontimber Revenues from a Rain Forest in Iquitos, Peru
(U.S. dollars per hectare)

Activity	Net present value at 5 percent
Fruit and latex	6,330
Selective logging	490
Subtotal	6,820
Clear-felling timber	1,000

Source: Southgate, Sierra, and Brown (1989).

- Tax credits are passed that allow farmers to use the costs of clearing forest land for cattle ranching to offset income in the tax regime
- Subsidized credit is available to develop crops and livestock
- Road infrastructure is built to establish political boundaries (Binswanger 1989; Mahar 1989; Repetto and Gillis 1988).

Equally important in the bias toward clearance is the status of land tenure. Forest dwellers rarely hold secure rights to the land, so outsiders can readily establish rights through clearance. Indeed, in many cases, the land must be cleared in order to claim land rights (Southgate, Sierra, and Brown 1989). Agricultural colonists invariably win the competition for land rights. Ensuring secure land tenure for indigenous peoples may be one of the most important ways of conserving tropical forests. Conferring security of tenure on colonists, however, acts like a magnet for outsiders wishing to clear land for agriculture.

Clearing forests for ranching is socially irrational: without subsidies, revenues from Brazilian beef cattle ranching cover only one-third of the costs of setting up the ranches, as table 5-10 shows (Browder 1988a, 1988b). The subsidy system explains why an activity that is privately profitable is socially unprofitable. The combined costs of tax credits, subsidized credit, and the timber revenues forgone because a forest is

Table 5-10. Cost Structure of a Typical Beef Cattle Ranch
in the Brazilian Amazon, 1979–84
(U.S. dollars per hectare)

Expenses	Amount invested	Percentage of the total
Capital investment		
Land cost	31.7	13.1
Forest clearance	66.0	27.3
Pasture planting	26.4	10.9
Fencing	19.4	8.0
Cattle acquisition	90.9	37.6
Other	7.4	3.1
Subtotal	241.8	100.0
Operating costs		
Labor	26.2	15.2
Herd maintenance	21.0	12.1
Pasture maintenance	47.3	27.3
Infrastructure	74.3	43.0
Other	4.2	2.4
Subtotal	173.0	100.0
Total costs	414.8	100.0
Total revenues	112.5	100.0
Revenues as a percentage of costs	n.a.	27.1

n.a. Not applicable.
Source: Ruitenbeek (1989).

destroyed are estimated to have been $4.8 billion between 1966 and 1983. Both market forces and government price distortions seem to explain why the forest was cleared for agriculture and livestock. While large ranches collected subsidies, small ranches did not. Yet small ranches expanded rapidly, which suggests that financial returns to smaller ranches may be quite high.

ECOTOURISM VALUES. Tropical forests are attracting a growing number of tourists searching for adventure or a place to appreciate nature. Ecotourism promises to be a major development capable of generating substantial revenues such as those earned in African countries from wildlife viewing and game drives. European package explorer holidays to the Peruvian Amazon, for example, cost around $2,300 per person for twenty days.[11] In Costa Rica, Ecuador, the Philippines, and Thailand, tourism ranks among the top five industries and brings in more foreign exchange than exports of timber and timber products (Gradwohl and Greenberg 1988, pp. 66–67). Thus Costa Rica earned $138 million in 1986 in what was mainly nature-based tourism. The number of tourists arriving in Manaus, Amazonas, Brazil, increased from 12,000 in 1983 to 70,000 in 1988. Tourism is expected to be the largest single source of income in Brazil's Amazonas State in the 1990s (quoted in Dogse 1989). The potential for tourism in Central America and Latin America remains largely untapped (Dourojeanni 1985; Leonard 1987). Obviously, not all tourism to these countries can be credited to forest areas, but some unquestionably is. Additionally, tourism brings its own external costs in the form of pollution, overexposure of wildlife to tourist vehicles, and so on.

Ruitenbeek (1989) suggests tentative values for tourist benefits in the Korup Forest in Cameroon. On the basis of assumptions about the rates charged both tourists and researchers, annual net income to Cameroon would, once rates were stabilized, be an estimated $180,000.

Of course, not all tourists originate from other countries. As real income per capita increases, so does the incipient demand for recreation in the developing countries. In Tunisia, for example, Lake Ichkeul and its associated marshes, which have been designated a national park, are particularly rich in wildlife, especially birds. A visitor survey in 1988 showed that, on a single day, 1,500 persons visited the park, and only 200 of them were from overseas. Tunisians were also prepared to travel long distances to visit the park: 60 percent of the visitors had come from Tunis, and 4 percent had traveled more than 350 kilometers (Thomas, Ayache, and Hollis 1989).

USES OF WILD FLORA AND FAUNA. Tropical forests act as the habitat for an enormous variety of species. The production of meat from wild animals in Peru amounted to some 13,000 tons in 1976 (Dourojeanni

1985, p. 420); fish and game comprise 80 to 85 percent of all animal protein intake in the lowland Amazon region outside urban centers. Legal exports of hides and skins from Peru amounted to 5 million and 0.5 million, respectively, between 1965 and 1976 (Dourojeanni 1985, p. 423). The trade in live animals is significant and, sadly, unsustainable due to excessive exploitation. As with tourism, fine distinctions frequently separate what is and is not sustainable.

Tropical forests act as the source of genetic material for modern food crops. Crossbreeding with wild varieties is essential for producing crops that resist diseases and pests. Myers (1983) suggests that such crossbreeding has already saved sugarcane, banana, and cocoa from major damage. Tropical forests are home to many insects that are the natural enemies of plant-damaging pests and to plant chemicals that are used as insecticides. No reliable estimates of willingness to pay for genetic material from tropical forests are available, and the informational needs for securing such estimates may be substantially greater than the information that exists in codified form (Brown 1986). Certainly, a valuation exercise should not be confused with simply looking at the value of the final product.

Placing value on the pharmaceutical use of tropical forest species is another formidable task. One out of four beginning materials for prescribed drugs originates in tropical forests, and the market value of drugs based on plants has been estimated.[12] But calculations of the market value of the prescriptions bought for a particular plant-based drug are not good estimates of the value of the plant used to manufacture the drug. What is required is the price drug manufacturers are willing to pay for the plant material plus a measure of consumers' net gains from using such drugs compared with those from using a substitute. The role of substitutes for plant-based drugs is thus crucial. Many modern drug manufacturers tend to focus more on the production of synthetic drugs using recent advances in molecular biology and biotechnology (Principe 1987). Put another way, their willingness to pay for retaining tropical forests as repositories of potential pharmaceuticals could be very low.

One study (Ruitenbeek 1989) has approached the value of genetic information in the Korup Rain Forest, Cameroon, by assuming that the value of patents can be applied to a guesstimated number of research discoveries in the forest area. Assuming ten such discoveries a year and an average patent value of $8,000, the annual benefits could equal $80,000, of which Cameroon would, of course, capture only a fraction.

Indirect Use Values

Tropical forests have many ecological functions. Valuation procedures tend to focus on either damage done or cost of replacement. Thus removing a tropical forest that protects a watershed can result in soil erosion, downstream sedimentation, and increased floods. This damage would then be a measure of the value of the watershed protection function, since such damage would have been avoided by conserving the forest. Alternatively, if the damage occurs, the amount spent reconstituting the affected area would be a measure of the protection function. If the damage cannot be reconstituted, it may be necessary to replace the protection function.

Although replacement cost approaches are useful because they provide an upper limit to the value of the resource or service to be replaced, they must be used with caution. Implicitly, they assume that making the replacement is worthwhile, which means that the benefits from replacement exceed the costs of replacement. Replacement costs are being used, however, to value the benefits of replacement, and this procedure automatically produces benefit-cost ratios of unity.

WATERSHED EFFECTS. The nature and extent of ecological functions that are lost from deforestation are disputed. Hamilton and King (1983) provide a survey, summarized in table 5-11, of claimed watershed effects and the empirical evidence for their existence; others, such as Myers (1983), dispute their assessment. Ecological impact depends on the use to which deforested land is put—that is, the nature of the agricultural system if deforested land is converted to agriculture, the nature of the logging regime, and so on. The argument is that forests are not unique in their watershed protection functions, and hence deforestation per se does not produce adverse effects. Rather the nature of the succeeding land use is what matters. In theory, forest clearance can have limited or negligible

Table 5-11. Assessment of the Ecological Impact of Tropical Deforestation

Impact	Assessment
Reduced rainfall	No evidence supports this claim, with the possible exception of recycling in the Amazon rain forest if permanent and large-scale deforestation occurs. Fog and cloud forests increase rainfall.
Reduced water supplies and reduced floods	Claim is based on the idea of forests as a sponge absorbing water in the wet season and releasing it slowly in the dry, but forests act more like a pump than a sponge. Cutting tends to increase the supply of water, but conversion to agriculture can lower the water table and reduce the river's flow during the dry season.
Soil erosion and sedimentation	Both effects are the result of conversion to unstable agricultural systems. Traditional shifting agriculture is not implicated in such damage, but modern slash-and-burn techniques (forest farming) are unstable.

Source: Hamilton and King (1983); Myers (1983); Salati and others (1979).

watershed effects if, for example, soils are allowed to secure a cover of grasses and shrubs. In reality, the forest clearer is often the same agent who subsequently uses the forest soils in an environmentally damaging way, such as cattle ranching or agriculture.

Ruitenbeek (1989) estimates the present value of forest protection for inshore fisheries in the Korup region of Cameroon as £3.8 million at an 8 percent discount rate. The benefits of flood control are an estimated £1.6 million.

Figure 5-2. Distribution of Inorganic Nutrients in Tropical Rain Forests above and below the Surface

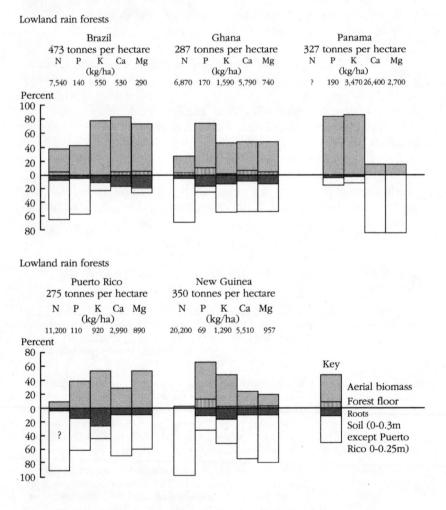

NUTRIENT CYCLING. Figure 5-2 shows a typical nutrient cycling diagram for a tropical forest. The nutrients in question include calcium, magnesium, and potassium, which are bound to soil and water, and elements such as nitrogen, which are interchanged with the atmosphere. Nitrogen, phosphorus, potassium, and, to some extent, calcium are stocked in the biomass. The carbon and sulfur cycles are considered separately below. Contrary to some discussions, we show that nutrients lie both below the surface and in the biomass.

The significance of nutrient cycling for valuation is twofold. First, disturbing the forest system releases nutrients into aquatic systems. In tropical forests, drainage water in the aquatic system is typically low in nutrients. Deforestation and, more generally, opening of the canopy cause a nutrient outflow, which itself can pollute river and coastal ecosystems (Furtado 1978; Furtado and Ruddle 1986). Second, and far more significant, however, the outflow of nutrients from deforestation drastically reduces the productive capacity of the area that had been forest. Forest soils are low in nutrients, and this explains why cleared forest land often sustains only limited livestock and crop production unless substantial amounts of artificial fertilizer are added. In short, nutrient lockup tends to impose irreversibility on the spectrum of land uses possible after deforestation.

CARBON CYCLING AND THE GREENHOUSE EFFECT. In the process of photosynthesis, growing forests fix carbon dioxide and give off oxygen. Once grown, forests no longer accumulate carbon from the atmosphere. Mature forests are said to be in a state of (approximate) carbon equilibrium, which means that they release as much carbon dioxide as they absorb. (The northern hemisphere's temperate and boreal forests may actually exhibit a slight net fixation of carbon, but tropical forests are in carbon equilibrium if they are mature, as is the case for the remaining primary forest.) Although their rate of carbon exchange with the atmosphere is zero, mature tropical forests lock up or sequester carbon as a stock. This distinction is important since it means that deforestation releases carbon dioxide into the atmosphere and thus contributes to the greenhouse effect. Indeed, deforestation releases other greenhouse gases such as methane. Tropical forests are major stores of carbon, and hence the use made of tropical forest land, and of the timber on the land, is an important factor in global warming.

It is important to distinguish what is being valued when talking of the carbon-fixing value of a tropical forest. The context is best viewed as one of the costs and benefits of alternative land use. Consider two basic options: to conserve tropical forest or clear it for agriculture.

- Conserving a mature forest in carbon equilibrium avoids the release of any carbon associated with the alternative land use (agriculture) and hence avoids the damage associated with that carbon release as well. The forest, then, has a carbon credit equal to the avoided damage.

- By clearing the forest for agriculture, deforestation occurs and carbon (and other pollutants) is released. The damage associated with that carbon release is, therefore, a carbon debit to that particular use of forest land.

However, it is not legitimate both to ascribe a credit to the conservation option and a debit to the clearance option. That would be double counting since credit and debit are the obverse of each other. Either conservation is credited with damage avoided or the agriculture option is debited with the damage done by deforestation.

A further complication is that the credit or debit depends on how the timber is removed, how it is subsequently used, and how the deforested land is subsequently managed.[13] Clearance by burning is associated with a total release of carbon dioxide and has no offsetting credits for the use made of the timber. If the land is subsequently managed so that carbon is once again fixed (for example, if it is converted to grassland), then that rate of fixation has to be offset against the loss of carbon from deforestation. Typically, forests contain 20–100 times more carbon per unit of area than agricultural lands. Thus, the offset due to subsequent land use will be much less than the loss from deforestation through clearance. The same goes for any downstream reappearance of carbon: by far the greatest portion of released carbon goes into the atmosphere.

If the forest is clear-felled and all the timber is used to make long-lived wood products (housing timbers and furniture, for example), the act of deforestation may release very little carbon because the carbon remains locked up in the timber products; this is known as product carbon offset. Subsequent land use may then fix some carbon, so that the overall effect of deforestation on the release of carbon could be very small: zero or even negative. This second kind of offset is land use carbon offset.

Most deforestation occurs through direct clearance or incidental damage. The estimates of deforestation in the early 1980s suggested that some 11.1 million hectares of tropical forest were being lost each year. Of this, 7.3 million hectares were being cleared directly for agriculture, usually by burning, and a further 3.8 million hectares were being cleared for a combination of agriculture and fuelwood. Selective logging was taking place on another 4.4 million hectares, and although selective logging is, in principle, consistent with regeneration (and hence with little change in the store of carbon over time), in practice it tends to be associated with extensive damage to the remaining tree stocks and produces carbon release (Repetto 1990). Although the extent of net carbon released by deforestation is specific to the location, little product carbon offset occurs overall. Both the land use offset and the product offset tend to be allowed for in the better studies of carbon release (such as Houghton 1990).

Taking the various offsets into account, carbon emissions due to deforestation in 1980 were estimated to be in the range of $0.4\text{--}2.5 \times 10^{15}$ grams, which equals 0.4–2.5 gigatons a year (10^{15} grams = 1 billion metric tons = 1 gigaton), with a mean figure of 1.8 gigatons a year (Houghton 1990; Houghton and others 1985). This compares with releases of fossil fuel carbon dioxide, which equaled 5.3 gigatons in 1984. Of this total (1.8 + 5.3 = 7.1 gigatons), around half remains in the atmosphere while the rest is absorbed by the oceans and other sinks. The net accretion is approximately 3.6 gigatons in the atmosphere. Tropical deforestation may therefore contribute about 25 percent of carbon dioxide emissions, which, in turn, contribute perhaps half of the total greenhouse gases. Tropical deforestation would therefore contribute 10–13 percent of all emissions of greenhouse gases. More recent estimates suggest that rates of deforestation have increased, and the amount of carbon released could be some 2–3 gigatons each year (Houghton 1990).

Two issues arise. First, what carbon credit should be given to tropical forests for their contribution to avoiding the global warming impact of deforestation (in other words, what is the carbon credit for conservation and hence the carbon debit for clearance)? Second, what contribution could afforestation make to containing the greenhouse effect?

In line with the valuation of damage avoided, a tropical forest should be credited with the value of global warming damage avoided by its conservation. Estimates of global warming suggest that the damage done, mainly the rising level of the sea, could equal $13 per ton of carbon (in 1989 dollars; Nordhaus 1991). Given the uncertainty regarding the speed, extent, and physical impact of global warming, these estimates must be regarded with care.

Table 5-12 shows some recent estimates of rates of deforestation and the resulting carbon releases for a single year, 1989. Most of the carbon is released in the first five years following deforestation. Focusing on a

Table 5-12. Rate of Deforestation and Release of Carbon, 1989

Country	Rate of deforestation (millions of hectares)	Release of carbon (millions of tons)	Carbon release per deforestation (tons of carbon per hectare)
Bolivia	0.15	14	93.3
Brazil	5.00	454	90.8
Guyanas	0.05	4	80.0
Indonesia	1.20	124	103.3
Viet Nam	0.35	36	102.9
Thirty-four countries	13.86	1,398	100.9

Source: Adapted from Houghton (1990).

single year therefore understates the total amount of carbon lost since release occurs beyond that year. The analysis helps illustrate the magnitude of the costs involved.

Table 5-12 indicates that, on average, deforestation of 1 hectare of land contributes some 100 tons of carbon to the atmosphere in a single year. At some $13 per ton, deforestation causes damage at a rate of $1,300 per hectare. Again, given the uncertainty of the estimated damage caused by global warming, this figure should be treated as a rough approximation. In reality, of course, the damage is higher than this because carbon continues to be released after the first year. Such carbon debits greatly outweigh the revenues generated by cattle ranching in Amazonia (table 5-10).

Sedjo (1989) has suggested that 1 hectare of new forest on a good site in the Pacific Northwest or southern United States could sequester 6 x 10 million grams of carbon each year (6 tons). If, hypothetically, afforestation programs were designed to take up, say, 3 of the 3.6 gigatons net accretion of carbon, 470 million hectares of new plantation would be needed, or around 10 percent of the current area of forest in the world. Given the obvious problems of such a massive taking of land for forestry, effort might be better devoted to raising the biomass of standing crops. The figures suggest that crop biomass would have to be raised 50 percent.

Myers (1990) suggests that a working mean sequestration rate of 10 tons of carbon per hectare a year is appropriate for tropical forests, making the required hectarage of afforestation around 300 million hectares. At 10 tons per hectare a year, the annual carbon credit would be $130 per hectare.

SULFUR CYCLING. The nature of sulfur cycling in tropical forests is imperfectly understood. Some authorities suggest that tropical forests contribute to acid rain (Samples, Gowen, and Dixon 1986). Others regard tropical forests as net scrubbers of sulfur.

CONCLUSIONS. The nature of the ecological functions of tropical forests is uncertain. In fact, the physical assessment of the impact of environmental damage or protection is often a greater problem than is economic valuation. Forests clearly generate positive economic value in this respect. Moreover, given the uncertainty, deforestation is inconsistent with risk-averse behavior since deforestation of closed canopy primary forest cannot be reversed. That is, the secondary forest that replaces primary forest, if the land is not converted to alternative uses after deforestation, is not the same as the primary forest. Nonetheless, irreversibility should not be exaggerated. Many of the protective functions of forests may be conserved by the land uses that succeed deforestation. As the secondary forest grows, much of the original biodiversity may be

Table 5-13. Nonuse Values for Unique Natural Assets, Mid-1980s
(U.S. dollars per adult)

Asset	Value
Animal species	
Bald eagle	11
Emerald shiner	4
Grizzly bear	15
Bighorn sheep	7
Whooping crane	1
Blue whale	8
Bottlenose dolphin	6
California sea otter	7
Northern elephant seal	7
Natural amenities	
Water quality (South Platte river basin)	4
Visibility (Grand Canyon)	22

Source: C. W. Clark (1980); Herrera (1985).

reintroduced. Rational behavior under uncertainty would dictate taking a very cautious attitude to deforestation.

Nonuse Values

The final category of value is nonuse value, the inherent value attached to the existence of tropical forests. The motivations for existence value need not concern us unduly.[14] Efforts to estimate existence value are based on contingent valuation studies, which use a questionnaire on willingness to pay. No study has been carried out for tropical forests, but table 5-13 reports estimates of average annual values per person taken from contingent valuation studies for selected animal species and natural amenities. Although limited in number, these studies offer consistent values. The animal values cluster in the $5–$8 range, with American national symbols—the grizzly bear and the bald eagle—in the $10–$15 range. The Grand Canyon similarly has a higher valuation as a major national heritage than, for example, cleaning up a river.

Could such values be borrowed for tropical forests? Tropical forests are unique assets, but they are generally located in developing countries. Allowing for this distance between the valuer and the object of value (which applies to the blue whale as well, for example), and the substantial global interest in tropical deforestation, a figure of $8 per adult a year seems very conservative. Allowing only for the valuations of the richest nations of the world, with some 400 million adults (Australasia, North America, and Western Europe), the valuation would be $3.2 billion a year. Of course, the $8 million may capture some of the indirect benefits of tropical forests, although it mainly captures existence value.

The opportunity costs of forest conservation are the development benefits forgone. As we have seen, these may not, in fact, be greater than the benefits of sustainable use of tropical forests. In order to assess the back-of-the-envelope guesstimate of existence value, however, one might look at the developmental uses of tropical forests to see what benefits accrue. If we take Amazonia as an example, the entire GNP of classical Amazonia is about 6 percent of Brazil's GNP, which was $200 billion in 1986. Thus Amazonia contributed $12 billion to the total. If each adult in wealthy countries would be willing to contribute $8 a year to an Amazon Conservation Fund, the resulting $3.2 billion would enable the people responsible for more than 25 percent of the economic output of Amazonia to be compensated for ceasing their activities.

Conclusions

The concept of total economic value offers a comprehensive framework within which to value tropical forests. Total economic value comprises use values, option values, and existence values. Direct use values include timber and nontimber products and ecotourism. Indirect use values include the ecological functions of tropical forests: their watershed protection and mineral cycling functions. Existence value relates to the intrinsic value of the forest unrelated to its use. Since all these values are given by people, the total economic value approach is totally anthropomorphic. It does not deny other rationales, such as natural rights, for conserving tropical forests. Resorting to such moral arguments may not be necessary. Economic arguments alone could justify a dramatic reduction in deforestation. A major issue, however, is that any mobilization of existence value must result in flows of cash or technology targeted to the people who make the decisions about resource use. If those individuals are small colonist farmers, for example, this fact would have formidable implications for the way in which any transferred funds are used in the receiving country.

Use values alone may favor forest conservation. Clearing forests for livestock agriculture, in particular, appears to have limited rationale. Doing so depends on substantial subsidies, which themselves introduce major economic distortions. Using forests as a source of products other than timber, such as minor forest products, appears to give higher financial rates of return than using them as a source of timber in some areas. Markets fail to allocate forests to their best uses because government intervention is inefficient, notably in the areas of subsidies and land tenure. The recreational use of tropical forests is only now beginning to be realized.

Indirect use values must be estimated. As yet, little effort has been made to value these indirect functions. Some of them are disputed, but there is no question that deforestation followed by unsuitable land use causes significant damage. Additionally, tropical forests should be given carbon credits for their role in containing the greenhouse effect. For existing forests the credit would relate to damage avoided by choosing not to pursue the development option, which is the benefit of conservation. This might total $1,000 per hectare for a single year, with similar benefits for about five years. For new forests, values might be $130 per hectare a year.

Existence values could be substantial and might dominate the use and indirect values. That would be consistent with other findings in the literature on total economic valuation. Assuming that the Amazon forest is valued at an average of $8 per adult in the advanced economies of the world, existence value could readily amount to $3 billion, or one-quarter of the entire contribution of classic Amazonia to Brazil's gross domestic product—including mineral extraction, timber, and agriculture.

Environment and Health

Environmental quality produces direct and indirect benefits. As a source of amenity, environmental quality is an important provider of direct benefits. It is tempting to think that this is only so in the industrial world, where amenity plays a large role in meeting the rapidly growing demand for recreation and wilderness. It is important in many developing countries, too, and as real income per capita increases, so does the incipient demand for recreation. The popular image that recreation does not matter in the developing world has to be resisted.

Arguably the most important and immediate consequences of environmental degradation in the developing world take the form of damage to human health. Not only is health an end in itself, but a healthy work force is essential to the development process as a whole. The economic effects of impaired health can be formidable. Diarrhea is a common occurrence in many developing countries, where 3 billion–5 billion cases are recorded every year. Each case is estimated to involve 3–5 days lost, so that 9 billion–25 billion working days could be lost in a single year. At a nominal $0.50 a day, the output lost could be $4.5 billion–$12.5 billion a year from this one disease (these are clearly guesstimates; see Meybeck, Chapman, and Helmer 1990). Table 5-14 provides data on the incidence of waterborne diseases. In Sri Lanka, 5.7 times as many males die from infectious and parasitic diseases, and 7.2 times as many females, as die in the United States. Similar ratios for other countries are 2.5 and 2.8 for Chile and 2.1 and 2.1 for Mauritius (data from the World Health Organization, which were reported in World Resources Institute 1990).

Costing Health Damage

An extensive literature exists on the economic cost of health damage from environmental degradation, most of it relating to the industrial world. The procedures used for valuation are often sophisticated. Those

Table 5-14. Morbidity and Mortality from Waterborne Diseases in Africa, Latin America, and Asia, 1977–78

Type of disease and infection	Number of infections (thousands per year)	Number of deaths (thousands per year)	Average number of days lost per illness	Relative disability
Waterborne				
Amebiasis	400	30	7–10	Able to work
Diarrhea	3,000–5,000	5,000–20,000	3–5	Able to function some
Polio	80	10–20	3,000+	Able to function some
Typhoid	1	25	14–28	Able to function some
Water hygiene				
Ascariasis (roundworm)	800–1,000	20	7–10	Able to work
Leprosy	12	Very low	500–3,000	Able to function some or able to work
Trichuriasis (whipworm)	500	Low	7–10	Able to work
Hookworm	7,000–9,000	50–60	100	Suffers minor effects
Water habitat with water-related vectors				
Schistosomiasis (bilharziasis)	200	500–1,000	600–1,000	Able to work or suffers minor effects
African trypanosomiasis (sleeping sickness)	1	5	150	Bedridden
Malaria	800	1,200	3–5	Able to function some
Onchocerciasis (river blindness)	30	20–50	3,000	Bedridden or able to function some

Note: The number of infections and deaths = $(10^3 \cdot a^{-1})$.
Source: Walsh and Warren (1979).

relating to morbidity tend to be different from those relating to mortality, but both tend to be part of a more general model known as a dose-response model or, sometimes, the damage function approach. This model traces a pollutant from its emission to its ambient concentration, which is called the dose. The response consists of a health impact, such as respiratory illness, that shows up as days lost from work, restricted activity days, and death. The valuation exercise only takes place when the epidemiological response is estimated. Statistics on diseases related to the environment offer a first-stage measure of the potential importance of the link between environment and health. It is not always easy, however, to distinguish the causes of disease. Lung cancers might, for example, be induced by airborne toxic substances, cigarette smoking, or a host of other factors. If the link can be established, the value of the health damage done—its monetary cost—becomes a second-stage environmental indicator. Rising monetary costs (in real prices) might indicate a path of unsustainable development.

As yet, monetary estimates of national health damage are few and far between. Freeman (1982) suggests that in 1978 the United States received a health benefit of $3 billion–$41 billion, with a best estimate of $17 billion, from policies on clean air and perhaps another $1 billion from improvements in the quality of water. Since the estimates relate to one year only, little can be said about trends.

Morbidity might be valued as a measure of the economic cost of a working day lost using the ruling wage rate. Mortality requires the use of what is misleadingly known as a value of human life. These values are, in fact, measures of willingness to pay for reducing risk or willingness to accept payment for increased risk. For example, such values might be taken from analyses of the extent to which wage rates in risky jobs compensate for the risks involved. Box 5-3 illustrates the dose-response approach for the United States. The example chosen uses what is known as macroepidemiology; that is, it relates large data sets on mortality and morbidity to factors thought to influence those rates.

Pollution and Health in the Developing World

Can the economic approaches to assessing health damage from environmental degradation be applied to developing countries? In principle they can, with two qualifications. First, data are usually not available to the extent required to model damage functions in the manner suggested. Second, valuation is more complex, particularly for mortality, because wages and health risks may not be linked in the labor markets of developing countries in the same way they appear to be in the richer world. Thus many studies of industrial countries value health damage by looking at the implicit valuation of risks in the labor market: the higher the risk of occupational accident or disease, the higher is the risk premium in wage rates expected to be. Labor markets in many developing countries will not adjust this way, and second-best valuation techniques, such as wages per day lost, may have to be used to value morbidity and perhaps lifetime income forgone for mortality.[15]

A further issue applies equally to the literature for industrial countries. The multiple regression approach relates a given measure of health damage to various indicators of factors that might be associated with that damage. That is, an equation is estimated of the general form: health damage = $f(V1, V2, V3 \ldots Vn)$. $V1 \ldots Vn$ are the variables thought

Box 5-3. Air Pollution and Health Damage in the United States

A 1976 data base covering 50,000 households was matched to pollution data and other information (Ostro 1983). Morbidity was measured by days off work—work lost days (WLD)—and restricted activity days—RAD, days in which activity was restricted because of ill health. Then WLD and RAD were regressed on various variables: indicators of chronic disease, race, marriage, temperature, population density, rainfall, cigarette consumption, and work status. There were no variables for air pollution other than sulfur oxides and suspended particulates nor any for water quality or diet. The results, showing just the estimates for the two air pollution variables, were as follows:

$$\text{RAD} = -0.83 + 0.00282 \text{ TSP} - 0.00008 \text{ SULF} + \ldots \text{ and}$$
$$\text{WLD} = -0.47 + 0.00145 \text{ TSP} - 0.001 \text{ SULF} + \ldots .$$

In these equations, the sulfur coefficients were not significant, which means that sulfur concentrations were not implicated in morbidity. This bears out earlier studies. The coefficients for TSP were significant and can be translated into elasticities, showing the percentage increase in morbidity for each percentage point increase in air pollution. The coefficients were 0.45 for WLD and 0.39 for RAD when expressed as elasticities. Thus a 1 percent improvement in air quality would reduce the number of working days lost 0.45 percent. Ostro did not estimate the monetary value of days lost or days of restricted activity.

A similar regression study (Kneese 1984) looked at mortality benefits. The regressions found that TSP was linked to deaths from pneumonia and influenza and that sulfur oxides were linked to early infant disease. Extrapolating these relationships to all 150 million urban dwellers at risk in the United States (experiencing similar exposure levels) and using a value of life of $0.34 million–$1.0 million based on wage-risk studies, the following results were obtained.

Table B5-3. Link between Air Pollution and Select Diseases, United States
(billions of 1978 U.S. dollars a year)

Disease	Pollutant	Value of a 60 percent reduction in air pollution
Pneumonia	Particulates	4.4–13.7
Early infant disease	Sulfur dioxide	0.7–2.2
Total	All	5.1–15.9

Source: For morbidity, see Ostro (1983), pp. 371–82. For mortality, see Kneese (1984). For a general discussion, see Pearce and Markandya (1989).

to influence health damage, and they include pollution indexes. The pollution measures usually refer to concentrations, for example, X parts per million of sulfur dioxide. A further stage—exposure—exists between ambient concentrations and dose that is determined by the period of time an individual spends in the polluted area. People actually spend a great

Table 5-15. *Air Pollution Emissions Produced by Different Fuels*
(kilograms of pollutants per 1 trillion joules delivered, unless otherwise indicated)

Type of fuel	Percentage efficiency	Fuel equivalent to 1 trillion joules	Total particulates	Sulfur oxides	Nitrogen oxides	Hydro-carbons	Carbon monoxide
Industrial boilers							
Wood	70	89[a]	500	53	400	400	450
Bituminous coal	80	43[a]	2,800	820	320	22	45
Residual oil	80	33,000[b]	94	1,310	240	..	20
Distillate oil	90	31,400[b]	8	1,120	83	..	19
Natural gas	90	28,200[c]	7	..	99	2	8
Residential heating stoves							
Wood	50	130[a]	2,700	30	100	6,800	17,000
Anthracite	65	49[a]	46	200	250	100	1,000
Bituminous coal	65	53[a]	550	1,100	270	530	5,300
Distillate oil	85	32,900[b]	11	1,170	71	4	20
Natural gas	85	30,000[c]	7	..	38	4	10
Residential cooking stoves							
Tropical wood	15	420[a]	3,800	250	300	3,200	34,000
Hawaiian cow dung	15	530[a]	10,000	3,200	—	—	44,000
Indian coal	20	220[a]	280	2,200	460	2,200	27,000
Coconut husks	15	480[a]	17,000	—	—	—	54,000
Natural gas	80	32,000[c]	0.5	—	10	5	250

— Not available.
.. Negligible.
Note: Actual efficiencies and emissions vary greatly according to the quality of the fuel and the combustion conditions. Combustion-derived particulates and hydrocarbons contain complex mixtures of hundreds or thousands of organic chemicals, many of which are mutagenic or toxic. Residential heating stoves were measured under conditions in the United States. Biomass and coal cooking stoves were measured under rural conditions in India.

a. Metric tons.
b. Liters.
c. Cubic meters.
Source: V. K. Smith (1987).

deal of their time indoors rather than outdoors, yet the pollution measures tend to be outdoor concentrations. For example, the major sources of exposure to air toxins such as benzene and chloroform are found inside, not outside. Even for traditional pollutants, the main source of exposure is often at home: for particulates, it is cigarette smoke; for nitrogen dioxide, it is gas stoves (these important findings are summarized in Smith 1988b).

This focus on exposure rather than ambient concentration is just as important in the developing world. Three-quarters of the world's population lives in the developing countries, and two-thirds of those persons live in rural areas. Yet rural dwellers in developing countries spend 60 percent of their time indoors, not outdoors. Assuming that rural dwellers are not exposed to air pollution is therefore wrong, since indoor pollution from open-hearth fires or stoves, for example, can be significant (table 5-15). The influence of cooking stoves using wood, dung, and crop residues is enormous. Formidable policy implications arise from this finding. Suppose the issue is whether or not to install particulate control technology in a coal-fired power station or how much of this technology to introduce (how much particulate matter is to be removed). It may be far cheaper to launch a program for cleaning up household stoves than to introduce controls at the power station. Smith (1988a) suggests that the same reductions in total exposure (individual exposure multiplied by the number of people at risk) could be achieved at only one-ninth the cost.

What are the risks from exposure to pollution in the developing world? In Mexico City deaths attributed to cancer, influenza, and pneumonia have increased sixfold since 1956, and deaths due to cardiovascular disease have quadrupled. Deaths to people over sixty-five years of age due to bronchitis, emphysema, and asthma increased 12 percent between 1978 and 1984. People suffering long-term mental impairment could double over the next few decades due to high concentrations of lead in newborns. Nor are the risks just from air pollution alone. Mexico City and the surrounding areas have 2,100 chemical plants. In November 1984 a gas storage plant exploded, killing some 650 people. Although disasters of this kind are perhaps extreme examples of pollution, chemical leaks in cities such as Mexico City are not unusual. Perhaps more than 70 percent of populations in urban areas live with unacceptable levels of air pollution (unpublished estimate of the World Health Organization and the United Nations Environment Programme, quoted in Weil and others 1990, chap. 4).

Appendix: Methodologies for Eliciting Economic Values

Numerous surveys now exist on the kinds of methodologies that may be used to elicit economic values (Bentkover and others 1986; Cummings, Brookshire, and Schulze 1986; Feenberg and Mills 1980; Freeman 1979, 1982; Johansson 1987; Kneese 1984; Mitchell and Carson

1989; Pearce and Markandya 1989; Smith and Desvousges 1986). Three broad categories of valuation techniques may be distinguished.[16] This appendix briefly reviews the main techniques and assesses their usefulness for the valuation of materials damage.[17]

Surrogate Markets Techniques

The surrogate markets technique involves finding a market in a good or service that is influenced by the nonmarketed good. The hedonic property price approach is based on this idea. Environmental quality affects the decision to purchase a particular house, and the price of the house should be influenced by the environmental attributes of the property. The price of the property, Hp, is dependent on site variables, S, accessibility, A, neighborhood characteristics, N, and environmental lack of quality, Q. Then,

$$(5A\text{-}1) \qquad Hp = f(S, A, N, Q).$$

The specific form of this equation is important, but if it is specified in log linear terms, a regression equation of the form

$$(5A\text{-}2) \qquad \ln \cdot Hp = a(\ln \cdot S) + b(\ln \cdot A) + c(\ln \cdot N) + d(\ln \cdot Q)$$

enables a direct estimate of the effect of Q on Hp to be determined independent of the absolute levels of Q and HP. The marginal willingness to pay to reduce Q is then

$$(5A\text{-}3) \qquad dHp \,/\, dQ = w.$$

Many hedonic price studies stop at estimating w, but theory technically requires that w should then be regressed on a set of household characteristics, such as income and family size, and environmental quality:

$$(5A\text{-}4) \qquad w = g(H, Q).$$

The area under this inverse demand function, between the relevant environmental quality levels, is an estimate of the benefit of improved environmental quality.

The travel cost method identifies the expenditures made by travelers as the surrogate market. A household's utility, U, depends on recreation, R, and other goods, E:

$$(5A\text{-}5) \qquad U = U(R, E).$$

The recreational services of site i are dependent on the number of visits to the site, Vi, the time taken to get there, Ti, and the attributes of the site, Ai:

$$(5A\text{-}6) \qquad Ri = R(Vi, Ti, Ai).$$

The household's budget constraint is

$$(5A\text{-}7) \qquad Y = wH + N + L = E + \{[Di + (Q \cdot Ti)] \cdot Vi\}.$$

Its time constraint is

(5A-8)
$$T = H + (Ti \cdot Vi)$$

where Y = potential income, N = nonwage income, L = income forgone due to recreation, Di = monetary cost of traveling to site i, Q = opportunity cost of recreational travel time, w = hourly wage, and H = hours worked. If

(5A-9)
$$Pi = Di + (Q \cdot Ti)$$

the demand function for R becomes

(5A-10)
$$R = R(P1, P2 \ldots Pi; Y).$$

From equation 5A-6, and assuming that the relationship between Vi and Ri is strictly increasing, we have

(5A-11)
$$Vi = Vi(Ti, Ai, Ri).$$

Next, assume Vi consists of two parts, one depending on Ti and Ri only, the other depending on Ai only. Then,

(5A-12)
$$Vi = G(Ti, Ri) \cdot H(Ai).$$

Equation 5A-12 says that the services of each site can be transferred into units $H(Ai)$ that are comparable across sites. An equal expenditure on two sites i and j will lead to visit rates Vi and Vj such that

(5A-13)
$$Vi / Vj = H(Ai) / H(Aj)$$

where $Vi / H(Ai)$ is now the attribute-adjusted number of visits.

Households are assumed to minimize the cost of securing a given level of recreational services, R. This means that the approach will equalize the unit costs per visit to each site:

(5A-14)
$$Pi / H(Ai) = Pj / H(Aj).$$

We can now write the minimum cost of securing R as C, where

(5A-15)
$$C = C[Pi / H(Ai), R].$$

The demand function for Vi given R is now dC / dPi. R, in turn, can be written as a function of attribute-adjusted prices and income (see equation 5A-10). Substituting this for R in equation 5A-15 gives

(5A-16)
$$Vi = V [Pi, H(Ai), Y].$$

This equation needs to be estimated:

(5A-17)
$$\ln \cdot Vi = a(Ai) + b(Ai)Pi + c(Ai)Y$$

where the coefficients a, b, and c are functions of the site attributes. Estimation tends to take place in two stages.

The hedonic wage approach also uses a surrogate market, the labor market, to value risks to life and limb. The assumption is that such risks will attract wage premia. A regression of the form

$$(5A-18) \qquad W = W(S, I, J)$$

can be established, where S refers to site-specific variables such as air pollution and crime; I refers to individual-specific variables such as race, sex, education, and job experience; and J refers to job-specific variables such as injury rates. Hedonic wage approaches have been widely used to value occupational risks of injury and death (for a survey of the findings of hedonic wage models, see Viscusi 1986).

Discrete choice techniques look at situations in which an implicit price is expressed for a nonmarketed good through the choice of a marketed good. The most notable example of valuation through discrete choice is the valuation of time. Someone using a travel mode A, say, and paying Pa for a journey time of Ta, may have chosen this mode over an alternative mode B with price Pb and journey time Tb. If $Pa > Pb$ and $Ta < Tb$, the implied value of time saved $Tb - Ta$ is $Pa - Pb$, and the value of a unit of time is

$$(5A-19) \qquad Vt = (Pa - Pb) / (Tb - Ta).$$

Market Creation Techniques

With market creation techniques individuals are asked directly about their willingness to pay (or be compensated) for a change in environmental quality. Such techniques are known as contingent valuation methods, although variations, including contingent ranking, exist.

Contingent valuation is founded directly on the theory of consumer behavior. Thus an individual is assumed to have a utility function:

$$(5A-20) \qquad U = U(a1, a2 \ldots an; Q1, Q2 \ldots Qn; X)$$

where $a1$ and so forth are activity levels, $Q1$ and so forth are environmental quality levels, and X is a composite commodity. The individual's expenditure is given by

$$(5A-21) \qquad E = (Pi \cdot ai) + X$$

where Pi is the price of a unit of activity ai. The minimum level of expenditure needed to achieve a utility level Uo is Mo, and this equals Y for the consumer's initial equilibrium. Thus,

$$(5A-22) \qquad Y = Mo = g(P1o \ldots Pno; Q1o \ldots Qno; Uo).$$

The valuation of an improvement in environmental quality Q that takes the consumer from Uo to $U1$, a higher level of utility, is then one of two measures: willingness to pay (WTP) to go from a lower level of utility to a higher level or willingness to accept (WTA) compensation for the improvement not to take place.

Contingent valuation techniques have been widely used to obtain measures of both WTA and WTP. Typically, they should diverge only slightly as long as the ratio of WTP or WTA to income is small. In practice, WTA estimates have often been much higher than WTP estimates. Ratios of 2–5 are not uncommon (see the discussion in Pearce and Markandya 1989, p. 26). Explanations for the differences range from statistical artefact (because contingent valuation experiments do not repeat valuations in the same way that consumers do when purchasing goods in a real marketplace) to prospect theory (in which consumers are regarded as having kinked valuation functions at a given endowment of environmental quality). Under prospect theory, increments in quality are valued lower than decrements since a decrement removes an entitlement to the initial endowment.

Much of the literature on contingent valuation methods is devoted to determining biases, which may be summarized as follows.

Strategic bias relates to the incentive to undervalue a public good that, if provided to one person, is provided to all. Individuals, it is assumed, understate their preference in the hope that the price charged for the good will be related to their stated maximum willingness to pay. The provision of the good depends on the aggregate willingness to pay that exceeds the cost of provision. This is the classic free rider problem.

Design bias relates to issues in the design of the willingness-to-pay questionnaire. Starting point bias arises when the initial bid is suggested by the interviewer, which biases the respondent's answers. Clearly, if the mean maximum willingness to pay is close to the questioner's starting point, this is a sign of potential starting point bias. Vehicle (or instrument) bias relates to the hypothetical means of payment: answers should not vary significantly according to the means of payment. In the same way, the degree of information given to the respondent affects the valuation. This is not clearly a bias, however, since valuations are influenced by the provision of information in real marketplaces.

Hypothetical bias is clearly a risk when a questionnaire poses hypothetical questions; in this case, the answers may not correspond to the amount that individuals are willing to pay when the time comes to express real values by paying up. Modern analysts discuss hypothetical bias in content, criterion, and construct validity (the definitive volume on contingent valuation is Mitchell and Carson 1989). Content validity relates to asking the right questions in an appropriate manner and can be assessed only as a matter of expert judgment. Criterion validity relates the hypothetical value to some real value, or market price. Some studies have sought to measure criterion validity by relating expressed WTP to WTP when actual money changes hands. Construct validity is the extent to which different measures of WTP agree with one another, none of which, however, is close to the criterion validity measure (convergent validity) or to theoretical expectations (theoretical validity).

Contingent ranking requires respondents to order outcomes for combinations of goods and payment requirements. Rather than directly asking for WTP, it infers WTP from the rankings. Thus a combination of environmental quality level $Q1$ and a price tag of $P1$ is compared to a combination of $Q2$ and $P2$, and so on. Respondents are then asked to rank the combinations (for a detailed discussion of contingent ranking, see Smith and Desvousges 1986; unfortunately, few studies of comparative ranking exist on which to base an empirical assessment). The rankings are then used to determine a valuation. It is not clear, however, whether attitude or behavioral intent is being measured.

Dose-response Relationships

Dose-response relationships, or production function approaches, are perhaps the most familiar valuation technique. Essentially, a link is established between, say, a pollution level and a physical response, for example, the rate at which the surface of a material decays. The decay is then valued by applying the market price (costs of repair) or by borrowing a unit valuation from nonmarket studies. Notable examples include the valuation of health damage. Once air pollution is linked to morbidity and morbidity is linked to days lost from work, the days lost can be valued, perhaps using a market wage rate. The main effort of the analysis is devoted to identifying the link between the dose and the response. Valuation itself tends to be fairly secondary to the research effort.

Notes

1. The literature on option value is extensive (see Bishop 1982, 1988; Freeman 1985; Johansson 1988; Plummer 1986). The sign of option value is indeterminate but may be expected to be positive if the future demand for the asset in question (the tropical forest, in this case) is certain and the supply is uncertain.

2. We do not dwell on the way in which TEV is derived here, but Hoehn and Randall (1989) have shown that estimating the component parts separately, and then summing them, is not formally identical to TEV estimated by a sequential procedure in which, say, existence value is estimated first, followed by site experience value, and then by activity-related values at the site. This is because the consumer surplus for a bundle of goods is not the same as the sum of consumer surpluses on individual goods.

3. Option value must be distinguished from quasi-option value (QOV). Arrow and Fisher (1974) introduced QOV to deal with the issue of project choice under conditions of uncertainty and irreversibility, where efficiency in decisionmaking may be influenced by the acquisition of additional information. Supply uncertainty, on the one hand, assumes that the valuer can control probabilities of the state of the environment in the future. QOV, on the other hand, relates to situations in which new information can be generated that will affect the assessment of costs and benefits. QOV would be relevant, for example, for assessing deforestation when genetic assets have unknown, or imperfectly known, economic value due to lack of research.

4. Dixon and others (1988) use land values for these outputs. This is misleading, however; whereas land values refer to the market price of the land, these outputs refer to the

value of output from the land. They are linked, of course, in that, under competitive conditions, the land value should equal the discounted value of the net profits from the land.

5. The scale of water vending in the developing world is substantial and perhaps unappreciated. In a study of Onitsha, Nigeria, Whittington, Lauria, and Mu (1989) found that households were paying $28,000 per day for 3 million gallons of water in the dry season to vendors who collected water from wells and resold it to other vendors, businesses, and households. In comparison, the public utility sold 1.5 million gallons per day for just $1,100.

6. Economic value should not be confused with financial or commercial value. Anything contributing to human welfare is deemed to be an economic function, and the flow of services may or may not be associated with a cash flow. Most of the functions of tropical forests do not have evident cash flows.

7. A detailed survey of systems for managing tropical moist forests concluded that only 1 percent of the 828 million hectares of productive forest is under sustained-yield management (Poore 1989, chap. 7). Sustained-yield management is consistent with two regimes that follow the completion of logging. One involves intensive silvicultural treatment. The other involves leaving the forest to regenerate on its own because the returns to silvicultural treatment are uncertain. Large areas of Malaysian forests are subject to this nonintervention approach, as are those of the forests of Cameroon, the Central African Republic, Congo, and Gabon. On this second basis, then, sustained-yield management is far more widespread. We are indebted to Jeff Sayer for this point.

8. For the view that sustained forest management should be based on clear-cutting and the maximum use of biomass, see Hartshorn, Simeone, and Tosi (1987). The analysis tends to assume that market conditions are right, which means that timber production takes place near to markets.

9. Leslie (1988) suggests that shadow pricing favors the more natural management systems.

10. We are indebted to Simon Reitbergen for this point.

11. One company advertises a tour with a two-day excursion into Amazonia. The excursion costs an additional $250 to the basic charge of $2,300. As a very rough guide, therefore, each visitor day could be worth $125.

12. Farnsworth and Morris (1976); Farnsworth and Soejarto (1985). A figure of $8 billion is quoted as the value of prescribed plant-based drugs for the United States. Principe (1987) calculates a figure for all countries in the Organisation for Economic Co-operation and Development of $43 billion in 1985, including over-the-counter drugs.

13. We are indebted to Jack Ruitenbeek for his assistance in clarifying the argument in this section. Much of the literature on the carbon value of tropical forests is misleading because it fails to take into account uses of the timber culled from deforestation and the subsequent use of the land. For an exercise in calculating carbon credits for temperate forests, see Pearce (1990a).

14. Some economists are concerned, however, that such valuations may be counterpreferential (inconsistent with the preference of individuals) in the same way that acts of duty or obligation are counterpreferential. If true, this may have implications for the underlying structure of the welfare economics used to evaluate resource worth. See Brookshire, Eubanks, and Sorg (1986).

15. These are second-best procedures because the measure required is the willingness to pay for a reduced risk. In fact, the link between the wages received for a day's work and willingness to pay to avoid losing that day is ambiguous. For further discussion, see chapter 6.

16. Some writers add other techniques, such as the use of expert assessments or values implied by past government decisions. These are not strictly valuation techniques, however, since they are rooted in the need to determine the valuations of individuals rather than those of representatives or experts. In the same vein, several authors regard opportunity cost as a valuation technique. This involves looking at, say, a development and valuing its benefits. The conservation sacrificed by the development is then valued as the benefits of the development. This is obviously circular reasoning.

17. This section is presented in formal terms. Readers wishing for more intuitive explanations of the various procedures should see an explanatory text on valuation, such as Pearce and Markandya (1989).

PART TWO

Resource Degradation:
Causes and Policy Response

6

Population, Resources, and Environment

Population growth is widely regarded as the dominant cause of environmental deterioration and overly rapid use of resources. Since deteriorating environments induce poverty, population change is linked to poverty through the environment. The links between population growth and the environment are more complex. Many factors give rise to environmental change, and many factors cause poverty. Citing population growth alone as the main cause of either poverty or environmental deterioration is therefore likely to misstate the problem. Environmental assets are also lost because of misguided government policies and the failure of market systems to account for external effects and the interests of future generations. Poverty may similarly manifest differences of political power within an economic system, and those differences can become self-perpetuating unless the power base is changed.

The generalized picture is depicted in figure 6-1, which illustrates some of the intermediary effects that population change may have on a specific sector, agriculture. Resources currently in use, such as existing cropland, urban land, forest resources, and rangeland, are distinguished from frontier resources, such as virgin forest or unused rangeland. Population growth tends to affect both types of resources. Existing resources might be used more intensively, resulting in shorter fallow periods and lower soil productivity. Population pressure might also force colonization of previously unused resources as forests are cleared, cattle are put on land

Figure 6-1. Links among Population, Environment, and Poverty

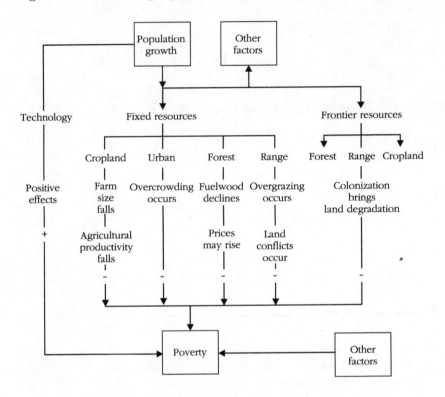

previously used by wildlife, and hillsides are cultivated. Erosion and overuse tend to follow because the land is intrinsically unsuitable for cultivation or because agricultural practices suited to inframarginal land are not suited to sloped land. All these effects contribute to soil erosion and lower soil productivity and, hence, to lower average yields. Incomes fall and poverty ensues. The induced poverty may itself lead to further land degradation as the poor seek to cope by extending farming margins, overgrazing livestock, and so on.

The feedback could also be positive. Population growth may encourage farmers to intensify agriculture by adopting technological change. Population has been the main stimulus to technological change in agriculture, but research and development, investment, prices, and management are the most important factors in modern agricultural growth.

World Population Growth

World population currently stands at some 5 billion people. By 2000 the earth will hold 6 billion people and by 2025 over 8 billion. The absolute increases will peak in the early 1990s at about 88 million a year. Total population growth and its regional distribution are shown in table 6-1. Asia (excluding Japan) has the largest share of the world's population (56 percent of the total), most of whom are in China (1,040 million people) and India (765 million). The fastest rate of increase is in Africa.

A long-run historical perspective reveals that population growth rates changed dramatically in the industrial world around the time of the industrial revolution. In Europe, the annual rate of change increased from 0.5 to 1.5 percent. In North America, the rate rose to 2 percent a year in the early nineteenth century due to high fertility, low mortality, and substantial immigration. Yet these rates of increase are low compared with the experience of developing countries in the twentieth century. Annual rates of growth below 2 percent are the exception, with average rates being closer to 3 percent, twice that of the industrial countries at a comparable stage of development. The contrast in historical experience is marked: population growth was correlated with increased material prosperity in the industrial countries as they developed, but population growth tends to be fastest in the poorest countries in the current developing world. In short, the historical experience of the industrial countries cannot truly be compared with the recent experience of the developing world.

World population growth is the result of marked and rapid reductions in mortality rates due to improved health care, education, and sanitation, especially in the developing world. For example, one-quarter of Sri Lanka's decline in mortality since 1945 has been attributed to malaria control (World Bank 1984, p. 69). Although birth rates have also fallen, they remain significantly higher than death rates in the developing world; in the industrial world, they are only slightly higher than death rates.

Table 6-1. World Population Trends, 1900–2100
(millions of persons)

Region	1900	1950	1985	2000	2025	2100
Developing world						
Africa	133	224	555	872	1,617	2,591
Asia[a]	867	1,292	2,697	3,419	4,403	4,919
Latin America	70	165	405	546	779	1,238
Subtotal	1,070	1,681	3,657	4,837	6,799	8,748
Industrial world						
Europe, Japan, Oceania,						
Soviet Union	478	669	917	987	1,062	1,055
North America	82	166	264	297	345	382
Subtotal	560	835	1,181	1,284	1,407	1,437
Total	1,630	2,516	4,838	6,121	8,206	10,185

a. Excluding Japan.
Source: Merrick (1986).

This factor provides the proximate explanation for the difference between the experience of the industrial and developing worlds. In the industrial world, reductions in mortality rates were generally accompanied by reductions in birth rates. Birth rates in the developing world have been reduced less than mortality rates and, in a number of cases, have hardly fallen at all. Nevertheless, in many developing countries an impressive decline in birth rates has occurred over the past twenty-five years.

What accounts for the historical difference that exists between the industrial and developing worlds in the profile of birth rates over time? The reasons are complex, and no explanation is universally valid for all countries. In Korea, fertility rates fell 44 percent between 1965 and 1982 as women increasingly delayed their age at marriage.[1] The 1982 level has continued to fall, but at a much slower rate because the average age of women at marriage is tending to peak. The potential for a further decline in fertility is thus constrained. In Costa Rica, fertility rates fell 48 percent between 1965 and 1987, and they are expected to fall another 25 percent by 2000. The signs point, however, to the existence of a lower limit to the desired family size. This suggests that fertility rates will not decline continuously as they did in the industrial world. The experience with family planning varies markedly. In India, the total fertility rate has fallen continuously, but contraceptive practice varies according to female literacy and the vigor with which contraceptive policy is pursued.

Population Growth in Africa

Some insight into the reasons that the decline in fertility is slower than expected in the developing world can be obtained by looking at the African experience.

The special problem of population growth in Sub-Saharan Africa is revealed in figure 6-2.[2] Whereas population growth rates are broadly constant or declining in all other regions of the world, annual growth rates in Sub-Saharan Africa are increasing steadily, from 2.5 percent in 1960 to 3.0 percent in 1983. This is the outcome of significant reductions in death rates and very little change in birth rates (indeed, some countries have experienced increased birth rates). Côte d'Ivoire, Kenya, and Zimbabwe have growth rates in excess of 4 percent a year, which, if sustained, would double their populations in less than eighteen years.[3] For Sub-Saharan Africa as a whole, the 1985 population of 485 million will double in just twenty-two years if current rates of growth are sustained.

Mortality rates have fallen dramatically in Sub-Saharan Africa, from just under 30 per 1,000 in 1950 to 16 per 1,000 in the early 1980s. This decline reflects the general increase in living standards, education, and

Figure 6-2. Population Growth Rates, by Region, 1850-2025

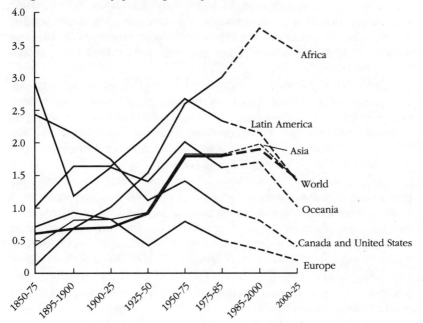

Average annual rate of population growth (percent)

Source: World Bank (1991b), p. 60.

public health programs. The birth rate has remained constant because of underlying cultural attitudes to the bearing of children and economic factors. As health improves, so does natural fecundity (the physiological ability to bear children). Age at marriage for girls in Africa has not declined significantly, breast-feeding and postnatal sexual abstinence seem to have declined, and the rate of using contraceptives remains extremely low. The birth rate continues to be high because of the following influences, which underlie the reasons already given (World Bank 1986b). First, the continuing agricultural bias in African economies provides incentives to invest in children, who serve as labor on the farm, assist with collecting fuelwood and water, care for other children, tend livestock, and perform other chores. Moreover, the amount of land that can be cultivated often depends on family size, creating further incentives for large families. The private benefits of increasing family size thus tend to outweigh the private costs, and this determines the size of the family.

The net private benefits tend to diminish, and eventually become negative above a limited family size, as educational opportunities expand, opportunities for off-farm employment increase, and patterns of land tenure and ownership change. State-provided education incurs private costs in the form of uniforms, books, and travel, making larger families more costly. Opportunities for urban work reduce the need for on-farm labor, and changes in tenure reduce the incentive to claim resource and land rights on the basis of family size.

Second, larger families provide social security through the extended family. Being a child frequently involves many obligations to other members of the family. Once again, investing in children becomes a way of ensuring care in old age. More generally, larger families mean wealth and influence. As state-provided social security systems are introduced, this motivation to have larger families will weaken.

Third, as long as women have an inferior social role to men any preferences they might have for smaller families will be underrepresented in the private cost-benefit decisions made about family size. Often, however, a woman's own status depends on childbearing so that many women appear to share the preference for large families. As education expands and other forms of emancipation increase, some women can be expected to change their preferences for large families, while others, with a prevailing but overruled preference for smaller families, can be expected to exert more influence.

Fourth, having few children and investing in their education is a high-risk strategy when infant mortality is high and the prospects for employment are poor. Once again, this risk aversion influences the private cost-benefit decision to favor large families. As employment prospects improve and infant mortality declines, the benefit-cost ratio can be expected to begin favoring smaller families.

Clearly, the social, economic, and cultural factors underlying decisions about family size are complex. They are also likely to vary from society to society. In general, however, the picture resembles that shown in figure 6-3. The private benefit-cost ratio favors large families at low levels of education, high levels of rural dependence, and low levels of state-provided social security. As these factors change, the ratio falls and begins to favor smaller families. The obvious problem in Sub-Saharan Africa is that these factors are changing much slower than the factors reducing the death rate.

It is also worth remembering that governments may not pursue policies to control population with great vigor. Some African leaders, for example, support population growth as a means of securing economies of scale. They may perceive that output per hectare does not diminish as new land is brought under cultivation; according to this view, more people mean bigger markets and hence a greater division of labor and a larger base for financing overhead costs (Cochrane 1985).

Figure 6-3. Private Costs and Benefits of Family Size

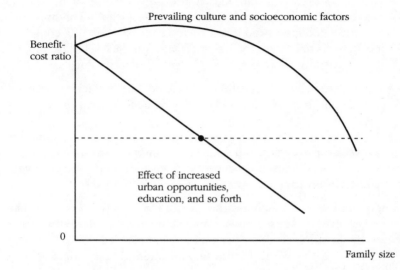

Note: As education increases, infant mortality declines, and rural dependence decreases. The social security provided by the state improves, and therefore the net private benefits of increased family size decline.

The Carrying Capacity and the Links between Population and Environment

Continued world population growth is inevitable. Controlling it requires extensive efforts to influence birth rates and to address the underlying reasons that families are large. One reason for increasing those efforts is to break the vicious circle of population growth, poverty, and environmental degradation. The influence that population growth exerts on resource availability and environmental quality contributes to poverty. At the global level also, more people mean more energy is consumed and more atmospheric pollution is produced. More people also mean a greater demand for cultivable and residential land and less forest and wetlands, contributing to further pollution and loss of biodiversity.

One way to assess the limits of population growth is to consider the carrying capacity of natural resources and land. Simply put, the carrying capacity of a given area is the maximum number of people that can be sustained by the resources on that land. The carrying capacity of a region is categorically not the desirable level of population unless the level of well-being at which that population is sustained is itself desirable. Usually, however, carrying capacity is defined as the maximum population that can be sustained at the minimum standard of living necessary for survival.

The most extensive analysis of the carrying capacity of the world was carried out by the Food and Agriculture Organization of the United Nations (FAO 1982; for a popular version, see FAO 1984). This approach looked at the potential production of food for each of 117 countries. Obviously, potential food production depends on the level of technology applied to agriculture. FAO categorized the level of technology as:

- Low level: using no fertilizers, pesticides, or herbicides, growing traditional crop varieties, and employing no long-term conservation measures
- Intermediate level: using basic fertilizers and biocides, some improved crop varieties, and some basic conservation measures
- High level: fully using fertilizers and biocides, improved crop varieties, conservation measures, and the best crop mixes.

For each of these technological scenarios, the potential output of calories was estimated. To estimate sustainable population, output was then divided by the calorific intake per capita recommended for each country by the FAO and the World Health Organization. These estimates were made for 1975 and the year 2000.

Table 6-2 summarizes the results in a convenient form. It shows the ratio of potential sustainable population to the expected population in 2000 for various regions of the world and at the three levels of technology. For example, for the developing world as a whole, if all cultivable land is devoted to food crops, at the lowest level of technology those lands could support 1.6 times the number of people expected in the year 2000. In Southwest Asia, the expected population will exceed the carrying capacity at both low and intermediate levels of technology. As the technological assumptions improve, so, dramatically, does the carrying capacity of the region.

The figures in table 6-2 suggest a fairly optimistic picture. Certainly, they highlight the role that technological improvement can play in vastly increasing carrying capacity. The picture is, nevertheless, far from optimistic, and it is important to understand why. First, carrying capacity relates not to the desirable standard of living, but to the maximum number of people that can be sustained with the given resource. Second, the carrying capacity relates to a minimum intake of calories; the approach makes no allowance for increasing the nutritional levels of even a single person. Third, the time horizon of 2000 does not permit the level of applied technology to change much, so the high-technology input scenario is of particularly limited relevance to what will actually be the case. Fourth, the approach assumes all cultivable land will come under food production or livestock pasture, which clearly exaggerates what is feasible. Allowing for nonfood crops, the average ratio of 1.6 in table 6-2 becomes 1.07, so that at a low level of technology the carrying capacity of the developing countries is only 7 percent more than the actual popu-

Table 6-2. Carrying Capacity in 2000, by Region
(population that can potentially be supported divided by the expected population)

Input level	Africa	Southwest Asia	South America	Central America	Southeast Asia	Average
Low	1.6	0.7	3.5	1.4	1.3	1.6
Interim	5.8	0.9	13.3	2.6	2.3	4.2
High	16.5	1.2	31.5	6.0	3.3	9.3

Source: FAO (1984), p. 16.

lation. Finally, making the transition to higher-yield technologies will itself involve major environmental impact.

In fact, the situation may be even worse than is suggested in table 6-2. The FAO study was concerned with carrying capacity in terms of food. Other resource scarcities may begin to exert an influence before cultivable land does. A notable example is the availability of fuelwood. In a study of the Sahelian and Sudanian zones of West Africa, Steeds (1985) computed the carrying capacity of various zones according to the limits set by crops, livestock, and fuelwood (table 6-3). The carrying capacity of natural forest cover—the main source of fuelwood—is much lower than that of crops using traditional technologies. Moreover, five of the six regions have already exceeded the carrying capacity for fuelwood, whereas only two have exceeded the carrying capacity for food and livestock. The regional picture presented in table 6-2 may therefore understate the problem of resource carrying capacity generally. What matters is which resource scarcity bites first.

Table 6-3. Carrying Capacity in Sahelian and Sudanian Zones of West Africa
(number of persons per square kilometer)

Zone	Sustainable population				Actual rural population	Actual total population
	Per crops	Per fuelwood	Per livestock	Per total		
Saharan	..	..	0.3	0.3	0.3	0.3
Sahelo-Saharan	..	..	0.3	0.3	2	2
Sahelian	5	1	2	7	7	7
Sahelo-Sudanian	10	10	5	15	20	23
Sudanian	15	20	7	22	17	21
Sudano-Guinean	25	20	10	35	9	10

.. Negligible.

Note: The Sudano-Guinean zone is the only region that has not exceeded the carrying capacity for fuelwood.

Source: Steeds (1985), p. 13.

Calculating carrying capacity is helpful up to a point. These estimates can be used to indicate the broad-scale seriousness of a problem, but they have drawbacks and should be used with caution.

- At the country or small region level, carrying capacity can be readily increased by trade. If calculated, the carrying capacity of, say, South Korea would show up adversely, yet by using its comparative advantage in technology and industry, Korea could import food and sustain a larger population.
- Population growth exerts a forcing effect on technology. This effect may, for example, lead to changes in how agriculture is practiced. Population growth generally explains the transition from shifting cultivation with long fallow periods to short-fallow farming that rotates crops with organic manure and, finally, to modern intensive monocultures based on high-yield crops, irrigation, fertilizers, and chemicals. Carrying capacity tends to be a static concept and thus cannot capture these dynamic, interactive effects.

Despite these drawbacks, a casual glance at the imbalance between the level of population and resources and the rate of agricultural growth suggests that as the pressure on natural resources grows, agricultural growth slows down. Table 6-4 shows this relationship for four groups of countries in Sub-Saharan Africa. Group 1 relates to countries where actual population exceeded the sustainable population in 1982; group 2 relates to countries where this will occur in 2000; group 3 to countries where it will happen in 2030; and group 4 to the remaining countries (those whose populations will not exceed their carrying capacities by 2030). In all cases, the measure of carrying capacity is that of the FAO. The data suggest that the closer a country is to its carrying capacity, the slower is its rate of agricultural growth. In turn, this suggests that the relation between population growth and food output might be reduced to the balance between two forces working in opposite directions: the role of population pressure in inducing technological changes that increase productivity and its role in encouraging wider resource degrada-

Table 6-4. Resource Pressure and Agricultural Growth in Sub-Saharan Africa

Country group	Year in which sustainable population equals actual population	Actual growth (annual percentage)
1	Before 1982	1.1
2	2000	2.2
3	2030	3.5
4	After 2030	1.5

Source: Ho (1985).

tion that reduces agricultural growth. The next section looks at these links.

Population Growth, Soil Degradation, and Technological Change

The historical evolution of agricultural systems is closely linked to changes in population density (important works establishing this link include Boserup 1981; Pingali and Binswanger 1984). Given the extensive forest cover of land in the earliest stages of man's development, primitive hunter-gatherer societies gave way to forest-fallow systems in which society cleared the forest, used the cleared land for a few years, and then relocated to new forest land. As population grew, fallow periods shortened and forest cover declined in density, giving way to bush and shrub cover and then grassland cover. Population growth eventually led society to abandon the fallow period altogether and thus to search for methods of restoring soil fertility, which the fallow period had achieved naturally. For soil fertility to be sustained or improved, therefore, the soil's natural regenerative capacity had to be replaced by other inputs and technology. One immediate reaction to declining fertility was, and is, increased labor inputs. Similar substitutions occur with the use of organic manure and, subsequently, artificial fertilizers, animal draft power, and, later still, mechanical power.

This process describes the general transition from extensive to intensive agriculture, but it is important to recognize that some agricultural ecosystems cannot support intensive farming technologies. Some soils are quickly eroded by mechanical tillage, for example. We must stop seeing agricultural development as a process in which soil degradation brought on by the loss of natural regeneration (due to declining fallow periods) competes with technological advance and begin considering the type of soil and ecosystem in place. Put another way, intensification and labor productivity are not necessarily closely correlated, particularly beyond certain thresholds. Moreover, empirical tests of the links involved are not conclusive. Population density does, however, appear to be closely correlated with farming intensity, as table 6-5 shows. The other link is between declining fallow periods and agricultural productivity. Various studies establish this relationship, although data tend to be sparse for Sub-Saharan Africa, where the ability of technology to compensate for declining fertility has been conspicuously slow to develop (some of the evidence is assembled in Ho 1985; see also Ruthenberg 1980, especially sec. 4.5).

The process therefore seems to be that population growth leads to reduced fallow periods and increased farming intensity. This, in turn, reduces soil productivity. Farmers react by introducing technological change. The relative speed with which technology evolves compared

Table 6-5. Population Density and Farming Intensity, by Farming System

Farming system	Farming intensity[a]	Population density[b]	Climate
Hunter/gatherer	0	0–4	Unknown
Forest fallow	0–10	0–4	Humid
Bush fallow	10–40	4–64	Humid or semi-humid
Short fallow	40–80	16–64	Semi-humid, semi-arid, high altitude
Annual cropping	80–120	64–256	Semi-humid, semi-arid high altitude

a. (Years of cultivation / years of cultivation plus fallow) x 100.
b. Persons per square kilometer.
Source: Pingali and Binswanger (1984).

with the rate of decline in soil productivity and the increase in population growth determines the rate of change in agricultural productivity. Technological change shifts the carrying capacity by enabling the land to support ever-increasing levels of population.

Population growth may thus force technological change and increase agricultural productivity and food supplies. It may also cause declining productivity if, for any number of reasons, technological change does not take place. Technological change may not occur because the soil in question cannot support such changes. If such limits to technology exist, the final farming system established must be capable of trading with other areas. For example, areas with soil suited only to rangeland may trade livestock with areas suited to arable crops and more intensive farming.

Population growth may, up to a point, benefit a given area through economies of scale. Essentially, fallow farming involves significant population movement. As fallow periods are reduced, the movement slows down and tends to be replaced by sedentary farming and settlement. This, in turn, makes introducing permanent infrastructure worthwhile, which in turn eases the transportation and marketing of produce. Moreover, as these changes occur, production can become more specialized as different areas begin trading with one another.

What are the policy implications of these probable links between population growth, technology, and soil fertility? It is tempting to draw a laissez-faire conclusion: there is no need to intervene to reduce population growth rates because those rates will generate feedback effects that ultimately increase food production. This is a dangerous conclusion. As we have seen, rates of technological change will not necessarily outweigh the deleterious effects of population growth on soil productivity. Although they have had this effect in the past, they will not necessarily do so in the future, particularly because the required agricultural revolution must take place in climatic conditions different from those in the past. Second, even when technology does achieve marked increases, as occurred during the green revolution, the technology itself can have significant negative environmental consequences. Examples are the effects of fertilizer runoff on water systems, of pesticides on human health, and of monocultural cropping on the resilience of ecosystems to shock and stress. Third, and perhaps most significant, securing technological change without rapid population growth is surely better than securing it with population growth. The fallacy in the optimistic interpretation of the link between population and agriculture is that it sees population growth as a necessary condition for improved agricultural productivity.

For these reasons at least, policy must continue to be directed toward both improving the application of technology and reducing the rate of population growth.

Population Growth and Resource Scarcity

The previous section discusses one causal link between population change and resource degradation: the impact of population growth on soil fertility via the development of agricultural technology. There are many other links as well. This section looks at several that have been highlighted in what is, to date, a limited literature.

Net Primary Product

An implicit link exists between population growth and use of the total amount of land available for different uses. As population grows and fallow periods decline, existing plots of land are occupied on an increasingly continuous basis. If efforts are made to colonize hitherto uncultivated land, the land available for other uses declines. These other uses include land used for recreation, wildlife habitat, and functions that generally protect the environment. One consequence of population growth, then, is that resources other than the fertility of agricultural land disappear. Ecologists characterize this effect as uses competing for net primary production (NPP) in the world's ecosystems. NPP is the change in the world's biomass that occurs as solar energy is fixed by the photosynthetic conversion of carbon dioxide into usable carbon compounds. Approximate calculations suggest that the standing stock of biomass in the world is 1,800 x 1 quadrillion grams, and that NPP is around 175 x 1 quadrillion grams a year (these estimates are taken from Woodwell 1985). Estimates put the amount of terrestrial NPP used for food, fuel, timber, and fiber for people, together with losses of NPP due to human alteration of ecosystems, at about 40 percent and the appropriation of terrestrial and aquatic NPP at 25 percent (Vitousek and others 1986). The significance of this ecological view is that population growth increases this proportion by increasing the demands on NPP needed to support food production and reducing NPP through forest clearance and conversion to agriculture, which is a displacement effect. The reduction in NPP occurs because agricultural land contributes less NPP than forest land so that a reduction in forest is not compensated wholly by its conversion to agriculture.

Some authors have noted the potentially alarming consequences of appropriating NPP at these levels. Taking the 25 percent figure, for example, means that if the human population were to double twice at the same rate of resource use per capita, the appropriation of NPP would be 100 percent, which is an ecological impossibility. Yet table 6-1 shows that the population is expected to double once before the end of the twenty-first century (see, for example, Daly and Cobb 1989). Technological progress that reduces human demands on net primary productivity is fundamental to changing these negative effects on world ecosystems.

Nonrenewable Resources

As population expands, the demand for nonrenewable resources, such as coal, oil, and metal ores, can be expected to rise. Consumption per capita is also likely to rise as living standards improve. Table 6-6 illustrates the relative contributions that population growth and rising levels of consumption per capita have on the demand for commercial energy (energy excluding woodfuels and other biomass energy). The relative contributions are computed by taking the level of energy consumption per capita for 1960 and multiplying it by the 1984 level of population. This calculation shows what the level of energy consumption would have been if consumption per capita had remained unchanged as the population grew. This change in the total energy consumed is then expressed as a percentage of the total actual change in energy consumption between 1960 and 1984.[4] The data also show the level of energy consumption per capita for 1960 and 1984. For the world as a whole, for example, energy

Table 6-6. *Population Growth and Energy Consumption, by Region, 1960–84*

Region	Percentage of increased energy consumption due to		Energy consumption per capita[a]	
	Population	Living standards	1960	1984
Africa	33	67	6	12
Asia	18	82	8	20
Europe	16	84	72	124
North America	51	49	—	—
Canada	—	—	164	286
United States	—	—	236	281
South America	37	63	16	28
World	46	54	38	55

— Not available.

a. Billions of joules per person.

Source: Computed from data contained in United Nations Environment Programme (1987).

consumption would have risen 46 percent between 1960 and 1984 if the world's population in 1984 had consumed energy at the 1960 per capita level. Thus 46 percent of the growth in energy consumption was due to population growth and 54 percent to rising levels of consumption per capita. Asia shows a marked increase caused by rising standards of living, and this is revealed also in its level of consumption per capita. Overall, then, population growth certainly has a significant impact on nonrenewable resources, typified here by energy. Rising income accounts for slightly more of the world's growing consumption of energy than does population growth. Rising income is especially important for explaining the growth of energy consumption in Asia and Europe.

The term nonrenewable implies a fixed stock of resources. In a literal sense this must be true. Actual recorded reserves of energy and minerals tend to increase over time because reserves simply record what has been proven to exist on a commercially exploitable basis. Reserves are therefore a subset of all the resources available. One way to discover whether population pressure is contributing to the exhaustion of resources would be to estimate total resources on the basis of known geological formations and their presumed mineral content. One could then estimate the world's future population at a given point in time, multiply it by an estimated per capita consumption of resources, and divide the resulting total into the figure for the total stock of resources. This would provide a very rough estimate of the number of years it would take for that resource to be exhausted (this is very much what the celebrated publication *Limits to Growth* did in 1972; see Meadows and others 1972). Such exercises are seriously misleading, however, because they fail to account for any of the adaptive and feedback mechanisms that tend to operate as a resource becomes physically more scarce. Such mechanisms include technological change that reduces the amount of the resource used per unit of economic activity and substitution between resources. A major inducement to such adaptations is price. As a resource becomes scarce, its price can be expected to rise, inducing conservation, substitution, and technological change.

Trends in the real price of natural resources traded in the United States have been analyzed in several publications. Hall and Hall (1984) suggests the results shown in table 6-7 (Barnett and Morse 1963, a classic work, argues that price and cost trends fail to support a hypothesis of increasing resource scarcity). Using two measures of scarcity—one based on costs of extraction and production, the other on real prices—Hall and Hall conclude that energy resources generally became more scarce in the 1970s, whereas nonferrous metals became more plentiful. Up until the 1970s, the evidence clearly supports the hypothesis that resources generally became less scarce.

Results of this kind should be interpreted with caution. Resource markets do not necessarily reflect anticipated scarcity well. Indeed, many governments have intervened in markets precisely because they do not believe that free markets correctly anticipate future scarcity. On the other hand, the price and cost indicators of scarcity are preferable to simple measures of resource availability since, as we have seen, these do not account for the various feedback mechanisms that ultimately determine the true scarcity of resources.

The importance of the impact that population change has on non-renewable resources depends on several factors. These include the weight that society should attach to the wants and needs of future generations compared with those of the current one and, once that has been decided, the extent to which resource depletion can be considered optimal. If nonrenewable resources are genuinely becoming less scarce in the economic sense, worrying about how population changes affect nonrenewable resources is unnecessary because future generations will have more access to those resources than the current one. Studies on trends in real prices suggest that some nonrenewable resources are becoming more scarce (table 6-7; Hall and Hall 1984). Hence continued concern makes more sense than indifference.

How far future generations matter is, as part one of this book shows, an ethical issue. The philosophy of sustainable development assumes that they do matter. Philosophers debate whether it is possible to speak about the rights of future generations to resources because rights tend to imply enforceability, and future generations cannot enforce their rights against current generations (see, for example, Steiner 1990). Deciding whether current rates of extracting nonrenewable resources are optimal or not depends on the goal that is set. Economists typically define optimality in this context as maximizing the present value of the flow of net benefits that comes from resource use (on concepts of present value, see chapter 3; for expositions of the problem of resource use set in these terms, see Fisher 1981; D. W. Pearce and Turner 1989). Maximizing net present

Table 6-7. *Cost and Price Measures of Natural Resource Scarcity in the United States*

Resource	Unit cost test		Relative price test	
	1960s	1970s	1960s	1970s
Coal	Down	Up	..	..
Oil and gas	Down	Up	Down	Up
Electricity	Down	Up	Down	Up
Nonferrous metals	Up	Down	—	—

.. Negligible.

— Not available.

Note: Up means increasing scarcity; down means decreasing scarcity. The unit cost approach uses a measure of the cost of inputs in the extractive process. The relative price approach uses real final prices.

Source: Adapted from Hall and Hall (1984).

values will not, however, be the relevant objective if intergenerational equity of the kind underlying the philosophy of sustainable development is a concern. If resource prices were accurate measures of scarcity, an equity objective would be consistent with keeping resource prices broadly constant.[5] Constant real prices could be interpreted as one measure of a constant capital stock. As we saw in part one, constant stocks can, in turn, be interpreted as implying fairness to future generations since the same capability to generate welfare exists.

Even if the objective of net present value is accepted, rising real prices are not evidence of optimality. The theory of optimal resource depletion predicts that real resource prices will rise at a rate equal to the discount rate (this is the Hotelling rule; see Hotelling 1931). Since we do not know what a global discount rate is, nor how the many factors such as technological change and new discoveries affect this general prescription, we cannot say whether the world is depleting nonrenewable resources optimally or nonoptimally (one study that looks at a single resource— copper—does assess what an optimal path of prices and extraction rates would be; see R. B. Gordon and others 1987).

Renewable Resources

Population growth has unquestionably affected the availability of renewable resources. Until World War II, the expansion of agricultural output was achieved mainly by expanding the area under cultivation. Table 6-8 shows broad estimates of changes in land use for the world's major regions between 1850 and 1980.

The picture is systematically uniform. Only in Europe has the area devoted to cropland remained static (it will, in fact, decline as agricultural price support schemes are phased out). This expansion has been at the cost of losses in forest land, wetlands, and grassland.

The links between deforestation and population growth have been investigated by several writers. A Finnish study produced an extensive

Table 6-8. Global Land Use, by Region, 1850–80
(percentage change in area)

Region	Forests	Grassland	Cropland
China	−39	−3	+79
Europe	+4	+8	−4
Latin America	−19	−23	+677
North America	−3	−22	+309
South Asia	−43	−1	+196
Southeast Asia	−7	−25	+670
Soviet Union	−12	−1	+147
Tropical Africa	−20	+9	+288
All regions	−15	−1	+179

Source: IIED and World Resources Institute (1987), p. 272.

Figure 6-4. Relation between Forest Coverage and Population Density in Sixty Tropical Countries, 1980

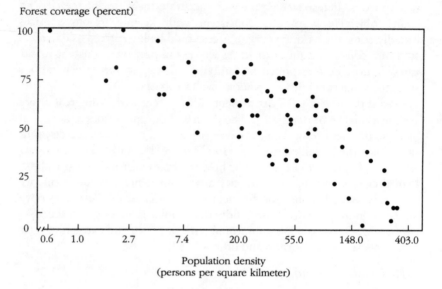

Forest coverage (percent)

Population density
(persons per square kilometer)

Note: The scatter shows a fairly close negative correlation between population density and forest coverage. As the number of inhabitants per square kilometer rises, forest cover falls.

Source: Palo, Mery, and Salmi (1987).

statistical test of the factors influencing deforestation in seventy-two tropical countries. Palo, Mery, and Salmi (1987) regressed a measure of deforestation in a given year on indicators of sensitivity to soil erosion, climate, accessibility of the forest area, extent of shifting cultivation and grazing, extent of fuelwood collection, various indicators of economic development, land tenure, and population pressure. Forest coverage was found to be very closely correlated with population density and population growth rates in all countries except eight arid African countries (figure 6-4). Food production was also correlated with deforestation, indicating that increased food output has been secured by clearing forests for use as agricultural land. To a limited extent, gross national product (GNP) per capita was also correlated with deforestation. Using the regression relationships, the authors project levels of deforestation up to the year 2025 under various assumptions. The general result is that very large-scale deforestation can be expected in the future, particularly in Latin America.

The Finnish study related to a single year (1980), and the analysis was therefore based on cross-sectional data. Because of its cross-sectional nature, it did not contain any price variables that might explain deforestation, such as export prices for logs. Capistrano and Kiker (1990) found that population was a less important explanation of deforestation than factors such as income, agricultural self-sufficiency, currency devaluation, and arable land per capita (see chapter 12). That study used time-series data, but in the absence of data on deforestation it used logging as a proxy. This may be unsatisfactory if logging is itself poorly correlated with deforestation generally. Moreover, one would expect price variables to be more relevant when logging is the particular change being explained.

One other statistical study of deforestation attempted to link population growth with deforestation, allowing for links between population change and agriculture. Allen and Barnes (1985) used panel data (a mix of time-series and cross-sectional data) for 1968–72; the models regressed were generally of the form DEFOR = F (POP, CULT, GNP, WOOD), where DEFOR is deforestation measured by the annual change in forest area, POP is annual population growth or population density, CULT is change in cultivated land area, GNP is growth in gross national product, and WOOD is change in the production of fuelwood and export of round-wood. Different specifications allowed for delayed effects on forest area. The results were as follows:

- Population change is more significant as an explanatory variable of changes in forest area in Africa and Asia than in Latin America
- The expansion of arable land is associated with forest loss and population growth
- GNP is not associated with reductions in forest area, nor is wood production per capita
- In the longer term, deforestation is higher in countries that use a high level of wood (as fuelwoods or for export); that is, deforestation is related to the past level of wood use.

Clearly, the studies do not wholly agree about how population change affects deforestation. Those that use direct measures of deforestation, which are subject to significant margins of error, tend to support a direct link between population and deforestation. Those that use logging rates as proxies for deforestation suggest that price variations and GNP are important and that population is relatively unimportant.

Deforestation is, however, a complex process caused by many interacting factors. Southgate has analyzed the factors at work in Ecuador (Southgate 1989; Southgate, Sierra, and Brown 1989). A simple Malthusian hypothesis linking deforestation with population pressure was rejected because the areas under study exhibited no secular increase in population density between 1974 and 1982, the period covered by the study. Land and resource tenure contribute strongly to deforestation since land claims can only be adjudicated if at least half of the settled land is cleared of vegetation. Fallow lands can also be claimed by agricultural colonists, which discourages existing arrangements that maintain fallow land under forest cover. Logging concessions were banned in 1982, placing the burden of supplying timber on colonists who depleted the forests inefficiently. The activity of these farmers has grown rapidly, which is revealed by the rapid increase in imports of chain saws. The Ecuadorian government has also banned log exports, which has kept timber prices low and, in turn, discouraged afforestation. Forest protection is also severely limited by the lack of forest rangers and low expenditure on research and extension. The studies link the extent of deforestation to the extent of agricultural colonization and an index of the extent to which formal land tenure is held. Land clearance was found to be affected by both population pressure and tenurial arrangements.[6] Simple relationships between population growth and the loss of renewable resources therefore tend to conceal the myriad factors contributing to resource degradation.

The evidence indicates what is intuitively clear: the use of renewable resources depends on many factors. Population growth alone is not to blame, although population pressure plays a major part in the loss of renewable resources.

Common Property

Population growth contributes to the overuse of common property and open-access resources, be they rangeland, the oceans, or the atmosphere. Atmospheric trace gases contributing to the greenhouse effect are strongly linked to energy consumption, which, in turn, is linked partly to population growth.

Most ocean fisheries are fully exploited, and a number are seriously overfished. Table 6-9 shows total catches by the major fishing nations between 1962 and 1986. The data are not totally reliable because a number of countries underreport catches, but the trends are clear: fish catches increased dramatically until around 1970, when their growth rate began to decrease, partly because of overfishing. Overfishing is, in turn, a result of demand induced by population and income growth. The figures for Norway and the United Kingdom illustrate the decline in the Atlantic herring and cod industry. The total catch of Atlantic cod has fallen from around 1.5 million tons in 1965 to about 600,000 tons in the 1980s. The haddock catch has fallen from 250,000 tons to just over 50,000 tons.

There is a complex link between population change and common property resources in which common property relates to resources that are owned and managed by a community. Traditional communal systems tended to regulate the rate at which resources were used, and many common property resources are effectively managed this way today (for example, Swiss mountain resources or Japanese village commons; see Repetto and Holmes 1983). Indeed, evidence suggests that communal management emerges in its strongest form where environments are most fragile, but the relationship is far from clear. Further evidence suggests

Table 6-9. Amount of Fish Caught by Major Fishing Nations, 1962–86
(millions of tons of freshwater and marine fish)

Region	1962	1972	1982	Average, 1984–86
Canada	1.2	1.1	1.4	1.4
Chile	0.7	0.7	3.8	5.0
China	4.1	3.7	5.1	6.9
India	1.0	1.8	2.4	2.9
Indonesia	0.9	1.3	2.1	2.4
Japan	6.8	9.9	11.0	11.8
Norway	1.4	3.0	2.7	2.2
Peru	7.1	3.5	2.5	4.4
Korea, Republic of	0.5	1.3	2.3	2.7
Soviet Union	3.8	8.2	9.9	10.8
Thailand	0.4	1.7	2.2	2.2
United Kingdom	1.0	1.1	0.9	0.9
United States	2.9	2.8	4.1	4.8
World	45.7	62.3	76.5	86.9

Source: United Nations Environment Programme (1990).

that population growth was itself managed to keep within the carrying capacity of natural environments or, where population growth occurred, that technological response took place to raise food output per hectare.

Common property systems have declined for many reasons, including population growth. Other factors include colonialism as a destroying force, acquisition of resources by national governments (70–80 percent of tropical forests, for example, are owned by the state), and ecologically unsound price signals that are set through subsidies to deforestation or irrigation.

Urban Pollution and Congestion

The rapid growth of urban populations clearly results in squalor, slums, and ill health. Unable to afford land in the town or city, poor households occupy the urban margins, which are invariably without sanitation or clean water supplies. Around 4 billion people are expected to be crowded into the world's urban centers by 2025. Each year 50 million more persons become urban dwellers (United Nations Centre for Human Settlements 1987, p. 51). The extent of overcrowding can be partially gauged by comparing population densities for major cities in the developing world with those for cities in the industrial world. Chicago has 2,500 persons per square kilometer; London has 4,000; Milan, 9,000; and Philadelphia, some 3,000. In contrast, Buenos Aires has 15,000; Cairo, 24,000; Casablanca, 12,000; Lima, 29,000; and Santiago, 17,000. At the top of the league are Mexico City with 34,000 persons per square kilometer, Manila with 43,000, Calcutta with

88,000, and Hong Kong with 100,000. Despite the immensity of these concentrations, progress is being made to connect urban populations to water and sanitation.

Air pollution has increased dramatically in many congested urban areas, although data for the developing world are very limited. São Paulo has shown an increase in the concentration of sulfur oxides, but a decrease in that of particulates (smoke), reflecting a policy of combating the more visible pollutant. Manila, on the other hand, has reduced sulfur oxides but increased particulates (World Health Organization 1984). Clearly, trends in air pollution are determined as much by policy measures and the nature of the urban economy as by population density.

Policy on Population and Environment

The evidence of this chapter indicates that population growth has two broadly counteracting effects on environment and development. By forcing adaptive and technological change, population growth may actually increase the prospects for development in the traditional sense of rising GNP per capita. By contributing to the depletion of natural resources, primarily renewable and common property natural resources, population growth impedes development in the traditional sense and certainly reduces environmental quality. The balance of these two broad effects favors the view that population growth, certainly on the scale now being witnessed, is detrimental to future human welfare.[7] Such growth threatens both the quantity and the quality of natural resources, including the capacity of the environment to assimilate waste. Moreover, to argue that population growth can be associated with advances in technology does not mean that technological advance will not occur without population change. Such a view overlooks the extent to which conscious decisions to invest in new technology can be made for reasons not associated with the need to feed, house, and supply with energy an increasing number of people.

Reducing population growth rates will contribute only partly to solving environmental problems. Many other factors generate resource degradation, especially misdirected policies concerning land tenure and prices. Major advances can be made by reforming government policy that directly or indirectly affects environmental quality. China, for example, has increased agricultural output dramatically by improving farmers' incentives and placing land under household management (for a general discussion of these efforts, see Repetto 1987). Malawi has increased agricultural output 7 percent a year since 1973 despite having the third highest rural population density in Africa. The potential for energy conservation is substantial in the industrial and developing worlds alike. Proper pricing and proper incentives offer the scope for substantial resource conservation. These issues are discussed at length in chapter 1.

To argue for the importance of policies other than those aimed at constraining population growth is not to downplay the importance of population control. Policies must be advanced on many fronts and should include major efforts to control birth rates, especially in Sub-Saharan Africa, where the traditional model of population control appears not to be working. Population policy requires not just investments in information about contraception and the benefits of reduced family size, but also a major effort to understand and modify the underlying economic and cultural factors that continue to favor large families. Ultimately, development will stabilize populations, but in many cases development itself is threatened by overly rapid population growth.

Notes

1. The fertility rate is a measure of the number of births per individual (or group or population). Broadly speaking, therefore, it is the number of children actually born to a woman of child-bearing age.
2. Sub-Saharan Africa relates to Africa other than Algeria, Egypt, Libya, Morocco, South Africa, Tunisia, and Western Sahara.
3. A population's doubling time, t, is given by the equation $e^{xt} = 2$, where x is the growth rate.
4. That is, we compute $(e_0 \cdot p_1) / p_0$ and subtract e_0. The result is then expressed as a percentage of $e_1 - e_0$, where e is total energy consumption, p is population, and the subscripts 1 and 0 are 1984 and 1960, respectively.
5. This argument is expounded in Page (1977a). See also Page (1977b). Page proposes a depletion tax imposed by each generation so that an index of real resource prices does not increase (either remains constant or declines). The arguments assume, of course, that real resource prices are accurate measures of scarcity. If they are, rising prices indicate that future generations will have access to less of the global resource.
6. More formally, the model has two equations. The first regresses the size of a canton's agricultural labor force on that of its nonagricultural labor force, the agricultural productivity of the soil, and the extent of the canton's all-weather road network. This equation then explains the extent of agricultural colonization. The second equation regresses deforestation on this measure of colonization and on land tenure. Southgate's findings are consistent with other work that places responsibility for deforestation on inefficient government interventions such as tax concessions for land clearance, tenure through clearance, and log export bans designed to capture rents for the domestic wood processing industry. See, notably, Binswanger (1989); Mahar (1989); Repetto (1988b); Repetto and Gillis (1988). For further discussion, see chapter 7.
7. For a strongly optimistic view, which argues that population growth is almost systematically beneficial, see Simon (1986). Simon's views are, in part, an extension of the population–technological progress argument presented in this chapter. He also argues that the greater the supply of people, the better the chance of finding inventors and scientists whose discoveries will increase human welfare in the long run. He omits to note that the same argument could be applied to the supply of individuals whose actions materially diminish human welfare, such as a Hitler or a Stalin.

7

Policy Failure:
Pricing below Private Cost

Economists distinguish two broad types of inefficiency in the management of modern economies. The first is market failure—the failure of freely functioning markets to reflect the full social costs of production in the price of traded products and inputs, and the failure of markets to exist for many inputs and outputs, especially environmental services. If input and output prices do not reflect full social costs, the economy cannot achieve maximum potential human welfare.[1] Market failure has been widely used to justify government intervention in markets, not just intervention in external costs, such as pollution, but also in sectors that have widespread external benefits, such as education and health. Indeed, the argument of external economy has been used to justify the provision of free education and health care because the external benefits—better information, improved capability to make decisions, improved nutrition and productivity, and so on—are thought to be very large. It is important, however, to assess whether government intervention bears any costs, since governments are not necessarily more efficient than imperfect markets.

The second kind of inefficiency arises from the failure of the government's policy or intervention. When governments intervene in the economy, they may produce less efficient outcomes than if they had allowed the market to allocate resources. Inefficient interventions may include subsidies, price controls, physical output targets, exchange controls, ownership controls, and so on. Even when intervention is justified, as it is in many contexts, the government should secure least-cost interventions, that is, use instruments of control that are not unnecessarily expensive or burdensome.

The analysis of government failure or policy failure is of considerable importance in both the industrial and developing worlds. In the industrial world, governments are relatively well informed about the effects of their actions, but this does not ensure that government intervention in the economy is efficient. Many interventions are clearly inefficient. Purely private markets in water are one example. Water is often a common property owned by no individual in particular, and using water often creates external effects such as downstream pollution. Moreover, intervention can be costly. Water supplied to the rich agricultural areas of the Westlands Water District in California comes from the Sacramento/San Joaquin Delta located some 150 miles to the north. The price of that water is so low that it no longer covers the costs of operating and maintaining the system. While the price of water is $10 per acre-foot, the cost of supplying it is $100 per acre-foot (see Frederick 1989). Much of the water is used for irrigated agriculture, and the implied subsidy averages some $217 per acre, with the average farm receiving a subsidy of around $500,000. These are only the financial costs. The water in the Sacramento/San Joaquin Delta can be used in other ways as well, and this full opportunity cost is likely to be larger than the financial cost of transferring water to the Westlands. The environmental effects of extracting the water are similarly ignored.

The price of natural resources is extensively controlled in the developing world, as we shall see, but, as the example of water indicates, policy failures are not confined to the developing world. The example of water can be easily replicated for forestry and energy (for interventions in forestry, see Boyd and Hyde 1989 for the United States and Hosteland 1990 for Scandinavia; for interventions in water in the United States, see Frederick 1986; for energy subsidies, see Goldemberg and others 1987). Although international agencies advise the developing world that interventions distort market signals and contribute to environmental degradation, they should also recognize that rich countries engage in similar policies.

This chapter looks at policies in developing countries that keep prices below the market price, while chapter 8 looks at divergences between market prices and full social cost prices. This chapter argues that below-market pricing generates inefficiency and, as a result, leads to excessive or wasteful use of natural resources.

Pricing for Cost Recovery

Many natural resources are priced even below marginal private costs. The effects of this underpricing can be seen in figure 7-1. MC is the

Figure 7-1. Inefficiency of Price Controls

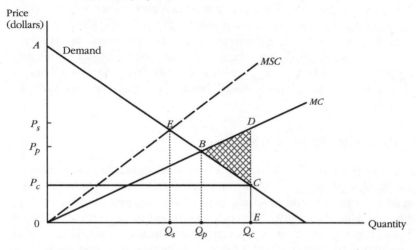

private marginal cost curve, and MSC is the marginal social cost curve. The socially desirable price and quantity are P_s,Q_s, where P = MSC. The private optimum is given by P_p,Q_p, but the optimum from the firm's standpoint when price is controlled at P_c is P_c,Q_c. Because its price is set below marginal cost, the resource is demanded in larger quantities than would occur if marginal cost pricing were adopted. The distortionary effect for quantity can be measured by the distance Q_c,Q_p. The distance Q_p,Q_s measures the extent of market failure.

Figure 7-1 shows the deadweight loss caused by price control. Overall, society experiences a net loss of efficiency because of the price control. Why, then, are price controls so widespread in developing countries?

Price controls are common for two main reasons. First, the price of essential goods must be low to benefit the poorest members of society. This explains why food and energy are frequently subsidized. Second, keeping the price of inputs low is thought to encourage industrial and agricultural activity. This explains why the price of fertilizers, irrigation water, and energy is generally controlled. Other policy considerations, such as protecting employment, also cause prices to diverge from efficiency prices. The costs of achieving these objectives can be very high since price controls mean that resources are used to subsidize the activities that produce the product whose price is controlled. These subsidies are often a serious drain on government revenues, and, of course, the revenue used for them could have been used for other purposes that also benefit the poor. The effect on the environment of expanding output from Q_s or Q_p to Q_c in figure 7-1 is to increase the potential demand on environmental quality by increasing the level of wastes disposed in the natural environment. Frequently, as we shall see, subsidies are applied to products that are particularly damaging to the environment: commercial fuels, transportation, fertilizers, pesticides, and irrigation water.

A measure of welfare lost as a result of the controlled price regime can be derived as follows. Areas under marginal cost curves are total costs. Areas under demand curves are measures of total willingness to pay, or total benefit. At P_p, Q_p net private gains are maximized at $\text{OAB}Q_p - \text{OB}Q_p = \text{OAB}$. At P_c, Q_c total benefit is increased by $Q_p\text{BC}Q_c$, but total cost is increased by $Q_p\text{BD}Q_c$, which is a net loss to society as a whole of the shaded area BCD. This is the deadweight loss from the price control.

Pricing in the Irrigation Sector

A survey of 149 World Bank projects was undertaken to see whether the Bank's pricing guidelines were being followed. In general, those guidelines recommend efficiency prices based on opportunity costs (Julius and Alicbusan 1989). For coal, an efficient price is either the border price (the export or import price) or the (long-run) marginal cost of production (the exact World Bank pricing guidelines are set out in Bentjerodt and others 1985). These rules ignore environmental considerations, but the issue here is whether even the narrower efficiency prices are being adopted. The survey found that cost-plus pricing rules were often used in an effort to protect high-cost mines from closing and that the coal industry in several countries was effectively being subsidized. Nonetheless, the overall judgment was that, in the case studies surveyed, efficiency pricing was adopted fairly faithfully.

The survey noted that pricing in the irrigation sector is generally feasible only when volumetric metering is possible (tubewell and pumped schemes, for example); when it is not feasible (or is rarely feasible, as in gravity-fed systems and canal irrigation), beneficiaries are sometimes taxed on land improvements or crop production in an effort to recover the costs of supplying irrigation. Distributional considerations typically militate against widespread charging for irrigation water, but since beneficiaries are often landowners rather than tenants, distributional concerns are not widely realized in practice. The actual prices charged were generally lower than the costs of supply and rarely provided an incentive to conserve water (for example, charges were set on the basis of irrigated acreage regardless of the quantity of water consumed). The result was that a number of schemes failed to recover even their operating and maintenance costs, let alone their capital costs. Cost recovery was around 7 percent of the total cost of supply.

One effect of charging such low prices is overwatering, which waterlogs irrigated land. Irrigation water is often applied in amounts that exceed design levels by factors of three. In India, 10 million hectares of land have been lost to cultivation through waterlogging and 25 million hectares are threatened by salinization (Repetto 1986). In Pakistan, some 12 million hectares of the Indus Basin canal system are waterlogged and 40 percent is saline. Approximately 40 percent of the world's irrigation

Table 7-1. Cost Recovery in Irrigation Schemes in Six Countries
(percentage)

Country	Ratio of actual revenues to operating and maintenance costs	Ratio of actual revenues to capital plus operating and maintenance costs[a]
Bangladesh	18	..
Indonesia	78	14
Korea, Rep. of	91	18
Nepal	57	7
Philippines	120	22
Thailand	28	5

.. Negligible.
a. Capital costs are moderate estimates only.
Source: Repetto (1986), p. 5.

capacity is affected by salinization. The amount that excess irrigation contributes to these totals is unknown: much waterlogging and saliniza-tion are caused by poor drainage systems.

Irrigation from river impoundments has had other environmental ef-fects as well. Large dams produce downstream pollution and upstream siltation as the land around the reservoir is deforested. People are moved from their homes and lands when the dammed area is flooded. Clearly, not all damage done by irrigation is due to low pricing, nor, by any means, can the environmental costs of large dams be debited to ineffi-cient pricing. But wrong pricing is clearly associated with environmental damage. Adopting prices that are too low increases the demand for irrigation water above the amount actually needed and exaggerates the need for major irrigation schemes. Even if a scheme is justified, an exces-sive amount of water will probably be used because the resource is not priced close to its true cost of supply. Table 7-1 shows two ratios for selected irrigation schemes: that of actual revenues to operating and maintenance costs and that of actual revenues to moderate estimates of capital plus operating and maintenance costs. Although some countries succeed in recovering most or all of their operating and maintenance costs, the highest recovery rate is only 20 percent of total costs.

The failure to charge market-clearing prices for irrigation water gives rise to rent seeking. Rent, or economic rent, is the difference between what a farmer is willing to pay for irrigation water and what he or she actually pays. These rents are frequently very large. Figure 7-2 illustrates the idea of economic rent. DD is a demand curve for irrigation water, and SS is a supply curve reflecting the costs of supply. Price is controlled at CC. Q_r shows the quantity of water that is rationed because demand is high at the subsidized price. Rent at this level of supply is the difference between the demand curve, which shows the marginal value of water to the farmer, and the price charged (the shaded area in figure 7-2).

Figure 7-2. Concept of Economic Rent

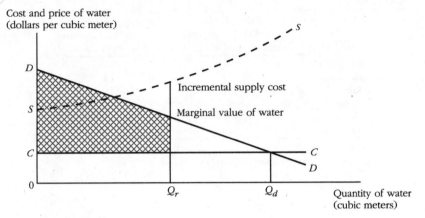

Source: Repetto (1986).

Rents are high in many developing countries. Table 7-2 shows charges as a percentage of estimated farmer benefits in several countries. In Indonesia, for example, charges amount to only 8–21 percent of benefits. Put another way, farmers secure 79–92 percent of their benefits for nothing. Repetto (1986, pp. 12–13) has drawn several conclusions from the data presented in table 7-2. First, farmers give marginal valuations for irrigation water that are very high, several times higher than the charges actually imposed. Second, raising charges by small amounts will not affect demand because the marginal values are so high. Third, the benefits from irrigation water arise from its availability not its low price. Raising the price will not, therefore, reduce the social benefits of irrigation. Other implications follow from looking at how irrigation systems operate. Underpricing encourages a wasteful attitude so that systems are kept in poor repair. Inefficient irrigation negatively affects agricultural output. Because charges are low, demand is excessive, giving a premium to those who can secure water rights by, for example, being the first in line to receive water. This premium can also be achieved by ensuring that the system irrigates particular parcels of land first, leaving poor farmers to secure whatever is left after wasteful prior uses. Moreover, water tends to be allocated by acreage, not crop requirements. This results in the phenomenon of rent seeking in which farmers seek to control the allocation system. High rents are capitalized in higher land values, which intensifies the incentive to compete for the allocation. But competition does not occur in the marketplace. It manifests itself as bribery to officials, corruption, expenditures on lobbying, political contributions, and so on. The allocators of rights similarly expand their own bureaucracies and secure benefits for themselves. Rent seeking obviously favors the rich

*Table 7-2. Charges and Rents as a Percentage of Benefits
in the Irrigation Sector, by Country*

Country and estimated benefit	Charges	Rents
Indonesia		
High benefit	8	92
Low benefit	21	79
Korea, Rep. of		
High benefit	26	74
Low benefit	33	67
Mexico		
High benefit	11	89
Low benefit	26	74
Nepal	5	95
Pakistan	6	94
Philippines	10	90
Thailand	9	91

Source: Adapted from Repetto (1986), p. 13.

and powerful and discriminates against the poor and unorganized.[2] Because it encourages waste, rent seeking harms the environment, adding to the social costs of policy failures in the price-setting sphere.

Pricing in the Energy Sector

Commercial energy—coal, oil, gas, and electricity—is widely subsidized in developing countries. As with irrigation water, these subsidies encourage wasteful uses of energy and add to the problems of air pollution and waste disposal. The economic effects of the subsidies tend to be more dramatic than the environmental effects: they drain government revenues and thereby divert valuable resources away from productive sectors. They also tend to reduce exports of any indigenous energy, thereby adding to external debt, and encourage energy-intensive industry at the expense of more efficient industry.

There are two measures of subsidy. The financial measure indicates the difference between the price charged and the cost of production. An economic subsidy measures the difference between the opportunity cost value of the energy source and its actual price. The opportunity cost value, or shadow price, is typically measured by either the price of the fuel at the country's border, if it can be internationally traded, or the long-run marginal cost of supply, if it cannot be traded. Typically this means that oil, gas, and coal are valued at their border prices (import or export values), while electricity is valued at its marginal cost of supply.

Financial subsidies measure the direct financial cost to the nation of subsidizing energy, but the economic measure is a more appropriate indicator of the true cost of subsidies since it measures what the country could secure if it adopted a full shadow pricing approach.

Table 7-3 shows the ratio of domestic to border prices for the main petroleum products—gasoline (petrol), kerosene, diesel oil, and heavy fuel oil—in a number of countries in the early 1980s. A ratio above unity indicates that the product is priced higher than the shadow price, while a ratio below unity indicates that the product is subsidized. The final column shows a weighted average of the four products. Some countries, such as Colombia, Ecuador, Egypt, Mexico, Peru, and Venezuela, subsidize all products. Kerosene is subsidized in India, Indonesia, Pakistan, Sri Lanka, and Tunisia; diesel, in Argentina; and fuel oil, in Argentina, Brazil, India, Kenya, Pakistan, and Tunisia. The biggest subsidies are in the oil-exporting developing countries (Ecuador, Egypt, Indonesia, Mexico, Peru, Tunisia, and Venezuela). Although the level of subsidy declined between 1981 and 1985 as countries began to pursue more rational pricing policies, subsidies remain widespread. Oil-importing countries tend to tax petroleum products and to use the high tax on gasoline to cross-subsidize other petroleum products.

The reasons for this subsidy structure are fairly easy to explain. Kerosene is widely used by low-income families as a source of energy, and raising its price is likely to have significant social consequences. There is, indeed, some evidence to support this view. A study by Hughes (1987) for Thailand found that taxing petroleum products generally has little effect on consumer price indexes and a suitable combination of lower import taxes and higher fuel taxes could, in fact, lower the price index. The exception was the tax on kerosene, which produced net losses of welfare for the poor. Other studies suggest that kerosene taxes may not be regressive since low-income households consume lower absolute quantities of kerosene than middle- and upper-income households (see Kosmo 1989a). The same distributional argument—that high energy prices harm the poor—is used to discuss subsidies to and, more generally, the low rate of tax on diesel because diesel fuel is used by public transportation systems. Most diesel fuel is used to run freight trucks, however, so manufacturing output, which is more likely to be consumed by higher- than by lower-income groups, is, in effect, subsidized.

Subsidies to heavy fuel oil are justified on grounds that they support manufacturing industry, sometimes using an infant industry argument. Even if gains can be secured by subsidizing energy, they are almost certainly offset by the incentives such subsidies provide for inefficient use.

As table 7-3 shows, gasoline tends to be taxed. Since cars are used by the richer social classes, the distributional objective here is sound. Nevertheless, gasoline taxes are also imposed to raise revenue that, in turn, finances part of the subsidies to other petroleum products.

Table 7-4 shows the size of the economic subsidy to energy in several oil-exporting countries. These subsidies have an additional distortion because they divert potentially exportable energy to the home market, thus adding to balance-of-payments difficulties and international indebtedness. The scale of the distortion can be gauged by looking at the subsidies as a percentage of energy exports and as a percentage of all exports. In Egypt, for example, these subsidies equal 88 percent of all exports and are worth twice the value of oil exports.

Pricing is similar for electricity, although the proper comparison is between price and marginal cost of supply. Table 7-5 shows the relation of price to cost for select countries. None of the countries sets the price at marginal cost. If they did, they would save the amount shown in the final column of table 7-5. The inclusion of the United States shows that economic subsidies are not confined to the developing world. Moreover, by adopting marginal cost pricing, the United States could save a staggering $60 billion. China and India could save $8 billion and $4 billion, respectively.

Public Policy and Tropical Deforestation

Tropical deforestation arises because land is cleared for agriculture and road building, logged to satisfy the demand for timber, fuelwood, and fodder, and damaged by single events such as fire (chapter 5 discusses the current rates of tropical deforestation). The underlying reasons that deforestation occurs include the pressure exerted by expanding and marginalized populations in search of land, the development process itself (logging and infrastructure), and government policy that deliberately or indirectly encourages deforestation. Determining the relative importance of each of the proximate causes is difficult because they tend to compound one another. Logging frequently opens inaccessible areas to agricultural colonizers. Forests regenerate if left alone, but the displaced primary forest is replaced with secondary forest that is not as rich. The regeneration process can be irreversibly destroyed if forest soils are used for inappropriate agriculture, such as cattle ranching.

Government Policy and Deforestation in the Amazon

Deforestation of Amazonia has attracted extensive public interest. Brazil alone has about 3.5 million square kilometers of tropical forest, about 30 percent of the world's total, and most of that is in the Amazon Basin, or Amazonia. Deforestation is extensive and has accelerated since 1975, as table 7-6 shows. Between 1975 and 1978 some 16,000 square kilometers were deforested each year; between 1978 and 1980 the rate increased to 24,000 square kilometers; and between 1980 and 1988 it accelerated to 60,000 square kilometers a year.

Table 7-3. Ratio of Retail to Border Prices for Select Petroleum Products in Industrial and Developing Countries, Various Years, 1981–85

Country and year[a]	Regular unleaded petroleum	Household kerosene	Diesel oil	Heavy fuel oil	Total[b]
Argentina					
1981	1.23	0.90	0.60	0.43	0.78
1985	1.91	0.97	0.81	0.74	1.18
Brazil					
1981	2.77	1.21	1.62	0.76	1.70
1985	1.60	1.09	1.24	0.78	1.25
Canada					
1981	1.10	0.80	1.27	..	..
1985	1.74	1.24	1.73	1.15	1.59
Chile					
1981	1.83	1.22	1.70	1.33	1.62
1985	1.63	1.51	1.51	1.26	1.49
Colombia					
1981	0.78	0.81	0.86	..	..
1985	0.71	0.63	0.79	0.58	0.71
Ecuador					
1981	0.54	0.22	0.32	0.43	0.43
1985	0.90	0.27	0.81	0.41	0.70
Egypt					
1981	0.55	0.15	0.13	0.05	0.15
1985	0.74	0.13	0.72	..	..
Ethiopia					
1981	1.96	1.02	0.89	0.91	1.13
1983	2.26	1.23	1.54	1.29	1.70
France					
1981	2.72	..	2.17	1.05	2.03
1985	2.85	..	2.55	1.23	..
Ghana					
1981	3.47	1.58	2.73	1.37	2.70
1983	3.80	1.69	2.99	1.57	3.05
India					
1981	2.21	0.63	1.07	1.12	1.07
1985	1.94	0.64	1.19	0.84	0.90
Indonesia					
1981	0.84	0.20	0.30	0.50	0.50
1985	1.67	0.72	1.03	1.25	1.12
Japan					
1981	2.26	1.19	1.54	1.05	1.43
1985	2.63	1.49	2.06	..	..
Kenya					
1981	2.28	1.01	1.58	0.89	1.49
1983	2.13	1.07	1.70	0.89	1.57

Table 7-3. (continued)

Country and year[a]	Regular unleaded petroleum	Household kerosene	Diesel oil	Heavy fuel oil	Total[b]
Korea, Republic of					
1981	3.48	1.27	1.28	1.34	1.40
1985	3.43	1.56	1.59	1.27	1.61
Mexico					
1981	0.43	0.24	0.18	0.11	0.26
1985	0.75	0.29	0.49	0.16	0.48
Morocco					
1981	2.51	1.39	1.47	0.90	1.33
1983	3.05	1.53	1.60	1.19	1.59
Pakistan					
1981	1.74	0.91	1.07	0.63	1.09
1983	1.69	0.84	1.10	0.54	1.05
Peru					
1981	0.88	0.16	0.62	0.62	0.61
1985	0.94	0.79	0.74	0.72	0.79
Philippines					
1981	2.16	1.29	1.34	1.19	1.33
1985	2.11	1.77	1.93	..	..
Sri Lanka					
1981	..	0.66	1.03	0.88	..
1983	..	0.73	1.17	0.95	..
Thailand					
1981	1.86	0.95	1.21	0.96	1.23
1985	1.80	1.10	1.30	0.91	1.29
Tunisia					
1981	1.95	0.37	0.79	..	..
1983	2.00	0.60	0.93	0.64	0.90
Uganda					
1981	2.97	1.63	1.83	1.16	2.06
1983	3.83	2.36	2.71	..	..
United Kingdom					
1981	2.53	1.33	2.72	1.40	2.20
1985	2.56	..	2.77	1.31	..
United States					
1981	1.18	1.09	1.09	0.91	1.13
1985	1.39	..	1.73	0.95	..
Venezuela					
1981	0.13	0.09	0.10	0.12	0.12
1985	0.77	0.41	0.30	0.25	0.55
Germany, Federal Republic of					
1981	2.52	..	2.28	..	..
1985	1.12	..	2.28	0.98	..

.. Negligible.

a. Figures are averages for the last quarter of 1985 or annual averages for 1981 and 1983.

b. Based on a weighted average of the four products.

Source: Kosmo (1989a).

Table 7-4. *Economic Subsidies to Energy in Select Developing Countries*

Country	Size (millions of dollars)	Subsidy as a percentage of all exports	Subsidy as a percentage of energy exports
Bolivia	224	29	68
China	5,400	20	82
Ecuador	370	12	19
Egypt	4,000	88	200
Indonesia	600	5	7
Mexico	5,000	23	33
Nigeria	5,000	21	23
Peru	301	15	73
Tunisia	70	4	10
Venezuela	1,900	14	15

Source: Kosmo (1989a), p. 248.

Clearing for agriculture is the single most important proximate cause of deforestation. Agricultural expansion was particularly rapid in Rondônia, northern Mato Grosso, Goiás, and southern Pará. Mato Grosso, Pará, and Amazonas have experienced the highest absolute levels of deforestation. Pasture is the main form of agricultural use, and the key to deforestation lies within the livestock sector (Binswanger 1989; Mahar 1989; see also Browder 1988a; Repetto 1988b). In turn, the conversion of forest to pasture occurs primarily in large landholdings. In Pará, Mato

Table 7-5. *Electricity Pricing in Select Countries*

Country	Ratio of price to marginal cost of supply[a]	Percentage of kilowatts per hour saved by marginal cost pricing[a]	Potential energy saved by marginal cost pricing[a] (millions of dollars)
Bangladesh	0.65	35	135
Bolivia	0.63	37	36
China	0.58	42	8,903
India	0.52	48	4,324
Morocco	0.63	37	301
Peru	0.45	55	324
Senegal	0.82	18	6
Tanzania	0.95	4	4
Uganda	0.15	84	21
United States	0.73	27	60,538

a. That is, long-run marginal cost (LRMC) pricing.
Source: Adapted from Kosmo (1989a).

Table 7-6. Area Cleared of Forest in Amazonia, Brazil, 1975–80
(square kilometers unless otherwise noted)

State or territory	Total area	Area cleared (percentage of total area)			
		1975	1978	1980	1988
Acre	152,589	1,165.5	2,464.5	4,626.8	19,500.0
		(0.8)	(1.6)	(3.0)	(12.8)
Amapá	140,276	152.5	170.5	183.7	571.5
		(0.1)	(0.1)	(0.1)	(0.4)
Amazonas	1,567,125	779.5	1,785.8	3,102.2	105,790.0
		(0.1)	(0.1)	(0.2)	(6.8)
Goiás	285,793	3,507.3	10,288.5	11,458.5	33,120.0
		(1.2)	(3.6)	(4.0)	(11.6)
Maranhão	257,451	2,940.8	7,334.0	10,671.1	50,670.0
		(1.1)	(2.8)	(4.1)	(19.7)
Mato Grosso	881,001	10,124.3	28,355.0	53,299.3	208,000.0
		(1.1)	(3.2)	(6.1)	(23.6)
Pará	1,248,042	8,654.0	22,445.3	33,913.8	120,000.0
		(0.7)	(0.8)	(2.7)	(9.6)
Rondônia	243,044	1,216.5	4,184.5	7,579.3	58,000.0
		(0.3)	(1.7)	(3.1)	(23.7)
Roraima	230,104	55.0	143.8	273.1	3,270.0
		(0.0)	(0.1)	(0.1)	(1.4)
Total	5,005,425	28,595.3	77,171.8	125,107.8	598,921.5
		(0.6)	(1.5)	(2.5)	(12.0)

Source: Mahar (1989).

Grosso, and Goiás, the principal livestock states, more than 70 percent of artificial pasture was on landholdings in excess of 1,000 hectares in 1980. Some conversion to pasture has also occurred as smallholders convert their farms to crops. The smallholdings are quickly abandoned, however, and taken over by large landowners for cattle raising. Much of the timber extraction in Brazil is associated with land conversion rather than direct clearance for logging. Areas newly opened up by agricultural colonizers are selectively cut by loggers, and the rest is burned and cleared.

The Brazilian government uses economic incentives to encourage the development of livestock. In the 1960s, the government began to open up Amazonia through Operation Amazonia, which has used various incentives to encourage settlement and development.

INVESTMENT TAX CREDITS. Investment tax credits allow Brazilian corporations to obtain up to a 50 percent credit against income tax liabilities if they invest the savings in Amazonian development. The projects must be approved by the Superintendency for the Development of Amazonia

(SUDAM). Initially, acceptable projects were confined to industrial ventures, but in 1966 livestock and service sectors were included as well. A 1979 rule designed to prohibit livestock development in rain forests was largely ignored. Of the 950 projects approved by SUDAM as of 1985, 631 were in the livestock sector, accounting for much of the deforestation in southern Pará and northern Mato Grosso and perhaps 10 percent of overall deforestation in the Amazon. Ranches average 24,000 hectares in size, and several cover more than 100,000 hectares. Little employment has been generated, and in some cases ranching has displaced workers who gather Brazil nuts and thus actually decreased employment. SUDAM has dispensed more than $700 million in subsidies. Despite this, only ninety-two livestock projects were awarded certificates of completion, and even those secured low average levels of production. Rates of return are intrinsically low because forest soils are simply unsuited to ranching. Stocking rates of 1 animal per hectare at the outset quickly fall to 0.25 animals per hectare after five years. Much of the clearance is undertaken purely to receive fiscal benefits or to speculate in land values. Clearance and occupation are the only way to ensure title to land.

SUBSIDIZED CREDIT. As noted, projects sponsored by SUDAM account for much of the deforestation in two regions, but not in the rest of Amazonia. Probably 90 percent of pasture formation is not assisted by SUDAM. Subsidized credit is, however, available for crops and livestock development. This credit has increased significantly over the years and has almost certainly diverted some developments to Amazonia from less fragile regions of Brazil. Perversely, since creditworthiness depends on holding title to the land, the poor and untitled cannot secure credit. In 1987 subsidies were abolished from rural credit, which should be environmentally beneficial except that removing cheap credit has forced some tree crop farmers to revert to using slash-and-burn techniques and raising livestock.

INFRASTRUCTURE. The Brazilian National Integration Policy, established in 1970, allocated significant funds to construct roads, including the 15,000-kilometer trans-Amazonia highway that runs east to west. A 20-kilometer strip was supposed to be kept clear on either side of the highway and used for agricultural settlement. The motives for the highway program were partly economic and social: to open mining areas and relieve poverty, especially in the Northeast. A dominant motive was to secure national boundaries. As it happened, very little resettlement took place because the soils adjacent to the highway were unsuitable for agriculture and because the clearance assisted the growth of mosquito populations. Agricultural inputs were expensive because supplies had to be transported across long distances, which also discouraged market sales. The environmental losses caused by the settlement associated with the trans-Amazonia highway have probably been small precisely because the policy failed.

By contrast, the Cuiabá-Pôrto Velho highway, which runs from north to south, did introduce uncontrolled settlement to the Rondônia area in the central and western region of Brazil. Substantial clearing for agriculture took place along the highway, but markets were still located at long distances, which discouraged farmers from growing tree crops, which are environmentally preferable to other crops and livestock. A regional development plan, POLONOROESTE, was aimed at encouraging the development of tree crops, reducing deforestation, settling some 15,000 new families in Rondônia, and benefiting an additional 30,000 families already there.

In practice, POLONOROESTE failed to reach its forestry and agricultural objectives. Deforestation continued apace because farmers exhibited a marked preference for livestock, population growth was encouraged by the paved highway, and institutional failure was involved. POLONOROESTE failed to enforce the rule that only 50 percent of a plot could be cleared. Subsidies for fertilizers to help farmers grow tree crops were not forthcoming owing to austerity measures. Moreover, clearing the land was encouraged because it is taken as evidence of land improvement and hence enables farmers to secure title. Rights extend to the cleared area multiplied by a factor of three up to a maximum of 270 hectares.

Land speculation is rife in Rondônia. One calculation suggests that by clearing 14 hectares of land, planting pasture and subsistence crops for two years, and then selling the rights of possession, a landowner could secure a capital gain of $9,000. The capital gains tax can be avoided by underreporting, while the income tax code generally exempts agricultural income from taxation altogether, making land acquisition more attractive still. Land speculation also encourages pasture formation because the costs of maintaining pasture are lower than those for growing crops. Farmers do not even have to purchase the fertilizers needed to grow tree crops.

Overall, the incentives provided by the Brazilian government are undoubtedly a major force encouraging the deforestation of Amazonia. The same is true for other parts of the Amazon region as well (see Southgate, Sierra, and Brown 1989).

Forestry Policy in Indonesia

In Amazonia, policies toward agriculture have generally accelerated the rate of deforestation. In other countries, policies toward forestry itself have encouraged deforestation (D. W. Pearce, Barbier, and Markandya 1990; see also Repetto 1988b). At the general level,

- Governments systematically overstate the value of forests for timber and understate the value of nontimber forest products and the general protective functions of forests

- The value of forests as reservoirs of genetic information and bio-diversity is largely ignored. Even timber that does not come from a few commercial species is damaged because its value is not recognized
- The value of forest soils for agriculture is seriously overstated
- Forests are used as spillover for crowded populations without examining their livelihood potential
- Investment in the forest sector is seriously deficient and used to secure doubtful employment and other benefits.

Deforestation has increased rapidly in Indonesia. In the 1980s, deforestation totaled some 8.5 million hectares, or 850,000 hectares a year. Shifting agriculture—which accounts for perhaps half a million hectares each year and nearly 60 percent of the total acreage—is the main cause. Agricultural conversion that is planned under official and spontaneous transmigration policies (which move people from Java to the outer islands) accounts for another 220,000–250,000 hectares or about 25 percent of the total, and logging accounts for some 140,000 hectares. Although it appears to be a significant factor, logging accounts for only 16 percent of all deforestation. Forest policies alone may cost Indonesia $1 billion–$3 billion a year.

Government policy accounts for much deforestation. Policies governing the timber industry have been directed toward creating and protecting Indonesia's domestic wood processing industry. This has been achieved partly by banning the export of logs, but the industry is inefficient and uses more logs than are needed to create a finished product (such as plywood). Lost rentals due to this inefficiency totaled some $136 million annually in the early 1980s (Gillis 1988). Even the finished product was sold below the cost of production at a further loss of perhaps $250 million annually (D. W. Pearce, Barbier, and Markandya 1990). By limiting production to what the domestic processing industry can handle, Indonesia may, nonetheless, have slowed extraction rates.

Government tax policies aimed at the logging industry are also inefficient. By taking too small a portion, the government allows others to capture rents. In theory, rental taxes can be very high since forest concessionaires gain economic rent for nothing. In practice, high rental taxes might cause concessionaires to move elsewhere, but Indonesia's taxes accounted for only 33–35 percent of rents in the 1979–82 period. Moreover, tax revenues accrue mainly to provincial governments that are in sore need of income, while the expansion of nature reserves frequently depends on the national government's forestry budget.

Policies on Pesticides

The misuse and excessive use of pesticides impose health and ecological costs. Such use is hazardous to human health, especially to the per-

Table 7-7. Pesticide Subsidies in the Developing World

Country	Subsidy as a percentage of retail cost	Total value (millions of dollars)	Value per capita (dollars)
China	19	285	0.3
Colombia	44	69	2.5
Ecuador	41	14	1.7
Egypt	83	207	4.7
Ghana	67	20	1.7
Honduras	29	12	3.0
Indonesia	82	128	0.8
Senegal	89	4	0.7

Source: Repetto (1989).

sons spraying crops, and creates ecological problems (Repetto 1985, 1989). Organochlorine insecticides and phenoxy herbicides have largely been phased out in the industrial world but are still widely used in the developing world. Thus, India consumed some 3,000 tons of DDT in 1981, 27,000 tons of HCH, and 400 tons of 2,4-D. J. A. McCracken and Conway (1989) quote the number of fatalities from accidental poisonings as 20 for every 100,000 persons in El Salvador, Guatemala, Nicaragua, and Sri Lanka, but severe underreporting means that true losses are much higher. A study of the Philippines reported a 27 percent increase in mortality among males in rural areas after the heavy application of pesticides was introduced with the green revolution in rice growing (Repetto 1985). Cases of poisoning rose a dramatic 250 percent, and deaths from associated conditions rose 40 percent.

Despite the hazards, pesticide use is widely subsidized in the developing world. Table 7-7 shows average rates of subsidy in several developing countries. Most of the subsidies were put into effect during the green revolution in an attempt to encourage small farmers to adopt the pesticide technology that was needed to grow high-yield varieties of crops. Subsidies now accrue mainly to large commercial farmers. Keeping the price of pesticides artificially low has two effects: it encourages excess applications and biases the choice of pest control technology toward pesticides rather than toward integrated pest management. Integrated pest management balances the use of chemical and biological methods of controlling pests with management practices such as planting resistant varieties of crops.

Pricing of Agricultural Output

In developing countries, governments tend to intervene in agricultural markets by controlling prices. This turns the terms of trade against agriculture and hence depresses the price of land. Farmers can be motivated

Figure 7-3. Possible Environmental Impact of Raising Agricultural Prices

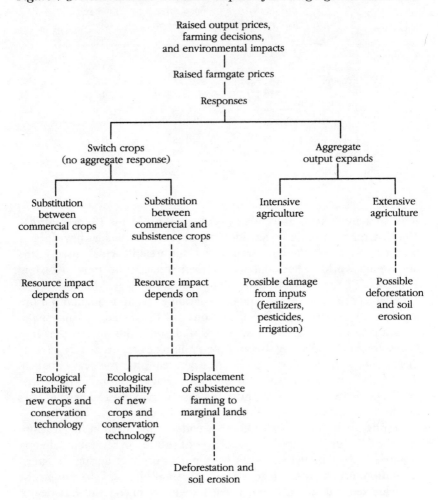

Source: Cleaver (1985).

to invest in soil conservation, tree planting, and so forth if the returns from such investments show up in capitalized form in land prices. By depressing agricultural prices, government policy lowers the rate of return to conservation measures.

Government policy also discriminates against export crops. Environmentalists frequently applaud this effect because export crops are generally thought to preclude the development of subsistence crops and to place farmers at the mercy of a volatile world market. This is the standard argument for food security, that is, for biasing investment toward the expansion of subsistence crops. Apart from other problems with the food security argument, export crops are often beneficial because they protect against erosion.[3] Compared with bare soil, for example, palms, coffee, and cocoa in West Africa have erosion factors that are 10–30 percent. Maize, sorghum, and millet, which are subsistence crops, have erosion factors of 30–90 percent. Groundnuts and cassava may reach 80 percent, whereas cotton and tobacco have a factor of about 50 percent (Repetto 1989).

Keeping agricultural prices down seems likely to inhibit long-run sustainable agricultural growth, but the relation between prices, agricultural output, and the environmental impact of agricultural change is far from conclusive. Figure 7-3 shows that increasing the price for a single crop could either increase aggregate supply or produce substitution between crops (in reality, both could occur). Where suitable agricultural land is scarce and intensification is not feasible because agricultural inputs are prohibitively expensive, extensification is likely to occur on ecologically fragile lands. This appears to fit at least some of the experience in Africa. In other cases, expansion of output might be secured through intensification, which, in turn, may be ecologically damaging if fertilizers and pesticides, for example, are used in excess.

The debate over agricultural pricing must be put in context. Raising yields has been the major source of increased food output in the past thirty years. Without those yield increases, extensification would have been even greater and the cost to the environment would have been substantial. Even though the relation between price and yield is uncertain, the policy implication is clear. If, for example, increasing prices was found to be inversely related to environmental degradation—that is, higher prices cause degradation—this finding would not be a recipe for keeping prices down. Raising farm incomes should be an end in itself. What it would mean, however, is that policies designed to raise farm incomes should be accompanied by measures to mitigate the effects that agricultural expansion has on the environment. This is an example, once again, of how environmental factors can never be neglected when discussing policies that seem to be purely economic.

Policies on Industrial Pollution

The general theme—that governments create economic distortions that frequently degrade the environment—is as true of industrial pollution as it is of agriculture and forestry. Subsidies to water encourage its excessive use and waste. Subsidies to energy encourage wasteful use and hence air, water, and solid waste pollution associated with the production and consumption of energy. There are other links too. Overvalued exchange rates make exporting difficult and reduce the availability of foreign exchange. In turn, limited foreign exchange inhibits the adoption of pollution control equipment.

In Egypt, for example, water for industrial uses costs only $0.005 per cubic meter compared with its marginal cost, which is some $0.025; thus the price is only 20 percent of cost (the following examples are taken from Kosmo 1989b). Raising water tariffs would, for example, make the treatment of cooling water at power stations economic (the electricity sector consumes some 80 percent of industrial water supplies). At low prices, the sector has no incentive to conserve or recycle water even though water is becoming increasingly scarce in Egypt. In the industrial sector, it would also reduce water pollution. Currently, the rate of reusing water is low: 18 percent in iron and steel and chemicals and only 4 percent in pulp and paper. Similar arguments apply to energy prices.

Also in Egypt, a major fertilizer plant does not recover ammonia and ammonium nitrate because the economics of recovery are unfavorable. The domestic price of ammonia is 48 percent of the world price, and that of ammonium nitrate is 45 percent of its world price, so controlled pricing is the policy that makes recovery uneconomic. The result is a waste flow containing unnecessary pollutants. Similar examples abound. Yeast cake is not recovered because the controlled price of yeast is low, yet waste containing the yeast is a major source of organic wastewater effluent in Lake Maryut. An excessive amount of air pollution is produced because cement factories do not recycle dust, and so on.

In Algeria, artificially low prices for natural gas encourage highly polluting industries that rely on natural gas feedstock, such as fertilizer and chemicals. An overvalued exchange rate discourages attempts to introduce pollution control measures using foreign technology. In Turkey, large subsidies are given to exporting industries, which, in turn, are often the largest polluters: chemicals, iron and steel, paper products, and non-ferrous metals. Yet Turkey has no comparative advantage in these industries. The same industries also receive protection against imports. The effective rate of protection for iron and steel, for example, is 6.5.[4]

Controlling urban waste also depends on proper pricing policies. In São Paulo, failure to coordinate the investments and actions of the municipal and industrial sectors has meant that the benefits of controlling water pollution have not been realized. Among other factors, a key issue has been how to charge industry for using municipal sewers and treatment plants.

Municipalities in developing countries are often bigger polluters than industry (gross pollution is a good indicator of hazards from water-related diseases). Even in cities as industrialized as Mexico City and São Paulo, for example, 60 percent of the flow and organic load from discharged wastewater originates with the municipality. Yet throughout the developing world, municipal sewage treatment and disposal are an abysmal failure. Pricing and financing policies are, once again, the reason. Municipal user charges are essential to achieving a balance between revenues and expenditures, but they also send important economic signals and provide incentives to households for conserving resources and reducing waste. In effect, user charges are an important surrogate for the "polluter pays principle" and send a consistent signal: households and industries that generate more waste pay more than those generating less.

Notes

1. Welfare, to the economist, is directly related to the satisfaction of wants. An individual's welfare increases in a new situation if he or she prefers the new situation to the old and decreases if he or she does not prefer it. Welfare economics analyzes changes in welfare for individuals and society. A good introduction to welfare economics is Boadway and Bruce (1984).

2. On the theory of rent seeking, see Colander (1984); Krueger (1974). Rent seeking is pervasive; it is not confined to the irrigation example given here, nor is it peculiar to developing countries.

3. See Barrett and Heady (1989), which shows that the availability of food is rarely the problem during famines, which are the major motivation for food security. Food is usually available, but people lack income and other means of acquiring it.

4. Rates over unity indicate protection. The effective rate of protection (EPR) is measured by $EPR = (V_p - V_f) / V_f$, where V_p is the domestic value added under the protection regime and V_f is the value added under free trade.

8

Market Failure:
Social Pricing Distortions

Chapter 7 investigated the environmental consequences of failing to price resources and products at their private marginal costs, that is, at the price that would rule if the market for products and resources was competitive. This is considered a policy failure because countries typically intervene in the workings of the marketplace to prevent prices from reaching a market-clearing equilibrium. (The failure to price goods and resources at private cost is only one form of policy failure. There are many others, and these are discussed in following chapters.) Even if markets were allowed to function freely, however, the allocation of resources within an economy would not achieve the highest level of social well-being. Markets tend to ignore costs (and benefits) that accrue to third parties from the actions of two parties engaged in an exchange. As a simple example, the buyer and seller of a packaged good do not consider that the packaging material must be disposed of in some way. The costs of a garbage collection and disposal scheme, if one exists, are not reflected in the price of the packaged good, and someone else—the local or national taxpayer—pays that cost. If no organized collection and disposal scheme exists, the garbage is simply disposed in the environment as litter or roadside waste or in unregulated landfill tips as waste. In many developing countries, for example, considerable amounts of waste are fly-tipped (disposed of anywhere) legally or illegally in rivers, on land, or in open bonfires. Health risks accompany all these practices. Just like the cost of disposing waste in a regulated scheme, these risks generate a third-party cost that is not reflected in the price of the packaged good.

In economic terms, these costs are an external effect. External benefits are possible but tend to be less common than external costs. External effects, or externalities, are market failures; that is, they are a distortion arising because markets fail to function efficiently (numerous texts demonstrate that social welfare is not maximized when externalities are present; see, for example, Kreps 1990). The distinction between market failure and policy failure is ambiguous. After all, governments can alter market prices to reflect, albeit approximately, the external costs of production and consumption. To that extent, their failure to do so is a policy failure: they fail to maximize social welfare. The important point is that reverting to free markets will not achieve maximum welfare. Markets may well need to be managed.

The presence of policy failures that set prices lower than market prices is one form of distortion. Market failures are another. The economics literature on inefficient resource allocation in the developing world tends to focus more on policy failure than on market failure for several reasons. First, reaching market prices is a first step toward correcting distortions. The second step is correcting further for full or social cost pricing. Second, the institutional framework for social cost pricing is frequently absent. For example, to attain social prices that are approximately correct, it is necessary to know the size of the distortion; this, in turn, means having some form of environmental monitoring agency assess the nature and extent of damage caused by using the product and resource.

Nonetheless, social cost pricing is not necessarily a distant or impractical prospect. Governments often have the means to effect approximate adjustments for external cost: they can, for example, raise gasoline taxes to account for the air pollution, congestion, and noise caused by vehicles.

Pollution and Resource Use

Environmental economics investigates both problems concerning pollution and issues concerning the rate at which natural resources should be used. Although distinguishing pollution from resource use is analytically convenient, they are not separable in practice.

First, the amount of pollution produced depends, in part, on the rate at which natural environments can receive and assimilate waste products. Sewage disposed in rivers, for example, will generally degrade and be converted to harmless products if the amount and quality of the sewage are within the assimilative capacity of the river. The assimilative capacity of natural environments is a natural resource. It is renewable, but like any renewable resource, it is capable of being degraded if the waste disposed exceeds its capacity to assimilate. Pollution, in the sense of undesirable changes in the receiving environment, thus depends on the relation between the wastes emitted and the environment's assimilative capacity.

Second, wastes, which give rise to pollution, are nothing more than transformed materials and energy used in the economic process. Carbon dioxide, nitrogen oxides, and sulfur oxides are gases emitted by burning fossil fuels. They are a by-product of the process in which heat is derived from fuel. The first law of thermodynamics assures us that the fuel generating the gases is equal in weight to the ash and gases produced by the fuel combustion process. We cannot destroy or create matter and energy. Hence, whatever we take out of the environment as a natural resource must reappear, sooner or later, as waste. In turn, waste causes pollution, depending on its relation to assimilative capacity. These are the essential elements of the materials balance equation.[1]

Pollution as Externality

The materials balance view of an economy demonstrates a general equilibrium analysis: it shows how economies and environments interact as a complex, integrated system. General equilibrium analysis focuses on all the effects of altering any variable in the economy. For example, altering the price of one good tends to alter the consumption of that good as well. It also alters the demand for substitute and complementary goods. If the good in question is an input to other goods, altering its price modifies the costs of producing the other goods, triggering further reactions. General equilibrium tries to capture the nature of these interactions. Each change that takes place tends to affect the environment. As prices change, the quantities purchased change, and hence the amount of materials and energy used in those goods changes. As natural resource quantities change, so does the flow of wastes corresponding to those resources, and hence so does the pollution profile of the economy. Extending the general equilibrium analysis to include the environment thus quickly generates a complex and extremely demanding amount of information.

Because of this complexity, it is more convenient to narrow the analysis to a partial equilibrium context in which the effects of a given change in, say, price are assessed by considering their effects on a few products and inputs and on the environment. In pursuing partial equilibrium, it is important to remember that we may be omitting important effects on the second, third, and other orders.

Environmental economics analyzes pollution as an externality. An externality is any impact on a third party's welfare that is brought about by the action of an individual and is neither compensated nor appropriated. Consider an upstream paper mill that discharges waste into a river, causing downstream pollution that damages fish stocks and reduces commercial and recreational fishing. The damage done is an external cost borne by the commercial and recreational fishermen. It shows up as reduced profits for the commercial fishermen and as a loss of welfare or utility for the recreational anglers. As long as the paper mill pays no compensation for the damage done, society suffers an overall loss of welfare compared with the desirable, or optimal, level of welfare. For an external cost to exist, then,

- The activity of one or more agents must cause a loss of welfare to other agents in the economy
- The loss of welfare must not be compensated.

A similar analysis also applies to external benefits. If an individual produces a product that benefits other people without exacting a price, a similar distortion arises in the economy. In this case, too little of the product is supplied, whereas in the case of external cost, too much is supplied. External benefits are not academic curiosities. A great many people obtain pleasure from knowing that a tropical forest is being preserved. They experience an external benefit from the preservation of the forest. Similarly, they experience an external cost if the forest is cut down. These observations have implications for how pollution and resource problems might be dealt with at the international level (see chapter 14).

Figure 8-1 shows how we can analyze the problem of an external cost. The diagram compares benefits and costs expressed as money with the quantity of the polluting good, Q. To avoid making the diagram overly complex, we assume that the amount of pollution is proportional to Q. Thus, as we move along the Q axis, pollution increases. In the upper part of the first diagram, MNPB is a marginal net private benefit curve. The easiest way to think of this is with regard to an industrial polluter (although it applies to any economic agent, firm, individual, or government). MNPB is simply marginal profits, that is, the extra revenue generated by producing an extra unit of the polluting product minus the extra costs to the polluter of producing the good. In other words, it is marginal profit, or marginal revenue minus marginal cost. MEC measures the extra cost of damage to the persons who suffer from the pollution. We show this extra cost rising as the output of the polluting product expands, but this need not be the case. MNPB slopes downward because costs tend to rise and extra revenue tends to fall as output expands. Left entirely to market forces, then, the polluting firm will settle at Q_p, which is the private equilibrium of the polluter. But Q_p is not socially efficient. The areas under the MNPB and MEC curves measure total gains and losses. By adding them, we can see that Q_p corresponds to overall net social gains of

$$A + B + C - B - C - D = A - D.$$

If the polluter were regulated so as to produce at Q_s, the overall net

Figure 8-1. Determining the Optimal Amount of Pollution

(a)

Benefits and
costs (dollars)

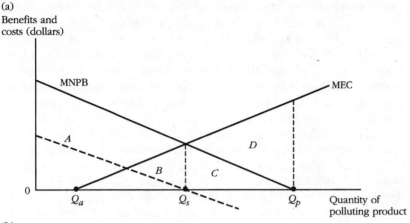

(b)

Benefits and
costs (dollars)

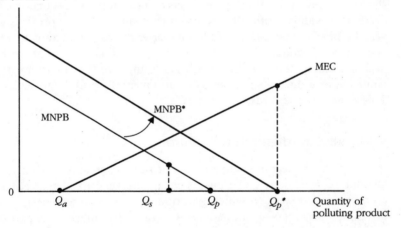

social benefits would be

$$A + B - B = A.$$

Since $A > A - D$, the private equilibrium is socially inefficient. Q_s is, in fact, a social optimum.[2]

The diagram also helps with other observations. First, the externality does not disappear. The amount B still exists as the optimal externality. The existence of a positive amount of optimal externality contrasts with the popular notion that pollution should be eliminated. Pollution can only be eliminated if the flow of wastes is kept below the assimilative capacity of the environment. In figure 8-1, that means staying to the left of Q_a, which corresponds to the level of waste at which no external cost occurs. Q_a is a sensible policy option only if MEC rises very steeply at point Q_a. This may, indeed, be the case for very toxic wastes or products with extremely high risks. Sometimes policymakers even talk about eliminating waste. The first law of thermodynamics shows us that making wasteless products is impossible. We could, however, prevent waste from reaching natural environments by recycling it. This is, indeed, an important policy option but subject to purely physical constraints again. The laws of thermodynamics also remind us that we cannot recycle energy or many materials, such as lead in gasoline, that we use in a dissipative way.

The second observation relates to the private optimum, Q_p. The one shown in figure 8-1 assumes that the costs and revenues of the firm are determined in the marketplace. But costs are frequently modified by government policy, especially in developing countries. Subsidies may be given for fertilizers or irrigation water or energy. The effect of a subsidy is to lower the private costs of production. The second part of figure 8-1 shows one way of illustrating the effects of a subsidy. As production costs decrease, MNPB is artificially increased to MNPB*—private profit is universally higher than before. The polluter expands production to Q_p^*, and the total amount of external cost is even higher. This important finding suggests that we can significantly improve the environment by removing or reducing subsidies to environmentally polluting industries. This is, in part, the thrust of chapter 7.

Market Paradigms and Pollution

The previous sections suggest that, to avoid creating an excessive amount of pollution, governments must intervene in a market-based economy. The extent to which governments should intervene is, however, very controversial. Individuals who favor free markets as part of a political ideology resist the idea that markets somehow fail to produce the right amount of environmental quality. Others argue that intervening to protect the environment places obstacles in the way of industrial progress and stagnates the standard of living. This argument is familiar in industrial economies. It is accorded even more importance in poorer countries. Many people believe that free markets cannot deliver a long-run increase in the standard of living. They argue that free markets are, in effect, manipulated by industry and that a poor country is easily diverted into producing or importing consumer goods when it should be building up its capital base. Markets also tend to favor the rich. The poor may simply be unable to buy at the prices determined in the marketplace. Indeed, this is often the argument mounted in favor of energy and food subsidies. It is helpful to investigate these ideas a little further.

The Unfettered Free Market Paradigm

Few people support totally free, totally unregulated markets, although arguments have been used to defend such a standpoint. Referring to figure 8-1, the argument might be as follows. Suppose the person who suffers from the pollution does not have property rights to the pollution sink—that is, the polluter has the right to pollute. The sufferer should still be able to approach the polluter and ask him what sum of money he requires to forgo polluting. A glance at the first part of figure 8-1 shows that, if we begin at point Q_p, the sufferer could bargain with the polluter to reduce pollution back to Q_s. This would be in the interests of both parties because the sufferer would be willing to pay any amount less than $C + D$, the cost he otherwise bears, while the polluter would be willing to accept any amount greater than C. The bargain results in Q_s, which, as we have seen, is the optimum. Suppose, however, that the sufferer has the property rights to the sink. Beginning at Q_a, the sufferer would not allow further production of the polluting product, but the polluter could pay the sufferer to accept the increase in production. The sufferer would agree to this as long as MNPB is above MEC. Once again, the bargain takes us to Q_s.

This bargaining outcome suggests that, regardless of who owns the property rights, individuals will create markets in externality. This is the Coase theorem: there is no need for the government to intervene (Coase 1960). In reality, the Coase theorem faces a great many difficulties. It does not work when other than competitive conditions apply in the economy (no proof is offered here; see D. W. Pearce and Turner 1989, chap. 5). It has little or no relevance to situations in which the sufferers are future generations, since they have no bargaining power. This is particularly relevant to global pollution such as the greenhouse effect. It is also at odds with observations that bargains are conspicuously difficult to find in practice. One response to this is that the absence of bargains is due to the costs of bargaining, the transaction costs of identifying polluters, organizing the suffering group, engaging in meetings and negotiations, obtaining legal surety for the bargain, and so forth. If bargaining is too costly, the benefits of the bargain must be less than the transaction costs plus the damage that would be avoided by securing the bargain. A moment's reflection shows that this argument produces a Panglossian outcome: everything is for the best in the best of all possible worlds. Very simply, if bargains produce net social gains, they will take place. If no bargains take place, no net social gains are to be secured. Whatever we observe is optimal, which raises the issue of what would have to occur for the world to be in a nonoptimal state.

Nonetheless, the bargaining approach does have relevance. In the international sphere, a great deal can be said for bargains concerning external effects. These might include bilateral deals where, for example, a country might receive aid in exchange for not reducing rain forest cover. Such bargains do take place and, to some extent, are manifestations of the bargaining solution.

Free market advocates in industrial economies also point to the advent of green capitalism. Under green capitalism, three sets of decisions are made in light of environmental awareness and consciousness. Consumers alter their demand for products and begin buying products that are less, not more, damaging to the environment. Investors alter their investments in companies and begin buying shares in companies with green images. Firms spontaneously alter their production processes out of environmental consciousness and, of course, out of concern for their shareholders and customers. Green capitalism raises the prospect that environmental problems can be solved simply by allowing environmental consciousness to influence market forces. This is a powerful idea but doubtful even in industrial economies. It does not guarantee that the right amount of pollution will result. With respect to figure 8-1, it does not assure that we will reach Q_s. It also leaves us with many consumers, investors, and producers who are not environmentally conscious and whose actions continue to impose external costs on others. Their actions alone may keep us from an optimal solution. Finally, it assumes a great deal about the information possessed by consumers and investors. Governments might still intervene to improve that information by mounting environmental campaigns, labeling products, and so on. Finally, green capitalism tends to be a phenomenon of industrial countries. It can impinge on the developing world insofar as it feeds back into the production processes of poorer countries. Consumers might discriminate against products from countries they judge to be pursuing unsustainable production processes, say, in forestry or fishing. This approach is weak because, in any event, rich countries use most of the world's resources.

Market-Based Regulation versus Command and Control

Once some form of regulation to maintain and improve environmental quality is acknowledged as essential, the issue devolves into one of how best to secure the regulation. Broadly, there are two standpoints: command and control versus market-based incentives.

COMMAND AND CONTROL. The central government can set environmental standards and design regulations to ensure that those standards are honored. The form of regulation contains a command, which says that polluters must not exceed a predetermined level of environmental quality, and a control, which monitors and enforces the standard.

Typically, polluters prefer this approach: the standards are usually in place for a determined period of time, and, depending on the degree of control, polluters can usually negotiate with the regulator to resolve special difficulties. Something can be said for a system that reduces the uncertainty associated with regulation. Regulation is, however, also more expensive than other means of control and therefore offends the principle of minimum cost. Regulation is more expensive for two reasons. First, the regulator must acquire information from the polluter, for example, about the costs of abatement technology. Second, the polluter has no flexibility. He must abide by the standard even when his costs of abating pollution are much higher than those of another polluter. Because both polluters face the same standard, the polluter with the lower costs of abatement cannot take a larger share of the control.[3]

We do have some idea of the excess costs of environmental regulation based on command and control. Tietenberg (1990) finds that the ratio of the costs of command-and-control approaches to those of market-based approaches in the United States is high, which means that command and control is significantly more expensive. Out of eleven cases, four had ratios of between 1 and 2, five had ratios between 2 and 10, and two had ratios in excess of 10.

Compliance cost savings become increasingly important as the cost of protection rises. Expenditures on environmental protection in countries of the Organisation for Economic Co-operation and Development (OECD) run at some 1.5–2.0 percent of their gross domestic product (GDP). The Netherlands National Environment Protection Plan anticipates that this share will rise to 3 or even 4 percent. The Netherlands is one country that has formulated a detailed strategy for obtaining a marked improvement in its environment. Interestingly, this strategy is based mainly on command-and-control policies. The percentage of GDP spent on environmental protection would almost certainly have been lower if market-based incentives such as taxes and tradable permits had been adopted instead.

Some studies have begun to suggest that command and control may impose significant burdens on the creation of wealth in its traditional form. Jorgensen and Wilcoxen (1990) estimate that in the United States the rate of growth of GNP would have been 0.19 percentage points higher between 1973 and 1985 without environmental control. Thus, an annual growth rate of, say, 2.5 percent would have been reduced to 2.3 percent because pollution control measures were based almost entirely on command-and-control measures. Focusing on how command and control affects GNP is slightly odd since GNP is now accepted to be a defective measure of changes in human welfare. Moreover, the benefits of environmental policy tend to show up as gains in welfare not captured by GNP: long-term health effects, gains in psychological welfare, improvements in amenity and biodiversity, and so on. We must resist the idea that losing a fraction of the growth rate of GNP is a net cost of environmental policy. Environmental policy has switched a small amount of measured GNP into generally unmeasured gains in human welfare. Nonetheless, for good and bad reasons, politicians and others worry about the impact that these policies have on GNP. The point here is not so much whether GNP is an adequate measure of human welfare, but the very high probability that the costs of environmental regulation in the United States could have been much lower if more market-based approaches had been used.

MARKET-BASED INCENTIVES. The same environmental standards can be enforced through incentive systems designed to get polluters to alter the technologies they use to manufacture products, or even to alter the products they produce, and to get consumers to recognize that polluting products have higher market prices than nonpolluting ones. The use of incentives defines the market-based approach to pollution control, which differs markedly from the unfettered market approach that rejects any form of regulation.

Looking once again at figure 8-1, we might set the environmental quality standard at Q_s if a cost-benefit approach to setting standards is used. In practice, standards are rarely set on the basis of cost-benefit considerations. Only a few countries mandate the regulatory process to use cost-benefit comparisons (the United States, for example, does so for some environmental issues). Most countries set standards according to public health criteria and the amount polluters can reasonably be expected to afford.[4] Only by accident, therefore, is the standard-setting procedure likely to produce an optimum such as Q_s. This lack of attention to the efficiency characteristics of setting standards is one of the main criticisms that environmental economists make of real-world environmental policy. Another criticism is that setting standards with partial reference to reasonable cost burden encourages industries to lobby against stricter standards. Above all, it may lead to static standards that offer the polluter no incentive to look for new technologies to reduce pollution further (these arguments are the subject of an extensive literature in environmental economics; for an overview, see Schelling 1983; for the analytics, see D. W. Pearce and Turner 1989; Tietenberg 1988).

Market-based incentive systems simulate market conditions using two basic mechanisms. The first alters the price of the polluting input or technology, the polluting product, or all of them. If coal combustion causes acid rain and greenhouse effects, the price of coal in the free market clearly does not reflect the use that coal combustion makes of environmental services supplied by the atmosphere. The price can be altered by imposing a tax or charge on the coal according to its sulfur and carbon content. An ideal tax from the efficiency standpoint is, in fact, equal to MEC in figure 8-1 at Q_s (the proof can be found in D. W. Pearce and Turner 1989). It is easy to see why this is so. Figure 8-2 repeats the structure of figure 8-1. If a tax is set equal to MEC at Q_s, the after-tax MNPB curve is shifted down to MNPB $- t$. Left to maximize its after-tax

Figure 8-2. Tax Solution to Pollution Externality

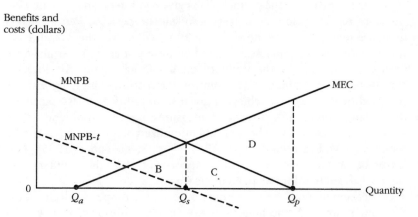

Benefits and
costs (dollars)

Note: A pollution tax is set equal to MEC at the optimum Q_s. This shifts MNPB downward to MNPB - t. By maximizing after-tax profits, the polluter automatically operates at Q_s, the optimum. To work ideally, the tax must equal MEC at the optimum, which means that we must have some idea of the monetary damage done by pollution.

profits, the firm automatically goes to Q_s. Such a tax, set on the basis of the monetary value of damage done by the pollution, is known as a Pigovian tax, after the Cambridge economist Arthur Pigou.

Pigovian taxes are attractive for many reasons. Most important, they are incentive taxes, which means that they are not designed to raise tax revenues. Put another way, they are most successful when they induce the polluter to introduce technologies that do not pollute and therefore enable him to avoid the tax. This feature of incentive taxes is widely misunderstood and explains, in large part, why pollution taxes are comparatively rare in practice—the idea of tax immediately suggests a weapon for reducing the after-tax income of firms and consumers. In fact, a pollution tax could be accompanied by measures to neutralize the tax burden on the nation as a whole, which means that it is revenue neutral. Another attraction is that by inducing the continual search for cleaner technologies, these taxes are dynamic, unlike the command-and-control approach.

The second mechanism that simulates the market is the marketable permit, also known as the tradable permit. All command-and-control regulations set some sort of standard, either for allowable emissions or allowable concentrations of pollutants. The marketable permit uses this fact by issuing permits that allow firms to pollute up to the level of the standard. The point of departure is, however, that the permits can then be traded between polluters. This requirement may seem, at first sight, to be redundant, but it enables polluters facing high abatement costs to bid in the marketplace for the permits. This gives polluters whose abatement costs are relatively low an incentive to sell the permits. Permit buyers therefore tend to pollute more than permit sellers, yet the overall environmental standard remains unaltered because just enough permits have been issued to achieve the standard quality in aggregate. Reallocating permits between polluters thus minimizes the costs of complying with the standard (using taxes to achieve a given standard is also less expensive than using command-and-control measures; see Baumol and Oates 1988; proof that marketable permits minimize compliance costs can be found in D. W. Pearce and Turner 1989, chap. 8; Tietenberg 1985). This is true because it concentrates the costs of control on the polluters who can best afford to adopt abatement measures.

Objections to marketable permits tend to focus specifically on how they might work. Some objections are simply misinformed. The most frequent objection is that issuing a permit allows polluters to pollute, which is ethically undesirable. The problem, of course, is that all regulatory approaches allow pollution up to the level of the standard. Marketable permits are no different. If intended to mean that there should be no pollution, this criticism would have to be justified by an objective other than efficiency. But even if this were the case, marketable permits would still be a cheaper way to achieve, say, Q_s in figure 8-1 than a command-and-control approach. If intended to mean that there should be no waste, rather than no pollution, this criticism is an impossibility according to the laws of thermodynamics.

Overall, then, market-based incentives are an attractive approach to controlling environmental pollution. Not least among these attractions is the likelihood that it will cost industry less to comply with standards backed by market-based incentives than to comply with command-and-control approaches. Moreover, since industry can always pass on some of the costs of controlling pollution to the consumer, the costs to the consumer are also lower under the market-based incentives approach. Keeping the costs of compliance down without sacrificing environmental standards is critical if, as seems likely, environmental costs will grow as global pollution worsens.

Environmental Taxes in Practice

In the industrial world taxes are often applied in the environmental context. Until recently, few, if any, could be said to have incentive objectives. Table 8-1 shows the kinds of tax and charge incentives in place in OECD countries in 1988. Although they are primarily designed to raise revenue, not alter the behavior of polluters, some recent taxes and charges are aimed specifically at altering the behavior of consumers and producers.

Table 8-1. Charging Mechanisms in OECD *Countries, 1988*

Country	Air	Water	Waste	Noise	User	Product	Adminis- trative	Tax differen- tiation
Australia	No	Yes	Yes	No	Yes	No	Yes	No
Belgium	No	No	Yes	No	Yes	No	Yes	No
Canada	No	No	No	No	Yes	No	No	No
Denmark	No	No	No	No	Yes	Yes	Yes	Yes
Finland	No	No	No	No	Yes	Yes	Yes	Yes
France	Yes	Yes	No	Yes	Yes	Yes	No	No
Germany, Fed. Rep. of	No	Yes	No	Yes	Yes	Yes	Yes	No
Italy	No	Yes	No	No	Yes	Yes	No	No
Japan	Yes	No	No	Yes	No	No	No	No
Netherlands	No	Yes	Yes	Yes	Yes	Yes	Yes	Yes
Norway	No	No	No	No	Yes	Yes	Yes	Yes
Sweden	No	No	No	No	Yes	Yes	Yes	Yes
Switzerland	No	No	No	Yes	Yes	No	No	Yes
United Kingdom	No	No	No	Yes	Yes	Yes	No	No
United States	No	No	Yes	Yes	Yes	No	Yes	No

Note: User charges (that is, charges for landfill waste, use of water, and so forth) were widespread in OECD countries, but effluent charges were comparatively rare in 1988. Charges for administering regulations were widespread, but less than half of the countries sampled used differential taxes (that is, taxes on leaded and unleaded gasoline) to encourage environmental improvement.

Source: Opschoor and Vos (1988).

Lead in Gasoline

Several OECD countries now charge different prices for gasoline containing lead additives and gasoline without them. Lead additives are known to affect health adversely, especially in children. Removing the lead from gasoline has benefits other than improved health, notably it reduces the cost of maintaining vehicles and increases fuel economy. The main political force behind changing the regulations was the effect of lead on children's health. While some countries altered the maximum allowable concentration of lead in gasoline, others adopted differential pricing. In January 1986, Sweden lowered the tax on unleaded petroleum 14 ore per liter and increased the tax on leaded petroleum 2 ore per liter, producing a price differential of 16 ore per liter. In the United Kingdom, a small differential of 3 pence per gallon of gasoline was increased to 10 pence per gallon in 1989, increasing the share of unleaded fuel in the gasoline market from 10 to 30 percent.

Energy Pollution Taxes

In Finland, a committee of the Ministry of Environment recommended in 1989 that Finland seriously consider introducing a carbon tax in order to reduce Finland's contribution to the greenhouse effect. The proposal

Table 8-2. Environmental Taxes on Energy and Transportation Fuel in Sweden, 1991
(kronor)

Type of fuel and unit taxed	Existing tax	New tax structure				Total
		Retained tax	Carbon dioxide	Sulfur oxides	Value-added tax	
Fuel oil (per cubic meter)						
Light	1,078	540	720	30	700	1,990
Heavy	1,078	540	720	210	..	1,470
Fuel (per ton)						
Coal	460	230	620	225	..	1,075
Liquefied petroleum gas	210	105	750	..	..	855
Natural gas (per 1,000 cubic meters)	350	175	535	..	..	710
Gasoline (per liter)						
Leaded	2.84	2.64	0.58	..	1.18	4.40
Unleaded	2.64	2.40	0.58	..	1.17	4.15

.. Negligible.

Note: 1 krona = $0.162. Sweden's environmental taxes on energy and transportation fuels were announced in late 1989 and scheduled to take effect in January 1991. Fuels with high amounts of carbon dioxide generally attract high carbon dioxide taxes, although the differential between coal and gas does not appear to be proportionately related to the content of carbon dioxide. Fuel oil attracts a higher carbon dioxide tax than coal, which attracts a higher rate of sulfur tax than fuel.

Source: D. W. Pearce (1991b).

also recommended encouraging competing countries to introduce such a tax. Sweden introduced the world's first carbon tax in 1991 at a rate of 0.25 Swedish krone per kilogram of carbon dioxide. In the energy sector, the tax is levied on oil, coal, natural gas, and liquid petroleum gas and replaces part of the previous set of energy taxes, which were reduced 50 percent. The net effect of the remaining energy tax and the new carbon dioxide tax is to raise the price of energy. In the transportation sector, the tax is imposed on gasoline, diesel, and domestic air traffic. A value-added tax, which was introduced in 1990, is levied on all fuel and electricity. Sweden also has a sulfur tax. Table 8-2 summarizes the proposed structure of Swedish environmental taxes on energy and transportation fuels.

Agricultural Input Taxes

In 1979, Finland introduced a tax on fertilizer for the purpose of generating revenue to pay for export subsidies extended to agriculture because of domestic overproduction. In 1989, a committee of Finland's Ministry of Environment, which was set up to investigate the potential use of market-based incentives for controlling pollution, recommended that fertilizer taxes be set so as to discourage water pollution caused by phosphorus and nitrogen loads. Sweden already had a charge on nitrogen and phosphate fertilizers and another on the acreage of land treated with pesticides. The Swedish taxes are used to support research in forestry, agriculture, and environment, but they also reduce the amount of fertilizer and pesticides consumed (Lidgren 1986).

Deposit-Refund Systems

Deposit-refund systems are variants of pollution taxes. The purchase price of a product contains a tax that is refunded when the product is disposed properly or recycled. In 1984, Sweden organized its system of charging for beverage containers by imposing charges on cans and bottles. In 1985, the recycling rate for aluminum cans—the ratio of returned containers to containers attracting deposits—was an estimated 66 percent. The government's aim was to achieve 75 percent. Bottles are reused an estimated fifteen to thirty-five times, although the exact number clearly depends on the rates of recycling and the nature of the bottle. Sweden also collects deposits on car hulks. The deposit is paid when the car is purchased and collected when it is disposed by the ultimate owner. The system apparently has not significantly increased the controlled scrapping of cars, even allowing for more durable vehicles, by and large because the rate of deposit is low (Lidgren 1986).

Overall, the use of taxes, charges, and deposit-refund systems has been fairly limited in the industrial world, largely because governments have resisted using the market-based incentives that should appear so attractive. But the climate of opinion is clearly changing. In 1990 the United Kingdom cautiously espoused environmental taxes as an element of environmental policy in the future. France announced plans for taxing nitrogen oxide and sulfur dioxide, increasing water discharge taxes, imposing charges on waste disposal sites to finance measures that reduce waste, and levying taxes on products to encourage recycling and waste reduction and on airports to reduce noise. Italy introduced an airport noise tax in 1989 and a tax on supermarket plastic bags; it is also considering imposing a tax on fertilizer and pesticides, a tax on carbon dioxide, and other measures. The Netherlands has announced that it is considering a carbon tax.

Marketable Permits in Practice

Marketable permits exist in the United States for air pollutants and were introduced briefly for lead in gasoline and for one case of effluent to a watercourse. The U.S. experience with air pollution permits is an interesting guide to the economic advantages that might accrue from using tradable permits.

The U.S. Clean Air Act permits emissions trading involving offsets, netting, bubbles, and banking. An emissions credit is traded that is, in turn, equal to the difference between permitted emissions and actual emissions. If a firm is allowed to emit X tons of pollutants, but in fact emits $X - y$ tons, it can trade the y tons. Trade can be internal—within the same plant or facility—or external—between sources in different plants. Sources are classified as existing (sources in place in the mid-1970s), new (sources introduced after the mid-1970s), and modified (existing sources that have been changed significantly). Finally, areas within the United States are categorized as attainment areas, which meet ambient standards, and nonattainment areas, which do not. The policy aims to maintain quality in attainment areas and bring nonattainment areas up to the same standard.

Netting allows modified sources to avoid the higher standards that would normally apply. This can be done by reducing emissions from another source within the same plant. The plant must generally have a net gain overall. Netting thus relates to modified plants and internal trading only.

Offsets, introduced in 1976, are used by new and modified sources in nonattainment areas and by some sources in attainment areas. New emissions in these areas can take place only if the firm obtains enough emissions credits within the same area. Internal and external trade are permitted.

Bubbles, first allowed in 1979, are used by existing sources in attainment and nonattainment areas. An imaginary bubble is placed over a multisource plant; the plant can increase emissions from one source provided it reduces emissions from another source and keeps its aggregate emissions within the limit. Effectively, this trades emissions credits among sources within the same plant. Bubbles tend to relate to internal trading but could relate to external trading as well.

Banking differs from the other forms of trading in that it allows a source to build up credits for future use.

Table 8-3 summarizes the type of trading available to each source. The level of activity in emissions trading varies according to the type of trade. The evidence suggests the following:

- Nearly all trading is internal. Only the offset system produces moderate external trading. Although the bubble system allows external trading, less than 150 bubbles have occurred and only two involved external trade. This appears to be due to the high costs of acquiring information about the willingness of other firms to trade and the costs of obtaining the regulator's permission to trade
- Banking is rarely used: only 100 or so transactions have taken place

Table 8-3. Emissions Trading in the United States

Type of source and area	Options	Nature of the trade
New		
Attainment	Optional offset	Internal and external
Nonattainment	Mandatory offset	Internal and external
Modified		
Attainment	Optional netting	Internal
Nonattainment	Optional netting	Internal
	Mandatory offset	Internal and external
Existing		
Attainment	Optional bubbles	Internal and external
	Optional banking	Internal
Nonattainment	Optional bubbles	Internal and external
	Optional banking	Internal

Note: Offsets are mandatory for firms in nonattainment areas that do not use netting. U.S. legislation allows trading to take place within a company (internal trading) or between companies (external trading). The options vary according to whether the source of pollution exists already, exists but is subject to modification, or is entirely new. It also varies by area of attainment. Nonattainment regions are defined as having failed to secure the air quality standards laid down in the U.S. Clean Air Act.

Source: Adapted from Hahn and Hester (1989).

- Netting—some 5,000 to 12,000 trades have occurred—is used much more extensively than bubbles, even allowing for the predominance of internal trades. This is surprising since bubbles apply to existing sources, whereas netting only applies to new or modified sources.

In theory, compliance costs should be lower under marketable permits than under a command-and-control system. Table 8-4 shows the actual level of trading for each type of permit in the United States and estimates the amount of costs saved. The effect on environmental quality ought to be fairly insignificant. The U.S. experience supports both expectations. Using permits has, by and large, neither improved nor degraded environmental quality compared with what it would have been without using them. It has, however, realized significant and even dramatic cost savings compared with using command-and-control measures. Best estimates suggest that bubbles have saved some $435 million; banking has achieved very small savings; and netting has saved between $525 million and $12 billion (Hahn and Hester 1989).[5]

The disappointing level of trading activity in the U.S. system of permits is difficult to explain. Commentators have suggested four main reasons. First, new sources are subject to far stricter regulations about emissions quality. This means that, when starting up a new source, firms are keen to adopt any offsetting procedure. Netting is the appropriate procedure in these cases, which explains why netting dominates the U.S.

Table 8-4. Economic Gains from the Use of Tradable Permits in the United States

Gain	Bubbles		Offsets	Netting	Banking
	Federal	State			
Number of trades	42	89	2,000	5,000–12,000	Less than 120
Internal	40	89	1,800	5,000–12,000	Less than 100
External	2	0	200	0	Less than 20
Costs saved (millions of dollars)	300	135	Large	525–12,300	Small
Impact on air quality	0	0	0	..	..

.. Negligible.
Source: Hahn and Hester (1987; 1989).

system. Moreover, existing sources have inherited abatement equipment, bought before the bubble policy was introduced in 1979, which means that the costs of adjustment are high.

Second, considerable uncertainty remains about just what emissions credits ensue under the banking legislation. Firms are not always sure how the regulator will determine baseline emissions or emissions credits. This uncertainty is heightened when the credits of other firms are being traded (that is, when external trading is involved). Firm A has to be sure that firm B really will reduce emissions to create credits that can be traded. In contrast, internal trading is far more secure because the firm is dealing only with itself.

Third, acquiring information about external trading is more expensive than acquiring it about internal trading since firm A needs to find out which other firms have banked credits and the price at which they are likely to trade them. Similar problems have arisen when other countries have attempted to establish waste exchange information services.

Fourth, firms do not seek to trade with other firms because the price of permits might rise. Instead, they hoard permits as long as the expected rise in price is greater than the cost of hoarding, that is, greater than the interest rate.

Fifth, hoarded permits can be used to deter new entrants. Although the environment may improve, the policy of competition is compromised.

Market-Based Incentives and Developing Countries

The idea of implementing pollution control measures through mechanisms such as charges and marketable permits is attracting attention in developing countries (see, for example, D. Anderson 1990; Bernstein 1990). Past neglect is hardly surprising given the limited attention afforded these techniques in the industrial world and the newness of environmental policy itself in many developing countries. Nevertheless, many developing countries have environmental agencies, and others are seeking advice on how to establish them. It is not too early to urge developing countries to begin considering a broad set of policy instruments. Many countries should perhaps establish their own instruments instead of simply borrowing the institutional structures already in place in the OECD nations. It seems likely, however, that they must gain far more experience before such instruments can be transferred as part of environmental policy in the developing world.

Attempting to adjust the price mechanism through Pigovian-style taxes may also be premature in other senses. The developing world often lacks the institutional basis for implementing such taxes. They may lack experience in environmental monitoring in general, have an inadequate legal system to back up a regime of fines, have problems collecting taxes, and so on. More important, as chapter 7 shows, pricing in developing countries rarely reflects the purely financial costs of production. In terms of the formula for social cost pricing introduced earlier ($P = $ MC $+$ MEC $=$ MSC), the problem is that $P < $ MC. Considerable environmental gains may be achieved by simply ensuring that prices reflect the financial costs of production. Setting P below MC produces several effects. First, it implies a financial subsidy, which drains central government resources. Second, it encourages excessive consumption, resulting in both financial waste and environmental degradation. Third, it creates rent, that is, large differences between the economic benefit obtained and the apparent cost of consumption. The existence of such rents encourages rent seeking—the creation of additional opportunities to create rent and therefore expand activity in the subsidized area.

Nonetheless, in many instances, charges could be implemented in a simple rule-of-thumb fashion, and the weapon of charging or taxing should not be overlooked. As traffic increases in the cities of many developing countries, so does the importance of the role that rising gasoline and diesel taxes can play in controlling the externalities associated with traffic, noise, congestion, and air pollution. Externality taxes are not intended to raise revenue. They are designed to offer incentives and work best when the demand for the product in question is fairly responsive to price, that is, when it is elastic. If demand is not responsive to price, taxes must be very large—which is not politically feasible—to have any effect. At the same time, modest environmental taxes on commodities with inelastic demand can be justified as a means of raising revenue in developing countries, whose tax base is often difficult to implement. Taxing a polluting product such as gasoline can be and is, however, done with comparative administrative ease. If doing so does not alter behavior much, it does, nonetheless, raise revenues that can either be used to supplement other sources of general government revenue or be directed to specific environmental purposes.[6]

In Mexico, for example, short-run elasticities of demand for gasoline are fairly low at perhaps 0.1 to 0.2 (see D. W. Pearce 1990c). This means that a 10 percent rise in the price of gasoline would reduce demand only 1–2 percent. In the longer run, however, elasticities are over 1, which means that a 10 percent increase in price would induce at least a 10 percent fall in demand. Using gasoline taxes to control pollution, which in Mexico City has a major, detrimental effect on health, is therefore both realistic and potentially powerful.

Notes

1. For a more extended discussion of materials balance, see D. W. Pearce and Turner (1989), chap. 2. The implications of materials balance principles for environmental policy were first spelled out in Ayres and Kneese (1969). The original source of the materials balance view is, however, Boulding (1966).

2. A formal proof is fairly simple but reveals one of the basic assumptions of this approach. MNPB = MR − MC, where MR and MC are the firm's marginal revenue and marginal cost, respectively. Under competitive conditions, MC = P, where P is price. Hence, MNPB = P − MC. At Q_s, MNPB = MEC. Thus P − MC = MEC. By rearranging this as P = MC + MEC = MSC, where MSC is marginal social cost, we have the fundamental equation of welfare economics: society maximizes its welfare where price is everywhere equal to the marginal social costs of production. The major assumption is that the economy is competitive, otherwise P would not equal MC because $P >$ MR.

3. The basic requirement for a minimum cost approach to regulation is that the marginal costs of pollution abatement should be equalized for different types of polluters. A tax that is the same for all polluters will achieve this result; each polluter will choose to abate rather than pay if abatement costs are lower than the tax, and each will prefer to pay if the tax is higher than abatement costs. A tradable permit system has the same property. If marginal abatement costs differ, gains can be obtained by having polluters with high abatement costs buy permits from polluters with low abatement costs.

4. Considering what industry can reasonably be expected to pay is formalized in a number of countries as the concepts of 'best practicable means' of pollution control or the 'best practicable environmental option.'

5. The wide range of estimates for netting reflects uncertainty about the number of trades (as they are necessarily internal) and the amount of savings per trade.

6. This is advocated by D. Anderson (1990). Economists have traditionally not favored earmarking because it introduces distortions into the economic system, that is, it forces revenues to be used for specific purposes rather than be allocated to their highest social use. Modern social choice analysts argue that earmarking fulfills a democratic requirement since it allows voters to keep track of how revenues are being used.

9

Planning Failure:
Socialist Planning and the Environment

In the late 1980s momentous political change occurred in the Soviet Union and Eastern Europe.[1] These countries began moving toward democracy, and more than forty years of centrally planned economic systems began unraveling. The changes will take many years to work through the economic systems of Bulgaria, Czechoslovakia, the former German Democratic Republic, Hungary, Poland, Romania, and the former Soviet Union, although some countries, such as Hungary, have already begun introducing market-based economic management. The process of democratization and openness has revealed environmental degradation as one of the major costs of physical planning. Although the picture remains unclear, the environment in all its forms has undeniably suffered as a result of centralized planning. This chapter looks at some of those environmental effects and some of the policies needed to bring about sustainable development in Eastern Europe.

The socialist philosophy of central planning maintains that it can cope with environmental degradation. In part, this assurance reflects Marxist philosophy, which argues that nature must be humanized to capture its inherent value to man. Engels, in particular, argued that taking an exploitative approach to nature should be avoided. In practice, Engels's concerns, which were not, in any event, dominant in his own thinking, have been put to one side in the belief that a humanized nature would be capable of supporting both increased population and rapid industrializa-

217

tion. Moreover, the centralization of power precludes any appreciation of the effects of environmental degradation. In the Soviet Union, these basic beliefs have materialized in various forms, such as the collectivization of agriculture in the 1930s. Others include construction of the canal joining the White Sea and the Baltic Sea and Khrushchev's Virgin Lands Campaign to increase agricultural output. In 1948, Stalin announced the Plan for the Transformation of Nature, which aimed to divert rivers to arid areas and to plant massive windbreaks and shelterbelts in the steppes. Natural resources were treated as free goods in an economic system heavily oriented toward producing material goods.

Two examples from the Soviet Union illustrate the effects of largely uncontrolled industrial and agricultural activities. One controversy surrounds the effects of large irrigation schemes that use water from the Amu Dar'ya and Syr Dar'ya rivers, which feed the Aral Sea, to irrigate the cotton fields of Uzbekistan. Some 60 percent of the Aral's water has been lost to these schemes, and between 1960 and 1989 the level of the lake fell 13 meters and its area fell from 69,000 to 39,000 square kilometers. The reduced inflow increases salinity in the Aral Sea, and, in turn, water returning from the irrigation systems exacerbates the salinization process. Salinity has increased threefold to 1 gram per liter and is expected to reach 3.5 grams per liter by the year 2000. The exposed bed of the Aral Sea covers 30,000 square kilometers, and wind erosion transmits salt and dust deposits over long distances (Medvedev 1990). Micklin (1988) suggests that 40 billion to 70 billion tons of Aral salt in aerosol form are transmitted to some 200,000 square kilometers surrounding the lake every year. Used extensively on cotton crops, fertilizers and pesticides have leached back into the rivers and lake. In the Kara-Kalpak Autonomous Republic, water intake is not treated or piped, and the result is increased infant mortality, liver disorders, typhoid, and cancer. Commercial fishing is no longer viable in the Aral Sea, and species diversity is markedly reduced. Even local climatic conditions have changed. Moreover, the system of planned quotas generates cheating. Cotton output has been exaggerated to attract centralized investment funds (see "Russia's Greens" 1989). One of the features of a planned system is that, all too often, the state is both regulator and polluter.

A twenty-year program of ecological revival for the Aral Sea was launched in 1988, but its outcome is highly uncertain: the Soviet Union is facing severe economic difficulties, and the program does not address the issue of cotton irrigation. Even more problematic, the Ministry of Land Reclamation and Water Resources is in charge of the revival even though it originally developed the area for cotton irrigation.

A similar controversy rages over Lake Baikal. The most voluminous and deepest freshwater lake in the world, Lake Baikal is of major scientific and human interest because of its biodiversity. Logging activities have produced soil erosion and sedimentation, while the wood processing industry has caused damaging effluent pollution. In the ten years from 1958 to 1968, an estimated 1.5 million cubic meters of logs ended up at the bottom of rivers feeding into the lake and of the lake itself; some rivers were 3–4 meters deep in lost logs. Oxygen was depleted as the logs began to decay. Combined with siltation and other pollution, the lake suffered a serious loss of fish stocks (Stewart 1990). A local fish, the omul, has stopped spawning naturally and must be sustained artificially. Other species of fish have lower growth rates and diminished egg production. Pollution may also be implicated in the death of freshwater seals.

Tree planting programs in the 1970s and bans on using tributaries to transport logs have helped restore Lake Baikal. Some areas are excluded from logging, but industrial effluent, notably from two pulp and cellulose mills, continues to pour into the lake, along with fertilizers, animal slurry, and pesticides from local agriculture. The effluent from the lakeside paper mill at Baikalsk has long been a source of public debate and political concern. After numerous purification measures in the 1970s and 1980s, the Baikalsk mill still takes in 400,000 cubic meters of water and discharges 230,000 cubic meters of effluent every day. As of early 1991, the future of the Baikalsk plant was uncertain because attempts were being made to phase out the worst polluting processes under a 1987 decree of the Central Committee and the Council of Ministers. The same resolution contains measures to control economic development around Baikal, quotas for fishing and seal trapping, and emissions reduction targets for industry. In April 1990, the Comprehensive Territorial Environmental Protection Plan came into being. This plan forbids virtually all development of any kind in a coastal strip and sets environmental controls that must be met for development to occur in the two remaining zones: the tributary valleys and the rest of the Baikal basin. The effectiveness of this plan remains to be seen.

These Soviet examples suggest that central planning poses serious risks for the environment and hence for sustainable industrial and agricultural production. The stress on meeting output quotas and the rewards for exaggerating performance work against environmental concerns, as does the emphasis on bigness, another legacy of the central planning doctrine that nature can and should be tamed.

The State of the Environment in Eastern Europe

Environmental statistics relating to Eastern Europe exist in scattered and unsystematic form. Their reliability is unknown since past governments clearly sought to conceal the processes of environmental degradation or, perhaps more often, simply ignored them. This section nonetheless compares Eastern and Western Europe insofar as the statistics permit (for overall data from the Council for Mutual Economic Assistance, two papers are particularly useful: Krawczyk n.d.; Olszewski, Bielanski, and

Kaminska 1987). Once again, readers are urged not to rely too heavily on the data shown.

Agriculture

A significant feature of Eastern European economies is the importance of agriculture. On average, agriculture in the CMEA countries (members of the Council for Mutual Economic Assistance, which are Bulgaria, Czechoslovakia, German Democratic Republic, Hungary, Poland, Romania, and the Soviet Union) accounts for some 19 percent of GNP compared with less than 9 percent in the twelve countries of the European Community (EC-12). Water uptake by agriculture is therefore important in CMEA countries, accounting for some 42 percent of total uptake in the six countries other than the Soviet Union (known as the CMEA-6) and 54 percent in the Soviet Union. This compares with some 24 percent in the EC countries. In both, approximately the same proportion of agricultural land is irrigated: 7.2 percent in CMEA-6 and 7.9 percent in EC-12.

Pesticide applications are 25 percent higher in the EC than in the CMEA-6: 5.8 and 4.6 kilograms per hectare, respectively. Only Czechoslovakia and Hungary have systematically increased their use of pesticides; other countries show significant variations. Fertilizer application rates grew more than 50 percent between 1972 and 1983 in CMEA-6 compared with a little more than 30 percent in EC-12. But fertilizer application rates in Czechoslovakia and Poland, at some 320 and 230 kilograms per hectare, respectively, are lower than the rates for EC: 364 kilograms per hectare in the United Kingdom, 424 in the Federal Republic of Germany, and 748 in the Netherlands. Agricultural pollution is thus a major source of pollution, ranking third in importance in Czechoslovakia, after industry and municipalities (Wilczynski 1990). The nitrate content is so high that water is unsuitable for babies and children in some areas, and a projected 50 percent of water will be unfit for human consumption by 2000.

Energy

Central planners have always been biased toward heavy industry (energy industries, metallurgy, and chemicals). As a result, energy consumption is critical for explaining trends in air pollution. In CMEA-6, some 0.78 tons of oil equivalent per $1,000 of gross domestic product (GDP) is consumed compared with 0.30 tons in EC-12. The resulting air pollution is significant, especially since many of the energy sources are low-grade coal (lignite). CMEA-6 produces some 18.3 kilograms of particulates per $100 of GNP compared with the 1.4 kilograms produced by EC-12. Gaseous air pollutants (sulfur and nitrous oxides) are perhaps twice as high per unit of GNP in CMEA-6 as in EC-12. Table 9-1 compares emissions levels for selected countries.

Table 9-1. Sulfur Dioxide Emissions in Europe, 1988
(thousands of metric tons)

Country	Sulfur dioxide emissions	Sulfur dioxide per square kilometer
Czechoslovakia	2,850	22.7
France	1,518	2.8
German Democratic Republic	4,990	46.1
Germany, Federal Republic of	1,890	7.7
Hungary	1,414	15.3
Netherlands	272	8.0
Poland	4,200	13.8
United Kingdom	3,780	15.6
Soviet Union–Europe[a]	10,000	1.8

a. European area of the former Soviet Union.
Source: Wilczynski (1990).

The energy-related air pollution produced by Czechoslovakia is fairly typical of the Eastern European countries. Low-quality brown coal with high ash and sulfur content is burned, producing high levels of pollution with serious concentrations in Central Bohemia, North Bohemia, North Moravia, and Prague. In North Bohemia—an ecological disaster area— thermal power plants based on open-cast lignite mines contribute a significant amount of pollution damage (Wilczynski 1990). Children from some parts of North Bohemia are granted an annual month-long holiday in Southern Bohemia to counteract their exposure to low-level pollution. In Chomutov, national ambient standards are exceeded 117 days in the year. Sickness rates are high, and the incidence of illnesses in Prague almost doubled between 1975 and 1990, in part due to air pollution.

Forestry

Forest areas account for about 28 percent of land use in CMEA-6 compared with 24 percent in EC-12. These areas are suffering considerable damage caused by air pollution. In 1986, some 57 percent of forests in the Czech Socialist Republic and 16 percent in the Slovak Socialist Republic had been damaged by air pollution. In Eastern Europe generally, heavy industry has expanded, displacing forest land, which is now used to mine gravel and open-cast lignite, and adding to the pollution burden borne by forests. The high demand for timber has also increased the rate of logging to well above sustainable rates. Between 1950 and 1980, the established limits for cutting timber were exceeded in Poland by 115 million cubic meters (Mazurski 1990).

The loss of forest land has been associated with marked increases in the rate of land subsidence and flooding. Damage from air pollution is not just generated within Poland: some 50 percent of atmospheric pollution is imported from the German Democratic Republic and

Czechoslovakia. The area of forest affected by air pollution has risen from 1,800 square kilometers in 1967 to 7,000 in 1987 and is projected to reach 40,000 square kilometers in 2000, or equal to about half of all Poland's forests.

Water and Water Quality

Some CMEA countries suffer water shortages as a result of the high demand for industrial and agricultural water. Water pollution has also made some water unsuitable for drinking and other uses. In Czechoslovakia, 70 percent of all watercourses are said to be heavily polluted with industrial effluent, disposed sewage, and agricultural run-off. Groundwater and well water are contaminated with nitrates, giving rise to health damage. Half of all drinking water does not comply with national standards (Wilczynski 1990). In Poland, wastewater generated by coal mining has produced salinization, and this is the largest factor making water unsuitable for industrial use (Kabala 1989b).

The state of Eastern Europe's environment clearly reflects the risks of attempting to industrialize rapidly without paying significant attention to the environment. Some caution is required, however, because the data are difficult to interpret. Reports on the nature of the environmental problems in Eastern Europe commonly portray widespread ecological disaster. A closer analysis reveals that just as Western Europe and North America have had (and still have) major polluted industrial areas, a limited number of heavily populated industrial regions or isolated hot spots merit priority attention in the Eastern European countries: Upper Silesia in Poland; North Bohemia in Czechoslovakia; the Borsod industrial region in Hungary; Copsa Mica in Romania; Dimitrovgrad, Srednogorie, and Devnya in Bulgaria; and Zenica in Bosnia. Some of the problems in these areas go beyond any western experience. For example, levels of lead in the blood of children in the most polluted regions are reported to exceed safe limits by as much as six times. Similarly, food contamination is recognized as a serious issue: the amounts of lead and cadmium in the soil of the Upper Silesian towns of Olkusz and Slawkow are the highest ever recorded in the world.

Even in some of these areas, however, levels of exposure to most of the major pollutants are not significantly higher than in other parts of Europe (figure 9-1 shows particulate concentrations in thirteen European cities; similar results are observed for sulfur dioxide). The problem is that the level of exposure has improved little in the worst Eastern European areas over the past two decades, while it has improved substantially in most of the OECD countries (especially for suspended particulates in the air). This is true even for areas whose record is not impressive. For example, in the most polluted region of Poland, maximum 24-hour ambient concentrations of black smoke during the heating season exceed the EC's standard more than sixfold, while in London, smog in 1952 exceeded the current EC standard more than ten times.

*Figure 9-1. Particulates and Urban Air Quality in
Major European Cities, 1977-87*

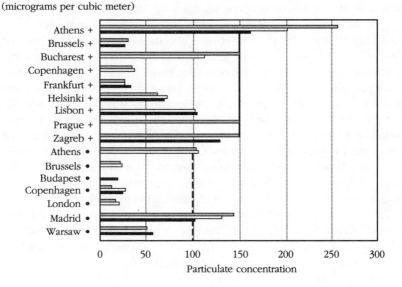

Mean annual concentration

(micrograms per cubic meter)

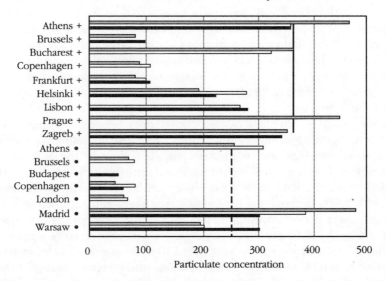

Concentration in the 98th percentile

Note: ▨1977-79; ☐1981-83; ■1985-87; —— EC standard (dust); – –EC standard (smoke).
Central city commercial locations: + dust measured by high-volume gravimetric methods;
• smoke measured by filter or reflectometry methods.
Source: Hughes (1990).

Economic and Environmental Reform in Eastern Europe

The process of economic transformation in Eastern Europe should involve the conversion of heavy industry to a more balanced economic structure as market forces remove subsidies and centralized planning targets. As individual preferences exert more influence over the economy, the changing structure of production will certainly result in a lowering of the coefficient between energy and output. As currencies gradually become convertible, some of the obstacles should be reduced to securing spare parts and modifying technology that is often antiquated, thus improving the chances of end-of-pipe adaptations. Western aid, especially through the European Bank for Reconstruction and Development, will include environmental investments concerned not only with improving the health of the people of Eastern Europe but also with reducing transboundary flows of pollutants from East to West and East to North.[2] Above all, competition should reduce the excessive waste of materials and energy associated with current technologies in Eastern Europe.

Three critical changes are needed to commence the process of improving the environment in Eastern Europe: changes in industrial structure; increases in the real price of energy; and increases in effluent charges. These points are illustrated next for Czechoslovakia.

Czechoslovakia

Czechoslovakia burns low-grade brown coal as its major source of energy. The air pollution effects of this practice are most dramatic in the northern Bohemian region, sometimes known as the Bermuda triangle of pollution. This region has concentrations of power plants, chemical factories, and open-cast mines. The yearly average concentration of sulfur dioxide is reported to be 50 micrograms per cubic meter, which actually compares well with U.S. standards of 80 and the World Health Organization (WHO) standards of 60. But the territory between Chomutov and Hrensko within North Bohemia averages 100–140 micrograms per cubic meter—above U.S. and WHO standards, but close to the limit of the European Community standard. A more disturbing picture lies in the daily concentrations, which usually exceed all standards: extremes of 2,400–3,000 micrograms per cubic meter have been recorded in some areas (these figures are contained in unpublished mission reports of the World Bank). A similar picture emerges for particulates: some areas have annual average concentrations of over 150 micrograms per cubic meter—the EC standard—and daily concentrations often three times higher than the EC daily standard. In the capital city of Prague, the average annual level of sulfur dioxide, 200 micrograms per cubic meter, exceeds the EC standard by around 40 percent. These pollution levels are bound to have adverse economic and health effects, but they are not as dramatically high as some media reports suggest.[3]

The forces of economic transformation alone may not reduce the burden of pollution in Eastern Europe. Specific policies that deal with natural resources must be changed significantly. The example of Czechoslovakia shows that pricing is one policy that must be changed. Energy is heavily subsidized, which, as the analysis in chapter 7 shows, encourages waste. Removing subsidies would promote both the transformation process and the environment. Czechoslovakia levies pollution and user charges for resources. A standard Kcs100 per ton of solid waste emissions is charged, and some parts of the country are subject to additional charges on carbon dioxide and nitrous oxide. Table 9-2 shows how charges related to air emissions compare with the cost of abating pollution to comply with the required standards; both are expressed as a percentage of production costs. Because the charges are almost universally lower than abatement costs, polluters have no incentive to abate pollution.[4] Water pollution fees are paid for the right to discharge wastewater to surface water. Once the accepted limit has been exceeded, the standard charge rises with the level of pollution. This would be required of a pollution charge that broadly obeys economic principles, but in Czechoslovakia the charge is inefficient because it is not high enough to induce industry to control pollution. Moreover, polluters are encouraged to discharge waste to rivers because the charge for discharging to sewers is much higher than the charge for discharging to rivers. To make matters worse, the charge for disposing waste in the sewer system is the same whether the wastewater is treated or not. New wastewater charges were introduced in 1989 with the aim of correcting this bias.

User charges tell much the same story. In Czechoslovakia, the supply of water faces problems not only of pollution, but also of availability. A charge of Kcs0.46 per cubic meter is made for water taken from surface water, and industry pays Kcs2 per cubic meter for water taken from groundwater. Both charges are fixed for the whole country regardless of regional variations in scarcity and quality. Drinking water is priced at Kcs0.6 per cubic meter for households and Kcs3.6 for industries; these charges do not cover costs. Finally, sewage disposed in the sewer system

Table 9-2. Charges and Abatement Costs for Air Pollution in Czechoslovakia
(percentage)

Industry	Pollution charge per production costs	Abatement costs per production costs
Chemical	0.007	0.88
Electricity	1.840	1.59
Fuel	0.590	0.88
Glass	0.002	1.75
Metallurgy	0.005	0.74

Source: Wilczynski (1990).

is charged at Kcs2.35 per cubic meter for industries and Kcs0.2 for households. Again, the charge is fixed across the country. New regional water and sewage disposal charges are, however, being introduced. These new user charges should reduce central subsidies and induce households and industries to conserve water.

The poor water quality is due to industrial and municipal effluent and agricultural runoff. Of the nearly 5,000 registered sources of water pollution in the Czech Socialist Republic, a mere 0.3 percent contributed 43 percent of the total biochemical demand for oxygen and 31 percent of the dissolved solids. Major advances in water quality could therefore be made by concentrating on a few major sources of pollution. A similar picture exists for the Slovak Socialist Republic.

Municipal sewage treatment has suffered from lack of investment. The law mandating the construction of new sewage treatment plants has not been applied in Prague, Bratislava, Hradec Kralove, and Usti nad Labem due to the severity of the problem. A significant part of the pollution of surface waters arises from agricultural runoff, including fertilizers, which have raised nitrate levels in surface and groundwater. Fertilizer use in Czechoslovakia is around 320 kilograms per hectare, which is higher than that in other Eastern European countries. Fertilizer runoff is exacerbated by weak practices in agricultural management, which have given rise to soil erosion; high fertilizer use also reflects the Soviet-style practice of establishing large farms.

Issues in Environmental and Economic Development in Eastern Europe

The major contribution to the damaging particulate air pollution in Eastern European countries does not come from tall stacks of industries and power plants, which disperse their emissions over a considerable area. Instead, they come from low-stack households and the service sector, which use more coal than is common in Western Europe. Except in Poland and Czechoslovakia, the share that coal has in generating electricity and industry is similar to its share in Western Europe.

The damaging pollution effects from low stacks show that the ambient level of exposure, not the total level of emissions, is important, since emissions and ambient air quality are not linked directly. Moreover, particulates (especially in conjunction with sulfur) are more damaging to human health than gaseous pollutants. Given the nature of the sources, relatively simple and inexpensive measures, such as switching residences and small boilers from coal to gas, would largely solve most of the severe problems of air quality throughout Eastern Europe. This is essentially what occurred in the heavily industrial regions of Western Europe and North America twenty years ago.

Controlling water pollution would be far more costly than controlling air pollution, and such investments are given lower priority, since water pollution generally involves few health costs except in limited geographical areas. In most Eastern European countries, the high levels of water pollution increase, above all, the capital and recurrent costs for infrastructure. Moreover, as in the West, nonpoint sources contribute a major portion of water pollution. Wastewater and nonpoint source pollution can be mitigated in large part through inexpensive, low-technology methods that increase the oxygen content of water and improve its self-purification properties (weirs, aeration equipment, and constructed wetlands); the typical high-cost western model for intensive wastewater treatment is not a good example.

Changing the industrial structure in Eastern Europe—above all, reducing the share of heavy industry—would solve many environmental problems but could increase others if the relative price of energy and natural resources is not systematically adjusted. In the OECD economies, the two oil price shocks of the 1970s made a significant fraction of the total capital stock obsolescent because it was poorly adapted to the new relative price of factors and resources. This capital was gradually replaced by new equipment that was more energy efficient and designed to meet much higher environmental standards. In contrast, Eastern Europe was largely insulated from the energy price increases in the West. Energy prices (combined with incentives to ensure a rapid response to higher energy prices, especially a hard budget constraint) are expected to be the single most important factor reducing the main diffuse air pollutants in CEE countries until the end of the century. Unfortunately, no similar instruments exist to reduce wastewater discharges. In the longer term, controlling water pollution will therefore require much larger investments than controlling air pollution. Figure 9-2 depicts the factors likely to reduce emissions in Poland up to 1995.

Any environmental action program must be based on a clear understanding of what would be achieved through price adjustments, industrial restructuring, and privatization, on the one hand, and explicit environmental policies and investments, on the other. How much of each policy is affordable socially and economically at any given time? How can sound environmental programs build on the benefits of adjustments and of reasonably predictable investments and technology? How can they correct negative environmental effects? How can short-term and long-term objectives be balanced, and what minimum financial resources will be required as increasingly stringent environmental policies are introduced? Which short-term environmental problems (hot spots) require immediate attention from a national, regional, or global perspective? Who should decide?

This task is complicated by the rapid changes and great uncertainty in the new democracies of Eastern Europe. The analysis must therefore evaluate different scenarios of economic and technological development

Figure 9-2. Sources of Reduced Emissions in Poland, Projected to 1995

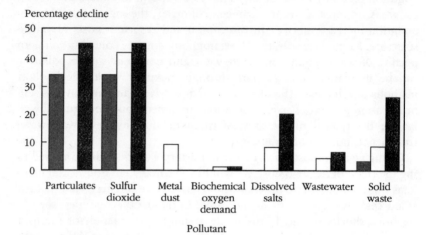

Percentage decline

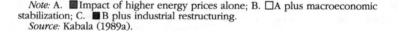

Pollutant

Note: A. ▉Impact of higher energy prices alone; B. ☐A plus macroeconomic stabilization; C. ▇B plus industrial restructuring.
Source: Kabala (1989a).

and the impact that the stabilization and adjustment programs now un-der way to varying degrees in the Eastern European countries are likely to have on the environment.

Eastern European countries have paid little attention to their weak institutions, limited absorptive capacity, and inability of their local cur-rency resources to match the limited hard currencies available even to-day. Throughout the region, quite high standards of technical expertise can be found, but decisionmaking and management capability are sorely lacking, as is knowledge of how to design and implement sound projects.

With the growing interaction of environmental experts from East and West, some countries are tending to adopt western models on a first come–first served basis without understanding the advantages and short-comings of the different systems (Hungary, for example, wants to adopt German emissions standards even though such an approach is inefficient and unaffordable for Hungary).

The rush to adopt western standards should be tempered by a careful evaluation of the costs and benefits over time and a clear determination of who should bear the costs and how the standards would be imple-mented in a phased multi-year program. So far, standards have not been based on a serious consideration of costs and benefits. Since many of their standards are quite strict but not enforced, the whole system of environmental regulations has not been taken seriously.

Most countries in the region have a fairly comprehensive system of permits, fines, and fees. In practice, these systems do not work because enterprises are more concerned about meeting their production targets than about improving their financial performance. Indeed, the price-setting regime allows them to build the cost of fees into the cost base used to determine the prices they charge for domestic sales. These prices are subsidized (by means of a so-called soft budget), and part of the subsidies actually support pollution. Further, the fees and fines are consistently well below the average cost of reducing emissions and are not system-atically adjusted for inflation. They are trivial in real terms.

This does not necessarily imply that environmental charges do not work in Eastern Europe, nor that they should be abandoned. Where fees and fines are sufficiently high, pollution has apparently been reduced, although this is hard to disentangle from the general process of economic downturn. Clearly, further efforts to make economic incentives workable are warranted, but major reliance upon them, particularly in systems in which prices in general do not adequately reflect costs and values, will not be possible for some years.

Privatization and industrial restructuring are being promoted with relatively little awareness of the potentially critical role that environmen-tal factors play in the process. Thus investors shy away from committing themselves (a) because they are afraid of being held liable for past envi-ronmental damage, (b) because the regulatory framework (including standards) is unclear, and they may be forced to change practices after making major investments in equipment, (c) because national or local authorities have established specific investment constraints based on a misguided ordering of economic and environmental priorities, and (d) because the environmental infrastructure makes meeting high production standards and attracting skilled labor impossible.

The political consensus in East and West is that transboundary pollu-tion should be rolled back progressively. Bulgaria complains about expo-sure to toxic fumes from industries just across the border, while Hungary must cope with heavily polluted surface water that flows into the country and accounts for over 95 percent of the available surface water. Finally, a substantial amount of transboundary air pollution is thought to acidify soils and destroy forests throughout Europe.

Numerous international legal documents commit the signatories to specific reductions in transboundary pollution fluxes within a given time period. In many cases, Eastern European countries have signed these protocols to appear as good citizens of Europe, without understanding the costs involved or knowing who would be the primary beneficiaries of the stipulated policies. These countries clearly need to (a) take stock of the various research programs on transboundary pollution; (b) identify as clearly as possible the sources and recipients of the pollution flows; (c) evaluate the costs and benefits of measures that could be undertaken at the source or where harm is suffered; and (d) propose acceptable criteria for external support that relate financial responsibilities to costs and benefits, ability to meet the financial obligations within a specified time frame, and realistic implementation and enforcement capabilities. For example, can offset arrangements be introduced in which some countries agree to reduce emissions and effluents over a given period of time? What is the most suitable process for negotiating this kind of arrangement, and how would its implementation be monitored and enforced?

In many respects, the growing number of environmental programs that focus on specific regions, such as the Baltic and Black seas, the Danube River basin, and the sulfur triangle, implicitly take these transboundary factors into account. Some regional programs also incorporate global concerns. However, as yet no explicit strategy addresses the regional or global environmental problems that should be given highest priority in Eastern Europe.

China

Even the briefest sketch indicates that China's environmental problems, and their causes, are similar to those of Eastern and Central Europe. With China, however, the issue is compounded by the very rapid growth of its population. Like all developing economies, China is suffering from environmental pollution and loss of natural resources. Water supplies are scarce in several places due to heavy industrial demand for groundwater; some sources are contaminated. China depends heavily on coal for its energy, and this dependence creates air pollution. Solid waste accumulates at the edge of cities, and a significant amount of untreated wastewater is discharged into rivers and watercourses. In rural areas, fertilizers and pesticides are used inappropriately; salt beds are forming as a result of irrigation and drainage problems; overgrazing, soil erosion, and loss of resources are common. Nevertheless, China has made significant environmental advances in recent years. The challenge has been to advance these improvements in the context of rapid population change and industrialization.

WATER POLLUTION. Some 27 billion tons of industrial wastewater is discharged throughout China, yet less than 30 percent is treated at all and only a fraction receives more than pretreatment. Municipal wastewater receives even less treatment: less than half of the stations for monitoring urban water quality show levels of biochemical demand for oxygen and dissolved oxygen that are higher than the minimum standards. The result is an unquantified, but significant, risk to the quality of urban drinking water. In rural areas, perhaps only one in seven persons has access to safe drinking water.

In rural areas, excessive use of fertilizers has produced nitrate pollution, although the extent is difficult to gauge. Fertilizers are subsidized and used for specific crops. In turn, central planning dictates that certain areas must produce specific crops, such as legumes, that use fertilizer. Excess use of irrigation water, which is associated with poor drainage, has subjected 7 million hectares of land to salinization and alkalinization. Untreated wastewater is used to irrigate some 1.4 million hectares, which are now contaminated with trade metals and toxins. Excessive use of groundwater has caused land near major cities to subside.

LAND DEGRADATION. The expansion of agriculture into marginal lands has caused substantial deforestation and soil degradation in the loss plateau, red soils area, northeast plains, and northwest grasslands. Degraded grassland extends to perhaps 86 million hectares and is expanding at a rate of 1.3 million hectares each year. These grasslands are being converted to crops or being overgrazed. Soil erosion, the result of deforestation and clearance of vegetation cover, extends to perhaps one-sixth of the total land area.

AIR QUALITY. Toxic emissions in the workplace give cause for concern, and outdoor air quality in the north frequently violates Chinese and WHO standards for air quality. Total suspended particulates in the north, for example, are some 525 micrograms per cubic meter compared with the WHO standard of 60–90 micrograms. In China, 26 percent of all deaths are caused by chronic obstructive pulmonary disease, and such diseases are linked to ambient concentrations of fine particulates.

Potentially significant environmental controls are in place that include requirements for environmental impact statements, best-technology standards for some industries, and central treatment of wastes. Economic incentives exist in intent if not in effective practice, and these range from tax rebates and taxes on polluting inputs to a pollution levy system. The levy system charges enterprises for any violation of emissions standards. Emissions that exceed the standard are multiplied by a fee to calculate the total levy. Repeated violations result in fines. Levies may be raised annually until compliance is secured. The fees are generally unrelated to the marginal cost of controlling pollution and offer polluters little incentive to adopt controls. Additionally, excess pollution is only computed for one constituent of pollution, namely, the largest difference between actual emissions and the standard. There is, therefore, no incentive to act on emissions that attract low charges. Finally, fees can be passed on as higher prices, so there is, once again, no incentive to avoid pollution as costs rise. The levies do generate revenue, however, and in 1989 they yielded some Y1.4 billion, or 0.1 percent of China's GNP.

Many of these policies are poorly implemented and exist in the context of controlled input prices, which tend to encourage overuse. An environmental improvement program not associated with such price reform is unlikely to have any significant success. The overlap between the state as the main polluter and the state as the regulator (the problem of the poacher and the gamekeeper) is troubling, although this may mean more efficient cleanup programs once the central authorities are persuaded that environmental improvement is necessary.

Notes

1. This chapter was written before the Soviet Union was dissolved in the fall of 1991. The situation throughout Eastern Europe is changing rapidly, and it is too soon to know how these changes will affect environmental policy. This chapter discusses policies of the Soviet Union and other centrally planned economies before that time.

2. The European Bank for Reconstruction and Development was established in 1990 to help emerging democracies in Eastern Europe move toward market-oriented economies. Members of the European Bank are likely to include all the European countries, Canada, Japan, the United States, and the Soviet Union.

3. The levels also tend to be compared to national standards. But, typically, Eastern European standards have been set absurdly low, well below the standards set by the European community, the United States, or the World Health Organization.

4. Thus if charges are above abatement costs, they can be avoided by installing abatement equipment. If charges are below abatement costs, it is cheaper to pay the charge and pollute. In an optimal system, one would expect some industries to face charges above, and others charges below, abatement costs; some variation will probably occur within each industry as well. Table 9-2 suggests that hardly any polluter faces charge rates above the costs of abatement.

10

Property Rights Failure and Renewable Resources

Previous chapters have sought to explain natural resource degradation by looking at scale factors, notably population; price factors, notably the failure to price at marginal private cost, but also the failure of markets to price at marginal social cost; and physical planning factors, illustrated by Eastern Europe.

The discussion also touches on so-called enabling incentives, which, if in place, assist the process of sustainable resource management. A good example is land tenure, which, if secure, enables the persons owning or using the land to respond positively to price incentives and even planning objectives. The absence of secure tenure is, then, an example of a property rights failure or an institutional failure.[1] In practice, as we shall see, the issue of property rights and resource management is immensely complex and very important. This chapter analyzes the problem of property rights in the context of renewable resources.

The Nature of Renewable Resources

The materials balance approach to studying how the economy interacts with the environment is mentioned in previous chapters. The approach reminds us that using natural resources and disposing waste products are two sides of the same coin. Whatever is taken from the resource sector is transformed into economic goods, which decay over time and become waste. Moreover, the processes whereby natural resources are transformed into economic goods themselves create wastes, such as overburden from mining and liquid wastes from chemical factories. Finally, the act of consuming goods creates waste: packaging materials, human waste, and so on.

Natural resources may be divided broadly into renewable and nonrenewable resources. Nonrenewable resources, as the name implies, are finite, so that using them at all depletes the stock over time. The economic issue with nonrenewable resources is the rate at which the stock should be run down over time. Renewable resources are capable of regeneration. Examples would be fisheries and forests. Their capacity for self-renewal does not, however, mean that they will, in fact, renew themselves. This depends on the management regime. A forest that is clearfelled and then used for livestock, say, does not typically renew itself. Even if the agricultural use is temporary, renewal may be impaired because the soil is eroded and nutrients are lost. A management regime that involves sustainable use allows the resource to renew itself and takes the sustainable yield of the resource. Thus, a fish stock can be fished by harvesting only the mature fish and leaving younger fish to age and breed and grow until they are ready for the next catch. If more than the sustainable yield is taken on a regular basis, the remaining stock has no chance to regenerate. The result is overuse, which threatens the resource with extinction. Extinction may be optimal in some circumstances, but extinguishing a renewable resource conflicts, at least potentially, with the philosophy of sustainable development. The economic issue with renewable resources, then, is the rate at which they should be used so that their stocks are maintained.

Resources that yield a constant flow of services through time, such as solar radiation or tidal or wave energy, are sometimes referred to as renewable resources. These are not, however, the subject of this chapter, which confines itself to biologically renewable resources. The following section analyzes the rate at which renewable resources should be used.

Renewable Resource Analytics: The Fishery

A fishery is a fairly straightforward example of a renewable resource. The first part of figure 10-1 shows a population growth curve that is a logistic function. At low levels of stock, the fish multiply rapidly, between A and B in the diagram. Then they begin to compete for food, and the growth rate slows (from B onward). Eventually, the stock converges on the maximum number that the habitat can sustain; this is the carrying capacity, shown as X_{MAX}. The growth curve begins at X_{MIN}, a minimum viable population, rather than at zero (X_0). This is because many biological populations require a discrete number greater than zero before they breed, Noah's Ark notwithstanding. If the population falls below X_{MIN}, it will tend to zero along the segment AC. For convenience, it is preferable to think of X_{MIN} as the origin—that is, to overlook section AC of the curve.

The second part of figure 10-1 expresses the same picture for rates of growth. That is, the curve shows the rate of change in X—which we write as $\dot{X}$ for time—against the stock of the resource. (The diagram now assumes no section similar to AC in the upper diagram.) The rate of growth is positive at first, reaches a maximum (corresponding to point B in the first part of figure 10-1), and then declines until it reaches the carrying capacity. For convenience, we have not included X_{MIN} in the diagram because doing so would complicate the analysis. Although we have not introduced any economic concepts, a concept of apparent eco-

Figure 10-1. Growth Curves for a Renewable Resource: The Fishery

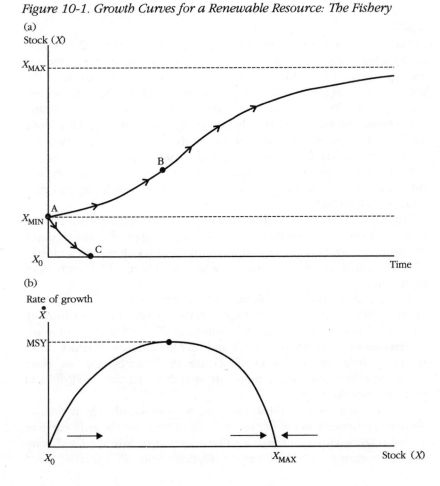

Figure 10-2. Equilibria in the Fishery under Various Management Regimes

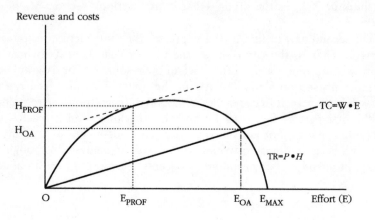

nomic interest already exists in the second part of figure 10-1, which shows a sustainable use curve. We can select any level of stock and the corresponding yield, which is equivalent to the rate of growth of the resource, that can be harvested without reducing the stock of the resource in the next period. One apparently obvious management solution is to choose the maximum sustainable yield, shown as MSY. This looks attractive because we can take the MSY each fishing period, leaving the stock to regenerate in between. Moreover, such a policy produces the highest possible catch. As we shall see, however, MSY is, invariably, not the optimal economic policy even though many resource managers continue to look for MSY.

Figure 10-2 repeats the earlier diagram but changes the horizontal axis to effort. Effort is a measure of the fishing inputs applied to the resource and could be measured in man-days, number of trawlers, and so forth. The diagram in figure 10-2 looks very similar to figure 10-1 apart from this change.

The actual transition is not of concern here (see D.W. Pearce and Turner 1989, chap. 16, for a diagrammatic approach to transforming figure 10-1 into figure 10-2). The intuition is that higher levels of effort correspond to lower levels of stock and that lower levels of effort correspond to higher levels of stock. Thus, the stock decreases as we move along the effort axis. E_{MAX} now corresponds to maximum effort and hence zero stocks (X_0).

With the aid of this transformation, we can supply an immediate economic interpretation of figure 10-2. We can convert the yield curve to a total revenue curve by assuming that each ton of fish harvested commands the same price. Then, harvest, H, times price, P, is total revenue.

The yield curve becomes a total revenue curve, TR $= P \cdot H$. We can also superimpose a total cost curve by assuming that each unit of effort, E, commands the same price, W. Then, TC $= W \cdot E$ is a total cost curve.

Two equilibria are of interest. First, suppose the fishery is owned by a single owner. This single owner will aim to maximize profits, and this will occur at E_{PROF}, where the difference between TR and TC is at a maximum. Note that E_{PROF} does not correspond to the point of maximum sustainable yield. It would do this only if costs were zero. E_{PROF} also looks fairly safe, at least for fish stocks. The equilibrium is a long way from E_{MAX}, which suggests that vesting ownership of a resource in an individual may well secure the conservation of that resource. This conclusion will have to be modified once time is more explicitly considered, but it does suggest one way of securing resource conservation. Notice also that it contrasts starkly with the view that private ownership necessarily leads to resource extinction.

Second, suppose that there is no single owner and that anyone and everyone can come and get what they want. This is the case if the fishery is in the high seas, where territorial rights do not exist. Such resources are known as open-access resources: there are no defined owners and no rules for using the resource. In the case of open access, everyone who realizes a profit by entering the fishery does so. Accordingly, wherever TR is above TC, new entrants come to harvest the resource. They stop only when TC exceeds TR, as it does to the right of E_{oa} in figure 10-2. Accordingly, E_{oa} is the open-access equilibrium. Notice that E_{oa} does not result in the extinction of the resource. Nonetheless, E_{oa} is quite close to E_{MAX}, so the danger of extinction is fairly high. Moreover, if the resource has a minimum critical size, E_{oa} could be even more risky. Finally, as the TC curve becomes flatter, E_{oa} is closer to E_{MAX}. Essentially, the lower the cost of harvesting, the greater the chances of extinction appear to be. This risk has considerable foundation in fact. African savannah elephants, for example, have traditionally been cheap to poach.

The risk of extinction associated with open-access solutions is sometimes referred to as the tragedy of the commons (Hardin 1968). The phrase is somewhat unfortunate because extinction does not necessarily follow (E_{oa} is an equilibrium at which a sustainable yield is taken) and use of common property is usually governed by rules and regulations. That is, under common property, a particular community owns the resource and this community frequently agrees to rules of behavior, including rules that regulate the rate at which the resource is used. A common property equilibrium is therefore likely to be somewhere between E_{PROF} and E_{oa}.

The diagram in figure 10-2 is fundamental to the theory of the optimal management of a renewable resource. Although simplistic, it enables us to posit the following general propositions. From the reasoning advanced so far, we can say that

- An open-access regime, in which no property rights are defined for named individuals or communities, risks extinction of the resource. Nonetheless, in theory, open-access equilibria can be stable, that is, consistent with sustainable use. In practice, open-access contexts reveal the serious risks facing resources such as blue whales, elephants, and many tropical forests
- Private ownership should maximize profits, which, in turn, should lead to restrictions on rates of exploitation and conservation of the resource. In practice, various factors, such as the uncertainty surrounding ownership rights, may lead to the overly rapid exploitation of the resource
- Common property regimes are likely to produce resource use rates somewhere between the solution of private ownership and that of open access. Common property carries much lower risks of resource degradation than open access, and the two should not be confused
- Although intuitively attractive, maximum sustainable yield is unlikely to be a rational management solution for renewable resources.

Introducing Time

The diagram in figure 10-2 is essentially static because it says nothing about how prices might vary with time and nothing about the resource user's discount rate (chapter 3 discusses discount rates). Discounting reflects our tendency to regard costs and benefits in the future as being less important than costs and benefits now. We do so for a number of reasons. We may expect to be richer in the future. If so, we value a dollar in one year's time less highly than a dollar now. In addition, we may be impatient and prefer benefits now to benefits in the future. Another factor is the productivity of capital: if we invest in a machine, that investment tends to yield a flow of services over time and those services have higher values than the cost of the investment. Whether we look at individual valuations over time (time preference) or at the capital market (capital productivity), we discount the future at a positive rate.

The discount rate is critical for determining the rate at which renewable (and exhaustible) resources should be used. Without going into the derivation, which is explained in detail in D.W. Pearce and Turner (1989), we may state a basic rule as follows:

$$\left(\begin{array}{c} \text{Marginal product} \\ \text{of the resource} \end{array} \right) + \left(\begin{array}{c} \text{rate of capital} \\ \text{appreciation} \end{array} \right) = \text{Discount rate.}$$

The marginal product is the resource's own rate of growth, in this case, the rate at which the fishery grows. The rate of capital appreciation refers to the possibility of collecting capital gains by leaving the fish unharvested. Such gains occur if the price of fish is rising through time so that their value appreciates when they are left in the sea.

The fishery should be harvested according to this rule. Consider some hypothetical numbers. Imagine that the discount rate is 10 percent, the growth rate is 3 percent, and prices are growing at 5 percent. The choice is between harvesting 100 tons of fish now at $100 per ton or waiting until later. The relevant calculations, in dollars, are as follows:

Indicator	Fish now	Wait
Revenue	10,000	10,815[a]
Discounted value	10,000	9,832[b]

a. The stock grows at 3 percent to become 103 tons, which are then sold at $105 per ton.

b. $10,815 / 1.1.

Waiting is not worthwhile, and the harvest takes place now. If the discount rate exceeds the combined growth of the fish and the capital gain, the resource is harvested sooner rather than later. If the discount rate is 6 percent, the calculations can be repeated to obtain the following:

Indicator	Fish now	Wait
Revenue	10,000	10,815
Discounted value	10,000	10,203

It now pays to wait because the discount rate is below the combined effects of growth and capital gain.

Finally, if the discount rate is equal to the sum of the effects of growth and capital gain, the discounted values are equal for fishing now or waiting. Thus if the discount rate in the above example is 8.15 percent, the discounted value of the catch obtained by waiting is $10,000, the same as harvesting the catch now. In essence, observing this basic rule precludes the resource owner from switching harvests between periods. A tradeoff exists between harvesting additional fish now and allowing the fish to remain in the water and thus increase future yields. At the optimum, the two contributions have the same present values (see Magrath 1989).

Applications of Fishery Economics

In reality, dynamic modeling of fisheries is far more complex than the previous section suggests (the definitive work on dynamic modeling is C.W. Clark 1990). Many works apply such models to actual fisheries and animal harvesting, and examples of these are given below.

Fisheries in Southeast Asia

Overfishing in Southeast Asia (mainly the countries of Brunei, Indonesia, Malaysia, the Philippines, Singapore, and Thailand) is well documented (Pauly and Thia-Eng 1988). Catch rates per unit of fishing effort have declined considerably since 1961 by at least a factor of ten for most species. Studies show that 60–70 percent of the decline in catches is due to overfishing. Most fishing is done by large numbers of small trawlers using nets with small meshes that catch many of the species' young.

Figure 10-3 shows clearly how, in the Philippines, fishery effort in the demersal and pelagic fisheries has moved the growth curves introduced earlier well beyond the point of maximum economic profit (rent) and toward effective open-access equilibria. As a result, rent in the fishery has dissipated totally, producing low average income for fishermen. Profits could be raised substantially if the fishery effort were restricted, as has happened in many of the world's fisheries. Some bans have been enacted in Southeast Asia. A ban was put into effect in the Southern Samar Sea in 1976, and Indonesia banned trawling in 1980. But factors other than effort also affect fisheries, including water pollution caused by industry and unregulated sewage, the destruction of mangroves, and sedimentation caused by erosion from logging.

The Pacific Seal Fur Industry

In the nineteenth century, North Pacific fur seals were harvested substantially as they migrated along the west coast of America to the Bering Strait (this section is based on Wilen 1976). These seals were an open-access resource, with vessels from Canada, Japan, the Soviet Union, the United Kingdom, and the United States taking part. In the 1890s massive exploitation occurred, followed by falling catches and the exodus of many firms from the industry. Various attempts to curtail catches were made, culminating in a 1911 treaty (which still exists today). The industry typifies what one might expect from an open-access situation. As we saw, open access can result in extinction. On the other hand, open access can also offer incentives to secure a common property approach by collectively regulating the catch. The question is whether the industry would have driven the resource to extinction, or whether it was already moving toward regulating itself as a form of common property?

A bioeconomic model of the industry was constructed to show the conditions under which firms enter and exit the seal fur industry. Basically, if profits are possible, firms enter the industry. If losses accrue, firms exit. By building in price data and using the number of vessels to measure effort, the model estimated the steady state stock (the stock that could be sustained indefinitely) to be some 580,000 seals, with a sustained maximum yield of around 80,000 seals. In fact, the stock of seals exceeded 1,200,000 in 1882 but fell to less than 400,000 just fifteen years later, when it had already begun to recover somewhat. Indeed, the number of vessels (the measure of effort) fell dramatically from 1892 onward. The path by which the changes took place suggests that the industry may well have been moving toward the optimal population by the very end of the nineteenth century. The industry was monopolized at

Figure 10-3. Overfishing in the Demersal and Pelagic Fisheries of the Philippines

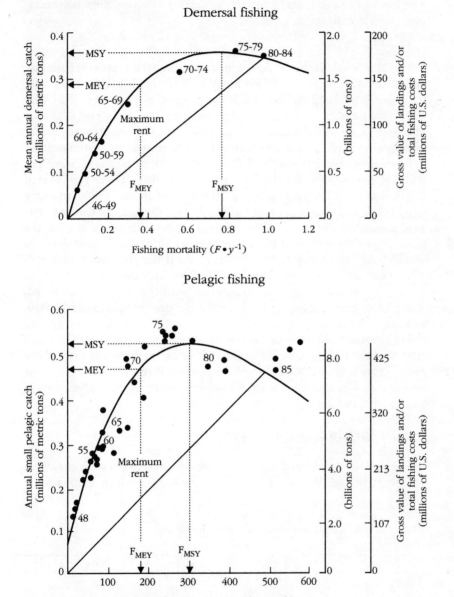

Note: Beginning in the 1970s, fishing effort went beyond the maximum economic profitability yield (MEY), and even beyond the maximum sustainable yield (MSY) and approached open-access catch rates. In both the demersal and the pelagic fisheries, the profit rate is zero. Significant increases in profits could be achieved by reducing catch rates.

Source: Pauly and Thia-Eng (1988).

the turn of the century and later regulated internationally. We shall never know, therefore, if the open-access solution was a stable equilibrium. The lesson to be learned, however, is that open access does not necessarily lead to extinction.

The Blue Whale

The blue whale is the world's largest creature (this section is based on Spence 1973). This fact alone justifies the efforts made to preserve it after the wholesale slaughter that took place especially between 1928 and 1938, when catches peaked at 26,000 whales a year (table 10-1).

Before human exploitation, some 220,000 blue whales were in the southern hemisphere and 8,000 in the northern. Current estimates put the remaining populations at 11,000 and 3,000, respectively. Some authorities suggest that the numbers are even smaller. Spence (1973) estimates that the maximum sustainable catch was around 9,900 whales a year, which was clearly exceeded in 1930–39, when annual catches averaged around 17,000 whales. An optimal catch, taking into account the costs of whaling and the commercial value of blubber, oils, and so forth, would have been some 9,000 whales a year if the population had been allowed to achieve its optimal level of 67,000. This could only have been done if all whaling had been abandoned until that level was achieved. The 67,000 figure is clearly far from the existing population of 14,000, or fewer, whales.

This exercise shows that on purely commercial grounds, the catch rates for blue whales were not optimal. The catches tended to reveal the open-access solution rather than the maximum profit solution. Given the scientific and existence value of blue whales, commercial analysis clearly dictates that the stock is too low.

Renewable Resources and Games

The previous sections distinguish common property resources (which are owned by everyone) from open-access resources (which are owned by

Table 10-1. Global Catches of Whales, 1910–87

Year	Catch
1910–19	26,819
1920–29	69,217
1930–39	170,427
1940–49	46,199
1950–59	35,948
1960–69	7,434
1970–79	23
1980–87	0

Source: Unpublished figures from the Bureau of International Whaling Statistics.

no one). Both are distinguished from private property resources, which are owned by someone. It might appear that, for resource conservation, private ownership is preferable to common property, which is, in turn, preferable to open access. If this is so, the implications for environmental policy are formidable because the conferment of resource rights could be a significant weapon for improving the environment. In light of this potential finding, it is important to analyze more closely the advantages and disadvantages of common property, open-access, and private property regimes.

Environmental property involves sets of rights that govern the use of resources, including the waste assimilation functions of receiving environments. These include the right to conserve, consume, sell, lease, bequeath, and exclude others from exercising those rights. In private property, the rights are conferred on individuals or corporations. Under common property, the rights are usually conferred on a fairly well-defined community, such as a tribe, village, or patriarchal or matriarchal group. Rights may cover specific resources, such as a particular kind of tree, crop residues for grazing, and so on. In the developing world, the structure of resource rights is frequently very complex, and simple prescriptions to privatize or communalize resources may be doomed to failure unless the structure of rights is carefully analyzed and understood.

Game theory can be used to assess the risk of a renewable resource held under common property or open access becoming extinct or degraded. Game theory analyzes the behavior of individuals or groups contingent on the reactions of other individuals or groups. What A does, for example, depends on how he thinks B, C, and D will react. Two models are particularly relevant to the problems associated with renewable resources; these are the prisoners' dilemma and the assurance game. An analogous presentation is also provided using a basic public goods model. Once a public good is provided to one person, it is automatically provided to others and no one can be excluded from receiving the benefits of access to it. In such circumstances, one would expect to find free riders—individuals who aim to secure the benefit without meeting the cost of providing the good.

The Prisoners' Dilemma

The original formulation of the prisoners' dilemma concerned two prisoners being held in separate cells and accused of a jointly executed crime. Each can confess or deny participation (the prisoners' dilemma is treated in many textbooks; see, for example, Varian 1987).

From prisoner A's point of view, it is always better to confess, regardless of what prisoner B does. If B denies involvement, A is freed. If B confesses, A gets three years if he confesses compared with six years if he denies involvement. For A, $-3, 0$ dominates $-6, -1$. Prisoner B has the same point of view: it always pays to confess. By confessing, B secures

$-3,0$, which dominates $-6,-1$. So, from the individual standpoint, it pays each prisoner to confess. But both prisoners are better off still if they refuse to admit any involvement in the crime. If both deny the crime, each gets one year in jail—the $-1,-1$ combination. The dilemma is that both will opt for an inefficient strategy (each could be better off; see the following matrix for payoff).[2]

Strategy of prisoner A	Strategy of prisoner B	
	Confess	Deny
Confess	$-3,-3$	$0,-6$
Deny	$-6,0$	$-1,-1$

The prisoners' dilemma is an example of a noncooperative game. Since the two prisoners cannot communicate, they are isolated (the game is also known as the isolation paradox). Even if they could communicate, however, each prisoner still has an incentive to defect from a cooperative strategy. Thus, the cooperative strategy produces the result $-1,-1$, but each prisoner can get off altogether by turning state's evidence and implicating the other. Any agreement must be binding.

The prisoners' dilemma is directly relevant to the problems of managing renewable resources. First, many renewable resources are not privately owned, so there are many actual or potential users. Second, each individual has an incentive to use more of the resource because this approach yields higher personal profits. This is the dominant strategy issue. Third, if all users behave in this way, the resource is at risk of being overexploited. Fourth, any agreement risks being unstable because of the incentive to defect.

If correct, this analysis has formidable implications for how renewable resources are managed. Either the resource must be privatized, which could mean dispossessing many users of their customary, or even legal, right to it, particularly if it cannot be divided, or the resource must be subject to some form of state regulation and control.

The picture changes somewhat if the game is repeated. Suppose resource user A defects from an agreement this year. If the game is played again next year, that is, if the same issue of resource use arises again, the other players can punish A by leaving him out of any agreement. Such threats might induce each player to adopt the efficient outcome the first time around, or perhaps each player will comply with the agreement after playing the game a few times. Such tit-for-tat strategies are often witnessed in international agreements that are renewed on a fairly regular basis. But, obviously, the force of such sanctions is limited if the game is played only a few times.[3]

The Assurance Game

Some writers have suggested that managing renewable resources in the context of common property is not best typified by the prisoners' dilemma (Hardin 1968 is famous for characterizing the problem of resource overuse as a game of prisoners' dilemma). Instead, the interdependence that exists between the players makes it more akin to an assurance game. The assurance game is shown in the matrix below. This time the players are partners, say, a married couple. One prefers to go to the ballet, the other to the cinema, but neither wishes to attend any event alone.

| Strategy of | Preference of prisoner B | |
prisoner A	Ballet	Cinema
Ballet	1,2	−1,−1
Cinema	−1,−1	2,1

Partner A prefers the cinema to the ballet; partner B prefers the ballet to the cinema (to check this, note that A gets 2 from the cinema if B goes with him and 1 from the ballet if B goes with him). But A would rather go to the ballet with B than go to the cinema alone. This game has two equilibria, whereas the prisoners' dilemma has only one. If both go to the ballet, the payoff is 1,2, and if both go to the cinema, the payoff is 2,1. The problem is to obtain the assurance of the other player that he or she will keep the agreement. Once this assurance is obtained, there is no incentive to defect (see Runge 1981, 1982; for a criticism of Runge's paper, see Mäler 1990).

Supporters of the assurance paradigm argue that overexploitation of renewable resources in open-access and common property situations can be solved by cooperative agreement. The conclusion of the prisoners' dilemma paradigm, that some form of externally imposed state control is required, is not warranted. Community management of the resource is, they argue, viable.

Extensions of Game Theory

Both the prisoners' dilemma and the assurance game offer insights into how renewable resource management should be structured. For example, if the situation is best characterized by the prisoners' dilemma game, incentive systems must be devised to discourage defection. Such systems need not consist of payments in cash or kind; incentives could include, for example, strengthening tribal or community bonds to decrease isolation. In the assurance game, institutions that encourage assurance may have to be established or strengthened. Both paradigms are, however, of limited value as complete descriptions of reality.

First, as noted, resource use games tend to be repeated over time. This opens up opportunities for coercing defectors in future games. Second, the examples have been of two-person games. The real world consists of multiperson (or *n* person) games. In multiperson games each individual has far less control over events, whereas in two-person games each player controls the outcome or shares control with a partner or opponent. In multiperson games, motives other than pure self-gain are likely to come into play. One such issue is the problem of free riding. Free riding arises when individuals think they can gain at the expense of others—for example, they do not pay for communal services that nonetheless benefit them as individuals. But the existence of free riders in the natural resource context is unclear. One bidding game failed to show that Nepalese farmers would spend all the money gained from a financial windfall on themselves. Respondents said they would devote around 50 percent of the windfall to village investments for the general good (Bromley and Chapagain 1984).

Although game theory analysis suggests various hypotheses, only empirical observation and testing offer real guidance for how resources should best be managed. The empirical literature on different resource management regimes and their relative success is very large. These works suggest that no single regime is universally best suited to the wise management of resources. In some cases, private ownership fares well, in others communal management works well. State ownership may work but frequently does not because it introduces objectives and bureaucratic aims that conflict with efficient or equitable use. The next section illustrates these points.

Resource Management Regimes

Using game theory to analyze resource management suggests that communal management may break down if there are incentives to ride free, that communal management might work if systems of assurances can be obtained, that privatization may be one solution to inefficient resource use, and that state control may be the only other stable regime. Table 10-2 shows the characteristics of rights and duties and privileges of four types of property regimes. Property is the right to a flow of benefits, and that right is secure only as long as others agree to honor the right. A privilege, in contrast, is a use not accompanied by a right, and that use can be exercised because others have no rights either: this is open access (the terminology is developed in Bromley 1989).

Privatization

Privatization is a frequent policy prescription for solving the problems caused by overusing resources under open access and common property (the theoretical literature underlining this proposition is developed in Cheung 1970; Demsetz 1967). Privatization may take several forms. For land, an option is for the authorities to confer title to individuals through documentation and to enforce that title. Title without enforcement is largely meaningless (see Lemel 1988). Documented land title is prescribed in contexts where owners may be threatened by outsiders with

Table 10-2. Definition of Property Regimes

Type of property	Definition
State	Individuals have a duty to observe the rules of use determined by the controlling agency. The agency has the right to determine those rules.
Private	Individuals have the right to undertake socially acceptable uses and a duty to refrain from unacceptable uses. Others have a duty to respect individual rights.
Common	A management group has the right to exclude nonmembers. Nonmembers have a duty to abide by that exclusion. Co-owners comprise the management group and have rights and duties related to the use of resources.
Open access	No users or owners are defined. Individuals have the privilege but not the right to use resources.

Source: Adapted from Bromley (1989), p. 872.

rival claims to the land or where land improvement raises land values, which act as a magnet to land speculators. However, land titling without enforcement has no particular advantages over customary ownership based on tradition.

Lack of formal title to land, in combination with factors such as the lack of transfer rights, the weakening of indigenous institutions, or the increasing scarcity of land, may result in various forms of uncertainty that could contribute to resource degradation (see Feder and Noronha 1987). First, in the absence of rights to sell or transfer land, the land "owner" may be unable to realize the value of any improvements and thus has little incentive to invest in long-term measures such as soil conservation. Second, if land values rise, the occupier may be unable to resist a takeover by land speculators or wealthier, more powerful farmers. Such groups may be even less interested in conservation, perhaps because land acquisition is a hedge against inflation or a means of securing tax concessions. Third, without title, land may not be sold on the open market, which means that it will not go to the highest value-added uses. This bias may or may not be conducive to resource degradation since high value added need not be synonymous with environmentally benign land use. Fourth, lack of title often means that the landholder has no collateral acceptable to the formal lending sector and is forced to borrow from the informal sector at very high interest rates. In rural Thailand, for example, Feder and others (1986) found that 90 percent of medium- and long-term loans were received by farmers with land titles even though such farmers constituted only 50 percent of the sample investigated. Legal owners offering land as collateral obtained between 50 and 520 percent more credit than farmers without collateral.

Interest rates on formal credit were one-third lower than those on non-institutional credit in the informal sector (Bromley and Cernea 1989, among others, question whether title to land is essential for obtaining access to credit since credit markets have operated for centuries without private ownership of land).

At the same time, the absence of title to land does not necessarily mean that landholders lack security. Attempts to give title to land in French West Africa were rejected by communities who preferred to rely on customary title (Lemel 1988). A review of traditional tenure systems in Ghana, Kenya, and Rwanda found that, under such systems, farmers enjoy transfer rights on their lands and that those rights are sanctioned by the community. Moreover, as circumstances change, so do tenure systems. Change usually occurs as a gradual evolution to individual rights, although these rights are not always equivalent to private property since other community members continue to have secondary rights to collect fuelwood or graze the land in question (Migot-Adholla and others 1991). Figure 10-4 summarizes how secure title may link land values and productivity.

The school of thought that favors privatization as the solution to open-access, common property problems believes that resource rights tend to become better defined as resource scarcity emerges. Thus, societies where population pressure is low have no need to establish exclusive rights to tracts of land that are not under immediate pressure. Effectively, the value of marginal land is zero. Such conditions favor usufructuary rights, which are rights to use the land but not to own it. There is no need for a right to sell or buy land because land is in excess supply. Land abandoned because it is no longer fertile is either left fallow, as with systems of shifting agriculture, or reallocated by tribal authorities to other potential users. Farm production and livestock systems necessarily use land intensively because land is the factor of production in excess supply. As population grows, pressure on hitherto open-access resources may result in the development of rules and conventions about resource use, effectively turning open-access resources into common property resources, as the assurance game paradigm predicts. Nonmarginal land comes under increasing pressure as population growth forces farmers to subdivide the land more and more to reduce the fallow periods.

As population pressure grows, property rights become even more precise until they encompass exclusive use and ownership by individuals. This view contrasts with the prisoners' dilemma phenomenon, which predicts that common property conventions will break down under population pressure and use of the resource will revert back to anarchic open access.

If this evolutionary view of how individual property rights develop is correct, the enforcement of individual rights should be greater in land- or resource-scarce countries or regions than in areas where the pressure on

Figure 10-4. Relation between Secure Title and Productivity of the Land

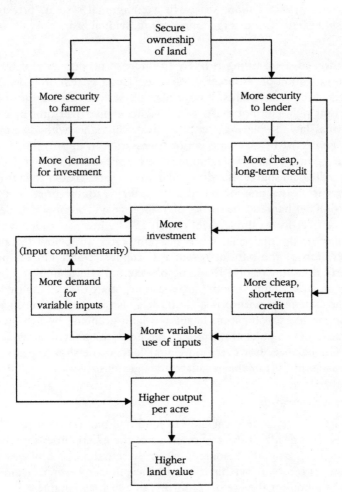

Source: Feder (1987).

resources is low. Ault and Rutman (1979) argue that this is the case for Africa:

> Differences in the land tenure systems described are attributable to the relative scarcity of land created by varying degrees of population pressure and reliance upon commercial agriculture. Tribal institutions governing land use and occupation respond to changes in economic conditions. As population pressure or the importance of commercial

agriculture increases, changes in the land tenure system should result in a system that defines the individual rights to the land more clearly. As land becomes more scarce in a communal system, private and social benefits will diverge unless the individual bears the full costs of his actions.

If enforced, land titling is likely to improve productivity of the land and conservation of resources when it replaces a system of ill-defined or nonexistent property rights. But the absence of documented title does not mean that rights do not exist. Many rights evolve over time as custom and tribal law. Replacing complex historical rights with documented rights conferred by the state is not necessarily an improvement at all. Moreover, individual ownership may be consistent with either depleting or degrading a resource. If individual discount rates greater than resource regeneration rates are combined with a high ratio of price to cost of extraction per harvest, the owner of a resource will optimally deplete the resource (see, for example, McConnell 1983). Indeed, resource extinction may be optimal even when discount rates are below the rate of regeneration of the natural resource (Cropper 1988). Finally, private property does not resolve the issue of external effects imposed by one owner on another unless both parties can negotiate the externality.[4]

Some experience with privatization has also been negative. In Kenya and Botswana, privatization facilitated land grabbing by new political elites after the colonial era. (Indeed, the practice imitated colonial practice.) On balance, however, individual land ownership appears to be consistent with sustainable resource management.

State Ownership

At first glance, state ownership of land and natural resources should address the tragedy of the commons since the externalities ingrained in the overuse of common resources become internalized to a single owner, the state. For state ownership to work efficiently, however, the state must be able to monitor the use of resources, establish acceptable rules of use by individuals and communities, and enforce those rules. Typically, this has not been the experience with state ownership.

In Nepal, faced with excess demand for fuelwood, fodder, and other forest products, the government nationalized all unregistered forest and wasteland in 1957. In 1961 the definition of forest land was extended to include all land adjoining forest areas that had been left fallow for more than two years. The aim was to establish sustainable use of the forest. In practice, the government could not supervise the use of forests because, throughout the country, access was frequently very difficult and government resources were minimal. Rules and regulations were impossible to enforce. For example, fuelwood was not supposed to be collected without the authority of a forest ranger. Timber for building houses required a permit from forest offices often located far from the forest. More significant, communities that had hitherto tried to protect their forests from outsiders now had no legal authority to do so. Because the forests were no longer theirs to own in the customary sense, the community had no incentive to protect them. The regulation allowing land left fallow for more than two years to be appropriated by the state simply discouraged farmers from practicing fallow agriculture, encouraging overcultivation and hastening soil degradation. The Nepal forest nationalization experiment was short-lived, and efforts were made in the late 1970s to hand the forests back to communities (Arnold and Campbell 1986).

Communal Management

Anthropologists and sociologists presume that local communities best understand their own environments and hence are best capable of managing natural resources in a sustainable way. Certainly tribal and peasant societies have formidable knowledge of soils, natural medicines, risk-minimizing cropping strategies, and so on. Similarly, these communities have elaborate rules and regulations to ensure sustainable use of natural resources. Mutual support within the community and storing produce for hungry days are but two examples (Noronha 1988). Although all this is true, such communities do not necessarily take care of nature. Many examples of successful communal management systems, where success is measured by survival, occur in communities that have no need to destroy their relatively abundant resources; because resources are abundant, the element of resource management per se never arises.[5] Communal systems vary substantially within broad types of land users—agriculturists and transhumants—so that generalizations are far from easy (box 10-1). Similar environments do not even correspond to similar social and political structures.

The prisoners' dilemma game predicts that communal management will break down. The assurance game suggests that communal management is feasible. The empirical experience tends to support both propositions, but communal schemes break down for many reasons not necessarily related to the tragedy of the commons (the conflict between individual and collective objectives). Various factors are often at work.

First, colonial rule has been implicated in the collapse of some communal management systems. Colonialism, it is argued, interfered with traditional systems of self-regulation and resource management and favored cash economies. To obtain surpluses to buy market products, farmers overused land and degraded resources, frequently moving subsistence production to marginal land, which was accompanied by the loss of forest and conflict with transhumants (Ciriancy-Wantrup and Bishop 1975). Colonialists found little favor with shifting agriculture and transhumance, even though both systems were suited to climatic and geographic conditions. The creation of forest reserves and game parks also

---

Box 10-1. Resource Rights under Traditional Tenure Systems in Africa

Under traditional tenure systems in Africa, ownership rights, management rights, and use rights often reside with different individuals. The same piece of land may be used by different people for different purposes. Notable differences, which can readily give rise to conflict in the absence of arbitration and control procedures, occur, for example, in

- The right of pastoralists to use the land of sedentary farmers
- The right to use trees, or tree products, on land farmed by someone else
- The right to use different products (such as crop residue) from a single piece of land.

A typical process giving rise to resource degradation is for sedentary farmers to claim land by clearing and cultivating it. Other users may then be forced onto marginal lands that are ecologically fragile. Pastoralists in particular become marginalized. Sedentary farmers may also vary their activities by introducing livestock, at the expense of transhumant herders who previously coexisted with them.

Fallow lands are the customary way of allowing cultivated land to regenerate. Traditionally, in many systems, fallow land reverts to the community and can be reassigned. As long as population pressure is moderate, such procedures are unlikely to cause significant disruption. When population pressure is great, however, cultivators fear their fallow lands will be reassigned, leaving them landless. The result is an incentive to shorten the amount of time land is left fallow and to cultivate plots continuously to keep them from being assigned to someone else.

Generalizations are impossible because tenure systems vary substantially, but traditional tenure systems seem to be consistent with good resource management as long as population pressure is low. As soon as population pressure is high, the incentives to defect from communal arrangements are also high, especially when migrants bring new practices and social norms to the area.

---

deprived traditional forest users of highly valued products (Noronha 1988). More generally, colonialism reduced the land available to indigenous populations, especially shifting cultivators and transhumants. In Kenya, for example, the Masai lost their best grazing lands to European settlers. In Zimbabwe, over 80 percent of class I lands were alienated for settlers. Institutions were interposed between the cultivator or livestock owner and the rule maker. Decisionmaking was thus removed from the local level and transferred to the center, and the distance meant that decisionmakers had less and less local understanding of resources and their links to human survival. Less obvious effects on resource use arose from restrictions on migration, which had enabled communities to adjust to local resource scarcity. The restrictions effectively forced communities to overuse resources since the safety valve of migration was less and less available.

Second, population growth obviously pressures communal systems as existing land is divided between an increasing number of people or is used by increasing herds of livestock. Picardi and Seifert (1976) argue that a period of relatively high rainfall in the Sahel, accompanied by public health measures and deep-water well technology, encouraged the population of humans and herds to expand. When rainfall fell below average, the use rate was too high for the available rangeland resources. Population growth is also linked to colonialism, which ended tribal wars, and the arrival of preventive medicine.

Third, technology can induce the overuse of resources, as with the introduction of motorized fishing boats in San Miguel Bay in the Philippines, chain saw technology in the Amazon forest, and high-velocity rifles for poaching elephants in Africa. But the record is not consistent because the effects of technology depend on the prevailing social values. Thus the introduction of steel axes among the Siane in Papua New Guinea did not increase destruction of the forest. Although axes reduced the time needed to clear and fence gardens, users chose to spend their new free time in prestige-enhancing activities rather than in planting and tending bigger gardens. Among the Machiguenga in the Peruvian Amazon, however, the introduction of steel tools did increase garden sizes and encouraged farmers to produce manioc rather than collect wild food (Noronha 1988).

Clearly, communal management systems break down for many reasons. Even when these factors are not present, would communal management break down in any event because social objectives frequently diverge from individual objectives? A study of forty-one villages in South India suggests that villages do provide public goods and services without the external sanction of government (Wade 1987). Villagers organize their own standing fund, which is distinct from local government monies, maintain village guards to protect crops, and pay common irrigators to distribute water to the rice fields. The villages also supply schooling, repair wells, rid themselves of monkeys, and so on. Oxen and buffalo are needed for traction, but the villages have no common land as such. The animals therefore graze close to the crops in the growing season, and livestock feeding is strictly controlled by field guards. Any animal found grazing on crops is arrested, and its owner must pay a fine to secure its release. Once the crops are gathered, the stubble becomes common property for livestock use. The use of this common property is regulated by detailed agreements between the village council and the herders. Livestock is allocated to land at night, and herders recoup the charges they pay for common grazing by selling the manure produced. Detailed and extensive regulations also apply to livestock.

Much the same form of regulation applies to irrigation water, a notable source of conflict. Common irrigators decide how to allocate the water. Each field is entitled to be adequately wetted so that no downstream user is placed at a disadvantage. What is the incentive for these examples of strict communal management? The main incentive appears to be the size of the collective benefit. Although incentives to defect, that is, to ride free, remain in existence, village authorities devote considerable time and effort to demonstrating that the returns to collective management are much higher. Moreover, the sanctions for defecting are enforced from within the system rather than from outside (which is what the prisoners' dilemma game predicts). Such rules are a necessary ingredient of communal management.

Conclusions

The following conclusions emerge for the management of renewable resources in the realms of open access and common property.

Open-access regimes contain high risks of resource degradation even though, technically, an equilibrium should exist at which average profits are zero and the resource is used sustainably. The risk arises because the resource stock may not be known with accuracy and because the minimum viable size of the stock is frequently quite high.

Open access must be distinguished from common property, in which sets of rules typically exist for the management and sustainable use of the resource. Even common property has built-in risks of overexploitation because the private good diverges from the collective good. If common property regimes break down, it cannot be assumed that they do so because of the internal contradiction between social and private benefit. Many other factors contribute to the destruction of common property systems: the insertion of alien values by colonialists, exogenous technological change, and population growth.

Privatization, the right of individuals to use or own resources, is attractive because it provides incentives for individuals to develop resources. Even if common property regimes are stable and sustainable, they may not cause incomes to rise over time. Privatization can provide dynamic incentives to improve land and resources but is also consistent with optimal resource degradation and the continued existence of externalities among owners.

Common property management regimes do work, especially when the incentives for communality are high. This is typically the case when the collective benefit is high, for example, the need to avoid the risk of total collapse.

Appendix: A Public Goods Model

An alternative way of showing the contrast between the cooperative and noncooperative solutions to a game is through a public goods model. (We omit the mathematics without losing continuity by going directly to the discussion of figure 10-5.)

Figure 10-5. Cooperative and Noncooperative Solutions in Common Property Management

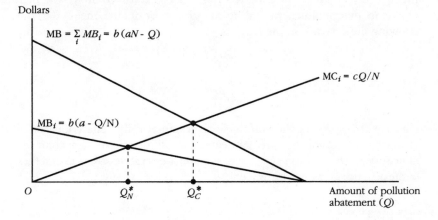

Imagine a group of producers who generate pollution in the same quantities. Each producer faces the same benefit function, that is, the benefits of abating pollution that arise when all producers do so. Specifically, following the example of Barrett (1989), let the benefit function for the *i*th producer be

$$B_i(Q) = b[aQ - (Q^2 / 2N)]$$

where Q is total abatement, a and b are parameters, and N is the number of producers. Each producer faces an abatement cost function:

$$C_i(q_i) = cq_i^2 / 2$$

where Q is the sum of q_i, and q is the level at which each producer abates pollution.

The global objective is to maximize net social benefits, that is, to maximize

$$S = b[aNQ - (Q^2 / 2)] - (cQ^2 / 2N).$$

Differentiating S from Q and setting it equal to zero gives

$$dS / dQ = baN - (2bQ / 2) - (2cQ / 2N) = 0$$

or

$$Q_c{}^* = aN^2 / [N + (c / b)].$$

Since Q equals Nq, we also have

$$q_c{}^* = aN / [N + (c / b)].$$

$Q_c{}^*$ and $q_c{}^*$ are the cooperative solutions for the socially desirable level of abatement and the desirable level of abatement by each producer.

The noncooperative outcome can be obtained as follows. Assume that each producer chooses his abatement level in the belief that the abatement levels of all other producers are given. Each country will then equate its marginal benefit with its marginal cost of abatement. Without showing the derivation, the result is

$$Q_N{}^* = aN / [1 + (c / b)]$$

and

$$q_N{}^* = a / [1 + (c / b)].$$

Figure 10-5 shows the solutions diagrammatically. The cooperative solution, $Q_c{}^*$, involves a greater degree of pollution abatement than the noncooperative solution, $Q_N{}^*$, yet the noncooperative solution emerges in the absence of a binding agreement.

Notes

1. Terminology varies, and many writers see these failures as instances of market or government failure. They argue that markets have failed to evolve for many resources and that governments frequently determine resource rights.

2. The payoff matrix illustrates some other technical concepts. Each player has a dominant strategy that will be pursued regardless of what the other does. Confessing is also a Nash equilibrium in which A's choice is optimal given B's choice, and B's choice is optimal given A's choice.

3. Strictly, cooperative agreements are more likely to be kept if the game is repeated indefinitely. Games with finite repetitions still face the incentive to defect, which is inherent in the prisoners' dilemma.

4. Defenders of the privatization argument generally argue that externalities between owners are the subject of such private bargains and that they preserve the optimality of the assignment of private property rights, that is, the Coase theorem.

5. Noronha (1988, p. 32) states that, "when resources are relatively widely available and trade is limited, there is no need to destroy resources which can neither be traded nor consumed. To convert limited technical capability and limited demand into a virtue of care is, therefore, quite misleading."

11

Poverty, Income Distribution, and Environment

Part one of this book focused on the meaning and measurement of sustainable development. For development to be sustainable, development policy must pay far more attention to natural and built environments. This, at its simplest, is the policy implication of sustainability. In discussing sustainability, part one places comparatively little emphasis on the issue of inequality, but in fact three types of inequality or inequity are important in this context:

- Inequality through time: intergenerational equity
- Inequality between nations at a given point in time: intragenerational equity between nations
- Inequality within a nation at a given point in time: intragenerational equity within a nation.

Sustainable development has clear implications for intergenerational equity; in fact, sustainability has been defined as some sort of intergenerational equity. Sustainability involves holding total capital stocks at least constant to ensure that future generations have the same capability to develop as current generations. Environmental capital is a vital part of that stock since it renders the life-support functions that make a reasonable quality of life feasible and, in some people's view, make existence possible.

But is sustainable development relevant to inequality now? Some authors distrust the emphasis that sustainability approaches give to environmental quality. This emphasis appears to some, for example, to be a conspiracy of the rich nations to conserve natural assets in the poor nations simply because those assets yield utility to the rich countries. On this view, not only does the asset generate benefits mainly outside poor countries, but conservation precludes poor countries from using the asset for development. Thus tropical forests yield the benefits of existence value and option value to rich countries, but these values do not translate into flows of cash for the poor, whereas development options might. This view contains a clear element of truth but misses much of the thrust of the sustainability approach.

First, sustainable development is concerned with inequality between countries. If the pattern of demand for traded natural resources in rich countries encourages unsustainable management of those resources in poor countries, that pattern of demand may threaten development prospects in the future. Those prospects are based on the comparative advantage that natural resources confer on the developing world. Hence, inequality between nations (intragenerational inequality) is relevant to the sustainable development of the developing world. On this hypothesis, inequality between nations may, in certain policy environments, foster unsustainable development. In other words, not only does sustainability affect equity, but inequality also affects sustainability.

Second, inequality within a nation may foster unsustainability because the poor, who rely on natural resources more heavily than the rich, would perhaps deplete natural resources faster if they had no real prospects of gaining access to other types of resources. This is the poverty-environment hypothesis. Moreover, degraded environments can accelerate the process of impoverishment, again because the poor depend directly on natural assets. As we shall see, this circular link between poverty, environment, and poverty is both far more complex and far more common than generally imagined.

There are differing views about the links between poverty and environmental degradation in the developing world. The received wisdom is perhaps summed up by the Brundtland Commission's remarks on the Sahel region (World Commission on Environment and Development 1987, p. 31):

> No other region more tragically suffers the vicious cycle of poverty leading to environmental degradation, which leads in turn to even greater poverty.

It is easy to see how environmental degradation induces poverty. The poorest people in the world depend directly on natural resources for their food, energy, water, and income. If grasslands are degraded, livestock suffers and income is lost. If woodlands and forests are cut, fuelwood becomes scarce. If soil is eroded, crop productivity falls.

But does poverty cause environmental degradation? The literature on the subject is sparse and frequently confusing. The effects of poverty are difficult to separate from those of population growth. Population growth can exacerbate poverty but also be a response to it as households invest in children for long-term security (see chapter 6). Population growth is also associated with environmental degradation as communities expand to ecologically fragile lands or urban peripheries. In this case, however, population growth, rather than poverty per se, generates environmental degradation.

There are no easy answers. Ideally, one wants to know what happens to environmental change when poverty increases or decreases, other factors (such as population change) being held constant. Moreover, short- and long-run associations must be distinguished. It is frequently argued that the very process of getting out of poverty through economic growth degrades the environment in the short run, but that in the long run higher incomes enable individuals and nations to afford a better, albeit different, environment. This process might even describe the economic history of the industrial economies. Initially, agriculture was intensified, often with environmental loss such as the removal of tree cover. Industrialization followed with all the consequent problems of pollution. Once industrialization was complete, the industrial economies began to restore and control the environment.

How far such a characterization of the economic growth process can be applied to today's developing world is open to question. The model tends to assume that ecological conditions are similar in the industrial and developing worlds; for example, it tends to assume that growth in a temperate climate can be imitated in tropical and arid climates. But a great many environments in the developing world are ecologically fragile. They are capable of sustaining certain levels of activity and certain levels of population, but exceeding that carrying capacity may well lead to growing poverty, as suggested by the Brundtland Commission.

This chapter thus concentrates on intragenerational equity within developing countries and explores the nature of the relations that link poverty, inequality, and the environment.

Income Growth and Distribution in the Developing World

Table 11-1 shows absolute levels and rates of change in real income per capita for broad categories of the developing and industrial worlds, and table 11-2 presents data for individual low-income countries. Although per capita incomes clearly grew between 1965 and 1989, the average annual growth rate for the poorest countries (other than China and India) was only 1.5 percent. In the 1980s both Sub-Saharan Africa and Latin America had negative growth rates, as did the severely indebted

Table 11-1. *GNP per Capita and Rates of Growth, by Global Region, 1965–89*

	1980			Average annual growth of GNP per capita (percent)					
Country group	GNP (billions of dollars)	Population (millions)	GNP per capita (dollars)	1965–73	1973–80	1980–86	1987	1988	1989a
Low- and middle-income economies	2,406	3,359	700	4.0	2.6	1.5	2.7	3.4	1.2
Low-income economies	784	2,459	320	3.6	2.4	4.0	3.9	6.8	1.8
Middle-income economies	1,622	900	1,760	4.6	2.4	0.1	1.8	1.1	0.8
Sub-Saharan Africa	213	362	570	3.0	0.1	-2.8	-4.4	-0.8	0.5
East Asia	586	1,363	420	5.4	4.4	6.6	8.0	8.7	3.1
South Asia	220	922	240	1.0	2.0	3.2	0.9	6.1	2.3
Europe, Middle East, and North Africa	590	335	1,740	5.6	2.1	0.8	-0.6	0.1	0.6
Latin America and the Caribbean	716	348	2,000	4.1	2.4	-1.6	1.5	-0.8	-0.8
Severely indebted middle-income economies	791	419	1,840	4.2	2.6	-1.5	1.2	-0.4	-0.7
High-income economies	7,923	742	10,740	3.5	2.2	1.7	2.5	3.5	3.1
OECD members	7,663	716	10,750	3.5	2.2	1.9	2.8	3.7	3.1
Total reporting economies	10,329	4,101	2,520	2.7	1.5	0.9	1.8	2.7	1.7
Oil exporters	964	479	1,980	4.6	2.8	-1.6	-2.5	0.5	—

— Not available.

Note: Low-income economies had real income per capita below $545 in 1988; middle-income economies, between $546 and $5,999; and high-income economies, above $5,999.

a. Preliminary.

Source: World Bank (1990c).

Table 11-2. GNP *per Capita and Rates of Growth in Low-Income Countries, 1965–88*

Low-income economies	GNP per capita (1988 dollars)	Average annual growth of GNP per capita, 1965–88 (percent)
Low-income economies[a]	320	3.1
China and India[a]	340	4.0
Other[a]	280	1.5
Afghanistan	—	—
Bangladesh	170	0.4
Benin	390	0.1
Bhutan	180	—
Burkina Faso	210	1.2
Burundi	240	3.0
Central African Republic	380	−0.5
Chad	160	−2.0
China	330	5.4
Democratic Kampuchea	—	—
Ethiopia	120	−0.1
Ghana	400	−1.6
Guinea	430	—
Haiti	380	0.4
India	340	1.8
Indonesia	440	4.3
Kenya	370	1.9
Lao People's Dem. Rep.	180	—
Lesotho	420	5.2
Liberia	—	—
Madagascar	190	−1.8
Malawi	170	1.1
Mali	230	1.6
Mauritania	480	−0.4
Mozambique	100	—
Myanmar	—	—
Nepal	180	—
Niger	300	−2.3
Nigeria	290	0.9
Pakistan	350	2.5
Rwanda	320	1.5
Sierra Leone	—	—
Somalia	170	0.5
Sri Lanka	420	3.0
Sudan	480	0.0
Tanzania	160	−0.5
Togo	370	0.0
Uganda	280	−3.1
Viet Nam	—	—
Yemen	430	—
Zaire	170	−2.1
Zambia	290	−2.1

— Not available.

Note: Low-income economies had real income per capita below $545 in 1988; middle-income economies, between $546 and $5,999; and high-income economies, above $5,999.

a. Figure is a weighted average.

Source: World Bank (1990c).

middle-income and oil-exporting countries. Eleven low-income countries experienced negative per capita growth in the past two decades. If poverty could be measured by income per capita and if a straightforward link between poverty and environment exists, we might expect those countries to be experiencing more general environmental degradation than countries with positive rates of growth. Unfortunately, testing this proposition is impossible in the absence of reliable, comparable environmental indicators for the countries in question.

The data on absolute levels of real income show that countries of the Organisation for Economic Co-operation and Development (OECD) have, on average, real income more than thirty times higher than that of low-income economies and six times higher than the average income of middle-income economies. A stark way of expressing the world distribution of income is to calculate what percentage of the world population receives what percentage of world gross domestic product. Figure 11-1 provides estimates of these percentages. Taking only countries that report to the World Bank, which excludes 364 million people in the Soviet Union and several other countries, almost 61 percent of the world's population is found in low-income countries and receives some 5 percent of the world's income. A further 23 percent is in middle-income countries and receives some 13 percent of world income, while just under 17 percent of the world's population is in high-income countries and receives 82 percent of world income.

Income Distribution within Nations

Measuring the distribution of income within the industrial and developing worlds on a comparable basis is difficult. Table 11-3 reports a measure of income distribution, but extreme caution must be exercised in making cross-country comparisons with the data shown. Some of the data suggest that as the poverty of a country increases, its income distribution generally becomes more unequal (the more equal the distribution, the closer to unity is the distribution measure shown). Countries such as Brazil, Kenya, Nepal, Panama, and Peru show considerable inequality, while some developing countries, such as Bangladesh, Indonesia, and Sri Lanka, show low levels of inequality comparable to those of the industrial world.

Poverty in the Developing World

The discussion of income distribution assumes that poverty can be measured by income per capita, although poverty is more complex than that. Certainly, income per capita is a factor in poverty. Another widely used measure is the incidence of energy-deficient diets. An energy-deficient diet is defined as being below a standard of either the amount of

Figure 11-1. Global Distribution of Income

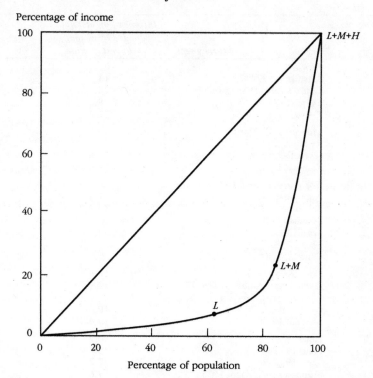

Percentage of income

Percentage of population

Note: The diagram shows a Lorenz curve. If distribution were equal, observations would lie on the 45° line, that is, 25 percent of the world's population would have 25 percent of the income, 50 percent would have 50 percent, and so on. The actual distribution, using just three observations, is shown by the curved line, which is plotted by first indicating the low-income country share (*L*), then adding the middle-income shares to the low-income shares (*L+M*), and then adding the high-income shares (*L+M+H*). Clearly, the global distribution of income is skewed. Low-income countries have 61 percent of the world's population but only 5 percent of global income; middle-income countries have 23 and 13 percent, respectively; while high-income countries have 17 and 82 percent, respectively.

Source: Adapted from data contained in World Bank (1990c).

calories needed to prevent stunted growth and serious health risks or the amount of calories needed to maintain an active working life. Table 11-4 shows broad estimates of the number of people who fall into these categories. The narrower definition would place some 340 million people below the poverty line, and the wider one, some 730 million (excluding China). Perhaps 40 percent of the poor are children under ten years of age; 75 percent live in rural areas; the poor spend some 80 percent of their income on food, which often includes very little meat; most are malnourished; most are susceptible to diseases. Of every ten children born to poor parents, two die within a year, another dies before the age of five, and only five survive beyond the age of forty (World Bank 1980).

Table 11-3. Distribution of Income within Countries, Various Years, 1970–86

Region, country, and survey year	Income of highest quintile divided by income of lowest quintile
Africa	
Botswana, 1974–75	13.4
Côte d'Ivoire, 1985–86	25.6
Egypt, 1975	8.3
Kenya, 1976	23.2
Mauritius, 1980–81	15.1
Reunion, 1976–77	21.0
Seychelles, 1978	12.6
Zambia, 1976	18.0
The Americas and the Caribbean	
Argentina, 1970	11.4
Bahamas, 1979	13.4
Bermuda, 1982	5.5
Brazil, 1972	33.3
1982	27.7
Canada, 1981	9.0
Costa Rica, 1971	16.6
Dominican Republic, 1976–77	12.6
El Salvador, 1976–77	8.6
Guatemala, 1979–81	10.6
Mexico, 1977	15.4
Panama, 1973	30.9
Peru, 1972	32.1
1977–78	7.7
Trinidad and Tobago, 1975–76	19.6
United States, 1980	10.7
1980	8.4
1985	9.5
Uruguay, 1983	7.6
Venezuela, 1970	18.0
Asia	
Bangladesh, 1973–74	7.0
1976–77	7.6
1981–82	6.9
China, 1984[a]	2.6
1984[b]	3.0
Hong Kong, 1980	8.7
1981	12.1
India, 1975–76	10.1
Indonesia, 1976	7.5
Israel, 1979–80	6.6
Japan, 1979	4.1
Korea, Republic of, 1976	7.9
1981	5.0
1981	4.9
Malaysia, 1973	16.0
Nepal, 1976–77	20.8
Philippines, 1971	16.1
1985	10.1
Singapore, 1977–78	7.6

Table 11-3 (continued)

Region, country, and survey year	Income of highest quintile divided by income of lowest quintile
Sri Lanka, 1980–81	8.4
Thailand, 1975–76	11.2
Turkey, 1973	16.2
Europe	
Austria, 1976	11.3
Belgium, 1978–79	4.6
Bulgaria, 1982	3.7
Czechoslovakia, 1981	3.6
Denmark, 1981	9.3
1981	7.1
Finland, 1981	6.0
France, 1975	12.5
German Democratic Republic, 1980	2.4
Germany, Federal Republic of, 1978	6.6
1978	5.3
Hungary, 1982	5.2
Ireland, 1973	5.5
1980	9.4
1980	8.1
Italy, 1977	7.1
Netherlands, 1981	5.5
1981	4.4
Norway, 1982	8.0
1982	6.4
Poland, 1983	3.4
Portugal, 1973–74	9.4
Spain, 1980–81	5.8
Sweden, 1981	7.3
1981	5.1
Switzerland, 1978	6.9
1978	5.8
United Kingdom, 1979	5.7
1982	7.1
1982	5.8
Yugoslavia, 1978	5.5
Oceania	
Australia, 1975–76	6.7
1978–79	6.0
New Zealand, 1981–82	6.8

Note: A quintile is one of five groups of households, each comprising 20 percent of all households. Thus the lowest quintile is the 20 percent of households with the lowest income, the highest quintile is the 20 percent of households with the highest income. Dividing the incomes of high and low quintiles produces one measure of income distribution. If there were complete equality, the ratio of the two quintiles would be unity. As the ratio grows, inequality increases.

a. Cities only.

b. County towns only.

Source: World Resources Institute (1989), table 14.4.

Table 11-4. *Prevalence of Energy-Deficient Diets in Eighty-Seven Developing Countries, 1980*

Country group or region	Below 90 percent of requirement[a]		Below 30 percent of requirement[b]	
	Share of population (percent)	Population (millions)	Share of population (percent)	Population (millions)
Developing countries (87)	34	730	16	340
Low-income (30)	51	590	23	270
Middle-income (57)	14	140	7	70
Sub-Saharan Africa (37)	44	150	25	90
East Asia and Pacific (8)	14	40	7	20
South Asia (7)	50	470	21	200
Middle East and North Africa (11)	10	20	4	10
Latin America and the Caribbean (24)	13	50	6	20

Note: The requirements set by the FAO and the World Health Organization are based on the standard amount of calories needed for a person to function at full capacity in all daily activities. The countries surveyed had 92 percent of the population in developing countries in 1980, excluding China. The numbers in parentheses are the number of countries in the sample. Low-income countries had income per capita below $400 in 1983; middle-income countries, above $400.

a. Not enough calories for an active working life.

b. Not enough calories to prevent stunted growth and serious health risks.

Source: World Bank (1986c), p. 111.

The role of women in poverty is significant. Among the poor of rural Africa and Latin America, households headed by women are poorer on average than those headed by men (see Binswanger and Pingali 1988). This underlines the need to target women in development assistance.

The problem of diet is not the global availability of food but access to food. The world's production of food has actually outstripped the world's growth of population (table 11-5). In Sub-Saharan Africa, in contrast, per capita food production has actually fallen. In general, the problem of energy-deficient diets is one of access, or food security, and food security is largely a problem of inadequate purchasing power (World Bank 1986c; Sen 1981 develops the idea that access to food, or goods in general, is the principal problem during famines).

The link between poverty and environmental degradation can be further investigated by asking where the poor are located (table 11-6 shows the geographical distribution of the poor). Within these broad regions, the poor are located either in ecologically fragile rural locations or in the peripheries of cities, which are also frequently fragile. Fragility means that the area is not resilient to stress or shocks such as climatic variations or population pressure. The relation between this resilience, or lack of it, and the demands made on natural resources is what matters. Thus parts of Western Europe, the corn belt of the United States, the Nile Delta, the Ganges floodplain, and the intensive rice-growing areas of Southeast

Table 11-5. Growth Rates of Food Production, 1960–80
(average annual percentage change)

Region	Total growth rate 1960–70	1970–80	Growth rate per capita 1960–70	1970–80
World	2.7	2.3	0.8	0.5
Developing countries	2.9	2.8	0.4	0.4
Low-income	2.6	2.2	0.2	−0.3
Middle-income	3.2	3.3	0.7	0.9
Sub-Saharan Africa	2.6	1.6	0.1	−1.1
East Asia	2.8	3.8	0.3	1.4
South Asia	2.6	2.2	0.1	0.0
Middle East and North Africa	2.6	2.9	0.1	0.2
Southern Europe	3.2	3.5	1.8	1.9
Latin America and the Caribbean	3.6	3.3	0.1	0.6
Industrial market economies	2.3	2.0	1.3	1.1
Centrally planned economies	3.2	1.7	2.2	0.9

Note: Production data are weighted by the unit price of world exports. Decade growth rates are based on the midpoint of a five-year average, except that 1970 is the average for 1969–71.
Source: World Bank (1986c), p. 58.

Asia have stable climates and alluvial soils and support very large populations with reasonably limited environmental problems.

Ecologically fragile environments are typified by tropical forests, where soils are acidic and subject to serious erosion once deforestation occurs; upland areas, where soil erosion is a serious risk; and arid and semiarid zones, where soils are light and easily eroded by wind.

Of the 700 million poor recorded in table 11-6, an estimated 250 million live in areas where agriculture could be intensified by applying fertilizers and using modern technology. In this sense, any fragility in the ecosystem can be substituted with capital inputs. Some 350 million peo-

Table 11-6. Geographical Location of the World's Poor, 1988

Region	Population (millions)	Percentage of regional population	Percentage of poorest people in developing countries
South Asia	350	33	50
China	76	7	11
East Asia	31	6	4
Sub-Saharan Africa	137	26	20
Near East and North Africa	34	13	5
Latin America	72	16	10
Total	700	18	100

Source: Leonard (1989a).

ple live in areas where such substitution generally is either much more difficult or not feasible because of climatic and soil conditions. The remaining 100 million poorest people live in peripheral urban areas, which, in turn, are often high risk because of landslides, floods, lack of sanitation, and lack of infrastructure. The 450 million people living in areas with a low potential to be productive and in urban margins constitute the marginalized poor (these broad estimates are taken from Leonard 1989a).

Theories of the Link between Poverty and Environment

The poorest of the poor thus occupy the least resilient, most threatened environmental areas of the world. The very fact of low resilience to stress and shock means that an exogenous event, such as a change in climate, could induce the poor to take actions that further degrade the environment. This happens when the poor are in some way confined to an ecologically fragile area and react to stress by intensifying their use of limited resources, that is, by deforestation and overgrazing. The stress in question could include population growth and economic signals from policymakers that diminish the incentives to maintain a stable equilibrium between the local economy and its environment.

On this analysis, poverty is not so much a cause, in the narrow sense, of environmental degradation, as a mechanism by which the true underlying causes are transformed into actions that degrade the environment. Put another way, poverty does not necessarily in and of itself lead to environmental degradation. That depends on the options available to the poor and on their responses to outside stimuli and pressures. Poverty, however, removes their ability to respond and adapt because the time horizon is typically short and few feasible options are available. This leaves only two types of reaction: they can attempt to supplement scarce assets by using free common property or open-access resources, or they can leave the land altogether and move to urban areas. The result of using up resources is to degrade the rural environment. The result of moving to urban areas is to swap one form of degradation for another, that is, rural for urban. Because poverty is also associated with poor health, the capability of responding to exogenous factors is further reduced by the physical effort involved. The association of poverty with illiteracy compounds the issue, since illiteracy also reduces the ability of individuals to respond to pressures. Poverty in all its manifestations keeps the poor from being able to respond to environmental degradation arising from other underlying causes; it thus becomes a disabling factor.

This idea of poverty as a disabling factor rather than an underlying cause of environmental degradation permits us to take into account other compounding issues. Population growth acts as both an underlying cause and a compounding factor. In Bangladesh, for example, population growth is reducing the average farm size, thus lowering productivity and deepening poverty (Mellor 1988). As poverty increases, the ability to escape environmental degradation is reduced even further. In Nepal, the same phenomenon leads farmers to clear and crop hillsides in an effort to maintain their income. Expanding agricultural area is associated with deforestation and with increased soil erosion (Kumar and Hotchkiss 1988).

The generalized picture of the links between poverty and environment must not be exaggerated. The existence of poverty does not mean that environmental degradation will necessarily follow. As the model suggests, if the underlying causes or shocks are absent, the state of poverty is likely to persist, but without environmental degradation. Comparatively few attempts have been made to trace the responses of the poor to stress and shocks over time. One set of case studies found little evidence that poor communities had degraded their rural environments (Jagannathan 1989, 1990; Jagannathan and Agunbiade 1990; Jagannathan, Mori, and Hassan 1990). These studies point to other factors causing environmental degradation, notably new roads that open up virgin territory and lead to agricultural colonization, misguided price and other incentives, and population growth. Illiteracy compounds the disabling effects of poverty. Instead of stimulating entrepreneurial activity and investment in rural areas, increasing literacy may quicken the exodus of the poor. It is sometimes argued that biasing public investments toward urban areas reinforces the trend of rural-urban migration by creating a large informal sector that acts as a magnet. In many ways, then, individuals in rural areas react to environmental stress by migrating to urban areas. As we saw, this shifts the type of poverty from rural to urban. This is particularly true if the informal sector cannot assimilate the flow but has real prospects for improving welfare if it can. Certainly, a bias may exist where cost recovery is not practiced and subsidies are not targeted. On the other hand, public investments in urban infrastructure are necessary if cities are to be a positive force in the national economy and provide jobs and income for "excess" rural labor. The important issue is to ensure that the beneficiaries of urban investments pay their fair share for those benefits and that indiscriminate subsidies do not end up in the pockets of the urban well-to-do.

Faced with declining real income because of, say, an exogenously determined decline in crop output, the poor may react in a number of ways.

- They may seek marginal lands on which to expand output—a direct link between poverty and environmental degradation if the marginal lands are ecologically fragile, as is likely.
- They may also seek ecologically sound ways of expanding output in ecologically sensitive areas, for example, by adopting terracing techniques or agroforestry on steeply sloped land. In Kano, Nigeria, for example, the pressure of famine did not seem to affect the preference of smallholders for tree conservation (Mortimore 1989).

- They may also seek income security rather than food security by obtaining employment off the farm or undertaking other activities that generate income. If so, they may well choose not to undertake activities that damage the environment (Jagannathan 1989 stresses this point and questions the ability of the poor to degrade the environment given their low nutritional status and lack of capital equipment).

Therefore, impoverishment by itself does not necessarily cause environmental degradation. Much depends on the coping strategies of the poor, and these depend, in turn, on the availability of options, cultural factors, and policies of local and national governments.

Just as significant, the factors giving rise to impoverishment may, however, be the underlying cause of actions that do degrade the environment. As economies grow and monetization is extended, the poor may become marginalized by changes in the structure of property rights. Common property, for example, may be privatized. This trend may be encouraged by the growing scarcity of land and water resources caused by population growth, as the poor are excluded from access to the privately owned land and forced onto marginal lands. This process has been observed in parts of India, for example (Jodha 1986). Poverty in the sense of powerlessness then becomes the means by which a more fundamental cause—centrally directed changes in property rights—gives rise to environmental degradation. From this point of view, the poor create degradation through misdirected public policies.

These general observations can be illustrated with some case studies. A study of Kabupaten Sukabumi, Indonesia, measured changes in land use by comparing two remote sensing images for 1976 and 1986 (Jagannathan 1989). In that period, some 27 percent of forest cover was lost, with about 40 percent of the conversion being to scrubland, 24 percent to mixed gardens, 10 percent to estates, and 25 percent to built-up areas. The switch to gardens and estates was caused by market incentives. The switch to scrubland responded to the demand for fuelwood. In turn, scrubland was converted to estates and mixed gardens, which may themselves have been converted to built-up areas or become severely eroded. The only link to poverty as such occurred when landless cultivators converted abandoned estates to farming. Because they lack title to the land, these farmers use destructive slash-and-burn techniques. Other land uses that have been environmentally destructive include mining for clay, gravel, and limestone. Deforestation was also marked in the areas immediately adjacent to new roads. Jagannathan (1989) concludes that the economic system (and by inference not poverty) is the key determinant of land and water use and that market incentive structures, public investments in infrastructure, and agricultural and macroeconomic policies appear to be the main causal factors behind observed changes in land use.

Similar studies in Gombe and Ekiti-Akoko, Nigeria, indicate that land clearance took place on the best soils, alongside roads, and around existing settlements. Human settlement growth was confined to existing towns. Although based on data and images of far less sophistication than the Java study, Jagannathan (1989) concludes that changes in natural resource uses appear to have been influenced by market forces (increases in food prices, changes in relative prices between food crops and tree crops), by infrastructural investments (road networks, health, and social infrastructure), and specific Agricultural Development Project policies, such as fertilizer subsidies, location of farm service centers, investments in rural water supplies.

Studies of Costa Rica, El Salvador, and Haiti (see Daly and Foy 1989) focus further on the role that distributional issues play in misallocation policies and population size. Haiti suffers from massive deforestation and erosion. A major factor is population growth, which simply causes a shortage of land and a demand for fuelwood that exceeds its rate of regeneration. In the late 1970s, emigration was officially encouraged to relieve the excess demand on natural resources. Misdirected public policies result in soil erosion. Thus coffee production is discouraged by high export taxes and the growing of maize, sorghum, and beans is encouraged. Yet perennial crops such as coffee are generally better for stabilizing the soil than grain and bean crops. The Haitian currency is systematically overvalued on the foreign exchange market, acting as a further disincentive to export crops such as coffee. Distributional considerations show up in interesting ways. Corruption in the public sector diverts valuable resources to the rich and powerful and creates extreme uncertainty about the possibility that the government will expropriate the land. This fear reduces the incentive to invest in soil conservation. The problem is further exacerbated by unequal distribution of land, although it is thought that redistributing land would add only marginally to the average size of holdings.

A similar picture of high population density, overvalued exchange rates, insecure land tenure, and coffee taxation applies to El Salvador. The significantly high rate of pesticide poisoning in El Salvador may be due to pesticide subsidies. Distributional factors are also relevant. Land ownership is very unevenly distributed—perhaps 80 percent of households are landless or nearly landless.

In Costa Rica, the present population pressure is perhaps manageable. Large-scale deforestation and land degradation are encouraged by implicit subsidies that offer cheap credit to cattle raising, although export taxes act as a disincentive to cattle production. Land ownership is once again skewed: perhaps 1 percent of landowners hold 25 percent of arable land. Poor farmers are marginalized onto forested lands, including the Corvocado National Park.

A study of deforestation in Ethiopia reveals the complex reactions of the poor to environmental change (Newcombe 1989). As population grows, so does the demand for fuelwood until, eventually, it outstrips the rate of growth of forests and woodlands. This breaches the first nutrient cycle in which trees fix atmospheric nitrogen (figure 11-2). The quality of the soil begins to diminish, but food production is not affected to any significant extent. Fuelwood becomes an even more important commercial good and is sold to other areas, especially urban centers. Rural peasants switch from using fuelwood to using dung and straw for fuel, but this begins to breach the second and third nutrient cycles in which dung and crop residues supply nutrients and organic matter to the soil. The quality of the soil is further diminished. Progressive deforestation and further commercialization of dung as a fuel accelerates soil erosion, and crop output declines. Eventually, farming systems collapse, and migration occurs. But for the poverty of the peasants, some of the effects on soil quality could be ameliorated by, for example, growing trees and using artificial fertilizers. The underlying cause of the deterioration is still population growth in excess of the carrying capacity of the natural environment.

The Policy Response to Poverty and Environment

The general theory of poverty and environment outlined above suggests that the link is not always straightforward. Often it can be direct and simple—reductions in real incomes do cause activities to expand into marginal areas, giving rise to environmental degradation. Disentangling this effect from population change and the influence of public policies is not easy. Frequently, however, policy measures and general population pressure dominate the processes that generate environmental loss. If this is correct, the policy response must, first, raise agricultural productivity in the most resilient and potentially productive areas, thereby improving the well-being of 250 million of the most impoverished poor and reducing the pressure exerted on marginal lands by populations who would otherwise be displaced from resilient areas. Leonard (1989a) describes this as the unfinished business of the green revolution. Second, the policy response must decrease the fragility of marginal areas through schemes of water conservation, agricultural extension, afforestation, and agroforestry. As with resilient areas, the policy mix must consist of investment, incentive schemes, infrastructure, credit, extension information, and institution building, including in many cases establishing or reinforcing resource rights through land and resource tenure.[1]

The first type of policy is likely to be more technological in character than schemes of the second type, which are likely to concentrate on institutions and incentives. The efforts to meet the poverty challenge have, in fact, witnessed just this kind of policy shift toward designing policies that are aimed at households and farms, communities, and local governments and that pay due attention to the centralized economic signals affecting choice of crops and type of economic activity. At the

Figure 11-2. Patterns of Deterioration in Ethiopian Agroecosystems

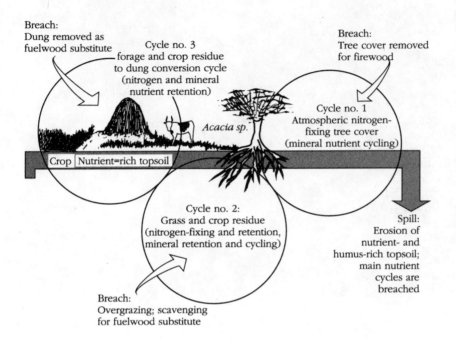

Source: Newcombe (1989).

investment level, considerable gains can be achieved by efforts to conserve the already fragile resource base, as with water harvesting techniques that conserve even low amounts of rainfall. It is important to recognize that urbanization is an important, positive force in reducing the pressure on rural lands. A link that should be stressed is the relatively low population growth rates associated with urban areas (which are related perhaps to such factors as improved social security and the existence of educational and job opportunities for women). Care must be taken, however, to keep urban centers from becoming pockets of future poverty. Appropriate urban policy is needed that promotes productivity, reduces poverty, and encourages environmental management.

Note

1. Lack of infrastructure tends to show up as obstacles to marketing produce that can otherwise be grown successfully or as inefficient distribution that lowers the farmgate returns to the farmer. In Bangladesh, for example, 12 percent of the population is below the poverty line in villages with good infrastructure, compared with 21 percent in villages with poor infrastructure. Employment per hectare of land is 4 percent higher, employment in nonagricultural activities is 30 percent higher, and wages are 12 percent higher. See Ahmed and Hossain (1987).

PART THREE

International
Environmental Issues

12

World Markets
and
Natural Resource Degradation

It is perfectly possible for a single nation to secure sustainable development—in the sense of not depleting its own stock of capital assets—at the cost of procuring unsustainable development in another country. An example might be when industrial economies import products from tropical forests in quantities that encourage deforestation in the exporting country without building up other forms of capital. The importing country effectively imports sustainability, while the exporting country exports it. The import and export of sustainability are partly an issue of international inequality. The traditional theory of comparative advantage, which says that countries export goods in which they have a comparative advantage and import goods in which they have a comparative disadvantage, must take into account the external effects and user costs of trading in natural resources.

How far this trade in sustainability is a matter of concern depends on (a) the balance between the trade and the resource endowments of the countries involved, (b) the extent to which revenues from exported resources are converted into other forms of capital, and (c) the extent to which the trade takes place at international prices that reflect the true social costs of resource depletion in the exporting country. Even when trade is in some sense responsible for environmental degradation, the appropriate policy may not be to restrict it. Trade accompanied by environmental policy is better than increased protection without appropriate environmental policies.

The Brundtland Commission's view is that world commodity trade frequently encourages resource depletion in the developing world (World Commission on Environment and Development 1987, pp. 80–81):

> The promotion of increased volumes of commodity exports has led to cases of unsustainable overuse of the natural resource base. While individual cases may not fit this generalization, it has been argued that such processes have been at work in ranching for beef, fishing in both coastal and deep-sea waters, forestry, and the growing of some cash crops. Moreover, the prices of commodity exports do not fully reflect the environmental costs to the resource base.

If, however, revenues are converted into other forms of capital, if this conversion is reflected in the proper user cost of the traded resource, and if prices reflect the true social cost of resource depletion, trade in sustainability presents much less of a problem. However, trade in products that are often environmentally benign tends to suffer from extreme price instability and a declining trend in the price per unit of exports relative to the price of imports (the terms of trade). This trade includes coffee, cocoa, tea, and citrus fruits, all of which benefit soil stability. Many products are environmentally damaging when produced on cleared forest or other marginal land. Products with this potential to damage the environment include cattle and root crops such as cassava and groundnuts. Trade in these products is often encouraged by special trade agreements with the industrial world. This chapter investigates the link between trade, environment, and sustainability.

Dependence of Developing Countries on Commodity Trade

Table 12-1 shows the share of renewable resource commodities being exported from developing countries and imported into industrial, developing, and nonmarket (centrally planned) economies. While the proportions change over time—with more trade among developing countries taking place—some two-thirds of the exports of renewable resources still go to the industrial world. Trade policies in the industrial world therefore have the potential to affect the developing world significantly.

Developing countries depend heavily on primary commodities for their export revenues. Some 66 percent of the world's trade in cocoa comes from Africa; 60 percent of coffee comes from Central and South America; 66 percent of tea comes from Asia, as does 50 percent of rice (table 12-2). Clearly, the price and volume of these commodities matter a great deal to the economies of the developing world.

Table 12-1. Destination of Renewable Resource Commodities Exported by Developing Countries, 1960–84
(percentage of exports)

Year	Industrial market economies	Developing countries	Nonmarket economies
1960	72.2	22.3	4.5
1970	73.4	20.0	5.7
1980	70.1	24.9	3.7
1984	64.3	29.6	4.8

Source: World Bank (1986a).

Some developing countries depend to a considerable extent on exports of renewable and exhaustible resources for their earnings of foreign exchange. Table 12-3 shows the ratio of earnings from thirty-three primary commodities to earnings from all exports. Shares of 60 percent are common.

Terms of Trade

Given the dependence of the developing countries in general on exports of natural resources or commodities based on natural resources, the prices at which those resources and commodities are traded is clearly

Table 12-2. Commodity Exports, by Region, 1985
(percentage of global trade)

Commodity	Central and South America	Africa	Asia	All developing countriesa
Beef	13	1	1	17
Cocoa	18	66	5	92
Coffee	60	23	7	92
Cotton	12	16	11	45
Groundnuts	9	18	30	60
Jute	..	..	96	96
Maize	9	5	4	19
Rice	5	1	50	55
Rubber	..	5	93	98
Sugar	51	6	10	69
Tea	2	15	66	85
Timber	2	4	18	28
Tobacco	15	10	13	51
Wheat	6	0	..	7
Thirty-six commodities	14	9	16	40

.. Negligible.
a. Includes other developing countries in Oceania and Southern Europe.
Source: Adapted from World Bank (1986a).

Table 12-3. Export Earnings of Natural Resources as a Percentage of All Export Revenues, by Region and Select Developing Country, 1981–83

Region and country	Percentage
Africa	
Botswana	18[a]
Central African Republic	63
Ethiopia	72
Kenya	45
Sudan	38
Asia	
Bangladesh	23
India	29
Indonesia	59
Nepal	63
Thailand	41
Central and South America	
Bolivia	36
Brazil	27
Costa Rica	61
Mexico	80
Paraguay	61

Note: Based on thirty-three primary commodities and total exports.
a. Excludes earnings from exports of precious stones.
Source: World Bank (1986a).

of major significance. A common measure of the purchasing power of exports is the terms of trade, which can be determined in several ways. The ratio of export prices to import prices is the barter terms of trade (or sometimes the net barter terms of trade). If export prices rise (the terms of trade improve), more imports can be purchased for a given volume of exports, which raises the standard of living. As this occurs, however, foreign demand may fall, reducing total exports. An alternative measure is the income terms of trade, which are the barter terms of trade multiplied by the actual volume of exports or, put another way, the value of exports deflated by the price of imports. Figure 12-1 shows movements in the barter and income terms of trade for developing countries from 1965 to 1988. The barter terms of trade fell a significant 50 percent over the period, while the income terms of trade rose 50 percent until the late 1970s and fell 50 percent from then until 1988. In other words, the income terms of trade were approximately the same in 1988 as they were in 1965.

Terms of Trade and Environment

Changes in relative prices tend to change production and consumption patterns and, hence, may affect the environment. Changes in the terms of

Figure 12-1. Volume of Exports and Terms of Trade of Developing Countries, 1965-88

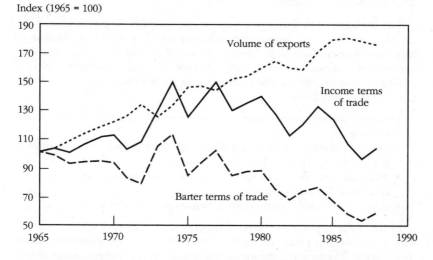

Index (1965 = 100)

Note: Barter terms of trade are the weighted export unit values of primary commodities deflated by the weighted import unit values of each region. Multiplying the barter terms of trade by the actual volume of exports yields the income terms of trade. Data are based on a sample of ninety developing countries.
Source: World Bank (1991b), p. 106.

trade are an important example of changes in relative prices; by extension, therefore, changes in the terms of trade will probably affect the environment. Nevertheless, there is little empirical evidence linking changes in the terms of trade to changes in the quality or availability of natural resources in the developing world. Primarily this is because specific hypotheses are difficult to test. Time-series indicators of resource quality and quantity are needed, together with a series of factors that might affect those indicators. One might, for example, try to relate the overall deterioration in an environment to measures of population pressure, changes in the terms of trade, and other factors. Box 12-1 reports on a study that attempts to approximate this approach.

The so-called Brundtland hypothesis about the link between the terms of trade and the environment is as follows. If the terms of trade decline, exporting countries must export more and more just to maintain foreign exchange earnings constant. In the specific case of crop exports, then, emphasis is placed on expanding acreage in order to increase exports. If the affected crops are environmentally hazardous—for example, groundnuts or maize—soils in land that is not marginal may be directly damaged. Damage to marginal soils would be even higher. Even if the crops are environmentally benign, efforts might be made to expand cultivation

Box 12-1. Testing the Factors Related to Trade That Give Rise to Tropical Deforestation

Data from forty-five developing countries were used by Capistrano and Kiker (1990) to test the factors giving rise to deforestation. The study related industrial logging—which is closely related to overall rates of deforestation even though it is not the major cause—to export prices of timber, income, population, levels of international indebtedness, and exchange rate adjustments. The expected relations might be as follows:

- Higher timber prices raise the opportunity cost of leaving forests unharvested
- Overvalued exchange rates may discourage the depletion of forests by making timber exports less attractive
- High indebtedness encourages the use of forest land for export crops, including timber and agriculture
- Population growth exerts pressure on unexploited forest land.

To test these hypotheses, rates of logging were regressed on indicators of various factors. The results are shown in table B12-1 for three specifications of the equation. The measures shown are elasticities—that is, the percentage change in forest depletion with each change in the variable of 1 percent. The results can be interpreted as follows.

In 1967–71, when exchange rates were relatively fixed, the export price of logs dominated the explanation of deforestation. Each 1 percent change in the price of logs was accompanied by a 1.5 percent increase in the area of forest logged.

In 1972–75 there was a worldwide shortage of grain. Countries sought self-sufficiency in cereals and deforested accordingly. Forest depletion increased 4.7 to 5.1 percent for every 1 percent change in cereal self-sufficiency. Real income growth was also important, with an elasticity of 2; in other words, each 1 percent rise in income was accompanied by a 2 percent increase in deforestation. The link between income growth and deforestation is positive, contrary to the popular hypothesis that poverty is a major impetus to deforestation (see chapter 11). Another finding contradicts popular views: the debt service ratio is inversely related to depletion so that increased indebtedness reduced forest depletion. The connection here may be that improving access to credit removed the pressure to raise logging rates. Agricultural prices generally rose in this period, giving some incentive to clear forests for agriculture.

In 1976–80, devaluation was strongly associated with forest depletion. Deval-

onto marginal lands by clearing shrub and forest land and adding to potential erosion through deforestation.

Some evidence for this relationship can be obtained from the experience of the Dominican Republic with coffee, which can be an environmentally benign crop when interspersed with trees in an agroforestry system. Veloz and others (1985) investigated the types of crops that should be grown in the watershed area of the Valdesia Reservoir, which is uations made exporting cheaper and importing dearer, perhaps raising the incentive to mine forests to secure foreign exchange advantages and find substitutes for dearer imports. Both income and cereal self-sufficiency exerted a continued impact during this period.

Table B12-1. Elasticity of Forest Depletion with Respect to Significant Variables, 1967–85

Year and variable	Model 1	Model 2	Model 3
1967–71			
Export price of logs	1.45**	1.49**	1.50**
1972–75			
Per capita income	2.18**	2.18**	1.96**
Agricultural export prices	0.86	1.11*	0.96
Debt service ratio	−1.15	−1.51	−1.46
Cereal self-sufficiency	5.12**	4.84**	4.71**
Population	0.26	0.26	0.26*
1976–80			
Per capita income	1.43	1.61*	1.29
Devaluation rate	4.10**	4.67**	3.16*
Cereal self-sufficiency	4.61	5.41*	4.19
1981–85			
Devaluation rate	1.40*	1.40*	1.02
Arable land per capita	3.74**	4.03**	2.86*

*Significant at the 5 percent level.
**Significant at the 1 percent level.
Source: Capistrano and Kiker (1990).

In 1981–85, real income per capita fell in most of the countries studied, yet forest depletion did not fall as a result. Real income ceased to be a significant explanatory factor. Cereal self-sufficiency was being actively discouraged as an economic objective, and it, too, ceased to be statistically significant. The expansion of arable lands became the most important factor explaining depletion, and exchange rate devaluations continued to have an impact. Note, however, that the study did not control for the role that domestic policies play in deforestation. Finding a variable to represent domestic policies is difficult, but some indicator of economic subsidies to deforestation is required. The results therefore must be interpreted with caution.

---

formed by a hydroelectric dam (see also Southgate 1988). The watershed area is located on a steep hillside: half of the total area has slopes greater than 40 percent. In order to avoid erosion, the crops grown on hilly areas in subtropical regions should be carefully chosen. Typically, hilltops and upper slopes should be forested, medium-sloped land should be allocated to agroforestry, and bottom lands could be cultivated with crops if conservation practices are followed. The investigators found that existing levels of erosion were very high, resulting in heavy siltation of the Valdesia Reservoir. The erosion was, in turn, related to cropping practices that did not follow the requirements for cultivating slopes. In particular, agroforestry and mixed cropping were not practiced. At prevailing prices, the costs and benefits of such practices meant that undertaking mixed cropping, especially with coffee and tree fruits, was not worthwhile, although the prevailing prices were distorted by an overvalued exchange rate. As the formula for the terms of trade shows, an overvalued exchange rate effectively turns the terms of trade against a country for commodities traded internationally.

The Dominican case illustrates how price distortions, in this case brought about by an overvalued exchange rate, affect the environment. Overvaluing the exchange rate turned the terms of trade against internationally traded products and in favor of subsistence crops. But in this case, the traded crops were environmentally benign, whereas the subsistence crops (beans, maize, and root crops) were erosive. The Dominican Republic deliberately overvalued its currency, adversely affecting the terms of trade. World supply and demand did not produce the adverse terms of trade, but in this example the effect is the same, that is, a currency overvaluation produces the same effect as a decline in the price of imports or a rise in the price of exports.

The Ivory Trade

The trade in elephant ivory is thousands of years old (this section is based on Barbier and others 1990). In only a few decades, however, the population of African elephants has been reduced so low that its future is cause for great concern (table 12-4 shows estimates of elephant populations in select African countries). World demand for ivory has induced massive slaughter and left perhaps 623,000 elephants alive compared with well over 1 million in 1981.

The demise of the elephant is the result of the demand for ivory artifacts such as carvings, personal seals, trinkets, inlay for furniture, even piano keys and gun handles. Table 12-5 presents the countries that export ivory, although these are often not the countries of origin due to the nature of the trade in ivory within Africa. Figure 12-2 lists the economies that import ivory. The role of the Far East is clear: Hong Kong, Japan, Macao, and Singapore dominate consumption. (The Belgian figures reflect entrepôt reexport trade because Belgium has been, for at least a century, a major center for receiving, grading, and reexporting ivory.)

Although live elephants definitely impose some financial costs because they damage crops, they also produce beneficial foreign exchange because they play a flagship role in attracting tourists. Tourist revenues are of considerable importance to the economies of several African countries, notably Kenya, Malawi, Tanzania, Zambia, and Zimbabwe. In

Table 12-4. Elephant Populations in Africa, by Select Country, 1981–89
(number)

Country	1981	1989
Central Africa	436,200	278,100
Central African Republic	31,000	27,000
Congo, People's Republic of the	10,800	25,000
Gabon	13,400	92,000
Zaire	376,000	103,000
East Africa	429,500	125,600
Kenya	65,000	18,000
Sudan	133,700	21,000
Tanzania	203,900	75,000
Southern Africa	309,000	203,300
Botswana	20,000	58,000
South Africa	8,000	8,200
Zambia	160,000	45,000
Zimbabwe	47,000	49,000
West Africa	17,600	15,700
Total	1,192,300	622,700

Source: Unpublished data from the African Elephant and Rhino Specialist Group.

Table 12-5. Countries That Export Elephant Ivory, 1979–87
(metric tons)

Country	Exports, 1986	Cumulative exports, 1979–87
Botswana	0	58
Burundi	90	488
Cameroon	1	28
Central African Republic	19	1,136
Chad	0	111
Congo, People's Republic of the	17	917
Kenya	2	131
Namibia	1	37
Somalia	61	105
South Africa	41	329
Sudan	78	1,452
Tanzania	70	653
Uganda	36	424
Zaire	23	640
Zambia	10	149
Zimbabwe	8	94
All exporters[a]	663	6,828

a. Includes other countries.
Source: Unpublished data from the London Environmental Economics Centre, Wildlife Trade Monitoring Unit.

Figure 12-2. Economies That Import Elephant Ivory, 1985-86

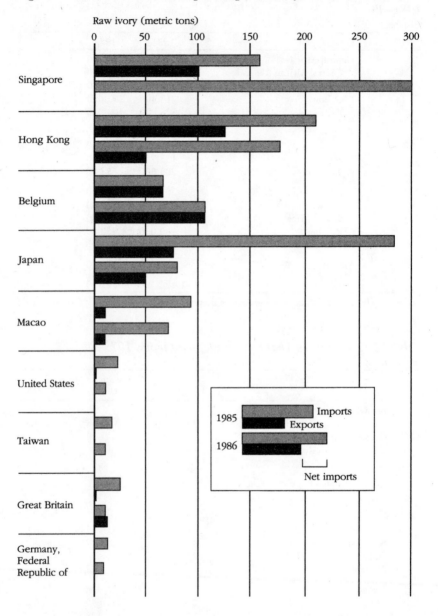

Note: Before 1989 the trade in elephant ivory was ostensibly managed by the Convention on International Trade in Endangered Species (CITES), but much of the regulation was ignored. In 1989 CITES agreed to place elephant ivory on appendix 1, introducing a ban on trade in raw ivory. The diagram shows the economies that consumed ivory before the ban was implemented. The effect of the ban on trade is not yet clear, although countries such as Kenya report a virtual cessation of ivory poaching.

Source: Unpublished data from the London Environmental Economics Centre, Wildlife Monitoring Unit.

African countries where tourism is far less fashionable or feasible, such as Central African Republic, People's Republic of the Congo, and Zaire, live elephants still have considerable earning potential because big game hunters are willing to pay high prices for the hunt. Managed sustainably, the resource could generate a significant amount of foreign exchange.

Since the world trade in ivory has decimated the African elephant population, policy measures must be aimed at altering both the inducement to supply and the sources of demand. The price elasticity of the demand for ivory—the sensitivity of demand to variations in price—appears to be low. This means that raising prices would have a comparatively limited impact on the demand, especially as the income elasticity of demand appears to be high. Thus an import tax is unlikely to be effective. Creating a cartel of the producers is unlikely because the few countries concerned have difficulty reaching an agreement.

The conservation community has been mainly, though not exclusively, concerned with imposing a total ban on the ivory trade, which would require the compliance of all importing and exporting countries.[1] Are such bans economically justified? Economists have long doubted the viability of bans on trade; in practice bans rarely work, and there are compelling theoretical reasons for why they do not.[2] The essence of the ivory trade is that some has been legal (sanctioned by the Convention on International Trade in Endangered Species [CITES]) and some has not. A ban affects the legal trade but leaves the illegal trade largely untouched. Some of the demand that was legal before the ban will even become illegal after it. Although overall demand will fall, the price of ivory may actually rise because the inflated illegal demand faces a smaller supply. Higher prices may induce smugglers to find more effective means of continuing their trade, notably the use of entrepôt countries outside the CITES system.

The Hardwood Trade

Almost without exception, forest management regimes in the developing world are not sustainable. Productive forest in 1985 probably constituted some 828 million hectares, but only 1 million hectares were under sustained-yield management (Poore and others 1988). The main suppliers of hardwood are shown in table 12-6.

Out of the 94 million cubic meters of timber imported globally in 1986, Japan consumed about two-thirds. Japan also consumed 50 percent of the world's imports of tropical hardwoods, while countries in the European Community consumed another 40 percent. The trade in hardwood products is summarized in table 12-7. Much of the trade in hardwood consists of whole logs imported from nonpeninsular Malaysia (Sarawak and Sabah). In 1970, Japan received some 35 percent of its hardwood log imports from the Philippines and 30 percent from Indonesia. In 1987, those proportions had fallen to nearly zero for both. In

Table 12-6. Principal Exporters of Hardwood, 1986
(thousands of cubic meters)

Country	Logs	Sawnwood	Plywood	Veneer
Brazil	9	375	218	50
Cameroon	704	103	10	27
Congo, People's Republic of the	287	23	..	46
Côte d'Ivoire	1,020	475	19	77
Gabon	883	3	46	8
Indonesia	..	2,160	4,618	91
Liberia	358	6	..	2
Malaysia	19,159	2,991	452	375
Papua New Guinea	1,400	15	1	..
Philippines	352	495	256	50
Singapore	..	741	575	38
Solomon Islands	349	3	..	..

.. Negligible.
Source: FAO (1986).

Indonesia, this occurred because log exports were banned in favor of the country's own domestic wood processing industry. Indonesia is now a significant supplier of plywood to Japan. In the Philippines, it occurred because the forests were exhausted as a result of agricultural clearance and overlogging that continue despite several attempts, on paper, to ban logging and log exports (Nectoux and Kuroda 1989).

Concern about unsustainable logging of the world's tropical forests produced the International Tropical Timber Agreement of 1983, which created the International Tropical Timber Organization (ITTO). Forty-two nations ratified the agreement, including the main consuming and producing nations. The ITTO seeks to "encourage the development of national policies aimed at sustainable utilization and conservation of tropical forests and their genetic resources and at maintaining the ecological balance in the regions concerned" (United Nations Conference on Trade and Development 1984). ITTO has already reviewed the various forest management practices of its member countries and initiated some pilot schemes for improving them.

How far a body such as ITTO can transform forest management from unsustainable to sustainable practices is open to question, particularly in the context of game theory. Essentially, if any one country adopts sustainable management practices, its supply of tropical hardwoods to the world market will be reduced. If the other main suppliers do not follow suit, the first country could be disadvantaged in the world market, losing revenues in the short run. Thus, in the short term, the incentive to secure sustainable management is limited unless a body such as ITTO can obtain a cooperative solution, that is, unless most or all of its members agree to implement such policies. This means that each country will have to make

Table 12-7. *Direct Imports of Tropical Hardwoods, 1984*
(thousands of cubic meters in roundwood equivalents)

Type of hardwood	Japan	United States	Western Europe
Logs	13,321	131	4,012
Sawnwood	1,143	772	5,163
Veneers	114	226	355
Plywood	147	2,519	2,239
Total	14,725	3,568	11,769

Source: Unpublished data from the FAO, Rome, and U.N. Economic Commission for Europe.

short-run sacrifices in order to receive long-run gains. This raises the issue of how countries view the future, which raises the issue of the discount rate (see chapter 3).

If discount rates are high, the short-term sacrifice will not seem worthwhile. Moreover, any one supplier can argue that it is depleting its forest resource in order to build up other forms of capital, thus securing sustainability in the sense of maintaining an overall stock of capital. These issues are common to many global and regional environmental agreements designed to secure sustainable use of the resource base.

In 1990 ITTO agreed to set the year 2000 as its target for achieving complete sustainability in the international trade of tropical timber. For some of the world's tropical forests, even this target, if it is achieved, will be too late.

The Cassava Trade

Cassava (also known as manioc and tapioca) is a root crop widely grown for human consumption in the tropics and a rich source of feed for livestock. It is highly suited to poor soils, is often the last crop in a rotation of crops, and requires comparatively little attention (Purseglove 1968). Until recent years, very little cassava was traded internationally. Currently some 8 million tons are exported from Thailand—where it is grown as a cash crop mainly in the low-income northeast highlands—to Belgium, Germany, and the Netherlands—where it is used as commercial feed for livestock, especially pigs. Exports from Thailand dominate European Community imports of cassava. (Intensive pig production also has significant environmental consequences in the Netherlands, where pig dung contributes to water pollution through runoff.)

Because cassava tolerates widely varying conditions, but prefers poor soils, small farmers in Thailand grow it as a commercial crop on previously forested land. Some authorities cite cassava production as a significant cause of deforestation, soil erosion, and soil nutrient reduction in Thailand (Myers 1986).

The reality is more complex. Cassava does not deplete the soil more than most other crops: it is usually planted ahead of the main rains and thus does not contribute to erosion from that source, but it does remove nutrients from the soil. When farming technology does not include artificial fertilizers, as is generally the case in northeast Thailand, cassava production depletes nutrients from the soil. Although cassava production was secured in Thailand by clearing forests, the reasons for doing so were complex. Building new roads for military purposes opened up the northeast uplands, and farmers began to grow cassava to meet the demand in the European Community. If they had not grown cassava, they would have grown another crop in an effort to escape considerable poverty. In short, deforestation would have occurred anyway. Cassava production takes place on some 25 percent of deforested land; most deforestation is the result of logging, followed by clearance for other crops, livestock, and so forth (see van Amstel and others 1986).

The Hamburger Connection

The hamburger is a legendary fast food in many countries, especially the United States. The meat used for hamburgers comes from grass-fed cattle, some of which is imported by the United States from Central America. Because cattle ranching in Central America often takes place on pasture cleared from forest, the idea has grown that U.S. consumption of hamburgers contributes directly to deforestation in Central America.[3] The reality is, once again, more complex.

Table 12-8 shows the amount of beef produced by and exported from Central America between 1961 and 1986. Exports comprised between 20 and 30 percent of a general increase in beef production, but exports specifically to the United States are no higher today than they were in 1966–70. Indeed, total exports declined after 1981 by some 40 percent. It is difficult, then, to link beef exports to increased deforestation, and harder still to link the demand for hamburgers to deforestation.

Nevertheless, forest has been cleared for pasture in Central America. Between 1960 and 1980 Costa Rica's forests declined in area some 6,000 square kilometers, and pastures increased the same amount. In Honduras, 30,000 square kilometers of forest were cleared, and pasture rose 14,000 square kilometers. For Nicaragua, the corresponding figures are 20,000 and 17,000 square kilometers, respectively (these figures are taken from Leonard 1987, table A34, p. 223).

Part of the mythology of the so-called hamburger connection is that U.S. imports are satisfied at the expense of per capita consumption of beef within Central America; however, domestic consumption accounted for some 80 percent of production in the 1980s, compared with 60–70 percent in the 1960s and 1970s. Indeed, per capita consumption within

Table 12-8. Central American Production and Exports of Beef, 1961–86
(thousands of metric tons, unless otherwise noted)

Year	Total production	Total exports	Exports as a percentage of production	Exports to the United States	Exports to the United States as a percentage of production
1961–65[a]	153	34	22	23	15
1966–70[a]	198	75	38	47	24
1971–75[a]	287	119	41	82	29
1976–80[a]	363	138	38	87	24
1981	356	101	28	67	19
1982	353	91	26	60	17
1983	351	81	23	56	16
1984	320	61	19	46	14
1985	315	66	21	52	16
1986	318	61[b]	19	50	16

a. Average.
b. Excluding Nicaragua.
Source: Leonard (1987), p. 87.

Central America is growing, as table 12-9 shows. The hamburger connection seems to be limited to a number of large ranches that supply the export trade. Browder (1988b), commenting on a similar view that the consumption of hamburgers is responsible for destroying the Brazilian rain forest, remarks that, "It is highly doubtful that even a single Brazilian rain forest hamburger has ever been consumed in the United States." Legal Amazonia supplied the United States with only 0.007 percent of its consumption of beef in 1982. In addition, U.S. health regulations prohibit the importation of fresh, uncooked beef from that source.

Table 12-9. Per Capita Consumption of Beef in Central America, 1960–84
(pounds)

Country	1960[a]	1972	1980[b]	1984
Belize	10	14	17	—
Costa Rica	27	19	36	36
El Salvador	17	12	14	13
Guatemala	19	15	24	15
Honduras	16	14	16	24
Nicaragua	32	29	29	25
Panama	42	52	45	52

— Not available.
a. Average for 1959–73.
b. Average for 1979–80.
Source: Leonard (1987).

European Community Beef and Range Degradation in Southern Africa

The European Community (EC) imports a guaranteed quantity of beef from Botswana each year through the various rounds of the Lome Convention, which govern EC's relations with the developing world. It has similar agreements with other countries such as Kenya and Swaziland. High agricultural support prices in the EC mean that Botswana secures more revenue from this arrangement than if the beef were sold at world prices. About 85 percent of Botswana's beef production is exported, half to EC countries (mainly Germany, the Netherlands, and the United Kingdom), 33 percent to South Africa, and 13 percent to other African countries (Cook 1988). Botswana beef is grass-fed and therefore leaner than the grain-fed beef typically consumed in the EC. This explains Botswana's ability to secure an export agreement with the EC, which otherwise produces a surplus of beef.

Botswana ranching has expanded considerably in recent years, frequently into relatively marginal savannah lands, where cattle compete with indigenous wildlife. The national herd probably doubled in size between 1964 and 1984; overgrazing is widespread, and range degradation is common (Arntzen and Veenendaal 1986; Ringrose and Matheson 1986). Much of the overgrazing is encouraged by fiscal incentives and subsidized services. Livestock owners receive various benefits from the government: animal health, extension, and research services; veterinary cordon fences; subsidies for slaughterhouses; and tax write-offs whereby agricultural investments and running losses can be offset against income from other sources. Having the EC as a guaranteed market simply adds to the list of existing domestic policy distortions that encourage increased stocking rates and more range degradation. That is, the price guaranteed for the EC acts as a further subsidy to livestock producers. According to Veenendaal and Opschoor (1986), a relatively small number of large-scale producers receives the greatest benefits from this multiple subsidy. In 1982, small, traditional farmers (94 percent of all cattle farmers) received an estimated 33 percent of the sales revenue from exports to the EC, traditional farmers (6 percent) received 22 percent of revenues, and commercial farmers (0.6 percent) received 45 percent of revenues, which indicates a highly skewed distribution of benefits.

Agricultural Protection in Industrial Countries

The agreement between EC and Botswana is just one example of trade links that have environmental consequences in the developing world. The industrial world protects its agriculture, generally keeping domestic agricultural prices above world prices. Developing countries practice the opposite, keeping domestic prices below world prices to benefit low-income (and, often, not so low-income) groups. Low domestic prices in the developing world are achieved through overvalued currencies, export taxes and quotas, and domestic price ceilings on food. This global price structure distorts world agriculture, biasing its production to the industrial (high-cost) world and against the developing (low-cost) world (this section relies heavily on Schuh 1990). Thus protectionism in industrial countries—in addition to misguided policy in developing countries—contributes directly to global income inequality.

To compound the problem, overproduction in the industrial world contributes directly to pollution from runoff and the destruction of habitats by removing hedgerow and using land that would otherwise be fallow. Currency overvaluation in the developing world encourages environmental destruction: while large farms can escape an implicit (or explicit) export tax by extending the amount of productive land, small farmers have no option but to mitigate the cost by cultivating marginal lands such as forests and hillsides.

Trade Links and Environment

Evidence regarding the effect of trade on the environment is mixed, as is apparent from the examples outlined above. Whereas the slaughter of elephants is clearly the result of global demand for ivory, deforestation and soil erosion in Thailand cannot be blamed wholly on international trade in cassava.

The trade in hardwoods, beef consumption, and agricultural protection in industrial countries suggest that environmental damage results from a combination of factors. These include domestic policy distortions in exporting countries, compounded by commodity exports and protectionism in industrial countries.

The relation between international trading and environmental quality has also raised the issue of whether or not free trade is necessarily a good thing. The issues are many. First, free trade is alleged to cause environmental degradation: hence liberalization of trade should be attenuated for environmental reasons. An example might be the trade in tropical hardwoods. Second, protection of domestic markets is said to cause environmental degradation: hence trade liberalization favors the environment. An example might be the Common Agricultural Policy. This point is clearly inconsistent with the first. Third, it is argued that trade should be restricted when it creates environmental degradation either by importing products that pollute the importing country (the case of unidirectional externality) or by encouraging production that may incur damages to both the exporting and the importing countries (the common property or mutual externality case). Fourth, it is argued that the existence of high environmental standards in an importing country is a nontariff barrier designed to protect the domestic market, and all countries should harmonize their environmental standards. Since richer countries tend to have higher environmental standards than poorer ones, this is frequently seen as an argument for lowering standards to permit development in poorer countries. On the other hand, countries with low environmental standards might be thought of as giving implicit subsidies to their exports since the costs of environmental degradation are not included in the price of those exports. This tends to be an argument for raising environmental standards in poor countries. Fifth, it is argued that other environmental policy instruments, such as environmental taxes or subsidies, also distort trade. Sixth, some international agreements retain trade discrimination as a weapon of compliance. That discrimination is thought by some to be contrary to the principles of the General Agreement on Tariffs and Trade (GATT). If so, and if GATT takes precedence, the implications for the design and effectiveness of international agreements are formidable.

Since GATT aims to ensure fair free trade, all the above issues are relevant to how GATT is designed and hence to the possibility of its reform. The implications are considered to be, according to the point of view, first, that GATT may result in environmental degradation by refusing to allow trade restrictions motivated by concern for the environment and, second, that GATT may remove a weapon of compliance for international agreements.

Since GATT was devised at a time when environmental awareness and concern were low, it is widely argued that GATT should be reformed in order to state explicitly the circumstances in which exceptions to trade liberalization should be made on environmental grounds.

The Benefits of Free Trade

Free trade is good, not as an end in itself but as a means of improving the world's standard of living. Some efforts have been made to quantify the gains from trade or, to look at it from another way, the costs of protection. Although many studies find that the annual costs of protection can run as much as 1 percent of gross national product (GNP), these estimates probably understate the true losses. The reason for this understatement is that these studies often use a partial equilibrium framework, identify immediate production and consumption losses only, and ignore other forms of inefficiency.

Production losses caused by protection arise because domestic producers can, with a tariff, produce at costs of production above the true world price. Consumption losses arise because consumers consume less at the new price, which includes the tariff. Together, these losses comprise the deadweight loss of welfare from protection. However, changes in the price and quantity of the protected good affect other prices and quantities in the economy. General equilibrium modeling provides an overall estimate of the gains and losses to the economy as a whole. Some general equilibrium studies suggest that protection may cost as much as 5 percent of GNP, while others estimate that it may cost less (Grais, de Melo, and Urata 1986; Shoven and Whalley 1984).

Protection entails other costs as well. It may encourage careless management of costs, resulting in X-inefficiency; it may encourage monopoly, which restricts output and creates further welfare losses; and it may encourage rent seeking and directly unproductive profit seeking. Rent seeking arises because import restrictions make the traded commodity relatively scarce and give rise to rents. Rent seekers then spend resources trying to capture these rents, through, for example, lobbying activity. Directly unproductive profit seeking embraces all activities that are unproductive but generate profit. This includes exerting pressure to create restrictions on trade in order to generate rent, which is then captured by rent seeking. In India and Turkey, profit sharing that is directly unproductive may equal as much as 7–15 percent of GNP (World Bank 1987).

Given the potentially large gains to be obtained from free trade, policies that restrict trade for environmental purposes must be approached with caution. Most important, all other approaches to reducing environmental damage should be exhausted before trade policy measures are contemplated.

Does Free Trade Cause Environmental Degradation?

The gains from trade are not without costs, and the environment might suffer as the result of liberalized trade in several ways.

First, free trade tends to increase economic activity, which tends to drag more materials and energy through the economic system (the materials balance principle). This is the growth effect of trade liberalization (Daly and Cobb 1989, chap. 11). Such an increase is likely but not necessary since it depends on what happens to the technical coefficients between economic activity and inputs. If energy inputs per unit of economic activity decline over time, as they have in industrial countries, expanding output need not increase energy consumption. Economic expansion is also likely to involve changes in land use that threaten natural environments. Sites that were once green will be converted to housing and factories, roads, and other developments. The EC Single Market, for example, has the potential to worsen environmental quality (Schneider and others 1989). As an example, the internal market is expected to increase transfrontier lorry traffic 30–50 percent.

Second, free trade may result in industrial and agricultural reorganization to capture the economies of scale made possible by larger markets. This might involve larger productive units: factories that are aesthetically unpleasing and farms that remove hedgerows and use intensive agricultural techniques.

Third, free international trade neglects the environment in the same way that domestic free markets fail to account for environmental losses. In other words, trade liberalization can be expected to increase market failure.

Fourth, freer trade removes subsidy systems since subsidies are barriers to free trade. This offsets the previous effects to some extent. Where subsidies take the form of price supports, overproduction tends to decrease, which may benefit the environment. The Common Agricultural Policy is a case in point, depending on how the use of land changes as the system of support is reduced over time.

Overall, then, trade liberalization is likely to produce negative environmental externalities, but also some environmental gains. The negative association between freer trade and environmental degradation does not imply that freer trade should be halted. It does suggest that the most cost-effective policies should be adopted to optimize the externality. Restricting trade is unlikely to be the most efficient way of controlling the problem, especially if trade retaliation may occur. The losses can best be minimized by firm domestic environmental policy designed to uncouple the environmental effects from the economic activity. This firm environmental policy may itself have international trade effects. The best way to correct externalities is to tackle them directly by implementing the "polluter pays principle," not restricting the level of trade. Where having the polluter pay is itself not feasible (when, for example, the exporter is a poor developing country), adopting cooperative policies—such as transferring clean technology or assisting with cleanup policies—will likely be preferable to adopting import restrictions.

GATT and the Environment

At this point, it is useful to establish how GATT approaches environmental issues. Since the environment was not an international issue in 1947 when GATT was signed, much depends on how the actual clauses of the agreement are interpreted. This judgment, in turn, calls for examining the deliberations of the panels in disputes that can be regarded as environmental.

The essence of the GATT approach to environment can be summarized as free trade principles and as exceptions to free trade. The free trade principles are as follows.

All domestic policies with trade effects are subject to two basic principles: most favored nation (article I) and national treatment (article III). Under most favored nation, any trade advantage conferred by one country on another must automatically be extended to all other members of GATT. Under national treatment, all contracting nations must treat imported goods in the same way as like or competing domestic goods.

Thus, they cannot tax an import if the same domestic good is exempted from the tax.

Under article II, any protection should be based on bound tariffs, that is, maximum tariffs for goods listed in an annex. In turn, these bound tariffs should decline over time as successive GATT rounds of negotiations are completed.

Article XI forbids the use of quantitative restrictions such as quotas, while article XVI deals with subsidies, which are, by and large, tolerated if they do not harm the export interests of other nations. There is a separate subsidies code (Agreement on Interpretation and Application of Articles VI, XVI, and XXIII) to which not all GATT members are signatories.

Exceptions to free trade also exist. For example, exceptions to the general free trade requirements can be made for severe balance of payments problems (articles XII and XVIII), national security (article XXI), and severe industrial effects (article XIX). Environmental exceptions come under article XX, which, in turn, sets out general exceptions to GATT principles. Article XX(b) allows exceptions for measures *"necessary to* protect human, animal, or plant life or health" (our emphasis), while article XX(g) specifies measures *"relating to* the conservation of exhaustible natural resources if such measures are made effective in conjunction with restrictions on domestic production or consumption" (our emphasis).

Reinstein (1991) notes that these clauses do not specify the location of the resources to be protected or conserved. In principle, therefore, they could relate to resources outside the country restricting the trade. However, it is difficult to construe article XX(g) in this way since the reference to similar treatment of domestic resources implies that the threatened resources are themselves domestic. Article XX(b) could be interpreted more generally. As we shall see, the resolutions clearly indicate that extraterritorial conservation—that is, conservation of resources outside national boundaries—is not a legitimate concern of GATT.

It is also important to note that all exceptions to article XX are subject to a general requirement that any restriction should not "constitute a means of arbitrary or unjustifiable discrimination between countries where the same conditions prevail, or [act as] a disguised restriction on international trade" (Reinstein 1991).

The Agreement on Technical Barriers to Trade—the Standards Code—deals explicitly with environmental standards. In principle, standards should not create unnecessary obstacles to trade, and countries can seek resolution of disputes that may arise. To date, however, no formal resolutions of disputes have been made (Reinstein 1991).

Although article XX(b) is being applied to environmentally induced restrictions, its original intent was primarily to cover quarantine and health cases (Hegenbart and Windfur 1991).

The most obvious interpretation of article XX(g) is that discrimination is justified if an import does not meet domestic environmental standards. The scope of the clause is however, largely untested.

The two clauses do have ambiguities. For example, the reference to exhaustible resources in article XX(g) is ambiguous because all resources, even renewable ones, are exhaustible when they are not managed sustainably. It is unclear whether GATT distinguishes between renewable and nonrenewable resources or recognizes that both categories are potentially exhaustible. Moreover, the meaning of health in article XX(b) appears to include the health risks posed by goods that are consumed voluntarily (for example, U.S. cigarettes are subject to an import ban in Thailand on health grounds), but the impact of this clause on, for example, aesthetics has not been tested.

The location of the environmental damage that warrants an exception is also unclear, although the article apparently refers to the environment of the importing country. Article XX(b) requires that the measures undertaken be necessary to protect health, but the meaning of necessary is unclear (does it mean, for example, that no other choice is available or simply that this is the most suitable measure?). Article XX(g) also implies that conservation per se need not be the prime concern provided the restrictive measure is in some way related to conservation. Indonesia's ban on the export of whole logs was primarily intended to capture the value added by domestic processing, not to conserve forests (indeed, through inefficient processing, deforestation has almost certainly been accelerated; Repetto and Gillis 1988). Yet Indonesia has used article XX(g) to defend the ban. The argument is weak, however, since Indonesia has neither instituted measures to conserve forests domestically nor restricted domestic production or consumption, as article XX(g) requires. The exact status of social objectives, such as the protection of health, compared with the objectives of free trade is open to question. The case of Thailand's ban on tobacco imports suggests that other objectives have status equal to or greater than that of free trade: the GATT panel declared that article XX clearly allows parties to give priority to human health over trade liberalization (Sorsa 1992), although the requirement that the exceptions in article XX should not be used to discriminate arbitrarily or unjustifiably may elevate free trade above other considerations. Whether environment has the same status as health for defending restrictions remains unclear.

Overall, then, GATT treats any environmental case for restrictions as an exception to be dealt with either under article XX or through the Standards Code. Moreover, the presumption in favor of free trade is reinforced by the procedures for settling disputes, which require that a disputes panel look first for any incompatibility of the restriction with GATT rules. Once incompatibility has been eliminated, then the panel looks for compatibility with article XX. That is, a trade restriction is presumed to be wrong, and the burden of proof rests with the defender of that restriction. Nonetheless, there is sufficient ambiguity in article XX and elsewhere in GATT for confusion to arise and inconsistent rulings to be made on exceptions.

Environmental Disputes under GATT

Only a few cases that can be termed environmental have been raised under articles XX(b) and XX(g). The case concerning Mexican tuna is discussed here. The case of a Thai ban on cigarettes is included to illustrate article XX(b).

In 1988, the United States amended its Marine Mammal Act to restrict imports of tuna that are caught using purse-seine methods, which also catch dolphins at a higher rate than the average for the U.S. fleet. The restriction was confined to the eastern Pacific where, the United States argued, dolphins are endangered. The restriction thus had a heavy impact on Mexico and almost no effect on U.S. fishermen, who had, in the main, given up fishing in the region. Mexico appealed to GATT on several grounds: the measure was protectionist and designed primarily to protect U.S. fishermen, much fewer dolphins were killed in Mexican nets than had been killed historically by the U.S. fleet, the dolphin kill rate was declining rapidly, and the national treatment clause was breached since the average kill rate for dolphins is known only at the end of the season and Mexico would not know until then whether it could sell tuna to the United States.

The issues in the case were as follows:

- Was the restriction primarily for conservation or industrial protection?
- Was the restriction necessary for conservation?
- Did article XX(g) cover processes (methods of catch in this case) as opposed to products, which are judged to be relevant to article XX(g) under the Superfund judgment?
- Were restrictions on quantity allowed?

The panel ruled that article XX(g) does not allow restrictions that protect natural resources outside the jurisdiction of the country doing the restricting. Although from an economic point of view, the United States can be argued to have suffered an externality (through the impact that this form of fishing has on the concern of individuals and the nation for wildlife, regardless of where it is located), GATT effectively ruled that the externality must be territorial. Moreover, the panel reaffirmed its previous ruling that restrictions cannot be justified if they relate to the process of production rather than to the product itself.

Although not obviously environmental, the case of Thailand's ban on cigarettes illustrates article XX(b). Thailand restricted imports of U.S. cigarettes on the grounds that they were a risk to public health. The argument was that Thailand had a general need to reduce consumption and that U.S. cigarettes were more harmful than Thai cigarettes. The United States countered that no restrictions on a comparable domestic industry existed and that national treatment was thus at stake. The World Health Organization became involved, indicating that the Thai public health system could not counteract the marketing might of the U.S. tobacco multinationals and, by implication, that Thailand could not take effective alternative measures. The panel ruled against Thailand but acknowledged that human health might have priority over trade liberalization. The measure was not necessary within the terms of article XX(b) because other measures, such as bans on advertising, could be taken that were consistent with GATT.

These case studies could be taken to suggest that GATT, as it stands, does not, despite the exceptions indicated in article XX, permit the use of trade restrictions to further environmental objectives. However, the cases in question were not judged to have environmental objectives as their main concern; that is, they were judged to be protectionist first and conservationist only second. It is not clear, therefore, what would happen if a measure that had a small degree of domestic economic benefit and a significant conservation benefit were brought to GATT's attention. Most environmental measures clearly have some incidental protectionist element, whether it is a domestic environmental standard or a restriction on imported logs. Deciding when protection or conservation is the primary motive could be very difficult. For that reason alone, article XX should be clarified at least. Moreover, as several commentators have pointed out, GATT panelists are not environmental experts.

Another reason for seeking clarification is that it is not clear what would happen if an appeal against trade sanctions were allowed under international agreements, such as the Montreal Protocol. Some commentators fear that sanctions would have to be removed as a weapon from all such agreements (Arden-Clarke 1991). Significant differences separate the essentially bilateral trade restrictions that have been tested so far under GATT and the restrictions that would come into play under an international agreement:

- International restrictions would be collectively enforced; that is, they would be enforced by more than one country on a defaulter
- The environmental objective should be clearly primary in international agreements, whereas it may not be in bilateral agreements.

GATT, as it stands, offers no guidance on these possibilities and as such must be clarified.

A third concern arises from the presumption that the gains from trade exceed the losses from environmental damage that may be associated with the trade. This is an empirical issue that has not, as far as we know, ever been tested. Essentially, it would be tested by comparing the welfare gains from liberalized trade with the welfare losses in both the exporting and importing countries from all associated environmental degradation, regardless of where it occurs.

The final issue is GATT's distinction between environmental damage arising from the product and that arising from the method of production. In economic terms, there is a legitimate externality in either case, so that the distinction appears to be artificial. We might, however, distinguish between damage and externality (welfare loss). The damage may be caused in the exporting country (deforestation, say), but the welfare loss may be suffered in the importing country, which disapproves of the deforestation. The next section investigates this issue in more detail.

Trade Restrictions: The Case of Unidirectional Externality

A unidirectional externality arises when the exporter of a good imposes an environmental cost on the importer of the good. Two possibilities exist:

- The externality arises when the good is consumed in the importing country
- The externality arises when the good is produced in the exporting country.

Examples of an externality that arises when the good is consumed tend to occur when the import fails to meet domestic environmental standards. Suppose, for example, that the importer has set standards for the ability to recycle a product and that imports fail to meet that standard. If the import is allowed to enter the country, it imposes an externality on the importing country, which cannot recycle the product. The importer might then seek to restrict the nonrecyclable import on environmental grounds. Other examples include the United States's temporary ban in 1989 on all fruit imported from Chile after a health scare arising from a pesticide-contaminated shipment of Chilean grapes and the EC's ban, also in 1989, on the importation of U.S. beef containing growth hormones.

Examples of an externality that arises when a good is produced in the exporting country include the hardwood trade where, even if the exporting country does not recognize an externality to itself, the importing country deems the resulting deforestation to be unacceptable. The externality arises when the damage done by the process or the product in the exporting country causes a welfare loss in the importing country. As noted in the discussion of past disputes, GATT clearly intends to rule out any externality arising from production. Only consumption externalities arising from the product are relevant.

Consumption Externalities

Cases of consumption externalities have been tested within the EC. Outside the environmental context, Germany attempted to ban French imports of crème de cassis on the grounds that its alcohol content did not meet German standards, and the case went before the European Court of Justice in 1979. The Court rejected Germany's case because it did not feel that this kind of standards-induced consumption externality could justify the trade restriction. In the environmental context, Denmark secured the opposite judgment against the EC when the Court ruled that its ban on the import of nonreturnable beverage containers was justified on environmental grounds.

How do the rules of GATT apply to such consumption externalities? First, a country would have to demonstrate damage and externality, that is, demonstrate that the effects are sizable. Health risks have been established as acceptable externalities, but environmental risks unrelated to health are still not clearly acceptable externalities.

Second, any restriction—whether a restriction on quantity, a tax, or a subsidy—must be shown to be necessary (according to article XX[b]) or related to the externality (article XX[g])—that is, the restricting country could not reduce the externality any other way. The case dealing with tobacco, for example, concluded that Thailand had legitimate concerns with health, but that weapons other than banning trade were available to it, such as mounting an information campaign.

Third, if the restriction differentiates between sources of the import, that differentiation must not be arbitrary or unjustified. From this it follows that GATT's interpretation would be that a consumption externality is, at first glance, a legitimate reason for restricting trade under article XX provided there is evidence of the externality, provided the trade restriction is efficient in some sense, and provided the restriction is uniformly applied.

Is this interpretation consistent with economic analysis? By and large, it is since GATT rules could be interpreted to suggest that trade restrictions should only be used if the net gains in welfare are positive and secured at least cost. However, this interpretation has two problems:

- Cost-efficiency may not be a relevant interpretation of GATT's requirement that a restriction be necessary to protect life or health; that is, the GATT rules may require that a more costly measure be taken if it is available. From an economic standpoint, the relevant comparison would be net gains and losses in welfare (K. Anderson 1992).
- The requirement that a restriction not discriminate against other nations could actually be economically inefficient since under the "polluter pays principle," it would be optimal to discriminate between imports according to the damage done (which means that a tax should be related to the damage caused; Rauscher 1991).

Production Externalities

Externalities that arise in the process of production are likely to be the most important challenge to GATT. An obvious example is acid rain that is transported internationally, although the production externality is much wider than the direct impact of acid rain. In the case of logging and deforestation, for example, the externality may be distributed between exporter and importer. The exporter may suffer because clear-felling increases soil erosion and sedimentation of water systems, which, in turn, reduce water productivity by, for example, reducing fish catches. The importer may suffer because of concern over the loss of biological diversity (loss of use, option, and existence values; see Pearce and Turner 1989). The issues arising are whether the importer can justify an import restriction on the grounds of the externality suffered in the importing country, the externality suffered in the exporting country, or both. The unidirectional case is best served by concentrating on externality suffered in the importing country. Austria and the Netherlands already have import bans on tropical timber that is produced unsustainably. Externality suffered in the exporting country is not irrelevant, however, since, although it may be best dealt with by domestic policies in the exporting country, a number of cases arise in which the importer could be acting on behalf of a minority or persecuted group (such as Indians in the Amazon).

GATT clearly dismisses externalities arising from production as opposed to consumption and does not allow them as an exception. In economic terms, however, the nature of the externality is not important. Both consumption and production externalities generate welfare losses in the importing country. Differentiating the types of externality therefore arises only from some notion of property rights, for example, the notion that no importing nation has a right to interfere with the production technology of another country. This principle supports the ruling of extraterritoriality in the case dealing with Mexican tuna.

GATT does not allow production externality in principle. The issue is not whether trade restrictions are the most efficient way of reducing the externality. In most cases, they certainly are not. The issue is the domestic policies of the exporting nation. But if a process of political persuasion fails to alter those policies, should importing nations be able to discriminate against products from countries producing, say, acid rain? If the principle that the restriction must be necessary to protect life or health is invoked, the importing nation must demonstrate that all other reasonable measures have been taken. The problem is more complex than this, however, since if an exception is allowed, the product that could be the subject of the restriction is not clear. Acid rain comes from power generation, and electricity is embodied in virtually all products. If the electricity itself is not traded, the trade restriction cannot be against the product directly produced by the polluting technology. It would have to be against other products, which raises concerns about blanket import restrictions.

Thus, although there appears to be no intrinsic difference between production and consumption externalities, there are formidable problems associated with allowing exceptions for production externalities. It is not clear where the process would end.

Trade Restrictions: The Case of Mutual Externality

Mutual externalities arise when the pollution from an exporting nation affects a common resource such as the ozone layer, the atmosphere, and the oceans. Typically, controlling such externalities requires an international agreement, and such agreements may use trade sanctions as a weapon to ensure mutual compliance, that is, to prevent free riders. For GATT, the issue becomes how to determine the necessity of such measures. Reinstein (1991) suggests that the need for trade restrictions arises not just because an agreement must be secured for environmental purposes, but because the agreement imposes costs on the participating parties that are avoided by nonparticipating parties. Thus, participants may bear some competitive disadvantage. In those circumstances, only collectively enforced trade restrictions will produce the desired result.

Under the Montreal Protocol on protection of the ozone layer, article 4 controls trade between signatories and nonsignatories in chlorofluorocarbons (CFCs) and in products containing them. It includes the threat of banning trade of products made with CFCs but not actually containing them—a clear example of a production externality. As Reinstein notes, if implemented, this would affect all trade in electronic equipment since CFCs are widely used to clean semiconductor chips. Compatibility with GATT was extensively discussed at the time of the Protocol, and the negotiations recognized a consistency between the Protocol and the GATT's article XX because the headnote to article XX states that the exceptions are subject to "the requirement that such measures are not applied in a manner which would constitute a means of arbitrary or unjustifiable discrimination *between countries where the same conditions prevail,* or a disguised restriction on international trade [our emphasis]." The argument was that conditions in the nonsignatory countries were different from those in the signatory countries, and hence the justification for trade restrictions was consistent with article XX.

As noted above, the role of collective discrimination against nonsignatories or defaulters might be used to distinguish trade restrictions from other restrictions in international agreements. Combined with the requirement that the same conditions prevail, which is contained in article XX, and the view that the need for restrictions can thus be more easily demonstrated in such cases, this suggests that trade restrictions under international agreements would be generally compatible with GATT. However, this is far from guaranteed, and, once again, some clarification would be valuable.

GATT and the Instruments of Environmental Policy

Environmental policy is secured through standards, taxes, and subsidies. How compatible are these with GATT? Standards and taxes are compatible with the "polluter pays principle." Subsidies are not unless they are transitional or linked to taxes (for example, deposit-refund systems; OECD 1975). GATT has a Code on Subsidies and Standards but no explicit guidelines on taxes. Thus the "polluter pays principle" is potentially compatible with GATT. The main source of incompatibility lies in the distinction between consumption and production externalities. Having the polluter pay is wholly consistent with taxing a production externality, and an import tax may therefore fulfill that function. As we have seen, GATT does not allow production externalities to qualify for exceptions.

Standards

Domestic environmental standards can clearly be barriers to trade. The standards impose higher costs on both domestic industries and their competitors if imports are treated the same as domestic products. GATT has an Agreement on Technical Barriers to Trade, the Standards Code, that permits environmental standards to be established provided they do not act as trade distortions when the same conditions prevail. It is legitimate to set standards to protect human, animal, or plant life and the environment. The Standards Code therefore refers explicitly to the environment, whereas article XX does not. The Code does not, however, define the term environment.

The Code recommends the use of internationally agreed standards, which means that it supports the idea of harmonized standards. Stricter standards can be justified, however, because countries can enact domestic standards that are higher than those enacted in other countries. Generally, although not explicitly, the Code apparently does not allow standards that are lower than the international norm, but this is not clear. Recent discussions have contemplated allowing countries to have standards that are lower than international standards when climatic, geographical, or technological problems arise. Whether a country can insist on imports having the same standard as domestic products is not clear. The Code appears to discuss products only, although article 14.25 mentions process and production methods. Most probably, as with the main articles, production externalities are excluded from consideration since the standards in question must be shown to be necessary and in keeping with scientific evidence. Thus the EC claimed that since the Code did not cover processes and production methods, its ban on hormone-fed beef from the United States was outside the scope of GATT. The United States argued that GATT was relevant to processes. GATT never resolved the issue. Recent discussions have centered on the idea of proportionality—standards should be in proportion to the environmental objective.

The Standards Code remains ambiguous particularly in the area of standards for process and production method (production externalities). Given the ruling governing Mexican tuna, the Standards Code probably will not be extended to process and production method, although the possibility is being discussed. As Sorsa (1992) notes, the case dealing with Mexican tuna raises issues about the nature of allowable standards. For example, if a standard on fishing technology had been agreed internationally for tuna—a standard related to a process—and Mexico did not agree to it, would the U.S. ban on tuna imports be justified?

Since the interpretation of the Standards Code is open to much latitude, assessing its compatibility with economic principles is difficult. Certainly the presumption that international environmental standards should be harmonized is not consistent with economic analysis. Countries might legitimately have different standards in order to reflect different tastes and preferences for environmental quality and different assimilative capacities (Siebert 1985; Siebert and others 1980). As with all GATT issues, the problem is to balance the gains from trade against the imposition of externalities.

Taxes

Under GATT, domestic taxes can be applied to imports of like products so long as they are applied equally and are not designed for protection. The ruling in the case of the Superfund Tax suggests that the impact of pollution does not have to be domestically located for the import tax to be justified. The precise compatibility between this extraterritorial impact and the extraterritorial impact in the case dealing with Mexican tuna is not clear.

In order to qualify as a tax that allows border tax adjustments, the tax must be borne by the product: it must be in the nature of an excise tax or an input tax in which the input is embodied in the product. Such taxes directly raise consumer prices, so that imports are not placed at a competitive disadvantage. Taxes like income taxes are excluded, as is a tax on fuel inputs, which is levied on the process, not the product. Such taxes could be absorbed by the product without increasing domestic prices. If they were then applied to import prices, imports would be at a competitive disadvantage, and this would be contrary to the principles of GATT. Thus, indirect taxes can be extended to imports, but process taxes cannot.

This rule implies that only a pollution tax levied on the pollution content of the product could be extended to imports. Even then, the principle of the polluter pays would allow discrimination between imports according to the effects of their environmental damage, whereas article I of GATT precludes this form of discrimination by disallowing discrimination between like products. Put another way, it is not possible, for the present, to argue that products are dissimilar because they have different pollution profiles. Moreover, GATT does not define what constitutes a like product. Case-by-case approaches have so far been used. If discriminating against like products is not allowed, one could argue that discrimination against polluting products is justified because the products are not alike precisely because they have different pollution effects. Most commentators seem to feel this is an unlikely scenario.

GATT initially appears to accept Pigovian-style pollution taxes, which, in turn, can be efficient. However, the continuing distinction between product and process limits the compatibility, as does precluding taxes on products differentiated by their environmental impact.

Subsidies

Subsidies are typically frowned upon under the "polluter pays principle." Until the recent Uruguay Round, GATT was ambivalent on subsidies. The main factor bringing subsidies to the fore has been the U.S. insistence that agricultural subsidies in Europe constitute unfair competition. The United States argues that such subsidies justify countervailing duties. One immediate problem is to determine what constitutes a subsidy (Snape 1991). Many argue that the absence of environmental regulations constitutes a subsidy to exports no different from financial subsidies actually transferred.

GATT prohibits export subsidies that make export prices for manufactured goods lower than domestic prices. As Snape (1991) notes, however, this test of a subsidy generally does not embrace production subsidies. Subsidies on primary products have typically not been addressed by GATT in other than vague language, while agricultural subsidies have generally been outside GATT since a waiver to the United States in 1955. Where a subsidy is proscribed, GATT rules allow countervailing duties no greater than the amount of the subsidy if a material threat exists to the domestic industry.

The Subsidies Code attempts to codify what is and is not allowed, but only some thirty countries (out of ninety contracting to GATT) have signed it. Export subsidies outside agriculture are technically prohibited, but not for the exports of developing countries. Agricultural export subsidies are supposed to be limited so as to avoid taking a share of world export trade that is more than equitable. This is a generally vague requirement. GATT has issued a general call against using subsidies to the detriment of other countries, but subsidies in developing countries are generally excluded from even this requirement.

By and large, then, environmental subsidies appear to be allowed under existing GATT rules. The Uruguay Round considered some more precise text in which subsidies to adapt existing facilities to new environmental standards would qualify as compatible with GATT, as would subsidies for research and development into even stricter environmental technology. As it stands at the moment, the argument that lack of standards constitutes a subsidy could be valid in GATT terms, which means that it could constitute grounds for countervailing action. Such an interpretation of a subsidy could have dramatic implications for developing countries, where environmental regulations are often minimal and the cost of adopting such standards could be significant. At the same time, however, no implicit subsidy has been tested, and authorities differ in their opinion of the likelihood of success if one were. The test would, for example, require the inclusion of an affirmative duty to protect the environment in the first place (Komoroski 1988; Shrybman 1990). Clearly, there is a need for extensive clarification.

Do Environmental Regulations Inhibit Competitiveness and Do Firms Move to Pollution Havens?

One major argument for harmonizing environmental standards across nations is that variable standards discourage competitiveness in the regulating country and encourage industries to migrate to countries with the lowest standards. The relevance to GATT is limited since GATT does not concern itself with regulating the behavior of multinational companies nor with an individual country's competitiveness. The relevance to environmental policy is stronger because industries threaten to relocate when lobbying against stricter environmental standards. The issue is linked to the more general one of whether environmental regulations cause firms to lose their competitive advantage.

Loss of Competitiveness

Dean (1991) surveys the literature on competitiveness and concludes that past and existing environmental regulations have little effect on competitiveness. This is because regulatory abatement costs are a small proportion of total costs and thus not significant, little output is lost, and the effects on trade are minimal. Walter (1973, 1982) found that, for U.S. industries, abatement costs for exports were only 1.75 percent on average compared with 1.5 percent for imports. Yezer and Philipson (1974) found that the reductions in output due to environmental regulations amounted to less than 1 percent. Mutti and Richardson (1976) found that environmental regulations increased prices 1 percent and reduced output 1.5 percent. Robinson (1988) also found that environmental regulations cause small changes in U.S. trade. Tobey (1990) calculates user costs at under 1.85 percent of total costs for forty industries, and from 1.85 to 2.89 percent for twenty-four industries, and shows no statistically significant difference between the exports of strictly regulated and those of leniently regulated firms. Overall, then, there is no evidence that industrial competitiveness has been affected by environmental regulation.

Pollution Havens

The interest in pollution havens is primarily political and strategic. Since countries vary in their environmental endowment and preference for environmental quality, it would be economically efficient if firms did relocate to areas where relatively lax environmental standards genuinely reflected differences in endowments and tastes. In practice, those who suffer the externalities tend to complain that they are being treated unfairly and that polluting technologies are being deliberately foisted on them.

As it happens, there is very little evidence to suggest that firms move in response to variable environmental policies. The reasons include those given for the loss of competitiveness: environmental regulations generally have very little impact on price and output. Even when the effects are significant, however, relocating is only profitable if the difference in actual and expected environmental costs is greater than the costs of relocation. Leonard (1989b, 1991) has surveyed the literature and carried out case studies. He found that overseas investment by U.S. manufacturing firms between 1970 and 1987 did not respond to domestic environmental legislation. In fact, investment was highest in industries with low pollution control costs. Some industries were pressured to move. These included manufacturers of toxic products that were unable to meet domestic standards—notably asbestos, arsenic trioxide, benzidine-based dyes, some pesticides, and some carcinogenic chemicals. In a number of cases, however, the temporary relocation of industry or of sources of supply was halted when consumption fell within the United States. In other cases—copper, zinc, and lead processing—some industries moved to other countries, but the role of environmental regulation was limited since factors relating to the requirement for processing in the country of origin and the availability of raw materials were also present. Some chemical activities may have moved, primarily because of workplace safety legislation, but other market factors were also at work. Leonard did not find any industry facing expanding demand or possessing technological superiority choosing to relocate. For many firms, technological innovation, use of new raw materials or substitute products, reclamation of waste materials, tighter processing and quality controls, and other adaptations are generally better responses than flight (this message is delivered in Warford 1987).

Using Economic Policy to Manage the Environment: Structural Adjustment Lending

The materials balance approach to the economy allows economic policy to be used to modify environmental quality. In the industrial and developing world, substantial attention is paid to economic policies that aim to modify the major economic aggregates such as GNP, the external trade balance, the rate of inflation, the money supply, and so on. Price setting is also widely used in the developing world to influence aggregate responses, such as agricultural output and export performance, and the distribution of income. The prospect arises, then, of thinking about national planning in the developing world as a means of securing environmental objectives that, in turn, are designed to secure long-run welfare objectives or sustainable development (Sebastian and Alicbusan 1989).

Environmental impact is rarely considered, but when it is, environmental policy is generally determined on a project by project basis. An investment in a particular area is checked for its environmental impact and may be modified to minimize environmental damage, or projects may be specifically designed to improve the environment (table 12-10). This approach is inadequate. First, projects often do not achieve their intended results since they depend on a mixture of good design, careful management, and continued management after teams from the donor agency cease to participate. Second, projects tend to be specific to a sector or a location; although they can affect the entire economy, that is not usually the case. Environmental degradation tends to be pervasive and therefore requires pervasive policies that reach throughout the economy. The most powerful tools for doing so are price controls and regulations. Projects exert an important influence but must be combined with macroeconomic policy reforms.

The flow of funds from official lending sources to developing countries has thus made increasing use of structural adjustment and sectoral adjustment. The aim of adjustment lending is to secure desirable adjustments in the borrowing economy and to mitigate the effects of the adjustment, particularly on the balance of payments. An adjustment program is agreed with the borrowing country, and lending is phased in order to monitor the achievements of the adjustment program. In this way, the loans have conditionality—that is, phased payments are conditional on achieving the agreed objectives. Table 12-11 indicates the extent of adjustment lending by multilateral agencies between 1983 and 1988.

The idea that structural adjustment should focus more on environmental conservation is of recent origin and contrasts with the criticism that structural adjustment loans (SALs) are an instrument of environmental destruction. Because they shift economic activity within the borrowing country, SALs may, it is argued, cause environmental degradation. Table 12-12 shows the type of adjustment that a SAL may request.

The evidence does not support the view that SALs have been environmentally destructive. Table 12-13 reviews the experience of SALs extended by the World Bank between 1979 and 1987 (Sebastian and Alicbusan 1989).

In twenty-three of the forty-three cases reviewed in table 12-13, adjustment policies raised agricultural prices. The impact of increased farmgate

Table 12-10. World Bank Loans with Environmental Components, 1989

Sector	Total number of loans	Number of loans with environmental components	Environmental loans as a percentage of total loans
Agriculture and rural development	51	39	76
Forestry	3	3	100
Irrigation and drainage	5	5	100
Area development	10	9	90
Research and extension	10	8	80
Agroindustry	5	2	40
Other	18	12	67
Energy	23	12	52
Oil, gas, and coal	6	4	67
Power	17	8	47
Transportation	22	7	32
Water supply and sewerage	10	7	70
Industry	14	5	36
Industrial development finance	16	3	19
Small-scale industry	5	1	20
Urbanization	12	3	25
Telecommunications	7	0	0
Education	19	2	11
Population, health, and nutrition	12	2	17
Technical assistance	13	0	0
Nonproject	21	4	19
Sectoral adjustment	14	4	29
Other	7	0	0
Total	225	85	38

Source: Warford and Partow (1989).

prices is not always clear, but in the countries in question, the increase tended to be for perennial crops that provide a continuous root structure and canopy cover. Such crops assist soil stability on sloping land and include bananas, cocoa, coffee, palm oil, rubber, and tea. Food crops not intended for export—for example, cassava, maize, millet, and sorghum—are often erosive. In general, SALs encourage environmentally benign crops more than erosive ones. Potentially damaging crops, such as cotton and tobacco, tend to be produced under sustainable conditions by commercially oriented organizations. SALs also lowered the price of some food crops that are environmentally damaging: maize, rice, and sorghum in Panama, and cotton, foodgrains, and tobacco in Turkey, for example. Although the motive for these price reductions was not

Table 12-11. *Adjustment Lending by Major Multilateral Donors, 1983–88*

Donor	Adjustment lending as a percentage of total lending				Cumulative
	1983–85	1986	1987	1988	
World Bank					
Annual average, 1979–88	13	18	23	25	—
Amount (billions of dollars)	—	—	—	—	15.3
Number of loans	—	—	—	—	121
African Development Bank					
Number of loans, 1984–88	—	—	—	—	13
Asian Development Bank					
Percentage of all loans, 1984–88	—	—	—	—	5

— Not available.
Source: Hansen (1988).

environmental—their principal aim being to reduce public expenditure caused by high support prices—their effects were probably environmentally beneficial.

In 28 percent of the cases studied, SALs adjusted agricultural export taxes. An export tax is equivalent to lowering farmgate prices since if the tax did not exist, farmers would receive higher prices. In Haiti, SALs attempted to remove export taxes on coffee and to reduce incentives to grow erosive grain crops on hillsides. In Malawi, by contrast, export taxes on tea increased under SALs. Although tea is a perennial beneficial for protecting the soil, in Malawi tea is cured using fuelwood obtained through deforestation. The increased taxes, designed to generate higher public revenues, probably benefited the environment overall. However, 35 percent of the SALs studied did reduce export taxes on erosive crops such as maize, sorghum, and tobacco. The overall effects depend on the mix of policies. Increased foodgrain production need not be environmentally damaging if production methods are managed carefully. In other cases, incentives to produce foodgrains reduced price supports for crops, such as sugarcane, that are erosive.

Currency devaluations were undertaken in 37 percent of the cases studied. Once again, the effect was to raise farmgate prices, and the net effect on the environment depended on which crops were encouraged.

When environmental policy is in place, SALs generally improve the environment. Put another way, SALs produce significant benefits. When the environmental consequences are negative, policymakers should not abandon structural adjustment but should encourage positive environmental policy.

At first sight, setting and controlling an exchange rate appear to have nothing to do with maintaining or improving environmental quality.

Table 12-12. Nature of Adjustment Lending in Select Countries

Country	Macro policies			Sectoral policies	
	Balance of payments reform	Fiscal reform	Financial reform	Agriculture	Industry
Chile	All qualitative restrictions eliminated; tariff reduced to uniform 10 percent; devaluation	None	Rescue financial institutions	None	Restructure to increase ability to compete
Colombia	Low export promotion and import reform; devaluation	Major tax reform	None	Separate credit operations from supply of physical inputs	None
Côte d'Ivoire	Strong trade reform	Public enterprise reform	None	None	None
Ghana	Trade reform; devaluation	Increase public spending	Rescue financial institutions; raise interest rates	Reduce overstaffing	None
Jamaica	Strong trade reform; export promotion; devaluation	Major tax reform	None	None	None
Malawi	Devaluation	Increase excise and trade taxes	None	Emphasis on smallholder producer prices	None
Mexico	Strong trade reform; export promotion; devaluation	None	None	Link farm prices to internal prices through a price band	Restructure to increase ability to compete
Morocco	Strong trade reform	Increase excise and trade taxes	None	Limit power of agencies in the sector	None
Pakistan	Remove quantitative restrictions on inputs; export promotion; devaluation	Public involvement in infrastructure for private sector	None	None	None
Thailand	Reversed reduction of protection; export promotion; devaluation; trade reform	Increase excise and trade taxes	None	None	None
Turkey	20 percent quantitative restrictions and tariff protection; export promotion; devaluation	Public involvement in infrastructure for private sector	None	None	None

Source: Sebastian and Alicbusan (1989).

Table 12-13. *Effects of Structural Adjustment Loans Extended by the World Bank, by Region, 1979–87*

Policy	Asia		Latin America, Central America, Caribbean		Europe, Middle East, North Africa		Africa		Total	
	Number	Percent	Number	Percent	Number	Percent	Number	Percent	Number	Percent
Countries reviewed	6	14	11	26	4	9	22	51	43	100
Change in relative price										
Adjustments in agricultural producer prices	1	17	4	36	3	75	15	68	23	54
Subsidy removal or reduction of prices on agricultural inputs	3	50	5	46	4	100	16	73	28	65
Tax adjustments on agricultural exports	1	17	5	46	0	0	6	27	12	28
Improved terms of trade on agricultural products	0	0	5	46	3	75	8	36	16	37
Adjustments in energy prices	3	50	3	27	2	50	7	32	15	35
Trade and industry policy reforms	6	100	8	73	4	100	11	50	29	67
Changes in the public expenditure program										
Agriculture or forestry	2	33	2	18	4	100	11	50	19	44
Energy	2	33	1	9	2	50	3	14	8	19
Industry	3	50	0	0	3	75	2	9	8	19
Institutional reforms										
Agriculture or forestry	3	50	7	64	3	75	16	73	29	67
Energy	3	50	3	27	2	50	5	23	13	30
Industry	5	83	5	46	3	75	9	41	22	51

Source: Sebastian and Alicbusan (1989).

Showing that doing so can have a significant impact on the environment is the first step toward demonstrating the link between macroeconomic policy and environment. Developing countries overvalue exchange rates in order to turn the terms of trade against agriculture and depress agricultural prices. Much overvaluation arises from the incidental effects of expansionary fiscal and monetary policy and from policies aimed at protecting domestic industry, thus raising the price of domestic industrial goods above world prices. Since agricultural sectors are the main exporting sectors in developing countries, overvaluation is, in effect, a tax on agricultural exports. This effect is what is meant by turning the terms of trade against agriculture. Overvaluation tends to reflect the push to industrialize and is left over from the days when import substitution was widely advocated. Since an overvalued rate lowers the domestic price of imports, overvaluation does not encourage import substitution. Hence, countries tend to have several rates of exchange. Overvalued rates tend to apply to capital items that are inputs to domestic industry. Freer rates of exchange apply to consumer items, which may also be subject to substantial import taxes.

Donor agencies frequently recommend that recipient countries raise the price of their agricultural output as a means of stimulating agricultural growth. The effects on the environment, and hence on medium- to long-term agricultural growth, are ambiguous, however. As box 12-2 shows, much depends on how the agricultural response occurs. If the response consists of substitutions between crops, the environmental impact depends, in part, on the nature of the higher priced crops that are substituted. If it consists of an aggregate increase in supply, much depends on whether the increase is achieved by using new land or by using existing land more intensively.

The policy implications are not straightforward. Certainly, analyzing, as far as possible, the effect that devaluing the currency has on the environment is important. But it is not possible to say how large the environmental impact will be nor to generalize across locations. If a significant effect is detected, the macroeconomic adjustment policy itself will probably not be modified—that is, devaluations are unlikely to be rejected as policy options because they may affect the environment negatively. It does, however, raise the possibility of designing other policies to offset the negative effects and reduce the incentive to deforest or degrade soils in an effort to increase agricultural supply. Examples might be subsidizing fertilizer applications or investing more in agricultural extension services.

Agricultural subsidies are often concentrated on credit and inputs such as fertilizers, pesticides, irrigation, water, and mechanization. Underpricing encourages misuse, which can harm the environment. In 65 percent of the cases studied, SALs reduced subsidies. Table 12-14 summarizes the experience of SALs with adjusting the price of inputs. Reducing the

Box 12-2. Effects of an Overvalued Exchange Rate

Suppose country A, a developing country, exports to the United States. Given a free market in exports and imports, the exchange rate would settle at, say, Rs20 per $1. Country A overvalues its exchange rate by setting a rate of Rs10 to the dollar. An item costing $10 in the United States could then be sold in country A for Rs100 instead of Rs200. Imports are cheaper because the domestic currency is overvalued. At the overvalued rate, U.S. importers would have to pay $0.10 for every item costing Rs1 instead of only $0.05 at the free market rate of exchange. Thus, A's exports are now more expensive. In this sense, overvaluation taxes exporters and subsidizes importers.

Empirical studies, such as Cleaver (1985), tend to show high supply elasticities for farmgate prices. Overvaluing the exchange rate has the same effect as lowering the farmgate price for agricultural produce. Farmers can therefore be expected to reduce output as effective farmgate prices fall. Cleaver's study of exchange rate overvaluation in Sub-Saharan Africa revealed that agricultural output fared less well in countries with appreciating currencies than in countries with exchange rate depreciation. A 1 percent annual rate of depreciation of the currency was associated with a 0.15 percent annual increase in agricultural output. Although other policies inhibited agricultural growth more than currency appreciation, overvaluation was important.

What impact does overvaluing the exchange rate have on the environment? Although it is not easy to tell what the impact will be, figure B12-2 shows some possible responses. First, the response may be to switch crops rather than to alter aggregate supply. Aggregate supply seems to increase as price increases, but the issue is still being debated. If farmers respond mainly by switching between crops, the environmental impact will depend on what type of crop is substituted. Tree crops (such as tea and coffee) tend to stabilize soils but, of course, affect the environment negatively when they are grown on land that is cleared, such as forests. Second, even if there is an aggregate response, we need to know how it is achieved. If the response is to extensify agricultural output—that is, to acquire new land—the effects could be negative as, for example, when forests are cleared. If the response is to intensify, the effects are more likely to be environmentally benign, especially if they are secured through soil conservation measures. The case study of Sub-Saharan Africa found that the supply response was to expand in areas under cultivation rather than to increase output per unit of land. As Cleaver (1985) notes:

> The problem with dependency on expansion of cultivated area is that arable land is increasingly unavailable. . . . More cultivation of marginal areas is causing soil erosion and desertification in many African countries.

subsidies on pesticides encourages less wasteful use, which is environmentally beneficial. Clearly, this effect is limited if reduced usage inhibits optimal pest control. Reducing the subsidies on fertilizers encourages the substitution of organic manures in integrated crop and livestock systems and discourages wasteful use by large agribusiness. Once again, price

Figure B12-2. Effects of an Overvalued Exchange Rate on the Environment

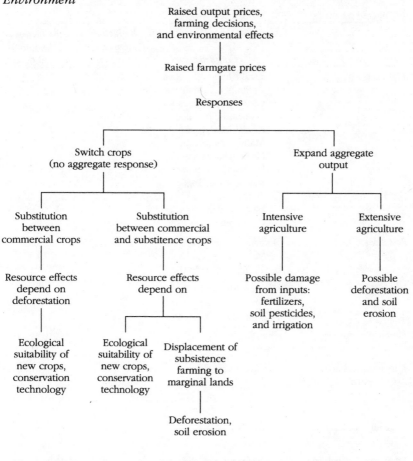

increases might damage environments if application rates are suboptimal. Reducing the subsidies on farm machinery discourages inappropriate land use such as some forms of mechanized agriculture (for example, in Sudan farm equipment compacts the soil) and forest clearance. Credit subsidies can be particularly damaging to the environment, as in the case of Brazil, where credit subsidies contribute to deforestation. The net effect of reducing credit subsidies in the ten countries shown in table 12-14 cannot be evaluated without detailed study of each case.

SALS often reduce energy subsidies to producers and consumers, encouraging less wasteful use and energy conservation, which produce less pollution than would otherwise be the case. Institutional measures designed to encourage conservation or the use of alternative energy sources

Table 12-14. Structural Adjustment and Changes in the Price of Agricultural Inputs
(number of countries)

Input	Countries	Reduction or removal of input subsidies	Reduction of import duties
Fertilizers	Central African Republic, Colombia, Costa Rica, Côte d'Ivoire, Ecuador, Guinea, Republic of Korea, Madagascar, Malawi, Morocco, Nepal, Niger, Nigeria, Pakistan, Philippines, Sierra Leone, Togo, Tunisia, Turkey, Zambia (Argentina, Colombia)	20	2
Pesticides	Ecuador, The Gambia, Madagascar, Pakistan, Turkey (Colombia)	5	1
Insecticides	Central African Republic, Ghana, Turkey (Argentina)	3	1
Herbicides	Tunisia, Turkey (Argentina)	2	1
Agricultural equipment, spare parts, implements	Côte d'Ivoire, Niger, Sierra Leone (Central African Republic, Colombia, Tunisia)	3	3
Machinery or tractor rental services	Kenya, Somalia, Sudan, Zambia	4	0
Interest on agricultural credit	Colombia, Costa Rica, Ecuador, Panama, Philippines, Sierra Leone, Somalia, Tunisia, Turkey, Zaire	10	0
Seeds and planting materials	Côte d'Ivoire, Ecuador, The Gambia, Guinea, Jamaica, Kenya, Morocco, Sierra Leone, Tunisia	9	0
Land rental rates	Sudan	1	0
Animal feed and livestock services	Kenya, Morocco, Tunisia	3	0

Note: The countries in parentheses have policies that reduce import duties on agricultural inputs.
Source: Sebastian and Alicbusan (1989).

are also important. The costs of production increased in eight of the countries presented in table 12-14, consumer prices increased in fifteen countries, and institutional reform occurred in thirteen. At the same time, some alternative energy sources, notably hydroelectric power, are environmentally very controversial, while raising liquid fuel prices could encourage some substitution by fuelwood, which is environmentally unsound (Cummings 1990; Dixon, Talbot, and Le Moigne 1989).

Trade liberalization policies can change the relative price of manufactured goods, remove obstacles to external trade, and encourage exports. In table 12-14, 67 percent of the sample liberalized trade. Liberalization policies could encourage the manufacturing sector to pollute, depending on the extent to which environmental regulation is pursued. They may also attract developing countries with weak environmental regulations. The evidence concerning pollution havens does not, however, support the view that firms move to developing countries in order to capture the benefits of lower environmental standards. Price increases under a regime that makes the polluter pay tend to be small, the effects on output limited, and the effects on trade negligible. When industries relocate, the countries receiving foreign investment in polluting industries such as chemicals, paper, metals, and so forth tend to be other industrial countries, not developing countries (the evidence is summarized in Pearson 1987; an extensive and valuable study is Leonard 1989b).

Reductions in public expenditures characterize a significant number of SALS. Insofar as they attempt to divert expenditure to forestry, extension, and the development of rural roads, such programs may be environmentally beneficial. Overall reductions in expenditure could cause a loss of welfare services to the poorest sectors of the community, adding to the pressure already being exerted on free natural resources. Indeed, some commentators argue that SALS have focused too much on short-to-medium-term macroeconomic adjustment at the cost of increasing poverty for sectors unable to adopt adjustment strategies (see, for example, Cornia, Jolly, and Stewart 1987; for an evaluation involving World Bank structural adjustment, see Demery and Addison 1987). If this is true, SALS may be environmentally unsound given the links between poverty and environmental degradation (see chapter 11). The challenge, then, is to design SALS that include environmental protection and other programs aimed at cushioning the impact of adjustment on the poor. Countries that reduce public expenditure, for example, may also reduce environmental protection measures, which they often regard as dispensable in times of austerity.

Institutional reform tends to dominate SALS. Over 80 percent of the sample in table 12-14 contained reforms to agriculture and forestry, industry, and energy. Reforms tend to focus on privatizing firms, encouraging foreign investment, increasing research and extension, improving marketing, and reforming land tenure. Most of the reforms are favorable to the environment. Thus squatters in the Philippines and West Bengal were given the right to plant trees in degraded forest land. Land tenure reform in Jamaica encouraged farmers to invest in soil conservation. Some tenurial reforms have failed, however, as in Rondônia, Brazil, where granting land rights and building new roads attracted an excessive influx of poor farmers, giving rise to extensive deforestation.

In sum, the effect of SALs on the environment is mixed. On balance, the environment has probably gained from SALs, although improving environmental conditions is not their aim. As such, there is a real risk that SALs will be designed in such a way that they inadvertently damage environmental quality. This risk can readily be reduced by ensuring that all SALs are monitored and evaluated for their environmental effects and that they are designed specifically to enhance environmental quality. It is clear, however, that SALs, even as they are designed at present, do not necessarily damage the environment.

Recognizing the necessary interaction between macroeconomic policy and environment is the first step toward achieving an environmentally sensitive economics in the developing world. Once this recognition has been achieved, there are no easy answers or prescriptions. In some cases, the positive or negative environmental effects of policies are reasonably clear. In other cases, the analyst and policy advisor must expect the effects to be specific to the location, which means that generalizations are unlikely to be fruitful. In still others, economists simply do not understand the implications of policies. Finally, we know too little about the character and volume of physical effects. This paucity of knowledge often poses problems that are as great as, if not greater than, those posed by the valuation issues examined in chapter 5.

Notes

1. The ivory trade was subject to a quota system administered by CITES, the Convention on International Trade in Endangered Species. But quotas were frequently ignored, not because countries exceeded them, but simply because they failed to certify trade so that a considerable proportion of it took place outside the CITES system. CITES introduced a ban on the ivory trade in 1989, the effect of which has yet to be evaluated.

2. The discussion here is a variant of one that undergraduate economists know as the parrot smuggling problem in which a ban on the capture of South American parrots increased the number of birds killed in transit. The ban increased the chances that smuggled parrots would be detected, so the number actually smuggled fell. Smugglers reacted to the ban by capturing even more parrots and hiding them in small containers, killing many in transit. Thus the penalty decreased smuggling but induced a smuggling technology that encouraged smugglers to capture even more birds in order to get a given number of live birds to market. See Varian (1987), pp. 409–12.

3. For example, Myers (1986, p. 296) writes that, "Here we have an example . . . of the way in which developed world consumerism can serve to foster environmental degradation in the developing world. It is often suggested that tropical deforestation is due primarily to the pressure of growing human numbers in the Third World. In the case of the 'hamburger connection' it has been due almost entirely to the pressure of growing consumerism in advanced nations thousands of miles away."

13

Transfrontier Environmental Issues

The previous chapters tend to assume that environmental problems are confined to national boundaries. Taking action on such problems then becomes a matter for national governments, aided, when appropriate, by donor agencies. Most international aid identifies a sovereign nation as the recipient of funds and as the agent responsible for policy. Nevertheless, a great many environmental problems cannot be resolved by one nation alone, and many do not respect political frontiers.

Waste emissions in one country can affect other countries. Known as transfrontier pollution, examples include acid rain, pollution of a sea or international lake, and pollution of a river that flows through several countries. In the same way, resource degradation in one country can affect well-being in another. Such transfrontier problems require at least bilateral negotiation and often multilateral cooperation.

It is helpful to classify international environmental problems by their externalities. An externality exists when one economic agent imposes a cost or benefit on another agent without providing the appropriate compensation or benefit. Table 13-1 offers one such classification. Two basic forms of interaction exist: unidirectional and reciprocal. With unidirectional interaction, damage is caused by one agent and imposed on another, as when an upstream nation pollutes a river serving a downstream nation or withdraws water so it is unavailable downstream. With reciprocal interaction, damage is caused mutually because the resource is

Table 13-1. International Environmental Problems as Externalities

Type of externality	Generator and sufferer (number of countries)	Examples
Unidirectional	One — > one	United States–Canada, acid rain
	One — > few	Upstream country in multicountry watershed
	Few — > one	Transportation of toxic waste
	Few — > few	Baltic, North Sea whaling
	Few — > many	Whaling, deforestation
	Many — > few	None
Reciprocal	One < — > one	None
	Few < — > few	Mediterranean, acid rain
	Many < — > many	Climate change, ozone layer, biodiversity loss

shared, such as the atmosphere or an ocean. In this case, use by one nation imposes a cost on another nation, and use by that nation imposes a cost on the first. Reciprocal externality therefore tends to be a common property problem.

In reality, international externality can be a mix of unidirectional and reciprocal interactions. Acid rain, for example, may emanate from country A and cause damage to countries B and C. Country A may also damage itself while at the same time suffering damage from countries B or C.

This chapter addresses some externalities that affect more than one country but stops short of issues with global impact. The final sections of this chapter deal with the question of international transfers for financing conservation measures. The final chapter looks at global resources and their protection.

An Acid Rain Game

Acid rain is an international externality that is both unidirectional and reciprocal (this analysis draws on Mäler 1989a, 1990). Acid rain in North America is unidirectional, moving between the United States and Canada, while acid rain in Europe is more reciprocal.

Acid rain begins with the deposition of acidic pollutants, mainly sulfur dioxide and nitrogen oxide and dioxide (known as nitrogen oxides). Once emitted into the atmosphere, these pollutants may be absorbed in their dry state by surface water, land, and biomass (especially crops and trees). This is dry deposition. Wet deposition occurs when pollutants are washed out of the atmosphere by rainfall (a washout) or mix with rain droplets in cloud formations (a rainout). When mixed with rain, they form sulfate and nitrate aerosols. Both dry and wet depositions are acidic. Although the terminology is somewhat confusing, acid rain typically refers to both phenomena.[1]

The nature of the damage caused by acid rain is the subject of debate. Broadly, the effects are alleged to be the following:

- Reductions in the ambient pH values of lakes and rivers, causing loss of aquatic life in commercial and recreational fisheries
- Direct damage to the leaf surfaces of trees and crops
- Increased solubility of soil ions, stripping forest soils of nutrients and producing toxic ions—notably aluminum—that reach aquatic life through runoff. Drinking water may also be affected.

Because sulfur dioxide and nitrogen oxides can travel in airsheds, it is perfectly possible for emissions in one country to result in depositions in another region of the same country or in another country altogether. Thus acid rain becomes an international or transboundary pollutant, and this international dimension is of immediate interest. The two major examples of transboundary acid rain are North America and Europe/Scandinavia.

In North America, acid compounds located in the atmosphere of the northeastern United States and Eastern Canada have allegedly increased because of emissions in the central and southern United States. About 180 lakes in the Adirondack Mountains in New York State have lost their trout populations because of acid rain. These lakes are more acidic than surrounding lakes, and the source of that acidity appears to be nitrates and sulfates. Wide-ranging surveys suggest, however, that acid damage to lakes is fairly limited (the evidence is usefully surveyed in Harrington 1988). The evidence that forest damage in North America is due to acid rain is less persuasive. Although extensive, forest damage may arise from other factors such as drought and, more probably, tropospheric ozone pollution (the ozone is formed by the reaction of nitrogen compounds and hydrocarbons, which suggests that vehicle pollution may be an important factor in ozone pollution).

Emissions in the central belt of Europe and in Eastern Europe adversely affect areas in the northern area of mainland Europe and in Scandinavia (figure 13-1). Acidic deposition is thought to be important in acidifying soils in southern Scandinavia and central Europe (this summary of European results is taken from Harter 1988). Forest damage has attracted the most attention, particularly in Germany, where over 50 percent of the total forest is damaged. The causal process is complex, however, and acid rain may be only part of a sequence of causes, including ozone pollution, aluminum mobilization through soil acidification, heavy metal pollution, and other factors. Nevertheless, acid rain is clearly implicated even if it is not a primary cause of forest damage. Water acidification does appear to be linked to acidic depositions in Europe.

Since acid rain does cause damage—albeit with uncertain impact—and is transported across national frontiers, securing international agreement

Figure 13-1. Transfers of Acid Rain within Europe, 1980

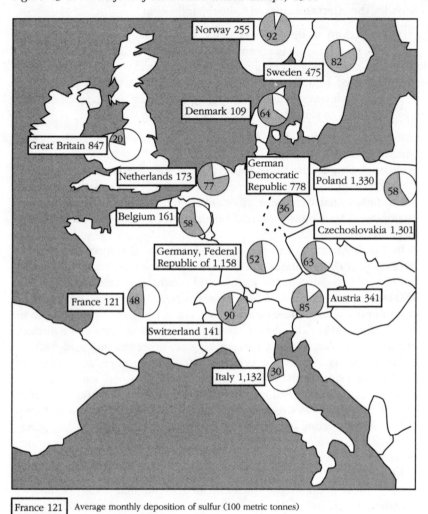

| France 121 | Average monthly deposition of sulfur (100 metric tonnes) |

Percentage of deposition received from other countries

Note: The map shows European country imports of acid rain (as sulfur) and the extent to which each country s own emissions are deposited within its own national boundaries. Thus, the United Kingdom imports 20 percent of its acid rain depositions, whereas Norway imports 92 percent and the Netherlands imports 77 percent.

Source: Environmental Resources Ltd. (1984).

becomes an issue. Sulfur dioxide and nitrogen oxides are found in various sources. Globally, approximately 60 percent of sulfur dioxide emissions come from burning coal and lignite and about 30 percent from burning oil. Nitrogen oxides come from burning fossil fuel, especially in vehicles, and from fertilizers and industrial processes. An international policy to control acid rain would have to be directed at sources such as electric power stations and motor vehicles that use industrial fuel.

It is possible to illustrate the benefits that can be gained by cooperative efforts to control acid rain emissions. First, some emissions have been estimated, and meteorological models can be used to estimate the proportion of a country's emissions that is transported to other countries. This is a transport model.[2] Second, the costs of abating sulfur emissions are known to a broad degree of accuracy. Indicators of the monetary value of damage done would then be helpful for measuring the gains from cooperative efforts. In practice, no such measures exist, although damage could be measured indirectly by assuming that sulfur dioxide emissions are in equilibrium in a particular year; that is, as long as other countries emit equilibrium levels of sulfur dioxide, any single country should emit its equilibrium level.[3] This implies damage functions in the sense of revealed government preferences for reduced sulfur emissions.

Table 13-2 shows one set of results of a cooperative solution to control acid rain in Europe. It shows the percentage reduction that each country would have to undertake in order to secure an outcome in which the sum

Table 13-2. Reduction of Acid Rain and Net Benefits from European Cooperation

Country	Percentage reduction in sulfur dioxide	Net benefits (millions of deutsch mark)
Bulgaria	43	−7
Czechoslovakia	75	152
Finland	14	−2
France	10	879
German Democratic Republic	80	11
Germany, Federal Republic of	86	328
Italy	33	−83
Netherlands	62	565
Poland	27	599
Soviet Union	2	1,505
Spain	14	−29
Sweden	4	606
United Kingdom	81	−336
All Europe	39	6,290

Source: Mäler (1990).

of the net benefits across all countries is maximized. It also shows the net monetary benefits accruing to each country. The estimates highlight an important point. The net benefit column shows the difference between the benefit gained from reduced environmental damage and the costs of abating sulfur dioxide. For all the countries studied, other than Finland, Italy, Spain, and the United Kingdom, net benefits are positive. For Europe as a whole, net benefits are positive at some DM6 billion, corresponding to a 40 percent reduction in sulfur dioxide. The size of the average reduction in emissions is part of the solution of the cooperative game: it is determined by maximizing net benefits and then calibrating the transport model until this objective is achieved.

According to game theory, Italy, Spain, and the United Kingdom have no incentive to play the game unless they can be compensated for the net cost they suffer. If they are not compensated, each of these countries will gain by becoming a free rider—they will gain by allowing other countries to abate sulfur emissions, collecting the benefit of some reduced damage, and paying nothing in costs. In game theory, such collusive behavior is known as a coalition. According to table 13-2, a coalition of Finland, Italy, Spain, and the United Kingdom would result in net gains for the defectors. What is more, any country could gain by being a free rider. That is, as long as it could be assumed that other countries would seek a cooperative solution, an individual country could gain by not signing a cooperative agreement.

The situation, then, is that having a cooperative agreement on acid rain makes Europe collectively better off but gives individual countries no incentive to sign because they could gain more by being free riders. The problem arises because the net benefits of reducing emissions are very unevenly distributed among countries. Some system of incentives must be devised to induce the potential losers to cooperate. Such incentives, termed side payments, effectively bribe potential losers to cooperate. International agreements do not typically offer side payments, at least not in the explicit form of cash transfers. But side payments can be made in ways other than cash transfers. These might include technical assistance to help poorer countries reduce emissions or invest in cleaner technologies. Note that side payments in the case of acid rain involve payments from sufferers to polluters. We therefore have an example of the "victim pays principle," which is different from the "polluter pays principle." The "victim pays principle" seems unethical, but it does have the virtue of acknowledging the real world situation in which incentives to cooperate are frequently absent at the international level. The results are illustrative. For example, the costs of removing sulfur dioxide vary with fuel and technology. Additionally, as the discussion of the prisoners' dilemma in chapter 10 shows, games rarely occur once. The participants usually play other games, giving scope for modifying the outcome.

The Mediterranean Basin

The Mediterranean Sea has long been the subject of environmental concern (this section is based on Batisse 1990; Grenon and Batisse 1989; World Bank and European Investment Bank 1990). Essentially land-locked and surrounded by countries with various combinations of rapid population growth, industrialization, and development, the Mediterranean Sea has suffered extensive pollution. The river basins serving the sea and the coastal areas have also been subject to massive changes in land use, further affecting the environments of the sea itself and of the surrounding countries. In 1975, the relevant countries formed the Mediterranean Action Plan, which was adopted at a regional conference in Barcelona and coordinated by the United Nations Environment Programme, as a forum for discussing common environmental problems.[4] One of its studies, the so-called Blue Plan, investigates the potential impact that population growth, economic change, and demands on use of the land, sea, and water will have on the future of the Mediterranean region. In the late 1980s, the European Investment Bank and the World Bank joined forces to create an Environmental Program for the Mediterranean aimed at implementing investment policies and strengthening institutions in the region.

State of the Environment

Environmental degradation is extensive in the Mediterranean (box 13-1 lists the main problems). Some of the accompanying problems are issues of shared resources, such as marine pollution, overharvesting of migratory fish, loss of habitat for migrating birds, and loss of marine mammals and sea turtles. Others are shared by a few countries, such as North Adriatic pollution (which affects Italy and Yugoslavia). Both types of problems are reciprocal externalities that require bilateral or collective action. Many more problems affect a single country and can be addressed by that country alone. Nevertheless, since countries in the region have similar physical and social conditions, regional cooperation would still be useful for transferring solutions.

Marine pollution arises from municipal and industrial wastewater, agricultural runoff, oil and chemical spills from ships, and poorly disposed industrial and other solid wastes, especially plastics. The deteriorating quality of water threatens recreation, municipal water supplies, and agriculture and wildlife. The effects are extensive. The northwestern Mediterranean is heavily damaged by pollutants from France, Italy, and Spain; the Adriatic is similarly polluted, mostly by Italy. The southern Mediterranean is less polluted, but some 90 percent of effluent is untreated. Seawater poses health risks to bathers and other users, and shellfish can

Box 13-1. Environmental Problems in the Mediterranean Basin

Common problems are shared by two or more countries in the region and require collective action.

- Marine pollution. Oil discharge and spills into the marine environment; discharge of nutrient-rich agricultural, urban, and industrial wastes, causing eutrophication and, as a result, algae blooms, oxygen depletion, fish kills, and odors; discharge of industrial pollutants, especially heavy metals
- Floating plastic and other debris.
- Endangered species. Loss of endangered marine mammal and turtle populations and reduction of habitat
- Migratory birds. Pressures on migratory birds, including endangered species, because of habitat destruction, especially in migration bottleneck areas, and unregulated hunting and trapping
- Air pollution. As indicated by initial studies, transboundary air pollution, especially in the northern Mediterranean, and forest death associated with acid rain
- Fisheries depletion. Depletion of many commercial fish stocks owing to poorly controlled fishing, destruction of habitat (for example, seagrass beds and coastal wetlands), and, to some extent, pollution
- Tourism development. Difficulty, because of international competitiveness, in taxing this growing industry to cover infrastructure costs and environmental improvement
- Migration. Semipermanent or seasonal migration of large numbers of people within the region
- Regional trade. Concerns, as regional trade increases, about protection of livestock and plant species from introduced pests and diseases and about pesticide and pharmaceutical residues in export crops

Similar problems occur separately in several countries and may be addressed on a country basis, but the solutions to them may be transferable, given the

be contaminated. Fisheries in the Mediterranean generally have declined because of pollution and overfishing. Approximately 80 percent of organic pollution in the northern Adriatic can be traced to the Po river system, which contains 20 million people, 3,100 municipalities, and 200,000 industries. The economic impact of pollution is potentially severe in certain regions such as Italy's Emilia-Romagna at the mouth of the Po, which alone receives some 40 million tourists each year and contributes 20 percent of Italy's fishery yields. High levels of nutrients in wastes lead to eutrophication, and excessive algal growth has caused several major tourist scares. Sewage treatment programs are under way to reduce the pollution loads.

Wetlands in the region have been progressively drained over the past centuries, and the land reclaimed. One result has been the loss of wildlife countries' similar physical, biological, and social conditions and common heritage.

- Coastal pollution from urban and industrial sources.
- Water quantity. Depletion of freshwater resources, which contributes to seasonal water scarcities and inadequate supplies, especially in coastal and island areas
- Water quality. Deterioration of quality of surface and groundwater owing to inadequately controlled discharges from urban, industrial, and agricultural sources; multiple-purpose use of available water complicates the situation
- Degradation of drylands. Deterioration of land resources in semiarid and arid portions of the southern and eastern countries owing to deforestation, overgrazing, and agricultural development of marginal lands. This leads to loss of fertility and erosion of drainage basins, with effects on irrigated agricultural areas and coastal areas. In its extreme form, this process ends in desertification
- Coastal zone management. Development pressures on many coastal areas, including beaches and wetlands. Much development is unplanned, with inadequate provision of services
- Degradation of cultural properties. Direct damage to or destruction of cultural properties (including archaeological and historic sites and traditional urban centers), owing to agricultural, urban, and tourism development, air pollution, and rising water tables
- Solid and hazardous wastes. Problems of varying severity in the collection, treatment, and disposal of wastes. Solid waste generation is increasing rapidly principally from industrial and agrochemical sources, and wastes are frequently disposed of improperly, causing contamination of water supplies and posing direct threats to health

Source: World Bank and European Investment Bank (1990), table 2.1.

---

habitat, particularly for migratory birds. Wetlands also act as buffers by filtering out pollutants, reducing floods, and capturing sediment; they are rich sources of fish.

Coastal areas suffer from the expansion of urban, industrial, and tourist development and the consequent loss of forests and natural habitat and increase in pollution. Water deficiencies are serious in some areas, and water disputes are common, with different end users demanding water from the same source. Figure 13-2 shows an exploitation index for water, measured as the current annual use of water divided by the available supply. Roughly one-third of the population in the south has inadequate drinking water, and even more suffer inadequate sanitation. Cyprus and Malta face serious problems of water supply and, together with Libya, are already using groundwater sources faster than they can re-

Figure 13-2. Exploitation Index for Water Resources in the Mediterranean, 1985

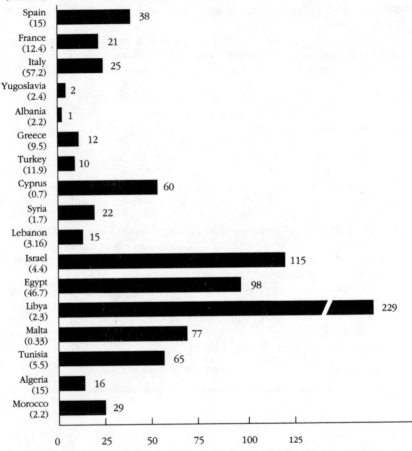

Country and population of Mediterranean watershed (millions)

Percentage of annual use per supply

Note: The exploitation index, expressed as a percentage, is the ratio of an area's annual use of water to its annual supply. Thus, an index of 100 percent would indicate that an area is using its total annual supply of water. An index above 100 percent, like that of Israel and Libya, indicates that the communities situated in the Mediterranean watershed are using unconventional water resources, such as nonrenewable fossil aquifers, recycled water, and desalinated water.

Source: Grenon and Batisse (1989).

charge themselves. Perhaps twenty of the twenty-nine drainage basins discharging into the Mediterranean have doubtful levels of water quality.

Soils are also suffering. Rangelands are being degraded as livestock herds increase while available rangeland decreases. Perhaps 130 million hectares of rangeland have degenerated in North Africa and the Mediterranean Basin. Overgrazing and overcultivation deplete the soils, while the forests in the region are among the most degraded in the world. Some 5 percent of irrigated soils in the Basin is subject to extensive salinization; over 30 percent of the Nile Delta and Nile Valley are affected by water-logging and salinization. In Syria, 12 percent of the Mediterranean watershed is similarly affected.

Solid waste is poorly managed in many countries. In Algeria, for example, hazardous materials have been found in municipal dumps, and stockpiles of dangerous chemicals, acids, solvents, contaminated sludge, and heavy metals await disposal. In several countries, waste has been washed into river basins and into the sea.

Air pollution is a major problem not only because it directly affects the health of town and city dwellers, but because it contributes substantially to pollution of the sea. Some 90 percent of the lead that reaches the Mediterranean originates in the atmosphere, and the sea is contaminated in equal measure by heavy metals from the air and from rivers.

The Causes of Environmental Degradation

How has the current environmental state of the Mediterranean come about? The main factors are likely to be population growth, economic policies, and institutional failure, all of which are relevant in the Mediterranean region.

POPULATION. Population growth is at the heart of the problem. Figure 13-3 shows past and projected population trends for the region. Population growth is expected to stabilize by 2000; by 2025, however, the 1985 population of 350 million persons could have increased by 200 million. Although the total population in the southern and eastern countries is roughly equal to that in the north, the northern population is expected to decline around 2000.

ECONOMIC POLICY. Energy is subsidized in a number of countries, giving rise to wasteful energy consumption and excessive air pollution. This is particularly true of Turkey and Yugoslavia, both of which rely heavily on low-quality coals. In Turkey, 90 percent of coal production comes from lignite, and the production of coal is expected to double between 1987 and 2000. Subsidies to irrigation water are also important, especially in Algeria, Egypt, and Yugoslavia, where prices are only some 20 percent of the marginal costs of supply. In Izmir, Turkey, water is supplied mainly by groundwater sources, but the municipality is not permitted to charge for water extracted from private wells. Firms pay only pumping costs, which are well below the costs of bringing water from distant sources.

INSTITUTIONAL FAILURE. Tenurial arrangements contribute to land degradation. Traditional resource rights often conflict with the govern-

Figure 13-3. Actual and Projected Population Growth in the Mediterranean Region, 1950-2025

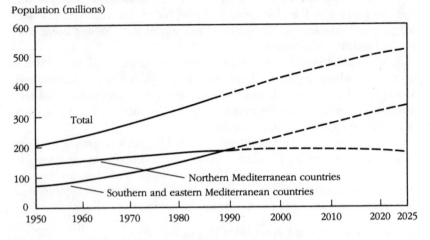

Population (millions)

Note: ——— Actual; ——— · Projected. Northern Mediterranean countries include Albania, France, Greece, Italy, Monaco, Spain, and Yugoslavia. Southern and eastern Mediterranean countries include Algeria, Cyprus, Egypt, Israel, Lebanon, Libya, Malta, Morocco, Syria, Tunisia, and Turkey.
Source: Grenon and Batisse (1989).

ment's priorities for land use. Landholdings are increasingly fragmented as population grows, and these diminishing plots of land are being over-cultivated. Controls over development are weak in many areas, notably Spain, where a new coastal law was implemented in 1988 in an effort to contain the deterioration brought on by high-rise development. All Mediterranean coastal countries face formidable threats to their coastlines.

Public awareness is a prerequisite for taking effective environmental action. Although political awareness of environmental issues is high in the northern countries, it is weak in the south and may be further depressed by a false sense of security. As land and water resources are depleted, food imports increase to compensate for low domestic productivity. Having to depend more on local natural resources might force countries to appreciate the increasing fragility of those resources. Table 13-3 summarizes the problems, the causes, and the solutions to the Mediterranean Basin's environmental woes.

Action on the Environment

Environmental problems in the Mediterranean reinforce the general policy prescriptions for improving the environment in the developing world. As far as possible, population pressure on limited resources must

Table 13-3. Causes, Effects, and Probable Solutions to Environmental Problems in the Mediterranean Region

Kind of degradation	Effect	Cause	Possible solution
Coastal and marine water pollution	Closed beaches and lost tourism revenues; lost aesthetic value; health consequences; eutrophication; contamination of fish and shellfish	Shipping and oil spills; poor solid waste management (litter, plastic); water pricing and poor operation and maintenance of wastewater facilities; input pricing, regulations, and enforcement (industrial wastes); agricultural runoff; detergents	MAR POL and MED POL: solid waste management; water pollution control (municipal and industrial wastewaters); industrial input pricing (energy, water, hazardous materials, and the like); port reception facilities, treatment technology and administration
Depletion of freshwater resources	Depletion of groundwater; increasing marginal cost	Pricing regulations; perception of water as a free good	Improved pricing; integrated watershed management; improved technologies
Degradation of quality of fresh water	Poor quality surface and groundwater; health effects; cost of water treatment; high cost to industry; saline intrusion; increased marginal cost of potable supply	Industrial and urban pollution; pollution of groundwater; overpumping of groundwater	Revised pricing; regulation of groundwater extraction; integrated watershed management
Solid wastes	Health hazards; amenity impact; pollution of beaches and wetlands; groundwater contamination	Inefficient management (especially disposal); no market for recycled materials	Improved collection and disposal technology and management; programs
Hazardous wastes	Pollution of ground and surface water; contamination of soils	Inadequate regulations and management; pricing of inputs into industries producing wastes	Licensing; recycling (changing pricing of inputs and outputs); improved collection

(continued on next page)

Table 13-3 (continued)

Kind of degradation	Effect	Cause	Possible solution
Land degradation	Poor drainage; erosion and siltation; desertification; loss of fertility	Deforestation; overgrazing; agricultural practices; pricing distortions affecting agricultural inputs and outputs; land tenure system; enforcement regulations	Sustained approach to management of agricultural production; soil conservation; improved markets
Degradation of coastal areas	Haphazard development; using up beachfront (natural resources); pollution (sewage and litter); wetlands degradation	Low market price for land in relation to long-term value; absence of planning controls	Measures to put incentives right (prices and taxes); better planning
Degradation of ecosystems	Damage to wetlands (rich genetic diversity, hydrologic aspects), plants, birds (breeding grounds for migrating birds), and shellfish	Water pollution; low market price for land in relation to true value; lack of controls on development; agricultural practices; solid waste disposal	Taxation; development planning and regulation; national preserves; activities of nongovernmental organizations
Air pollution	Health problems; damage to built environment	Urbanization; industrialization; increased vehicle ownership; home heating fuels	Preventive measures; enforcement of standards; emission charges; conversion from lignite as fuel

Source: World Bank and European Investment Bank (1990), p. 36.

be contained. Tenurial conflicts must be reduced. Resource prices must be brought into line at least with private marginal costs and, more appropriately, with social costs. Institutions must be strengthened so that effective environmental laws can be implemented, and the high economic cost of environmental degradation must be made apparent not just to the public at large, but to government as well. In particular, action on the environment should focus on adjusting economic policy. Energy and water pricing thus become prime candidates for attention. Raising prices is politically unattractive in many cases but should be the ultimate goal:

> Even where it is politically difficult to increase prices quickly, economic pricing concepts can provide guidelines for environmental policy—in choosing rationing techniques, for example. In the long term, appropriate resource pricing is a cornerstone for resource conservation and sustained development (World Bank and European Investment Bank 1990, p. 52).

In addition to pricing policy, investing carefully in pollution abatement is required, but the temptation to invest in large-scale abatement equipment while leaving the original polluting technology in place must be resisted. The returns to public health from investments in wastewater treatment can be very high. Legislation should be implemented to protect critical environmental resources and tighten control of hazardous waste in countries with limited knowledge of stored wastes or the hazards they present. Planning the use of land should be strengthened so that important environmental assets are protected and all significant development is subjected to some form of environmental assessment.

The Himalayas

The Himalayas extend from Nanga Parbat in the northwest, above the Indus Gorge, to Namche Barwa in the east, above the Brahmaputra. More liberally interpreted, they include the Hindu Kush, at the far western end, and the Hengduan mountains. Many popular analyses of environmental problems in the region point to a process of environmental degradation that could only be resolved through a major regional initiative.

Essentially, pressure on natural resources in the mountainous regions, especially Nepal but including India and Bhutan, is thought to have brought about massive deforestation and the subsequent movement of peasants to marginal lands. Both these effects of population growth are said to have caused soil erosion and increased siltation in downstream river systems, especially in Bangladesh. River levels during the annual monsoons then rise, causing flooding. Crudely put, it is argued that Bangladesh's flood problems originate elsewhere. As one ex-minister put it, "Bangladesh is being destroyed by its neighbors" (quoted in Singh 1989, p. 8). More generally, low-lying areas are placed at risk by environmental degradation in the mountainous regions. If such a view is correct, a regional solution involving Bangladesh, Bhutan, India, and Nepal is clearly needed. Although this situation, if it is properly formulated, is a problem of unidirectional externality rather than of a shared resource, the required collaborative solution places it in a discussion of regional management.

More recently, a number of experts have questioned what they call the Theory of Himalayan Environmental Degradation, which blames mountainous regions for lowland problems (see especially Ives and Messerli 1989). This theory has the following elements:

- Population growth was accelerated in Nepal by modern health care and medicine and increased immigration from India
- Approximately 90 percent of the population consists of the rural poor who make significant demands on fuelwood, timber, fodder, and land
- Population growth has caused deforestation, which has, in turn, caused soil erosion
- Erosion has caused high runoff during the summer monsoons and dried up water resources in the dry season
- The increased sediment load has extended the Ganges and Brahmaputra deltas
- As agricultural land is lost in the north through soil erosion, new lands are being opened up through further deforestation. Animal dung is diverted from the soil and used as fuel. The nutrition and health of women decline as the women must walk farther and farther to obtain fuelwood.

The various parts of this theory are considered next.

Population growth in Nepal is rapid and projected to remain high at around 3 percent a year. Growth in the Terai (lowland areas) is expected to be faster than in the mountains or hills. One result is that the availability of cultivated and cropped land per person will decline as projected in table 13-4 (Ives and Messerli 1989, p. 200, stress that the data are extremely uncertain; for the view that uncertainty is imposed partly by the wide variety of analysts investigating the Himalayan problem, see Thompson, Warburton, and Hatley 1986).

Table 13-4. Availability of Cultivated and Cropped Land in Nepal, 1985 and 2005
(number of hectares per capita)

Year and location	Cultivated area	Cropped area
1985		
Mountains	0.15	0.25
Hills	0.12	0.20
Terai	0.17	0.28
2005		
Mountains	0.08	0.11
Hills	0.06	0.11
Terai	0.11	0.22

Source: Ives and Messerli (1989).

The lessons to be drawn from these trends depend on the reliability of the data on population growth and deforestation and on where the population growth is focused. Recent studies of forests suggest that the area devoted to forest in the middle mountains of Nepal has changed little since 1950, but that the quality of the forest, measured by crown cover, has declined.[5] Thus, from 1964 to 1979, forest area fell at an annual rate of some 2 percent in the Terai, but at a rate of 0.4 percent in Nepal as a whole and not at all in the middle and high mountains. Between 1979 and 1985, the area of the high mountains did not change at all, while the decline in the middle mountains was 0.3 percent a year, that of the Terai was 3.9 percent, and the average for Nepal as a whole was 0.5 percent. These are hardly the dramatic rates of change implicit in the popular theory. Forest crown cover has, however, declined. Between 1964 and 1979, the amount of forest with crown cover of more than 70 percent fell from 40 to 13 percent in the mountains, from 41 to 12 percent in Siwaliks, and a modest 44 to 37 percent in the Terai (these estimates are from official sources in Nepal).

Although the popular view of widespread deforestation appears untenable, could the reduction in crown cover account for soil erosion? The question assumes that the soil is, in fact, eroding even though data on erosion are not particularly reliable. Ramsay (1986) found annual erosion rates varying from about 8 tons per hectare to 200 tons per hectare (Ramsay 1986). The high estimates relate to degraded grazing land. Sloping terraces that are poorly managed also have high erosion rates. But several questions arise. Are these loss rates excessive? What is the extent of the degraded land? What happens to eroded soil?

Experts differ in their views, but even the upper limit of the estimates should be compared with annual rates well above 200 tons per hectare in mountainous countries such as Ecuador and Madagascar. The extent of degraded forest and grazing land is disputed, but degraded forest land was put at only 5 percent of the total in 1986, although it was as high as 9 percent in the middle mountains (estimates of the Nepalese government). Under these circumstances, the extent of severe land degradation seems unlikely to be associated with substantial downriver transfers of sediment. Soil from terraces does not appear to travel far and often only reaches the lower terraces. The efficient management of terraces in Nepal is a subject of varying views, but photographic evidence suggests that terraces are generally well managed and even significant landslides are quickly terraced again.

A second check on the issue of land use and erosion is the extent to which downstream sedimentation occurs. Sedimentation rates have been fairly well studied, but the important question is the extent to which they arise because of anthropogenic rather than natural factors. Himalayan rivers are characterized by very high rates of erosion compared with other river systems, but separating out natural from man-made factors appears to be impossible (Ives and Messerli 1989, table 5.4).

The reality in the Himalayas, then, is unclear. The available evidence certainly does not support the popular theory advanced at the beginning of this section and may even contradict it. Calls for regional management of the Himalayas are therefore likely to be at best premature and at worst extremely wasteful of the resources of governments, donor agencies, and the people affected. But resource degradation exists, regardless of its cause, and should be the real focus of concern since the measures needed to control it are reasonably well understood.

The International Transfer Issue

As has been said, a feature of international environmental problems is that degradation in any one country may affect the well-being of another. This transboundary effect sets the stage for resolving environmental problems through mutual cooperation. Without that cooperation, countries tend to use more of the resource in question than they do with it. The result is overuse. The main issue, then, is to devise an efficient system of incentives that will induce cooperation between the relevant parties. Clearly, international environmental problems require international environmental policy and incentives.

At the early stages of development, the perceived value of natural environments frequently appears to be low. Priority is given to industrialization and development programs, which often damage the environment. In contrast, environmental values in the richer, industrial countries appear to be high. Environmental concerns are often high on the political agenda of all political parties. Figure 13-4 shows, for example, the relation between willingness to take action to perfect the environment and gross domestic product (GDP) per capita in European countries. The link is fairly systematic: the higher the level of real income per person, the more willing are individuals to act. This discrepancy between the perceived value that industrial and developing countries give to the environment raises the issue of transfers to finance action on international environmental issues.

An illustration can be made using the example of tropical deforestation. A poor deforesting country, P, may judge the benefits of deforesting, B^{DP}, to be greater than the costs it bears, C^{DP}. A richer country, R, secures little or no benefit from deforestation in P but may well suffer costs in the form of effects on climate, concern over loss of biological diversity, and so on. The richer country then suffers costs, C^{DR}. If decisions regarding deforestation are made within P, deforestation will occur as long as

$$B^{DP} > C^{DP}.$$

But if global well-being is to be maximized—and the world is made up of countries R and P—deforestation is not justified unless

Figure 13-4. Average willingness to Take Action to Protect the Environment as a Function of GDP per Capita, 1985

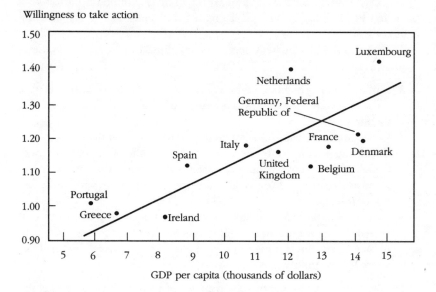

Willingness to take action

Note: GDP per capita is based on purchasing power parity in countries of the European Community.
Source: Based on unpublished data from EUROSTAT, Brussels.

$$B^{DP} > (C^{DP} + C^{DR}).$$

Not surprisingly, the poorer nations seeking the benefits of rapid industrialization may well resent the implication that they need to take into account the costs to wealthier countries of environmental degradation. This raises the issue of transfer payments for international environmental degradation.

The direction of the transfer, however, is not a straightforward issue. For example, country P imposes an external cost on country R by deforestation. Application of the "polluter pays principle" suggests that P should pay R for the damage caused. But since the forests belong to P, property rights are vested in P, which suggests that R should pay P not to deforest. This is an example of the "victim pays principle" and illustrates Coase's theorem, in which the loser compensates the gainer. This principle tends to apply when there is no supranational body to determine property rights: national sovereignties turn the issue into a bargaining context.

The application of both principles to unidirectional externalities is fairly clear. When the damage is reciprocal, or is a mix of reciprocal and unidirectional externality, the principles are more difficult to derive. Nevertheless, bargaining offers both countries opportunities to gain. The assumption that all parties, or at least the main or dominant parties, can gain by bargaining is at the heart of international environmental cooperation.

The international transfers necessary for mutual gain can be made in many ways:

- Lump sum payments can be transferred directly to compensate a country for not developing a resource. These are known as side payments.
- Compensatory resources can be transferred to a country that avoids degrading a resource by developing along some other, environmentally less destructive route. The transfer may take the form of technical assistance and loans that are specific to environmentally benign projects.
- Industrial countries can make transfers to developing countries that reduce some of their debt obligations in return for an agreement to reduce their environmental destruction and manage natural resources sustainably.

As yet, pure side payments—the transfer of resources without specifying how they might be used—have not occurred. Examples of the second and third types of international transfers are many. The most notable among them are proposals for international funds to assist environmentally benign development and debt-for-nature swaps.

The following sections discuss each type of transfer. For such transfers to take place, they must channel funds to agents whose behavior has to change. If, for example, the actions of small colonist farmers are causing degradation, transferred funds should be used to change the incentives giving rise to environmental loss.

International Conservation Financing

In light of the evolution toward greater environmental sensitivity in existing lending, one study addresses the need for new initiatives and suggests a number of ways in which international conservation financing can be developed from new and existing sources (New World Dialogue on Environment and Development in the Western Hemisphere 1991).

First, domestic funds must, realistically, be made available primarily by redirecting resources away from unsustainable activities and adopting policies that assure economic reform, promote private savings and investment, reverse capital flight, and encourage debt-for-nature and debt-for-development swaps. Much of the capital needed for sustainable development could be supplied by private sector investment if governments set incentives properly. Furthermore, government should encourage civic and local community associations, green movements, and other such organizations to contribute even more to sustainable development. International institutions could help by supporting domestic and international private voluntary organizations that seek to fight poverty and improve the environment, by institutionalizing their own participation in policy-making, and by encouraging cooperation among countries.

Second, military budgets no longer needed for national security in the post–Cold War era could be redirected to environmental, economic, and human security budgets, enabling countries to reduce national debts and pursue sustainable development strategies.

Third, using public and private international debt creatively and recycling interest payments could provide additional monies. The repayment terms for debtors could be made more flexible, allowing interest payments on debt to be used for development purposes. Economic and environmental conditions imposed on debtor countries could be replaced by symmetrical commitments for sustainable development in both developing and industrial countries.

Reducing private debt, which accounts for most of the debt crises, could be pursued by creating an inter-American debt management authority, which would purchase outstanding debt on the secondary market and forgive it selectively and gradually, depending on performance in fulfilling environmental and macroeconomic policy commitments. Negotiations or international consortia, such as those contained in the Brady Plan, could provide debt relief on a case-by-case basis, providing flexibility and relief to encourage investment in sustainable development.

Fourth, a sustainable development facility could be created within the Inter-American Development Bank to provide the special support needed to increase the number and quality of sustainable development projects, including coastal protection, sustainable agriculture, energy efficiency, pollution prevention, and so on. Meanwhile, the United States and Canada could increase their foreign aid devoted to reducing poverty and promoting socially, economically, and ecologically sustainable development.

Fifth, new funding for these initiatives could come from an ecofund. Resources for the fund would be raised through an agreement among nations, based on the "polluter pays principle," to levy a special tax on oil and the carbon equivalent in other fossil fuels. Such taxes could raise large revenues and would be automatic, that is, they would be determined by a formula and would not depend on voluntary contributions from governments.

The international nature of many environmental problems clearly necessitates international transfers of resources from rich nations to poor nations, but not necessarily from the polluting or resource-degrading country to the suffering country.

Global Environmental Facility

As we have seen, environmental improvement frequently pays a single country net benefits. The general lesson is to ensure that costs and returns are correctly evaluated. However, many actions that a country can take to improve the environment will also benefit other nations, or the global community as a whole. According to a purely national comparison of costs and benefits, it may not pay a single country to invest in that improvement: the costs are borne nationally, whereas the benefits accrue to the world as a whole. Efforts to control global warming are an obvious example, since, by and large, other countries will also benefit from, say, a measure to increase energy efficiency in a single country.

In 1990, the World Bank, together with the United Nations Development Programme and the United Nations Environment Programme, established the Global Environment Facility (GEF). The GEF provides concessional assistance to the developing world for investments that would

- Protect the ozone layer
- Reduce greenhouse gas emissions
- Protect international water resources
- Protect biological diversity.

The GEF offers aid to help developing countries undertake the measures required in the Montreal Protocol to protect the ozone layer. To reduce greenhouse gases, the main focus is on investments in cleaner fuels and technologies in the energy power sectors and lower-waste technologies in the industrial and power sectors. Accelerating the development of natural gas is an area that would, for example, qualify for assistance. Investment in forests, particularly programs to create sinks for carbon dioxide, is also eligible for such aid. International waters would benefit from similar investments to prevent oil spills and toxic waste pollution, which damage shared water resources. To preserve and improve biodiversity, the GEF may seek to encourage debt-for-nature swaps and the conservation of tropical forest areas. As of 1991, no adequate mechanism had yet been found to deal with the recurrent financing of GEF projects. Figure 13-5 illustrates how the GEF is supposed to work in efforts to reduce carbon dioxide. At the heart of the analysis is the concept of marginal abatement costs (MAC) and corresponding marginal benefits. Economic theory indicates that an efficient solution will be found where marginal benefits equal marginal costs.

Figure 13-5 provides a diagrammatic exposition of the situation facing a single country. The upward-sloping MC curve shows, in a stylized way, the marginal cost of each new method of avoiding carbon dioxide emissions. Some of them—those below the axis—have direct benefits that outweigh their costs. Examples might be the introduction of more efficient appliances or vehicles, the use of surplus energy in efficient ap-

Figure 13-5. Choosing the Optimal Abatement of Carbon Dioxide for an Individual Country

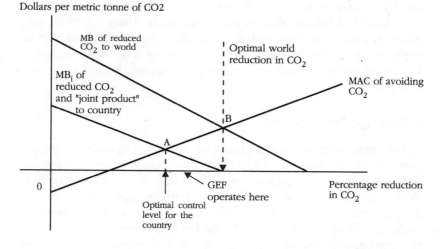

pliances or vehicles, or the use of surplus energy in efficient industrial combined heat-and-power schemes. Some are inexpensive enough that the local benefits from reducing carbon dioxide and creating joint products exceed the costs. But once these initial projects have been exhausted, projects that make larger reductions possible have rising costs.

The two downward-sloping curves show the marginal benefits of reducing carbon dioxide (and counterpart reductions in other joint products), first, to the country concerned and, second, to the world. Point A, where MBi equals MAC, is the optimal control level for the country, while point B, where MB equals MAC, is the optimal level for the world. GEF's role is to encourage movement from A to B. Policies that yield greater benefits for the individual country are often dubbed no regrets, although this term is sometimes confusing. Here, no-regrets policies are those where MBi > MAC, although some commentators use the term to refer to policies where MAC < 0.

One of the key issues that will need to be addressed by developing countries is the relation between the options existing to the left and right of point A in figure 13-5. Many of the options available to achieve GEF's objectives may require the existence of infrastructure, such as better transmission, and a strong relation between the costs of initial and subsequent changes. For example, a large hydroelectric storage plant may have costs that locate it in the region between A and B, but its output cannot be used without developing the transmission system, which can be fully justified by its local benefits. However, when task managers are assessing policies to improve the global environment, this prerequisite does not exist and the feasible set of options is, therefore, constrained. Similarly, the early development of a new technology may be justified by local benefits (they may lie to the left of point A), but subsequent use of that technology in more difficult areas may not be. Using this technology to satisfy global objectives will, then, be either more constrained or more expensive than when all points to the left of point A have been achieved. In the real world of developing countries, of course, this will be a recurrent problem.

Debt-for-Nature Swaps

The outstanding international debt of all developing countries totaled some $1,300 billion at the end of 1987. This is equal to about 50 percent of the GDP of developing countries. Just under half the total outstanding debt (about $600 billion) is to financial markets, that is, to the private banking sector rather than to official sources, such as governments, or multilateral lenders, such as the World Bank. Indebtedness is highest in the upper middle-income countries, but low-income countries have some $330 billion of debt, of which $67 billion is to financial markets. South and Central America owe some 63 percent of their debt to commercial sources, Asia, 42 percent, and Sub-Saharan Africa, 20 percent (see OECD 1988). The sheer scale of indebtedness, overlending by the commercial banking sector in the 1970s (when revenues of the Organization of Petroleum Exporting Countries were recycled to the banking world), domestic economic mismanagement, world recession, and the vagaries of international commodity markets have led to various debt crises in which borrowing countries have defaulted, or threatened to default, on their loans. Mexico failed to meet its debt obligations in 1982, and other countries followed. This situation called for various approaches to debt relief, which aims to cancel or reduce debt, and debt rescheduling, which aims to reschedule the period of repayment.

One reaction to the risk of default has been to resell debt within the banking sector. Debt, as opposed to equity, involves paying an agreed sum at regular intervals regardless of economic fortunes. Any one bank can spread its risks by selling high-risk debt to other banks at a discount. This discounted debt is known as secondary debt. Essentially, discounted debt means that a dollar of debt owed by an indebted country can be bought for less than a dollar on the secondary market. The discount arises because owners of the debt doubt that they will be repaid. In 1989, for example, Yugoslavian debt could be bought at less than 60 percent of its face value. The comparable figures were 35 percent for Poland, 30 percent for Nigeria, under 30 percent for Brazil (prior to their default), under 20 percent for Argentina, and only 5 percent for Côte d'Ivoire. Moreover, prices of secondary debt fell fairly systematically during the

1980s. This secondary loan market developed after Mexico's default crisis of 1982.

The same market also handles debt conversions, which account for around half of the secondary loan market. A conversion swaps some secondary debt for an asset in the indebted country. If the swap is with equity, it is a debt-for-equity swap. Debt can also be converted to local currency or even to claims on exports. The advantage of such swaps is that the lender gains access to creditors in the indebted country rather than simply to the population at large. The indebted country may gain some relief by reducing regular debt payments and perhaps negotiating overall debt relief when the swap is made. Debt-for-equity swaps may take place when an investor wishes to invest in the indebted country. Secondary debt may therefore be traded between banks and between banks and others. All debt conversions relate to commercial debt only, there are no conversions of official debt owed to governments or multi-lateral agencies.

One variety of debt conversion is a debt-for-nature swap. Instead of acquiring equity, the holder of discounted debt agrees to help the indebted country conserve a natural resource, such as a tropical forest. As with debt conversions generally, there are various types of debt-for-nature swaps. One variant is the debt-for-sustainable-development swap whereby debt is swapped for a more general agreement to undertake actions beneficial to the environment. Debt-for-nature swaps have occurred in many countries, and the literature on these swaps is considerable; see Conservation International 1989; Dogse and von Droste 1990; Hansen 1989; Hultkrans 1988; Jansen and Opschoor 1988; J. Walsh 1987; World Wildlife Fund 1988. Some examples are briefly described below.

Bolivia

Conservation International, an environmental organization in the United States, used funds donated by the Frank Weeden Foundation of Connecticut to purchase $650,000 (at face value) of Bolivian debt in 1987 for $100,000 from an affiliate of Citibank. It then swapped the debt for an agreement with the Bolivian government to establish and legally protect three conservation areas totaling 2.7 million acres adjacent to the Beni Biosphere Reserve—established in 1982—and to enhance the legal protection of the reserve itself. Apart from containing thirteen of Bolivia's endangered species, the reserve is also home to Bolivia's Chimane Indians. Under the agreement, half the forest area was protected for scientific investigation and indigenous rights, and half was scheduled for sustainable logging. The Bolivian government established an endowment fund of $250,000 in local currency toward the cost of managing the reserve, of which 60 percent came from USAID (the United States Agency for International Development). Conservation International agreed to assist Bolivia with technical expertise, staff training, and coordination of other international assistance. Major activities included training in the sustainable management of the forest, training and assistance for local botanists and biologists, and education programs.

The effective cost of the agreement was an initial $350,000 ($100,000 of debt purchase and $250,000 of management funds) to protect 2.7 million acres, or around $0.13 per acre. The debt retired was trivial, at 0.01 percent of Bolivia's total debt.

The logging provision of the agreement has come under a great deal of criticism. Reports in 1990 indicated that local Indians were not satisfied with the impact of the swap on their lives (see, for example, F. Pearce 1990). The sustainable management of the forests involved logging companies, which, the Indians alleged, opened up the forest, alienating them from their traditional rights and causing soil erosion. The logging provision has been absent from other debt-for-nature swaps.

Costa Rica

In 1987 and 1988, the World Wildlife Fund for Nature and other agencies donated funds to purchase $5.4 million (at face value) of Costa Rican debt.[6] The $5.4 million figure was a ceiling set on such swaps by the Costa Rican government. The donations were used to establish a Natural Resources Conservation Fund in Costa Rica. The debt was then converted at 75 percent into local currency bonds. The purchase price of the secondary debt was $0.15–$0.17 per dollar, so that the acquisition cost was less than $1 million. The local currency was then used to buy monetary stabilization bonds in Costa Rica. The bonds were given to a Costa Rican bank, which holds them in trust for the Fundación de Parques Nacionales and the Fundación Neotrópica, which are private nonprofit organizations that use the revenues to buy land for conservation, manage existing national parks, and train personnel.

The success of the first swap led the Costa Rican government to relax its ceiling on the amounts involved and produced three more swaps. In 1988, the Dutch Foreign Ministry purchased $30 million of Costa Rican debt at 15 percent for $4.5 million. The debt was then converted to bonds at 30 percent of their face value, that is, some $9 million of Costa Rican bonds were obtained. The converted bonds yield revenues, which, under the swap agreement, are to be used for agroforestry and reforestation. This was the first agreement to involve a government and also extended the asset purchased beyond land to be conserved.

In 1989, a consortium led by the Nature Conservancy purchased $5.6 million of Costa Rican debt. The government issued local currency bonds equal to 30 percent of the principal amount.

Finally, the Swedish government recently purchased $25 million of commercial bank debt to be exchanged for conservation bonds. The local currency bonds will equal 70 percent of the principal of the debt.

Ecuador

In 1988, the World Wildlife Fund purchased $1 million of Ecuadorian debt for $300,000, which was then swapped for non-negotiable stabilization bonds. The revenue generated by these bonds (the principal sum on maturity and the interest in the meantime) goes to Fundación Natura, a private organization in Ecuador, to protect and manage protected areas, advance environmental education, acquire some small nature reserves, and train conservationists. The Ecuadorian swap was initiated by the Fundación Natura, which had previously secured permission to operate swaps up to $10 million in value. The second tranche of the $10 million, some $5.4 million, was purchased in 1989 at a rate of just under $0.12 per dollar, which equaled some $650,000. The debt will again be converted to local currency bonds, and the interest will go to local conservation projects in western Ecuador, the Ecuadorian Amazon, and the Galápagos Islands. Fundación Natura will again manage part of the revenues. The remaining $3.6 million of the original $10 million ceiling on the swaps will be purchased by the Nature Conservancy.

Philippines

In 1989, the World Wildlife Fund completed a swap with the Philippines. The exchange of $390,000 of debt (at face value) formed part of a series of exchanges that will eventually total $2 million. The debt is to be converted to local currency at full face value and made available to the Haribon Foundation, a private conservation group, and the Department of Environment and Natural Resources. Proceeds are to be used for various projects and initially in two national parks.

Madagascar

In 1989, the World Wildlife Fund bought $2.1 million of Malagasy debt from private banks for $950,000, with an option to buy up to $3 million of debt. The USAID issued a grant of $1 million toward the cost. The swap involved Madagascar in spending local currency on conservation projects, including the provision of 400 park rangers.

Zambia

In 1989, the World Wildlife Fund and the Netherlands purchased $2.27 million of Zambian debt for $470,000. Over half the purchase price came from a Swiss donor. The proceeds are to be converted into local currency and used to help protect two wetland areas, support conservation education, and assist with wildlife protection in Zambia.

Conclusions

Debt-for-nature swaps have been criticized on several counts. First, they retire too little debt. To be effective, the swaps must be local in character, since they involve deals that cover the management of natural resources. But if they are local, they are never likely to be large and hence will have a negligible impact on external indebtedness. This criticism is not serious, however, since the swaps have never been conceived as having more than a nominal effect on indebtedness. Their objective is to enhance conservation and, perhaps more ambitiously, contribute to sustainable development.

Another criticism is that they interfere with national sovereignty. This criticism is rarely heard within the host countries themselves. Moreover, the Ecuadorian deal was initiated within the country. The Costa Rican government favors debt-for-nature swaps—the minister of Natural Resources personally promoted the swaps—as do vocal groups in the Philippines.

Debt-for-nature swaps are criticized as inflationary. This criticism might be credible if the amounts in question were large and the debt were converted to cash rather than bonds. In Ecuador and Costa Rica, however, the conversions were to bonds.

Some say that the resulting conservation displaces smallholders and squatters. There is obviously a risk that the activity funded will fail to take account of the interests of indigenous populations or agricultural colonists, who often rely on the conserved land for their livelihood. The focus of debt-for-nature swaps, however, is only partly on conservation in this strict sense. They are particularly concerned with promoting the sustainable use of land in protected areas. The concept of a buffer zone means that the area in the center of a set of concentric circles is protected, while the zones around that area are adapted for sustainable use.

The criticism that debt-for-nature swaps do not create additional funds for conservation but displace other conservation funds is difficult to evaluate. To be true, foreign conservation funds would have to be displaced. Since the current examples of debt purchase typically involve nongovernmental organizations, investment funds clearly have not been displaced. If nongovernmental organizations have difficulty transferring funds to indebted countries in other ways, debt-for-nature swaps may improve their ability to do so. The real problem is the valuation of debt. In advancing cash for conservation, it is possible to concentrate on the conservation rewards for a given sum of money. With debt-for-nature swaps, however, the sum actually advanced for conservation depends on the value of the debt in the marketplace, and the indebted country could easily affect this value by influencing how others perceive the possibility of default. This is a potential problem if debt-for-nature swaps begin to convert a significant amount of total debt.

Finally, some fear that host governments will renege on the management agreement. This danger is real. One solution is to negotiate agreements in which the flow of funds into the host country is annual and depends on some monitoring of performance. If the government defaults, payments can be stopped or reduced.

The real contribution of debt-for-nature swaps is likely to be different. Their greatest benefit will be raising environmental awareness in the host countries and increasing the dialog between local nongovernmental organizations and local governments. The criticisms advanced are not telling, but they might be if such swaps were to involve significant sums. If they were larger, they might prove inflationary and encourage debtor nations to play games with the price of secondary debt by, for example, threatening to default at the time of negotiations. On a larger scale, the swaps might occur at the expense of other types of loans or debt relief.

Notes

1. Acidity is measured by the pH scale. The lower the pH value, the higher the acidity. It is a logarithmic scale so that a pH value of 4.0 is ten times more acidic than a pH value of 5.0. A pH value of 7.0 is neutral.

2. In Europe, the best-known model is that of the Cooperative Programme for Monitoring and Evaluation of the Long-range Transmission of Air Pollutants in Europe, supported by the United Nations Economic Commission for Europe, the World Meteorological Organization, and the United Nations Environment Programme.

3. We are interested in the gains to be obtained from cooperation. The problem is set up as a game and can be analyzed using game theory. Games have equilibria, and a well-known form of equilibrium is a Nash equilibrium in which neither player has an incentive to change strategy. The strategy is determined by calculating the optimal behavior of other countries and hence the optimal response to their behavior. The game is a nonconstant-sum game because, by colluding, the players can alter the overall sum of net benefits (if they could not, it would be a zero-sum game). In a cooperative nonconstant-sum game, the assumption is that individual players can be made better off by collusion and no player need be worse off.

4. The Mediterranean Action Plan gave rise to the Convention for the Protection of the Mediterranean Sea against Pollution in 1976. The contracting countries were Algeria, Cyprus, Egypt, France, Greece, Israel, Italy, Lebanon, Libya, Malta, Monaco, Morocco, Spain, Syria, Tunisia, Turkey, and Yugoslavia. Albania joined in 1990.

5. Crown cover is the extent to which the crowns of trees cover the land below. Viewed from above the forest, crown cover would be roughly measured by the extent to which the ground can and cannot be seen.

6. The agencies were the Asociación Ecológica La Pacífica, Conservation International, Jessie Smith Noyes Foundation, MacArthur Foundation, The Nature Conservancy, the Organization for Tropical Studies, Pew Charitable Trusts, Swedish Society for the Conservation of Nature, W. Alton Jones Foundation, and the World Wildlife Fund.

14

Managing Global Resources

The world's population shares the use of global resources: the atmosphere—made up of the troposphere and stratosphere—and the oceans beyond the exclusive economic zones surrounding land masses. These resources are often known as the global commons because they are owned by the world at large. More correctly, however, they are closer to being open-access resources (see chapter 10). In general, the world does not manage them for mutual benefit, although in recent years, various attempts have been made to undertake global management through conventions regulating the dumping of wastes in oceans and international agreements on controlling the depletion of the ozone layer. The 1990s are likely to witness attempts to negotiate international agreements on controlling atmospheric gases—the so-called greenhouse gases.

Chapter 10 shows that common property resources have a greater risk of being overused than other resources, and that risk is larger still for open-access resources. It is now evident that the global commons are being used in excess of their economically desirable levels and, in some cases, in excess of their ecological carrying capacity.

This chapter looks at four global environmental issues:

- The global atmosphere in the context of the greenhouse effect
- The global troposphere in the context of depletion of the ozone layer

- The case of Antarctica
- Biodiversity.

Endangered species are, of course, located in individual countries or, if they are migratory, shared by several nations. As such, they do not fit under the category of global common property. Nevertheless, because the values they hold are shared by individuals across the world, it is appropriate to discuss biodiversity under the general rubric of global environmental issues.

The Greenhouse Effect

As a natural phenomenon, the greenhouse effect is a process in which energy from the sun (solar radiation) passes through the atmosphere fairly freely, but the heat radiated back from the earth is partially blocked or absorbed by gases in the atmosphere. This blocking or absorption occurs because energy is radiated from the earth at a lower frequency and thus can be, to some extent, trapped by atmospheric gases. Energy is radiated from the sun at a high frequency and thus is not absorbed well by the atmospheric gases surrounding the earth.

Figure 14-1 illustrates the process at work. For every 100 units of incoming shortwave solar radiation, some 31 units are reflected back from the air, clouds, and the earth's surface—the earth's albedo. This leaves 69 units to account for. Of these, 23 are absorbed by clouds, atmospheric vapor, ozone, and dust. The earth, including the oceans, absorbs 46 units (100 − 31 − 23), but incoming and outgoing radiation must balance. So, 100 units (incoming radiation) minus 23 (albedo) equals 69 units that must be reflected back as longwave radiation. The sums are complicated because longwave radiation going from the earth's surface does not pass through clouds, vapor, and atmospheric gases easily. This creates a bounce-back effect. This can be seen at the right-hand side of figure 14-1. Twenty-four units of longwave radiation are emitted as latent heat—heat carried into the atmosphere by water evaporating from the oceans and land surface waters. Another 7 units are emitted as sensible heat flux—the direct heating of the atmosphere by the warm earth. Because there is a bounce-back effect of 100 units, outgoing longwave radiation must be 115 units (since [115 − 100] + 7 + 24 = 46, where 46 is the radiation absorbed by the earth's surface).

The radiation absorbed by clouds, water vapor, and carbon dioxide produces the greenhouse effect, the warming of the atmosphere. The greenhouse analogy arises because the glass in a greenhouse, like the earth's atmosphere, admits solar energy but traps the infrared energy generated by the soil and plants. The temperature inside the greenhouse rises until the solar energy gained is just balanced by the heat lost from the greenhouse. This warming is natural: indeed, without it there would

Figure 14-1. Greenhouse Effect

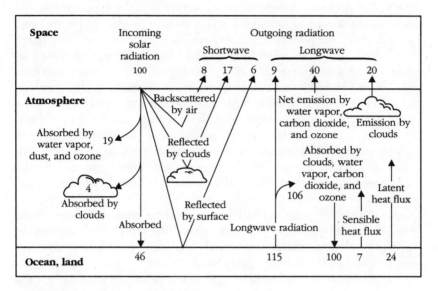

Note: Numbers represent an index of incoming solar radiation.
Source: McCracken and Luther (1986).

be no life on earth because the average temperature of the earth's surface would be below the freezing point of water, which is around −18°C, rather than at 15°C, as it is now.

Why, then, should this greenhouse effect be thought of as a problem? The additional warming is what causes concern. The atmospheric trace gases that trap the outgoing longwave radiation have been increasing, further reducing the ability of the radiation from the earth to travel through the gases and hence adding to the warming effect. Put another way, without these increased gas concentrations, the earth would maintain its existing equilibrium temperature. With the gases, the temperature will increase. This increased warming has many potentially damaging effects and some beneficial ones.

The gases producing this layer around the earth are water vapor, carbon dioxide, methane, nitrous oxide, some chlorofluorocarbons (CFCs), and ozone. These gases are a mix of natural events and anthropogenic factors, which are induced by humans. Thus methane is given off by natural processes of organic decay in the oceans and by herbivorous animals. Nitrous oxides are given off by microbial processes in soil and water. But both gases are also given off by the activities of people: the growing of paddy rice contributes to methane emissions, as does cattle farming. Nitrous oxides are produced by the use of nitrogen fertilizers and fuel combustion. Ozone is created naturally in the upper atmosphere through the actions of sunlight, but it is also the product of photochemical reactions with pollution, notably vehicle emissions, near the ground. Carbon dioxide is absorbed by plants in photosynthesis and is then released to the atmosphere naturally from organic decomposition and from the oceans (an important fact that we return to shortly). However, carbon dioxide is also released in large quantities as a result of burning fossil fuels and deforestation. Forests play an important role in the production of carbon dioxide: the burning of forests (usually to clear land for agriculture in tropical countries) contributes to carbon dioxide, cleared forests may increase the albedo (the cleared land reflects radiation back), and forests act as carbon sinks, taking in carbon dioxide while giving off oxygen.

Determining the relative contributions of these gases is complex. Table 14-1 shows the relative importance of the different gases as assessed by the United Nations Intergovernmental Panel on Climate Change (IPCC), a body set up in 1988 to investigate global warming.

Table 14-2 shows the broad sources of the individual trace gases; table 14-3 shows the geographical sources. Most of the carbon dioxide and

Table 14-1. Contribution of Greenhouse Gases to Global Warming, 1990
(based on 1990 emissions levels)

Type of gas	Carbon dioxide equivalence	1990 emissions (millions of tons)	Percentage share over 100 years
Carbon dioxide	1	26,000	66.0
Methane	21	300	16.5
Nitrous oxide	290	6	4.5
CFCs			12.0
CFC-11	3,500	0.3	—
CFC-12	7,300	0.4	—
HCF22	1,500	0.1	0.4
Other	—	—	0.6

— Not available.

Note: Carbon dioxide is of considerable importance, contributing around 66 percent of the total warming effect of greenhouse gases. But the roles of methane (16 percent) and CFCs (about 12 percent) are also substantial (methane having 21 times, and nitrous oxide 290 times, the impact of carbon dioxide). Although concentrations of CFCs in the atmosphere are small, they are important because they are even more powerful in their radiative effects than carbon dioxide—many thousands of times more powerful; they persist in the atmosphere for long periods of time; they destroy stratospheric ozone, and this may enhance the greenhouse effect; and their emissions increase at a very high rate. How far their control under the Montreal Protocol will reduce their role as greenhouse gases is open to question because a substantial stock of CFCs has already been released to the atmosphere and has yet to release the chlorine that damages the ozone layer.

Source: Unpublished data of the Intergovernmental Panel on Climate Change (1990).

nitrous oxide emissions are, technically, under the control of man, whereas perhaps only half of the methane emissions could be subject to some form of management. All new CFC production could be controlled, but, like carbon dioxide, past emissions still affect future global warming. In effect, the world is committed to a certain degree of global warming in the future even if anthropogenic production of all greenhouse gases were to cease today. This cannot be prevented; the world's only choice is to adapt to committed warming.

Committed warming exists because the oceans store carbon dioxide. The oceans already hold fifty times more carbon than the atmosphere.

Table 14-2. Source of Global Emissions of Greenhouse Gases Produced by Human Activities, 1985
(millions of metric tons a year)

Source	Greenhouse gas emissions	Carbon dioxide–equivalent emissions	
		Amount	Percent
Carbon dioxide emissions			
Commercial energy	18,800	18,800	57
Tropical deforestation	2,600	2,600	8
Other	400	400	1
Total	21,800	21,800	66
Methane emissions			
Fuel production	60	1,300	4
Enteric fermentation	70	1,500	5
Rice cultivation	110	2,300	7
Landfills	30	600	2
Tropical deforestation	20	400	1
Other	30	600	2
Total	320	6,700	20[a]
Total CFC-11 and CFC-12 emissions	0.6	3,200	10
Nitrous oxide emissions			
Coal combustion	1.0	290	Above 1
Fertilizer use	1.5	440	1
Gain of cultivated land	0.4	120	Above 1
Tropical deforestation	0.5	150	Above 1
Fuelwood and industrial biomass	0.2	60	Above 1
Agricultural wastes	0.4	120	Above 1
Total	4.0	1,190	4
Total emissions	—	32,880	100

— Not available.

Note: Carbon dioxide–equivalent emissions are calculated from the figures on greenhouse gas emissions by using the following multipliers: carbon dioxide, 1; methane, 21; CFC-11 and CFC-12, 5,400; nitrous oxides, 290. All entries are rounded because the exact values are controversial.

a. Total does not sum due to rounding errors.

Source: Adapted from the U.S. Department of Energy (1990).

*Table 14-3. Estimated Anthropogenic Emissions of Greenhouse Gases,
by Source, 1985–2050*
(percentages unless otherwise noted)

Type of gas and source	1985	2000	2015	2050
Carbon dioxide				
United States	21	19	16	12
Other OECD countries	22	19	16	12
Soviet Union and Eastern Europe	22	22	19	18
Centrally planned Asia	10	13	16	21
Other developing countries	25	28	32	37
Commercial energy	86	87	89	92
Tropical deforestation	12	11	9	6
Other	2	2	2	2
Total emissions (millions of metric tons)	5.99	8.05	10.27	16.95
Methane				
United States	12	11	9	8
Other OECD countries	13	12	12	10
Soviet Union and Eastern Europe	13	14	14	15
Centrally planned Asia	17	16	17	19
Other developing countries	46	47	49	48
Fuel production	18	22	26	32
Enteric fermentation	23	24	23	22
Rice cultivation	34	31	29	24
Landfills	9	10	10	14
Tropical deforestation	6	6	5	4
Other	9	7	7	5
Total (millions of metric tons)	320.1	399.5	476.8	710.5

They exchange carbon with the atmosphere, but that exchange is not quite balanced, or so it is thought; the oceans receive perhaps 105 billion tons of carbon each year from the atmosphere and release 102 billion tons to the atmosphere. The carbon released to the atmosphere is subject to time lags—that is, carbon received by the oceans is released over a period that may range from twenty to sixty years. Moreover, the oceans appear to be a net sink, which means that they receive more carbon than they release. As the global climate gets warmer, this accumulation process could be reversed, thus accelerating the greenhouse effect. Much depends on the imperfectly understood exchange that occurs between oceans and the atmosphere. CFCs are similarly stored in the atmosphere, breaking down over what are often very long periods of time.

Understanding how changes in climate are predicted is critical because it reveals a fundamental feature of the greenhouse effect—uncertainty. Just when global warming will occur, and how much warming will take place, depends on the level of committed warming, on future emissions of trace gases, and on the sensitivity of climate to changes in concentra-

Table 14-3 (continued)

Type of gas and source	1985	2000	2015	2050
Nitrous oxide				
United States	14	12	11	9
Other OECD countries	13	14	14	12
Soviet Union and Eastern Europe	14	15	14	13
Centrally planned Asia	13	16	14	15
Other developing countries	46	47	47	52
Commercial energy	25	26	29	36
Fertilizer use	38	43	44	41
Gain of cultivated land	10	8	8	6
Tropical deforestation	13	11	10	9
Fuelwood and industrial biomass	5	4	3	2
Agricultural wastes	10	8	7	6
Total (millions of metric tons)	4.21	5.85	6.87	8.85
CFC-11 and CFC-12[a]				
United States	24	18	17	12
Other industrial countries	41	24	24	21
Soviet Union and Eastern Europe	16	14	14	13
Countries using 0.2 kilograms per capita[b]	6	14	15	19
Other developing countries	12	30	30	36
Total (thousands of metric tons)	642.1	837.8	755.1	828.5

Note: For carbon dioxide emissions, the average annual growth is 1.6 percent; for methane gas, 1.2 percent; for nitrous oxide, 1.2 percent; and for CFC-11 and CFC-12, 0.4 percent.

a. Assuming no further controls beyond the Montreal Protocol.

b. Nations whose use of CFCs is between 0.1 and 0.2 kilograms per capita and is likely to reach the 0.3 kilograms per capita limit set by the Montreal Protocol before 1990.

Source: Unpublished data from the U.S. Council of Economic Advisers (1989).

tions of trace gases. Just how the climate will vary geographically is another complex issue.

Two features of global warming have now been highlighted: uncertainty and a commitment to some degree of warming. Two policy responses have been identified: prevention (to reduce trace gas emissions) and adaptation. We return to these points later.

Climatologists distinguish between equilibrium warming and transient warming. If trace gas emissions were to cease immediately, some warming would still occur because a time lag occurs in the system by which the ocean and the atmosphere exchange carbon and because CFCs are being stored in the atmosphere. If no further trace gases are emitted, the climate will change until it reaches a steady state equilibrium. The temperature would be warmer, but the warming would settle down at this equilibrium value. Similarly, if trace gas emissions continue to rise, there will be a new equilibrium warming level, some time in the future, for each level of emissions. This equilibrium warming is of interest insofar as it should be possible to estimate the level of warming to which the world is already committed, or to which it would be committed if trace gas emissions were halted at some stage in the future.

Transient warming refers to the actual change in temperature that occurs because of trace gas emissions. At any point in time, the observed temperature will differ from the equilibrium temperature because of the time lags that characterize the system of exchanging carbon between the ocean and the atmosphere. A snapshot for the year 2030, say, would show us the transient warming, but further warming would still occur until the system reached a steady state. Transient warming is therefore below equilibrium warming as long as we can assume positive feedbacks. A feedback effect arises if the increase in temperature itself triggers a reaction that either accelerates the warming (positive feedback) or decelerates the warming (negative feedback). An example of a positive feedback is a reduction in sea ice and snow cover as the temperature rises. This, in turn, reduces the amount of heat being reflected back into space (an albedo effect) and increases the warming of the earth's surface. An example of a negative feedback is the effect of temperature on cloud cover. As the optical properties of clouds increase, incoming radiation may be reduced, offsetting the warming to some extent. Existing models tend to predict a preponderance of positive feedback effects, that is, the warming process will give rise to effects that increase warming further. Thus transient warming tends to be some proportion of equilibrium warming.

Scientists use general circulation models to illustrate these interactions. Despite their apparent complexity, these models are still fairly primitive for modeling the various feedbacks that occur. To build in all the feedbacks requires three-dimensional models, which are being developed. Until these models are complete, we therefore have one source of scientific uncertainty about what will happen.

Figure 14-2 shows the projected effects of greenhouse gas emissions under various scenarios prepared by the IPCC, whose Working Group 1 was responsible for analyzing the scientific evidence for global warming and projecting the expected changes in global temperature under various assumptions. Under scenario A—business as usual—no controls are exercised over current rates of emission growth. This gives rise to increases in global mean surface temperatures of 0.2°C–0.5°C a decade in the twenty-first century, with a best guess of 0.3°C a decade. Essentially, then, doing nothing will increase global mean temperatures 1°C by 2025 and 3°C by 2100 compared with temperatures in 1990. To understand the significance of this projection, temperatures during the last Ice Age 18,000 years ago were only 4°C–5°C colder than they are today. In the mini ice age experienced by Europe between 1400 and 1800 AD, temperatures were 0.5°C–1.0°C colder than today.

Under scenario B, deforestation is halted, natural gas is substituted for coal, which has a higher carbon content, and energy conservation mea-

Figure 14-2. IPCC Scenarios for Changes in Global Temperature, 1850-2030

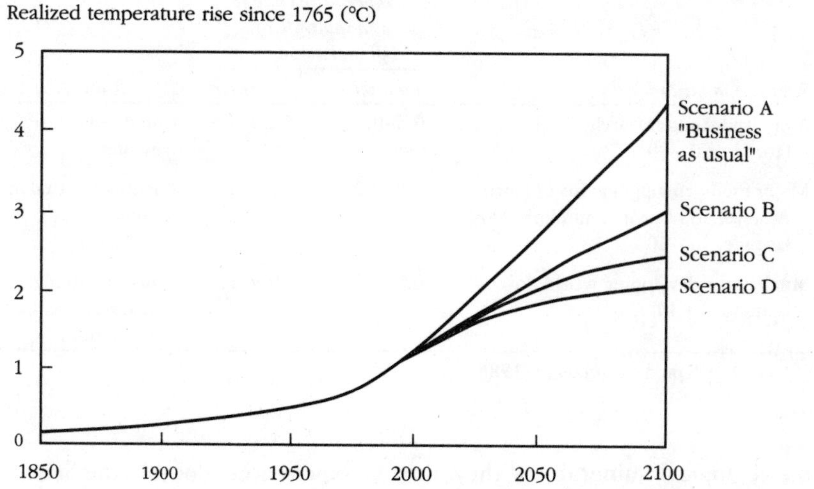

Realized temperature rise since 1765 (°C)

Note: The following numbers are based on high-resolution models, scaled to be consistent with an estimated global mean warming of 1.8°C by 2030. For values consistent with other estimates, the following estimates of a global rise in temperature should be reduced 30 percent for the low estimate and increased 50 percent for the high estimate. Estimated precipitation is also scaled in a similar way. Confidence in these regional estimates is low.

In Central North America (35°-50°N and 85°-105°W), the warming varies from 2°C to 4°C in winter and 2°C to 3°C in summer. Precipitation increases 0 to 15 percent in winter but decreases 5 to 10 percent in summer, when soil moisture decreases 15 to 20 percent.

In Southern Asia (5°-30°N and 70°-105°E), the warming varies from 1°C to 2°C throughout the year. Precipitation changes little in winter and generally increases 5 to 15 percent in summer, as does soil moisture.

In the Sahel (10°-20°N and 20°W-40°E), the warming varies from 1°C to 3°C. Mean precipitation increases, and mean soil moisture decreases marginally in summer. Throughout the region, some areas have increases and some have decreases in both parameters.

In Southern Europe (35°-40°N and 10°W-45°E), the warming is about 2°C in winter and varies from 2°C to 3°C in summer. Precipitation seems to increase in winter. In summer, however, precipitation decreases 5 to 15 percent, and soil moisture decreases 15 to 25 percent.

In Australia (12°-45°S and 100°-115°E), the warming ranges from 1°C to 2°C in summer and is about 2°C in winter. Summer precipitation increases around 10 percent, but the models do not produce consistent estimates of the changes in soil moisture. The area averages hide large regional variations within the continent.

Source: Unpublished data of the IPCC (1990).

sures are adopted. The result is a rise of 0.2°C per decade. In scenarios C and D, increasingly strict abatement measures are undertaken, and energy from fossil fuels is aggressively replaced by renewable energy. Under scenario C, warming is held to 0.1°C, and under scenario D, warming is eventually stabilized.

The scenarios show only the changes in global mean temperature. The regional variation around this mean is uncertain, but table 14-4 shows IPCC's best guesses in the business-as-usual scenario. Substantial uncertainty surrounds these figures. Nonetheless, even if they are only broadly correct, some areas of the world will experience a dramatic worsening of

Table 14-4. *Possible Changes in Climate, by Region and Season*

Region and latitudes	Temperature change as a multiple of global average		Rainfall
	Summer	Winter	
Arctic and Antarctic areas, high latitude, 60°–90°	0.5–0.7	2.0–2.4	Enhanced in winter
Major food-growing regions of North America and Europe, middle latitude, 30°–60°	0.8–1.0	1.2–1.4	Possibly reduced in summer
Much of the developing world, low latitude, 0°–30°	0.9–1.7	0.9–1.7	Enhanced in places that have heavy rains today

Source: Adapted from Jaeger (1988).

the ecological vulnerability they already experience—notably the Sahel, where warming is projected to increase, and the Mediterranean area, where increases in temperature are expected to be accompanied by significant reductions in rainfall.

The Effects of Global Warming

The effects of global warming may be classified in the following terms: changes in average regional temperature and rainfall, average rise in sea level, and frequency and severity of weather events.

RISE IN REGIONAL TEMPERATURE. Regional variations in temperature rise are difficult to predict because general circulation models are not yet sophisticated enough to provide the required detail. Table 14-4 shows some possible broad regional scenarios and reveals some important potential effects. The mid-latitude regions include most of the world's major crop-growing areas, such as Argentina, China, Europe, New Zealand, and the United States. Thus, some 65 percent of the world's cereals output comes from the 30º–50º zone, 75 percent of maize, 74 percent of wheat, 86 percent of barley, and 38 percent of rice. Just how these areas will be affected by global warming is uncertain. Summer soil moisture may be reduced, and crops could be affected by summer droughts. One significant impact could be the reduction of water supplies, both of surface water and groundwater aquifers.

Evapotranspiration can be expected to increase, but this may be offset by increases in rainfall. Overall, the main impact on agriculture is likely to be caused by changes in hydrological regimes, but little scientific study has been conducted to establish just what the effects might be. In addition to the scientific uncertainty about climatic sensitivity to concentrations of trace gases, and forecasting uncertainty about the way in which trace gas emissions will behave in the future, we have dose-response uncertainty about the way in which hydrological and other regimes will respond to variations in temperature and rainfall. Crosson (1989, pp. 107–18) reviews impact studies and concludes that the studies of the impact of climatic changes on crop yields do not suggest a major threat to global agricultural capacity by mid-twenty-first century. His view is that even if yield loss were at the high end of the range, this would be small compared with the doubling or more of yields that might be expected from future advances in technology and management.

RISE IN SEA LEVEL. Projections of the global mean rise in sea level are perhaps more certain than projections of temperature and rainfall. Global warming will affect the sea level by thermal expansion of the oceans, by melting mid- and high-latitude small glaciers and ice sheets, perhaps by melting the Greenland and Antarctic ice sheets, and possibly by disintegrating the West Antarctic floating ice sheet. The IPCC studies suggest a global mean rise in sea level of 6 centimeters a decade over the next century, with a range of uncertainty of 3–10 centimeters a decade for the business-as-usual scenario. It is important to note that the sea level would continue to rise after that date because of the dynamic role played by oceans and that in the past 100 years the sea level may have risen 10–15 centimeters. Sea level rises over the next forty years may, therefore, be three or even four times greater than they were in the past century.

Sea level rises vary regionally, in part because the level of land masses changes. The Mississippi Delta is already experiencing a rise in sea level due to decreased sedimentation, which is caused by human activity, and has resulted in subsidence. One obvious impact is the loss of low-lying land to the sea, but there are other effects as well. These include salt intrusion to freshwater systems and groundwater and storm surges that cause floods.

FREQUENT AND SEVERE EVENTS. Climatic changes are also likely to alter the frequency and variability of events related to the weather. Thus droughts, storms, and floods may be more frequent, and the severity of these individual events may be greatly increased.

The Impact on Developing Countries

The impact of climatic change on developing countries could be substantial. First, developing economies tend to be more dependent than industrial economies on natural resources, which themselves are sensitive to fairly moderate changes in climate: soil quality, woody biomass, and water for drinking and as a habitat for fish. Second, the agricultural systems of many developing countries are based on low-lying deltaic land fed by rich silt from river systems. These lands will be prone to flooding and the intrusion of saltwater. Third, many agricultural systems rely on natural rainfall rather than irrigation systems. Not only does the amount of rain matter, but so do the timing and distribution of rain across the growing season. Third, many small developing countries are island communities at special risk from severe weather events such as hurricanes and cyclones. Fourth, the very poverty of many developing countries will preclude them from undertaking the kinds of adaptive policies, such as sea defenses, that may be needed.

Semiarid tropical regions—Sub-Saharan Africa, Northeast Brazil, and parts of India and Pakistan—could be especially at risk from extended dry periods. Changes in hydrological conditions in the humid tropics could affect rice growing, especially in marginal lands. Agriculture in the temperate zones has already been mentioned. A possible scenario is the loss of U.S. cereal crops, although not on a significant scale, the increase of rice production in Japan, the improvement of wheat production in the Soviet Union (due to warming), and the expansion of cereal production in northern countries (see Parry, Carter, and Konijn 1988). In developing countries, a major impact will be on subsistence crops, which are frequently grown on marginal, and hence more climatically sensitive, land. Some illustrations are provided below.

GUYANA. Guyana, which is situated on the north coast of South America, has a land area of some 215,000 square kilometers and a population of about 900,000 (this section is based on Camacho 1988). The vast majority of the population (90 percent) live on the coastal plains, which comprise only 3 percent of the land area but contribute some 70 percent of the country's gross domestic product (GDP). The coastal plains rarely extend beyond 16 kilometers into the mainland, and much of the area is below the sea level at high tide. The coastline is protected by dikes built by Dutch engineers with slave labor in the eighteenth and early nineteenth centuries. Many of these old sea defenses are already breached by the sea.

Rising sea levels due to global warming would have the following consequences. A rise of 150 centimeters—which would, however, not occur for 150 years according to the IPCC's worst scenario for the global mean rise in sea level—would mean the following:

- Most of the existing agricultural areas would be flooded or subject to periodic intrusion of saltwater
- Since the main crops are sugar (44,000 hectares) and rice (72,000 hectares), industries processing these crops will be drastically affected
- Other crop losses would include various fruits, vegetables, and peppers

- Pasture would be lost (40,000 hectares) with little chance of being relocated inland, where the land is unsuitable
- The loss of residential and commercial property located on the coastal plains would be large
- There would be similar major losses of infrastructure.

A rise of 150 centimeters seems extreme in light of the scenarios previously discussed, but it must be recalled that a range of 17–28 centimeters is forecast for 2030, sea levels would continue to rise after that, and the rise in sea level would vary by region. Even if the focus were on 2030 only, a rise of 25 centimeters would still mean that drainage for agricultural areas must be improved substantially and sea defenses strengthened.

An approximate estimate suggests that the value of crops and residential housing in the coastal plains is some $790 million a year. A coastal protection plan would initially have to consist of additional sea defenses and enhanced gravity drainage (drainage that relies on water flowing out at times of low tide). Relatively long-term measures might include additional pumped drainage. The option of wholesale moves inland does not appear to be feasible because the land there is not suitable for agriculture. The costs of the protective measures required initially are speculative but could amount to some $20 million over five years.

TONGA. Tonga, in the Pacific, is a kingdom of some 150 islands, has a population of 95,000 people, and covers a total land area of 560 square kilometers (this section is based on Lewis 1988). Its capital, Nukualofa, which is located on Tongatapu Island, has a population of about 20,000 and was extensively flooded during hurricane Isaac in 1982. It has been estimated that if the sea level were to rise 50 centimeters, some 15 percent of the land area of the main parts of Nukualofa would be flooded, and a rise of 150 centimeters would flood some 38 percent of these areas.

Land in Tonga is not bought and sold. It is the property of the king of Tonga, who, in turn, allocates it to the nobility and all males on their coming of age. But land is leased, so a market does exist. For the rise of 50 centimeters, land that could be leased for some $T8 million would be lost; for the rise of 150 centimeters, the value would be on the order of $T23 million. These are land values only, not complete property values, which, if the market functioned freely, would also reflect the stream of future net benefits from economic activity on that land.

Areas lost to the sea for each scenario are estimated at 0.54 and 1.4 square kilometers, respectively. Thus the land value lost per square kilometer can be put at $T8 million/ 0.54 = $T14.8 million per square kilometer a year for the rise of 50 centimeters and at $T23 million/ 1.4 = $T16.4 million per square kilometer for the rise of 150 centimeters. Although foreshore sea defenses were constructed in the wake of hurri-

cane Isaac, their cost cannot be related directly to the land values preserved. Nonetheless, the cost of sea defenses is probably outweighed by
the land values preserved, partly because land is scarce and has high lease
values. Clearly, no firm conclusion can be reached on the basis of the
figures available. Nevertheless, the value of land preserved can be compared with the cost of sea defenses to approximate a cost-benefit approach to adapting to a rise in sea level.

BANGLADESH. Bangladesh's economy is heavily dependent on the
Ganges Delta (this section is based on Holdgate and others 1989; Milliman, Broadus, and Gable 1989). Half of Bangladesh lies at elevations
under 5 meters. The delta comprises 80 percent of the land area of
Bangladesh. The impact of a rise in sea level on local deltas will depend
on the relation between the rise induced by climate and the rise induced
by land subsidence or uplift. A tectonic uplift could counteract the rise in
sea level, while subsidence could compound it. Subsidence is normally
offset by the deposition of new sediment in the delta. Subsidence can also
be accelerated if groundwater is extracted rapidly for human use. The
overall impact of a rise in sea level thus becomes uncertain.[1]

Bangladesh's population of 112 million is mostly located on the low-
lying Ganges-Brahmaputra-Meghna River Delta, which has a 650-
kilometer coastline to the Bay of Bengal. Floods and storm surges are
frequent: 300,000 people lost their lives in a cyclone in 1970; 5,000 died
in 1985; 3,000 more were killed and 25 million made homeless in the
monsoon floods of August through September 1988. Another 5,000 died
in a cyclone in December 1988. A rise of 1 meter in the local sea level
would flood perhaps 10–11 percent of Bangladesh's land area, affecting
9–10 percent of its population and 11 percent of its agriculture. The
natural protection afforded by mangrove swamps is being lost as the
mangroves are removed. This is occurring even in protected areas such as
the Sundarban Forest in the southwest of the country.

But the effect of global warming on the behavior of the sea in the Bay
of Bengal is highly uncertain. The past events that have caused so much
damage and loss of life in Bangladesh arise from storm surges that increase the height of waves as storms are funneled up the Bay of Bengal.
These surges could increase in frequency and severity. The height of the
waves—the surge amplitude—could actually decrease as sea levels rise;
the deeper the water, the lower the wind stress.

Subsidence in the bay may be on the order of 1 centimeter a year,
although there is considerable uncertainty about this. The depletion of
groundwater may be contributing to the subsidence. The fate of sediment
flows is not known in detail. Milliman, Broadus, and Gable (1989) have
estimated a local rise in sea level in 2050 to be between 13 and 209
centimeters, an enormous range. The lower end of the range would
correspond to a 1 percent loss of land. The higher end of the range would

lead to an 18 percent loss of land that currently supports 15 percent of the people and produces 13 percent of the country's GDP. By 2100, the land lost would be between a few percentages and 34 percent. The effects would depend on the fate of the mangrove forests and the extent to which the flow of sediment is interrupted by dams. Warming of the climate may also intensify the cyclones that already affect the area.

THE NILE DELTA. The Nile Delta is Egypt's food lifeline since it contains nearly all the country's agriculturally productive land. Because of the Aswan Dam, little sediment reaches the coast and coastal areas have become degraded as the sea enters areas previously taken up by sediment. Large lakes that lie just inland of the coast supply much of the nation's fish. The lakes are protected by dunes, but these may be breached if the sea level rises. In addition, the delta is subject to subsidence, and this may accelerate under the pressure of groundwater extraction. Estimates suggest that the local rise in sea level could be between 13 and 144 centimeters in 2050. The effects of such a rise are summarized in table 14-5.

Policy on the Greenhouse Problem

Three broad policy stances may be undertaken to deal with the greenhouse problem. In each case, a single country could act alone or cooperatively. Acting alone is very unlikely to affect the damage from global

Table 14-5. *Predicted Effects of a Rise in Sea Level in the Nile Delta, 2050 and 2100*

Effect	2050			2100		
	Best case	Worst case	Absolutely worst case	Best case	Worst case	Absolutely worst case
Rise in sea level (centimeters)						
Global	13	79	79	28	217	217
Local subsidence	0	22	65	0	40	115
Total	13	101	144	28	257	332
Shoreline erosion (kilometers)	0	1	1	0	2	2
Percentage of habitable land lost	—	15	19	—	22	26
Percentage of population displaced	—	14	16	—	19	24
Percentage of GDP in affected areas	—	14	17	—	19	24

— Not available.

Note: The best-case scenario assumes a minimal rise in sea level; natural subsidence is offset by deltaic sedimentation. The worst-case scenario assumes a maximum rise in sea level and uncompensated natural subsidence since the Nile is completely dammed. The absolutely worst-case scenario assumes the worst case and also assumes enhanced subsidence due to the withdrawal of groundwater.

Source: Milliman, Broadus, and Gable (1989).

warming significantly, but a country may have other reasons for wanting to demonstrate that it is taking action. It could, for example, want to influence global bargaining, and its bargaining power could be improved by revealing a willingness to act unilaterally. The three policy actions are to do nothing and rely on natural adaptation, to reduce greenhouse gas emissions, and to invest in adaptation.

Even if no specific actions are taken, populations will adapt to the effects of climatic change. Much of the change will be gradual, and people will adapt by migrating, changing their lifestyles, and undertaking defensive expenditures such as using more fertilizer to offset reduced crop productivity. The scope for natural adaptation is obviously very uncertain. Research could still continue within this scenario. Although doing nothing sounds reprehensible, it may enable more cost-effective solutions to be found in the future. On the other hand, doing nothing also increases the level of committed warming. This is a fairly familiar outcome of a wait-and-see policy: the quality of the decisions that eventually must be made are improved because they are based on better information, but the damage may be more costly due to the delay.

Prevention and containment are another option. They include reducing carbon dioxide emissions by reducing the use of fossil fuels. This would require, in turn, a combination of the following measures: undertaking energy conservation, changing the mix of fuel to favor fuels other than carbon (for example, nuclear power and renewable sources of energy such as wave, wind, and tidal power), and reducing the concentrations of carbon dioxide by increasing the carbon sinks. This is done by increasing afforestation (since trees fix atmospheric carbon) and by reducing deforestation, especially of tropical forests. The consensus of analysts is that energy conservation has the highest potential for reducing the greenhouse effect.

Setting Targets: International Discussions

Table 14-6 shows the targets that individual countries have set for reducing greenhouse gases. Although the United States has set an overall target for greenhouse gases, it has not done so for carbon dioxide because some scientists express doubts about global warming and others express concern about the costs of combating it. Notable omissions from the target-setting countries are the former Soviet Union, Eastern Europe, and the developing world.

International discussion among members of the Organisation for Economic Co-operation and Development (OECD) other than the United States has tended to center on trying to stabilize emissions at the 1990 level by the year 2000 or 2005.

Setting Targets: The Acceptable Level of Global Warming

The world is already committed to some global warming because of the thermal inertia of oceans. Even if the emission of all greenhouse gases stopped tomorrow, some global warming would still occur. The Toronto Conference set a target that would reduce the current level of emissions 20 percent, which was thought to be consistent with a rate of warming of 0.1°C each decade (this limit is suggested by, for example, International Project for Sustainable Energy Paths 1989). This has been advanced as an ecologically manageable rate of increase in warming; that is, it is the rate at which nondisruptive ecological change will take place. The idea of using ecological limits is very much akin to the constant natural capital approach (see chapter 2). However, stabilizing carbon dioxide emissions at 1990 levels by 2000–05 is consistent with a warming level significantly higher than 0.1°C and perhaps closer to 0.25°C. Figure 14-3 shows a simulation of various policy measures in the context of hypothetical damage functions. The simulations are of the IPCC scenarios. An optimistic damage function might look like damage 2 in figure 14-3, while a pessimistic one might look like damage 3. In between is damage 1. If some scientists are correct, the area to the right of the O.1°C rate of warming contains major uncertainty. Indeed, the earth has not witnessed a combination of absolute warming higher than 1°C above the pre-industrial temperature level and a rate of warming higher than 0.1°C a decade. Business as usual (the IPCC scenario in which no action is taken) is shown to be consistent with a rate of warming of around 0.27°C a decade, way beyond the zone of safety. But even if the OECD countries were to take major actions, the effect on the rate of warming would be limited: stabilizing carbon dioxide emissions by 2000 in all OECD countries achieves only a modest reduction in the rate of warming.

The acceptable level of warming can be derived in another way. Costs and benefits can be compared in monetary terms; that is, a utilitarian approach could be adopted in which sacrifices made now are weighed against gains received later (see D. W. Pearce and Barbier 1990). Nordhaus (1991) has made a significant attempt to compute approximate costs and benefits (see also Walter and Ayres 1990).

Nordhaus suggests the picture of costs and benefits that appears in table 14-7. The figures should be read to find the greatest difference between costs and benefits, that is, the maximum net benefits from reduced emissions (and from afforestation as a means of fixing carbon dioxide). Thus, a 5 percent reduction in emissions is clearly worthwhile since the world would avoid about $3 billion in damages at a cost of only $600 million. Reductions are worthwhile up to a maximum net benefit corresponding to an 11 percent reduction in emissions; the net benefit is reduced beyond this. For cuts of around 20 percent, costs actually exceed benefits.

Nordhaus shows that this overall reduction should comprise a virtual phaseout of CFCs and a very modest reduction in carbon dioxide. The finding that CFCs should be phased out is wholly consistent with the existing international discussions, but the consistency ends there. Nordhaus refers to modest reductions in the level of carbon dioxide that

Table 14-6. *Commitments of OECD Countries to Controlling Global Changes in Climate, Various Years, 1988-2005*

Country and gases included	Type of commitment	Action taken	Base year	Commitment year	Conditions and comments
Australia, greenhouse gases and gases not covered in the Montreal Protocol	Target	Stabilization	1988	2000	Interim planning target; to be implemented if others take like action
		20 percent reduction	1988	2005	
Austria, carbon dioxide	Target	20 percent reduction	1988	2005	Still needs parliamentary approval
Belgium, carbon dioxide	EC agreement	..	..	..	..
Canada, carbon dioxide and other greenhouse gases	Target	Stabilization	1988	2000	..
Denmark, carbon dioxide	Target	20 percent reduction	1988	2005	Implementation plan adopted
Finland, carbon dioxide	Target	Stabilization	1990	2000	..
France, carbon dioxide	Target	Stabilization	1990	2000	Target of less than 2 metric tons of carbon per capita a year
Germany, Republic of, carbon dioxide	Target	25 percent reduction	1987	2005	Larger percent reduction in eastern states of former Federal Republic
Greece, carbon dioxide	EC agreement	..	..	..	..
Iceland, carbon dioxide	EFTA agreement	..	..	..	..
Ireland, carbon dioxide	EC agreement	..	..	..	..
Italy, carbon dioxide	Target	Stabilization	1988	2000	Nonbinding resolution
		20 percent reduction	1988	2005	Nonbinding resolution
Japan, carbon dioxide	Target	Stabilization	1990	2000	On per capita basis; implemented if others act likewise
Luxemburg, carbon dioxide	EC agreement	..	..	..	..

Netherlands					
Carbon dioxide	Target	Stabilization	1989–90	1995	Unilateral action committed
		3–5 percent reduction	1989–90	2000	..
All greenhouse gases	Target	20–25 percent reduction	1989–90	2000	Unilateral action committed
New Zealand, carbon dioxide	Target	20 percent reduction	1990	2000	..
Norway, carbon dioxide	Target	Stabilization	1989	2000	Preliminary
Portugal, carbon dioxide	EC agreement	..	..	..	..
Spain, carbon dioxide	EC agreement	..	..	..	..
Sweden, carbon dioxide	Target	Stabilization	..	..	Conditional on like action and only applies to sectors not subject to international competition
Switzerland, carbon dioxide	Target	At least stabilization	1990	2000	Interim target
Turkey	..	..	..	..	..
United Kingdom, carbon dioxide	Target	Stabilization	1990	2005	Conditional on like action. A 20 percent reduction in global warming potential of U.K. emissions of all greenhouse gases in 2005 compared with 1990 levels
United States, all greenhouse gases	Commitment to set of policies	Stabilization	1990	2000	Stabilization achieved in part by phasing out CFCs

Note: The following are members of the European Free Trade Association (EFTA): Austria, Finland, Iceland, Ireland, Norway, Sweden, and Switzerland. The following are members of the European Community: Belgium, Denmark, France, Germany, Greece, Luxemburg, the Netherlands, and the United Kingdom. Countries committed to the EC agreement are included in the target for the entire EC but have not yet set their own target.

Source: International Energy Agency.

Figure 14-3. Damage Functions of Policy Measures toward Global Warming

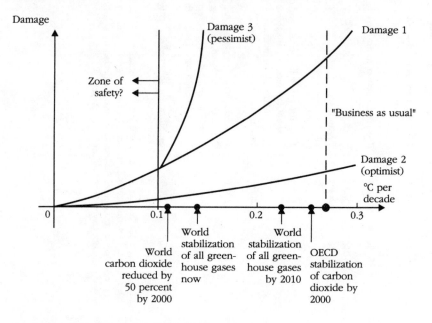

Source: Unpublished data of the IPCC (1990).

would otherwise exist in 2050. The implication is that the optimal level of warming is significantly higher, and hence the requirements for reducing emissions are substantially lower, than is countenanced in the current international discussions. Cost-benefit analysis would tell us not to take such drastic action.

Nordhaus's analysis may understate the degree of control required. First, his damage costs may be conservative if the potential for catastrophic events is realized. If the damages are higher (the benefits of reducing emissions are the same as the damages avoided), the optimal level of control is higher. This is the essence of the constant capital approach, which emphasizes the degree of uncertainty and hence the potential for irreversible losses. How far the potential for catastrophic damage is borne out by the scientific evidence is, however, open to question. Second, Nordhaus's estimates of the costs of control appear to ignore energy conservation measures that are cost-effective now without having to introduce measures that raise the price of energy through, for example, carbon or gasoline taxes. If this is correct, the lower costs of reduction mean a higher level of optimal control.[2]

What can we conclude about the cost-benefit approach to global

Table 14-7. Costs and Benefits of Combating Global Warming
(billions of 1989 dollars unless otherwise noted)

Reductions in emissions of greenhouse gases as a percentage of base level	Total cost of reduction	Total benefit of reduction
0	0.0	0.0
5	0.6	3.0
10	2.2	5.9
15	6.8	8.9
20	16.3	11.9
30	49.5	17.8
40	108.0	23.7
50	191.0	29.6

Note: The benefit figures are from Nordhaus's medium-damage scenario, corresponding to damage of some $7 per ton of carbon dioxide equivalent.
Source: Nordhaus (1991).

warming? At the very least, it should be pursued vigorously as a check on the economic implications of targets like those presented at Toronto. If the two approaches result in very different outcomes, attention should focus on why this is so. Moreover, existing negotiations focus on reducing emissions as the appropriate response to global warming. But it is very unlikely that formulating policies that only reduce emissions will be efficient. Adapting to global warming, through economic adjustment and defenses against rises in sea level, will surely play a part. The ecological limits approach tells us nothing about the optimal combination of prevention and adaptation. Cost-benefit analysis is expressly formulated for just such a purpose. What a more detailed analysis will show, however, remains open to question.

Achieving Global Warming Targets

The major issue is how to achieve whatever target is eventually set for an acceptable level of global warming. An obvious point is that the targets must be internationally agreed, initially through a framework convention. This would produce a statement recognizing the problem and showing intent to take action. The task of setting quantified targets would be a matter for one or more protocols. The convention should target aggregate emissions of greenhouse gases rather than carbon dioxide alone. Individual countries should be free to adjust their mix of emissions to meet the target because this would reduce the costs of complying with the target. For example, if it is cheaper—per radiative effect—to cut CFCs, that should be the first step taken. If energy conservation is cheapest, that should be pursued early on.

The idea of minimizing the costs of compliance is important. Negotiators should find the most cost-efficient way of achieving a given environmental target. This principle is easily confused with getting environmental quality on the cheap. The idea, however, is not to sacrifice environmental quality but to achieve a quality target at the lowest possible cost. This releases resources for other purposes, including other environmental purposes. The minimum cost principle is also important when considering the probable shape of environmental policy over the next two decades. It seems very likely that all nations will face a rising bill for securing environmental quality. This is very much a legacy of our failure to take action in the past two decades and a reminder that precaution is better than reaction. But if the bill is going to rise anyway, we must seek the most effective ways to minimize those increased costs. In this way, the cost burden to be borne by industrialists and consumers can be contained. This is not just a matter of wise husbandry; it is a matter of strategic importance to the environmentalist case. Inefficient expenditures will risk alienating industry and, for that matter, consumers. Keeping costs down will help minimize the risks of a polluter backlash.

Instruments for Achieving Global Warming Targets

There are only three routes to achieving internationally agreed global environmental targets:

- Command and control, whereby pollution standards are set and polluters are simply required to achieve that standard
- Pollution taxes, whereby the polluter is taxed according to the level of emissions produced
- Tradable permits, whereby polluters are given permits to pollute up to the standard and have the option of buying and selling permits in the marketplace.

The last two forms of regulation are market-based incentives, which are discussed more fully in chapter 8. Their particular feature is that they use market signals. Pollution taxes either alter the prices paid by industry and, by increasing the costs to industry, consumers as well, or tax consumers directly on their consumption of a polluting commodity. Tradable permits work through quantities; they allow polluters to switch between sources of pollution provided they honor an overall target for environmental quality.[3] Command-and-control approaches, on the other hand, do not use the market at all.

The three forms of regulation are not exclusive. In general, a sensibly designed environmental policy will be a mix of all three. Currently, and with odd exceptions, environmental policy is based on command and control. Regulation means setting targets for the polluters responsible for the initial emissions; this is the command. The control involves monitoring, inspection, and imposing penalties.

Typically, polluters prefer command and control, or regulation. There is a high degree of certainty, standards are usually in place for some period of time, and, depending on the degree of control, polluters can usually negotiate with the regulator over special difficulties. In addition, polluters prefer regulation because the private costs are lower: they do not have to pay for residual pollution, as they would with targets or marketable permits. They only incur abatement costs.

Two broad sources of inefficiency arise in the command-and-control approach. First, command and control requires the regulator to use resources acquiring information that polluters already possess. Second, polluters can abate pollution with varying degrees of ease. Put another way, their costs of control differ. Control does not concentrate on the sources that can abate pollution for the least cost. Yet, such a process of concentration would minimize the overall costs of complying with the standard.

This is the basic idea underlying tradable permits, introduced in chapter 8. First, an acceptable level of pollution is determined. This may be expressed as some allowable concentration of, say, lead in gasoline; a production or consumption target for chemicals, such as CFCs; or an allowable national emissions level, as is likely to be determined for carbon dioxide some time in the future. Permits are then issued for the level of pollutants up to the level allowed. If, say, 100 units of pollution are allowed, 100 permits each with a value of 1 unit of emission might be issued. There are various ways of determining how to issue the initial permits. Because alternative allocations might be disruptive, a popular initial allocation is based on historical levels of emission. Grandfathering, as this is known, bases the right to pollute on past emissions. But grandfathering is not the only way to determine the initial allocation.

Once the initial allocation is made, polluters are then free to trade the pollution rights. This tradability is the hallmark of the permit system since it keeps down the costs of complying with regulations. Basically, a firm that can abate pollution fairly inexpensively will find it profitable to sell its permits to a firm that finds abating pollution fairly expensive. Essentially, a firm will sell the permit at a price higher than the abatement costs it now has to bear because it lacks a permit. The polluter with high costs, on the other hand, will find it profitable to buy permits if the price is below what it would otherwise pay to abate pollution. Both polluters stand to gain from the trade. Moreover, the control of pollution tends to be concentrated among firms that find it cheap to abate. Permits tend to be held by firms that find it expensive to control pollution. Yet the overall environmental standard is safeguarded because the overall number of permits remains unaltered.

Although this description is simplistic, it captures the essence of the tradable permit system. One important point is that trade need not be between different polluters. It can occur between different sources within a single firm. The result is the same, however, because the firm will gain by concentrating abatement in its low-cost sources and concentrating permits in its high-cost sources.

If the above description is broadly accurate, permit trading should not reduce environmental standards but should reduce the costs of compliance compared with what would have been incurred in a command-and-control system. By and large, this is the experience of the United States, where a system of tradable permits forms part of the U.S. Clean Air Act. Nevertheless, the U.S. experience, which is evaluated in chapter 8, suggests that the level of trading activity between different polluters has been less than ideal. This may be due to the uncertainties endemic to the U.S. approach: uncertainties about the willingness of other firms to trade, the costs of obtaining the permission of regulators to trade, uncertainty about just what emissions credits are available under the legislation, and uncertainty about the prospect of rising permit prices.

In the United States, objections have focused on two main issues: whether environmental quality is sacrificed under a tradable permits system, and whether it is morally right to permit pollution even for a price. There is no evidence that environmental standards in the United States have been sacrificed by the trading system. Of course, it could be argued that without the permits system, standards might have had to be made tougher still, but this proposition cannot be tested. Nor would it follow that tougher standards would be cost-effective, if it were true. The second objection has to be countered by an educative process. All regulatory systems permit pollution, if pollution is taken to mean waste. No economic process is waste free. Nor could it be, by the laws of thermodynamics. The issue therefore must be whether a tradable permits system somehow allows more waste than a command-and-control system. As we have seen, there is no reason at all for this to be the case. Objections to a tradable permits system on the grounds that it permits pollution are deficient, but the political reality is that such false arguments have influence. It is important, therefore, to secure well-informed debate on permit systems, as well as on other market-based incentives.

The U.S. experience suggests that certainty about the regulatory system is highly valued. With command-and-control systems, the firm is, by and large, clear about the nature of the regulation and what is and is not permitted. This is also true for command-and-control systems that are less rigid, such as the system in the United Kingdom, which gives considerable scope for flexible adjustments by allowing firms to negotiate with the Inspectorate of Pollution. It is clear, however, that a tradable permits system should be designed so as to minimize the kinds of uncertainty that are endemic to the U.S. approach.

Regulators are naturally sensitive to the concerns of both environmentalists and industry. Nonetheless, they also have their own concerns, primarily arising from the costs of considering, formulating, and implementing any departure from the established command-and-control approach. It is worth remembering that the command-and-control mode of thinking is ingrained in environmental regulation in Europe, reflecting as it does the experience of over 100 years of public health, workplace, and environmental legislation.

The principles underlying a pollution tax are also introduced in chapter 8. If a tax aimed to control, say, carbon dioxide emissions, processes that emit carbon dioxide would be charged according to the carbon content of the fuels they burn. Coal would attract a higher charge than oil, which would attract a higher charge than natural gas. The effect of the tax would be to induce (a) substitution of relatively low-carbon fuels for high-carbon fuels; (b) substitution of energy other than carbon (nuclear power, renewable resources) for carbon energy; and (c) energy conservation. The essence of the tax would be to encourage tax-avoiding behavior. It is an incentive tax rather than a revenue raising tax. Nonetheless, revenues will be raised, and these can be used in a fiscally neutral way to reduce income or other taxes. This softens any burden that may exist under the tax option and reduces tax disincentives in the economy. Command-and-control procedures generate no revenue, so this option does not arise.

A tax solution has other virtues as well. To select just one, a pollution tax is a tax on all emissions. There is thus a systematic, continuing incentive to search for new technologies, which will reduce the tax burden by removing the basis on which the tax is assessed, that is, pollution. Again, the command-and-control approach does not force firms to seek new technology because it is invariably based on some concept of the best technology available. In principle, however, standards can be set to force the search for new technology. The pollution tax could be more expensive for industry, however, if it applies to all emissions, even optimal emissions.

Market-based Instruments and Global Warming

What is the relevance of market-based instruments for global environmental issues? A protocol on greenhouse gases would set a target for reducing greenhouse gas. But it is just as inefficient to set the same target for each polluter as it is to do so for each country. There is a real danger that a global warming protocol will make this mistake. It may seem fair for each country to achieve, say, the stable emissions target, but the fairness is illusory because the target is set regardless of differences in the costs of achieving it. The aim should be to bias the reductions toward countries that can most easily achieve them. The logic of this requirement is fairly simple: if one country has lower costs of abatement than another, it will be cheaper to require control in the country with low costs than in the one with high costs. A protocol that requires the same emissions reductions for every country offends this principle and hence incurs an unnecessary burden of aggregate cost. Equally, any burden-sharing arrangement must allow for the development needs of the developing nations.

It is conceivable that a protocol based on regulation could embrace the principle of minimum cost, but doing so would be complex and, as it happens, unnecessary because using taxes or issuing tradable permits would avoid the problem. Additionally, taxes and permits help solve the other dominant problem in international agreements, namely, how to devise incentives for cooperation.

Global warming affects different countries in different ways. A few may conceivably gain from a change in climate, but even if all lose, some will lose far more than others. Under these circumstances, it will be difficult to secure agreement on appropriate targets and on the allocation of emissions reduction targets among countries. More important, the avoidance or containment of global warming is an example of what economists call a public good. Reducing global warming will generally benefit all countries, and no country can be excluded from the benefit. Any one country could secure the benefit of a global agreement without sharing the cost. The United Kingdom, for example, could refuse to cooperate and wait for the rest of the world to solve the problem. The United Kingdom could avoid the costs, reap the benefits, and thus ride for free.

The potential existence of free riders means that any protocol must have built-in incentives to cooperate. We have already noted the problems of securing global cooperation on CFCs, and this is a comparatively straightforward agreement since relatively few countries are involved. Some studies have drawn attention to the dissimilarity between the ozone layer and global warming, contrary to the widespread view that all we need to do for global warming is follow the example set by the Montreal Protocol (Barrett 1989).

The benefits of safeguarding the ozone layer appear to be better defined and more tangible, in relation to the costs involved, than those of mitigating the greenhouse effect. Benefits from reduced global warming may appear dubious, and the costs large, given scientific and forecasting uncertainties. This could make securing international cooperation on the greenhouse issue difficult. Another main difference is that CFCs are produced by only a few firms, making monitoring relatively easy. The sources of carbon dioxide, on the other hand, are many, making enforcement more difficult.

Moreover, the Montreal Protocol is a game played by few nations. A global warming agreement, however, must account for not just existing polluters, comprising relatively few countries, but also rapidly growing polluters. In other words, there have to be many players in a global warming game.

In order to persuade the potential free riders, it is necessary to create incentives for them to cooperate. This involves transferring resources—funds, technical assistance, technology—to the countries not cooperating. The scale of these transfers could be large, and the world's leaders do not seem to understand the scale of the transfers that are likely to be required (the transfer issue is emphasized in Grubb 1989). In the ozone case, however, the transfers are relatively modest. Perhaps $1.8 billion—

$2.0 billion are needed to help developing countries create substitutes for CFCs (see Mintzer 1989). Much larger sums will be needed to help them find substitutes for coal, enforce energy efficiency, and so forth. In short, the critical feature of a global warming protocol has to be incentives for cooperation, and that means resource transfers.

The twin features of minimizing costs and transferring resources make the use of market-based instruments attractive for implementing a global warming protocol. Both the tax and tradable permits solutions need to be considered.

The International Tax Solution

In discussing an international tax solution, we focus on carbon dioxide, although a protocol allowing individual greenhouse gases to be traded off in ratios determined by their radiative properties would be more efficient. A tax administered internationally and collected by some central agency is too bureaucratic and would interfere with domestic sovereignty. A tax implemented by each government would run foul of the free rider problem since governments could easily offset a carbon tax by reducing other fuel taxes (Hoel 1990). The solution therefore has to be one in which a central agency taxes each country according to emissions levels. The same tax level would be set for each country. Tax revenues would then be reimbursed, that is, handed back to countries according to some formula of allocation. Each individual country would then act to minimize the sum of its tax payments and abatement costs. It prefers to pay the tax if the cost of abatement is higher than the tax, and it prefers to abate if doing so is cheaper than paying the tax. We would expect some combination of both actions.[4] The size of the tax would be determined by the agreed reduction in carbon dioxide emissions. Some countries will then be net payers of tax to the central agency, and some will be net recipients of tax revenues, depending on the reimbursement rule chosen. The net payers of tax will still be better off under the agreement than they were without it for they will have secured the benefits of avoiding some damage from global warming. Indeed, for the agreement to be successful, each country must be better off with the agreement, taking into account net tax payments, abatement costs, and environmental benefits.[5]

The rationale for reimbursing tax revenues arises from the need to transfer resources, as we have already demonstrated. Reimbursements should therefore relate to the costs of controlling carbon dioxide emissions and the damage likely to be caused by global warming. As the cost of control increases, so does the amount of reimbursement required. Coal-based economies such as China or India, for example, will tend to require large reimbursements. Countries that can switch easily from coal to gas-fired electricity will have low reimbursements. The United Kingdom might be such a country, although it has an incentive to focus a protocol on all greenhouse gases in order to minimize the extent to which adjustments will have to be made to carbon fuels and hence to its coal industry.

Countries that stand to lose most from warming, such as deltaic or island countries, are likely to cooperate because they will want the protocol to succeed. They will tend to require lower reimbursements from the tax revenues.

The problem of determining costs and benefits for each country arises with reimbursement. This may well be impossible to do to any meaningful degree of accuracy. Apart from the difficulty of determining costs, tax receipts may or may not be sufficient for this purpose, depending on the level of the tax, the abatement costs of the countries cooperating, and the number of countries not cooperating. In addition, such a solution would not solve the problem of countries enjoying the benefits without paying the costs.

If, as in the case of ozone, developing countries are the most likely not to cooperate, a formula that relates reimbursements to population or, inversely, to per capita income would be a prime candidate for the protocol. The resulting scale of transfer from rich to poor could be substantial and might arouse strong opposition because some industrial countries could be worse off with the tax than without it. Some authorities, such as Grubb (1989), doubt the acceptability of any international fund based on receipt of substantial carbon tax revenues; others, such as Bertram, Wallace, and Stephens (1989), doubt its political acceptability or its efficiency; still others, such as Hoel (1990), think such a fund is feasible and that, to secure cooperation, reimbursements should be based mainly on gross national product (GNP) and only partially on the basis of population.

Recent work in Canada suggests that a global carbon tax designed to secure the Toronto Conference's ultimate target of a 50 percent reduction in carbon dioxide could generate tax revenues of $600 billion, of which $480 billion would be reimbursed to developing countries (Whalley and Wigle 1989). To gather some idea of the significance of these figures, $600 billion would be equal to some 51 percent of the entire external debt of the developing world in 1989, to one-and-a-half times the entire external debt of Latin America, and six times all disbursements to developing countries in 1989. It is scarcely credible that any single international agency could manage such resource transfers. It seems more likely that an agreement would have to be reached on the total amount of the net transfer to developing countries. Within that constraint, tax receipts could then be allocated to both industrial and developing countries on the basis of, say, an inverse relation to income per capita. This approach would not, however, compensate the net costs of participating in the agreement nor assure that there are no net losers.

If a tax solution could be implemented, how big would the tax have to be? Table 14-8 shows the results of a number of studies. An international carbon tax should not be dismissed, but, as with any solution, there will clearly be formidable problems of design and implementation. The main reason for keeping such a tax on the agenda is that it is likely to be a more efficient instrument of control than country-by-country targets.

Internationally Tradable Permits

The last option for implementing a protocol is through tradable permits. In essence, the permit solution gives countries an incentive to trade permits with each other and make net gains in the process without compromising the overall emissions target. As with pollution taxes, countries have an incentive to trade their permits until the marginal costs of abatement are just equal to the price of the permits in the marketplace. If costs exceed price, the countries will try to buy further permits. If abatement costs are lower than the price of permits, they will sell the permits, collect the revenue from their sale, and use some of the proceeds to abate emissions. This is entirely analogous to trading emissions credits between companies in the United States, although here the trading partners are countries. A number of other trading systems exist, as with fisheries quotas in New Zealand and Iceland and milk quotas in the United Kingdom.

Several problems accompany the trade in permits. Some countries emit large amounts of carbon dioxide, notably the United States, the Soviet Union, and members of the European Community. This may adversely affect the efficiency of the tradable permit approach because the sales and purchases made by big countries will influence the price of permits on the open market (see Hoel 1990). In addition, while the tax solution penalizes countries that emit too much, the permits system penalizes countries that exceed the level permitted. This is particularly relevant to global warming since it is not clear what sanctions can be applied if countries persistently exceed their permitted emissions.

An overriding problem is how to allocate permits in the first place. This is akin to the problem of how to allocate tax reimbursements among countries. The grandfathering of permits, which allocates permits initially according to the existing level of emissions, favors the industrial countries and does little or nothing to create incentives for the developing world to cooperate. At the same time, any allocation other than grandfathering is likely to be resisted strongly by the major emitting nations.

Some authors favor a system that bases the initial allocation on GNP, but this again favors the industrial countries, as does using GNP per capita. Per capita allocations have found most favor, and an initial allocation based on such a rule would provide developing countries with a large quantity of permits that could then be sold to industrializing and industrial countries at a profit over the cost of abating greenhouse gas emissions (Bertram, Wallace, and Stephens 1989). Grubb (1989) suggests

Table 14-8. Results of Carbon Tax Studies

Study	Region	Carbon tax (dollars per ton of carbon)	Percentage of the price of oil	Reduction in carbon dioxide and year
Barker and Lewney (1990)	United Kingdom	145	92	18 percent in 2005
		516	327	33 percent in 2005
Barrett (1990)	United Kingdom	34	32	20 percent in 1988
		59	57	35 percent in 2005
Bye, Bye, and Lorentsen (1989)	Norway	126	75	20 percent in 2000
Chandler and Nicholls (1990)	United States	82	53	20 percent reduction in baseline
Cline (1989)	World	158	100	57 percent in 2050
				21 percent off 1985 emissions by 2050
Edmonds and Reilly (1983)	World	123	78	40 percent in 2050
Howarth, Nikitopoulos, and Yohe (1989)	World	623	103	26 percent in 2050
IEA (1989)	OECD	72	44	12 percent in 2005
Ingham and Ulph (1989)	United Kingdom manufacturers	87–205	57–128	20 percent off 1988 emissions by 2005
Kram and Okken (1989)	Netherlands	40	26	28 percent below baseline
Manne and Richels (1989)	United States	300	190	85 percent in 2100 or 20 percent off 1985 emissions by 2100
Manne and Richels (1990)	World	250	158	75 percent in 2100
Nordhaus (1991)	World	3	2	9 percent in 2050
		27	23	28 percent in 2050
Nordhaus and Yohe (1983)	United States	20	13	7 percent below baseline
		100	65	27 percent below baseline
		200	130	43 percent below baseline
		300	195	54 percent below baseline
Symons, Proops, and Gay (1990)	United Kingdom	96	62	20 percent off 1988 emissions by 2005
U.S. Congressional Budget Office (1989)	United States	28	18	Stabilize 1990 levels by 2000
		113	72	10–20 percent off 1990 level by 2000
Whalley and Wigle (1991)	World	460	300	50 percent off trend emissions
Williams (1989)	Sweden	160	104	63 percent below baseline
		250	162	74 percent below baseline

avoiding giving countries an implicit reward for overpopulation by counting adult populations only. Another suggestion is to allocate all permits to countries that do not pollute, that is, the world's poor, and allow trade thereafter. To keep rich countries from hoarding them, permits could be subject to renewal; that is, they could be leased rather than owned (Grubb 1989). Countries with a capacity to create carbon sinks, such as new forests, could secure credits under the system; they could be allowed to emit beyond the level of their permits provided the carbon sinks offset the excess.

The reality of the international political economy is likely to work against any system that allocates permits based on population. Such a system would require assurance at the outset that international trade in permits would take place, otherwise the burden of adjustment would fall heavily and rapidly on the countries with high emissions per capita, such as the United States. In those circumstances, such countries are unlikely to agree at the outset. Grandfathering of some kind is likely to be the only initial allocation acceptable to the existing polluters. The sheer newness of tradable permits on the international scene may, in any event, militate against them. If so, one essential message for international negotiators is that the system of permits should mimic as far as possible the efficiency of market-based approaches. To this end, allocated emissions reductions must bear some resemblance to the pattern that would emerge if they were allocated according to the costs of abatement. Even that requirement is formidable for international negotiation (for further discussion, see D. W. Pearce 1990b).

The Problem of the Ozone Layer

Stratospheric ozone blocks ultraviolet radiation from the sun, and depletion of the ozone layer increases the incoming ultraviolet radiation. In the mid-1970s researchers discovered that chlorofluorocarbons (CFCs) were depleting the ozone layer (for the history of the scientific discoveries, see Gribbin 1988). Threats of increases in skin cancer due to these higher levels of ultraviolet radiation led the United States to ban the use of CFCs in aerosol cans. In the mid-1980s, the discovery that the ozone layer above Antarctica was heavily depleted (that a hole was forming in the ozone layer) accelerated international efforts to secure a treaty controlling the production and use of CFCs worldwide. The need for an agreement was further strengthened because CFCs are also a greenhouse gas and thus contribute to global warming.

The most widely publicized effect of increased ultraviolet radiation is an increase in skin cancer. Malignant melanomas have reportedly increased, although their connection with increased ultraviolet radiation has not been established (the evidence is discussed in Arrhenius and Lundin 1990). Social behavior toward suntans has changed and may itself account for the increase. Moreover, reducing CFC emissions is unlikely to be a cost-efficient way of preventing cancer even if this is the relationship. More sensible human behavior toward exposure to ultraviolet rays would be cheaper. But increased ultraviolet radiation has other effects as well. It may be linked to suppressions of the immune system in the human body, to eye disorders, and to reduced or distorted growth in plants, especially in unmanaged ecosystems.

International action on the ozone layer was taken when the United Nations Convention on the Protection of the Ozone Layer was drawn in Vienna in 1985. The Montreal Protocol, which came into force at the start of 1989, is the actual agreement to reduce the use of CFCs. Under the Protocol, consumption of five CFCs (11, 12, 113, 114, and 115) was to be frozen at 1986 levels by 1989, cut to 80 percent of 1986 levels by 1994, and cut to 50 percent by 1988–89. The cuts in production were slightly less severe to allow for the needs of developing countries, with the aim being to allow 65 percent of the 1986 level by 1999. In addition, the consumption of three halons (1211, 1301, 2402) was frozen in 1986 and their level of production was frozen at 110 percent of the 1986 level by 1992.

Individual countries have already announced plans for complete phaseouts (the United States and the United Kingdom aim to phase them out completely by 2000, for example). An agreement reached in London in June 1990 produced even stricter controls and revised the Montreal Protocol to achieve cuts of 50 percent by 1995 and 85 percent by 1997. Some countries pressed for total phaseout by 1997. Halons will be cut 50 percent by 1995 and will be phased out by 2000. Carbon tetrachloride and methyl chloroform were added to the agreement, the former to be phased out by 2000, the latter by 2005. Developing countries have a grace period of ten years in which to achieve these targets. Virtually all industrial countries are now party to the Montreal Protocol, and these countries account for about 80 percent of the global consumption of the relevant CFCs and halons (see Markandya 1990). Although twenty-three developing nations have signed the Protocol, India and China only agreed to sign in 1992. The London meeting also established a special fund of $240 million to help developing countries adjust to the CFC phaseout (Markandya 1990 suggests that adopting CFC substitutes would cost developing countries $1.8 billion at 1990 prices).

Effectively, then, the Montreal agreement and its modifications seek to halt all production of ozone-depleting CFCs. Unfortunately, chlorine will continue to be released in the atmosphere for some time because time lags separate the production, consumption, and release of CFCs to the atmosphere. Nevertheless, the Protocol is as near as we can get to realizing the intent to treat the ozone layer according to the instrumental rule of maintaining constant natural capital. Intent is the operative word because the implications of the Protocol could be formidable if developing countries do not accede and significant even if they accede but increase their consumption of CFCs to the limit allowed under article 5 (Markandya 1990).

At first sight, the Montreal Protocol and associated events suggest that a carbon convention to control global warming might be possible. Moreover, the Montreal Protocol was drawn up and ratified in little more than twelve years after the depletion of the ozone layer was given scientific credence. But the Montreal Protocol and other agreements for controlling the ozone layer may not be relevant to the prospect of a carbon convention.

First, the Montreal Protocol was greatly accelerated by the discovery of a major hole in the ozone layer above Antarctica. This surprise event led governments to recognize that ozone depletion was not a uniform or slowly evolving event. Global warming will probably require a similarly large-scale event to trigger active concern. Yet another ten or twenty years may pass before anyone can be certain that existing global warming is explained by the greenhouse effect rather than natural warming cycles.

Second, securing agreement on CFCs is simple compared with the problems faced by a carbon convention. The reasons for this lie with the nature of international agreements according to game theory. Game theory studies behavior when one individual's actions depend on the behavior and reactions of other participants in the game. The atmosphere is common property. If country A takes action to reduce global warming, country A and all other countries benefit. Thus some countries will have an incentive to ride free—to play the game in such a way that they make little or no effort to reduce emissions (and thereby incur costs) while allowing others to take the emissions-reducing activity.

Broadly speaking, the fewer the players in the game, the more likely it is that a cooperative solution will come about. That fits the Montreal Protocol case because the number of CFC producers is very limited and the consumers are primarily the industrial countries. It does not fit the case of carbon, however, because the number of players is very large and includes major developing countries. An additional point is that cooperation is more likely to occur when the costs of doing so are comparatively small. Finding substitutes for many uses of CFCs, notably their role in aerosols, is simple and inexpensive compared with reducing carbon dioxide emissions. The reason for this, as we have seen, is that, even though energy consumption can be reduced significantly through conservation, securing those reductions may require the use of significant tax disincentives. The private costs to the players will appear to be high even though they are outweighed by the social benefits.

Third, CFCs are used widely, but not as pervasively as carbon fuels are. Changing the use rates of carbon fuels is therefore likely to have far more widespread implications than changing those of CFCs. The conundrum for greenhouse gas policy is as follows. Actions taken by individual countries may well set an example but will have very limited effect on global warming. Internationally coordinated actions are needed. The experience of the Montreal Protocol on the ozone layer appears very encouraging for the prospects of such an agreement, but further analysis shows that the game theoretic conditions necessary to spur cooperation were present in the ozone case: comparatively few players, manageable costs of substitution, and a dramatic event (discovery of the ozone hole). These conditions may not apply to carbon fuels, where the players are many, the costs of cooperation are perceived to be high, and significant climatic events in the next twenty years may still not be attributable to the greenhouse effect.

Antarctica

Antarctica has been described as the last wilderness (Laws 1989 offers an excellent introduction to the area; a useful collection of scientific articles is found in a special issue of *Ambio* [1989] dealing with the polar region). It is also unique because extensive international agreements have been reached about its use and the conservation of its resources. Antarctica limits are defined by the Antarctic Convergence, which marks the boundary between cold Antarctic surface water and the warmer sub-Antarctic water. At 14 million square kilometers, it represents 10 percent of the earth's surface and is the most glaciated continent in the world, with 90 percent of the world's ice and nearly 75 percent of its fresh water. Oddly, little snow falls, the average annual snowfall being less than 10 grams per square centimeter. The snowfall that does accumulate probably equals the volume of ice lost when icebergs split from the coastal ice shelves. Mean annual temperatures at the South Pole are -49ºC, and -89ºC was the lowest temperature ever recorded, at Vostock in 1983.

The resources of Antarctica are unique in many ways. Wildlife resources are extensive, and although the number of species is small, their populations are large. In addition to finfish, krill, mammals, and birds, the area contains potentially valuable mineral deposits.

Finfish are mainly adapted breeds of cod and herring, and fishing is generally confined to the areas of South Georgia and South Orkney islands and Kerguélen. Tonnages caught range from some 400,000 tons in 1970 to around 75,000–100,000 tons in 1987–88. The oscillations are largely explained by overfishing of single species, followed by concentrated effort in subsequent years on hitherto unexploited species, and so on. Thus, effort in the early 1970s was focused almost entirely on *Notothenia rossii* (the South Georgian cod), which was overexploited and is now protected in its depleted state. Scientific interest in the various fish species is considerable. The supercool fish have what is effectively an antifreeze in their bodies that prevents freezing. The icefish (*Chan-*

nichthyidae) have no hemoglobin in their bodies, making their blood translucent.

Krill are planktonic crustacea, very small shrimp-like creatures of fundamental importance to the Antarctic ecosystem because a wide range of predators are wholly dependent on them as food. The predators include five species of whale, three species of seal, three of squid, and a large number of birds. Predators avoid competition by differentially selecting krill according to age, location, and so forth. Krill are also caught by humans, mainly in the South Georgia area. Catches in 1987 and 1988 were around 400,000 tons, with the Soviet Union dominating the catch effort (77 percent of the catch in 1987/88), followed by Japan (20 percent). Most of the catch is used for animal feed, although some is sold for human consumption, especially in Japan. Krill catches are likely to be sustainable at around 400,000 tons, but the effect that even this level of consumption will have on predator populations is uncertain.

Antarctica has a wide range of whales, including the blue, which is the largest, the fin, humpback, minke, right, sei, killer (*Orcinus orca*), and sperm whales. Whaling began in Antarctica in 1904, and the familiar process of overexploiting a single species and then moving on to others began. The humpback whales were targeted first because they are comparatively easy to harvest, followed by the blue whales, the fin whales, and the sperm whales. In the late 1960s, the fin and sei whales were preferred until the International Whaling Commission closed them to whaling in the mid-to-late 1970s. In the 1970s, the minke whale was the most sought-after species. The International Whaling Commission now provides complete protection for the blue, humpback, fin, sei, and sperm whales. Blue whales are probably at under 1 percent of their stock before whaling began, humpbacks at 3 percent, and sperm whales at 20 percent.

Seals are abundant in Antarctica. The phocid seals are the most numerous and include the crabeater (numbering perhaps 15 million–30 million), elephant seals, leopard seals (220,000), Ross seals (220,000), and Weddell seals (800,000). Otarriid seals comprise fur seals and sea lions and include the Antarctic fur seal. In the nineteenth century, fur seals were exploited to the point of virtual exhaustion, and then elephant seals were harvested for their blubber. The fur seal recovered its population in the twentieth century. Crabeater, Weddell, Ross, and leopard seals have generally not been commercially exploited. Seals are protected under the 1972 Convention for the Conservation of Antarctic Seals, which came into force in 1978. The Convention sets low limits for annual catches of crabeater seals (175,000), leopard (12,000), and Weddell seals (5,000) and gives total protection to fur, elephant, and Ross seals.

The majority of Antarctica's birds depend on the islands as breeding grounds. The flying birds can be broadly classified as the coastal-based skuas, gulls, and terns and the ocean-ranging albatross and petrels. Penguins are flightless birds, and the Antarctic species are the Adélie, macaroni, gentoo, chinstrap, rockhopper, king, and emperor. Penguin populations have typically been stable or have grown (Adélie, chinstrap, and macaroni) probably because krill has become more available as the number of whales has decreased. The number of wandering albatross has declined, perhaps because they scavenge near fishing fleets and become tangled in lines and nets.

Much of the current debate about conservation in Antarctica centers on the issue of mineral exploitation. Onshore, there appear to be substantial deposits of iron ore in the Prince Charles Mountains and coal in the Transarctic Mountains. The Pensacola Mountains are of geological interest for more precious minerals. Exploitation conditions are so bad, however, that mineral developments on land seem unlikely. Offshore, there is some evidence of oil and gas deposits, albeit at depths that probably cannot be exploited by current technology.

Clearly, Antarctica exhibits the classic dimensions of the development versus conservation debate. It is a fragile ecosystem, and even the limited human presence there now has caused environmental damage. It also has potential development benefits, notably from mineral deposits and certainly from fisheries and krill fishing. In 1959, the Antarctic Treaty was signed by the twelve nations with a presence there: Argentina, Australia, Belgium, Chile, France, Japan, New Zealand, Norway, South Africa, the Soviet Union, the United Kingdom, and the United States. By January 1989, thirty-nine states had acceded to the Treaty. Twenty-two states are consultative parties.

The Treaty requires that Antarctica be used for peaceful purposes only, provides for freedom of scientific research and information exchange, and does not recognize any territorial claims or disputes (article IV). Article IV effectively acknowledges that territorial claims to Antarctica cannot be resolved. Its ambiguity is consistent with viewing Antarctica as genuine common property, that is, as a property owned by claimants or by claimants and nonclaimants or by no one. Seven of the original twelve signatories (Argentina, Australia, Chile, France, New Zealand, Norway, and United Kingdom) have territorial claims to Antarctica. These are the claimant states. Five of the original signatories are nonclaimants who refuse to recognize the ownership claims of the other seven.

The Treaty is supplemented by the 1972 Convention for the Conservation of Antarctic Seals, the 1980 Convention on the Conservation of Atlantic Marine Living Resources, and the 1988 Convention on the Regulation of Antarctic Mineral Resource Activities. The 1988 Convention is, however, the subject of a dispute that highlights the conservation and development debate. Concerned with restricting mineral developments, it accepted that mining could take place. Prospecting for minerals would not require authorization but would be subject to environmental and safety standards. Exploration and development would require authorization to grant exclusive rights to operators. Specific proposals would then be considered by a regulatory commission set up by the Convention. The commission would also monitor all exploration and development, and all development would have to be agreed by all signatory states to the Antarctic Treaty.

Environmental organizations have led the battle to have Antarctica declared a world park, which would allow only limited fishing and continued scientific research, but no development for minerals. In 1989, Australia and France announced that they would not sign the 1988 Convention but would urge instead the signing of a Comprehensive Environment Protection Convention for Antarctica. Effectively, Australia and France opted for the concept of a world park, and other nations have offered their support.

International agreement about the use of the Antarctic illustrates several principles in environmental economics. Ownership of Antarctica is unclear precisely because the Antarctic Treaty refuses to acknowledge existing or any other claims to territory. On balance, this is probably a virtue in that the original nonclaimants and subsequent signatories of the treaty feel they have as much right to influence the future of Antarctica as the original claimant signatories. As the number of signatories has grown, the likelihood that actual territorial claims will be pressed has perhaps decreased. On the other hand, the growth in the number of signatories threatens the management of Antarctica with excessive bureaucracy. The chances of reaching a consensus decline as the number of parties grows. If this is correct, the chances of securing a world park could be small and the lengthy process of obtaining it could threaten Antarctica because mineral development is not forbidden or regulated by the Antarctic Treaty. Moreover, many observers argue that the existence of the Treaty and its supplements demonstrates that common property need not suffer the fate of the tragedy of the commons. That is, common property under proper resource management and regulated by agreed conventions and rules is wholly consistent with sustainable use.

Others disagree and point to existing breaches of good environmental behavior in the Antarctic, such as debris from scientific stations, damaging airstrips, pollution, and, perhaps most conspicuously, overfishing. Indeed, overfishing has arisen from the lack of ownership. Under the United Nations Conference on the Law of the Sea, most nations have declared a 200-mile exclusive economic zone around their coasts. This limits entry to continental shelf fisheries and thus conserves stocks more than the previous open-access situation. No such exclusive economic zone surrounds Antarctica simply because ownership is not agreed. In the Atlantic, the 1980 Convention on the Conservation of Atlantic Marine Living Resources protects fishery resources, and in 1987 the Convention's regulatory commission set catch limits on one species of finfish. Nonetheless, the 1980 Convention operates by consensus, which means that any one nation can veto agreements. The Soviet Union has, in fact, vetoed major efforts at marine conservation.

An alternative route to creating a World Antarctic Park may be through the 1972 Convention Concerning the Protection of the World Cultural and Natural Heritage, the World Heritage Convention (this is argued, for example, in May 1988). World Heritage Sites, of which there are over 160, can be declared if the area represents a major stage in the earth's evolutionary history; represents significant ongoing geological or biological processes and human interaction with the natural environment; contains superlative natural environments, natural beauty, or geological formations; or acts as a habitat for threatened species of outstanding value. Antarctica clearly qualifies under all criteria, and the existence of the World Heritage Convention at least means that a new convention does not have to be negotiated.

The future of Antarctica is uncertain. It is already the subject of what many people regard as one of the world's most effective international agreements, but others see as poor protection against the pressures for development. At the heart of the problem are property rights. Conferring ownership rights could both damage and conserve the environment: doing so would damage it by removing the disincentive offered by international criticism of unilateral development proposals and conserve it by limiting access, especially to marine waters. Continuation of the de facto lack of ownership places a heavy burden on mutual responsibility for protecting what effectively becomes an open-access resource.

Protecting the World's Biodiversity

Just as the world has developed an international agreement on protecting the ozone layer, and is making efforts to do so for global warming, so have there been many calls for an international agreement to protect the world's biological diversity, or biodiversity. Biodiversity is the totality of genes, species, and ecosystems. The term is helpful for reminding us that it is not just the total stock of living things that matters, but the range of different living things. To lose one species, for example, may be more important than losing a proportion of each of several species. Protecting the world's biodiversity is clearly an enormous and impossible task. Thus it is important to establish the value of biodiversity to humankind so that priorities for protection can be determined. Such an approach is self-evidently anthropogenic—it affords no concept of inherent rights of species other than humans to exist. The problem with the rights-based approach to biodiversity conservation is precisely that it does not face the reality of limited resources for protection. One way or the other, a priority ranking must be developed. World governments understood that when they approved the World Charter for Nature in 1982. The Charter agreed that "all species and habitats should be safeguarded to the extent that it is technically, economically, and politically feasible."

To see that protecting all species is impossible, consider just how many species exist. The most widely discussed estimates suggest perhaps 30 million species, but the figure could be as high as 50 million (see McNeely and others 1989). Yet only 1.43 million species have been scientifically described. Most undescribed species inhabit the tropical forests, which suggests a further reason for conserving those forests: their total economic value is unknown and could be substantial (see chapter 5). The rate of loss of species is not known, and extinction is, of course, a natural evolutionary process. The 30 million species that exist today should, therefore, be put in the context of several billion species that have ever existed. Evidence suggests, however, that the rate of extinction has increased and that perhaps one-quarter of existing species are at risk of extinction in the next twenty to thirty years (McNeely and others 1989, p. 41). Table 14-9 shows one set of estimates of current species under threat.

In addition to species lost, habitats for wildlife are declining rapidly. Yet the most effective way of ensuring the survival of a species is by protecting its habitat. In Sub-Saharan Africa, some 65 percent of all wildlife habitat has been lost, with ranges of 35 percent in Gabon to 89 percent in the Gambia. In tropical Asia, total loss of habitat is 65 percent, with a range of 24 percent in Brunei to 94 percent in Bangladesh (and 97 percent in Hong Kong; see McNeely and others 1989, p. 47).

The causes of biodiversity loss are familiar from earlier chapters of this book. Population growth, ill-defined land and resource rights, and market, planning, and government failures all explain the destruction of environmental assets and hence the loss of biodiversity. We now turn our attention to ways in which conservation can take place. Self-evidently, if the above factors explain habitat loss, their reversal or containment will assist the conservation process. That is, pricing inputs and outputs properly, curtailing population growth, offering more informed and better-directed technical assistance will all help. In addition, attitudes to the

Table 14-9. *Status of Threatened Species*

Species	Extinct	Endan-gered	Vulner-able	Rare	Indeter-minate	Total
Amphibians	2	9	9	20	10	50
Birds	113	111	67	122	624	1,037
Fish	23	81	135	83	21	343
Invertebrates	98	221	234	188	614	1,355
Mammals	83	172	141	37	64	497
Plants	384	3,324	3,022	6,749	5,598	19,078
Reptiles	21	37	39	41	32	170

Notes: In addition to these threatened species, many other populations are declining, as is their genetic variability.

Source: McNeely and others (1989), p. 42.

relations between communities, individuals, and conserved habitats also must be changed.

Occasions will always arise in which environmental assets are so fragile that outright protection from human interference is required. The concept of outright protection has also served to alienate people. Two concerns arise. First, the concept of protected area, most usually evident in the idea of a national park, takes control of resources away from the people whose livelihoods depend on them. Governments feel, often wrongly, that local communities cannot manage protected resources, partly because the whole ethos of the national park concept is that people must not interfere in any way with nature and partly because they have other motives, including the extension of central government influence into boundary areas. The second concern is that national parks must be demarcated, and this means fences and controls. Fences, in particular, interfere with the migratory habits of many wildlife species; they also give the impression that whatever is inside the fence is protected and whatever is outside can be used as the inhabitants see fit. As a result, according to McNeely and others (1989, p. 49), "park managers in many parts of the world have developed a 'siege mentality,' feeling encroachment from all sides. The dilemma of how to conserve wildlands in a sea of hostile interests is a serious one."

McNeely and others (1989), the most authoritative review of the problems facing protected areas, conclude that

- National development objectives fail to give sufficient value to living natural resources
- These resources are exploited for profit and not for meeting the needs of people
- The species and ecosystems on which people depend are still poorly known
- The available science is poorly applied
- Conservation activities are too narrowly focused
- Conservation is poorly funded (see also Ledec and Goodland 1988).

Modern habitat management experts tend to favor the idea of community involvement in protected areas, but the traditional concept of outright protection still influences most conservation activity. As an instance of the modern approach, consider one experiment in wildlife management in Zimbabwe. Under the Communal Area Management Programme for Indigenous Resources (CAMPFIRE), wildlife resources in two districts of the Zambesi Valley are subject to communal proprietorship. The scheme gives local communities responsibility for managing wildlife in return for secured benefits.

The Zambesi Valley contains abundant wildlife resources and has high tourist attraction (Lake Kariba, Victoria Falls, and Mana Pools). Wildlife are harvested legally by big game safari hunting and cropping and illegally through subsistence hunting and poaching of rhino horns and ivory. Development schemes within the valley tend to emphasize the benefits of ranching, though they rarely estimate actual returns to livestock (see D. Jansen 1990). The benefits of wildlife management tend to be poorly documented and advocated.

The threat to wildlife in the valley arises from two processes. People are being resettled from areas that are already beyond their human carrying capacity due to rapid population growth, and cattle grazing is being extended as the threat of the tsetse fly is being reduced by eradication campaigns. The incentive to remove wildlife is growing due to the absence of any financial gain and the presence of financial costs from crop damage caused by wildlife.

Under CAMPFIRE, local natural resource cooperatives are established with what are effectively rights of group ownership of the resources. Each community member is a shareholder, and profits can be used for communal capital or distributed to individuals. The CAMPFIRE experiment is very recent, and it may be too early to evaluate the experience properly. In the Nyaminyami District, for example, a wildlife management trust was established in 1988. The scheme has already determined sustainable offtake quotas—0.7 percent for elephants, 6–8 percent for lions and leopards, and 2 percent for buffalo. A small number of guards were hired to protect crops and people against problem animals and to deter poachers. Revenues from hunting permits (the dominant source of income) and sales of wildlife products have been partly used to compensate residents for crop damage, thus reducing the perception of wild animals as imposing costs rather than conferring benefits. Impala were cropped for local consumption, a further benefit. For the first year of operation, revenues exceeded costs by a substantial amount; 80 percent of the surplus was distributed to local wards and 20 percent to reserves and levies. For households, gains from this distribution could amount to 15–25 percent of annual household income. In another district, Guruve, however, similar surpluses were retained for investment, and only 37 percent of the surplus was distributed to the communities. In each case, the sum was thought to be too small to distribute to individuals and was thus spent on community projects.

If community-based projects like CAMPFIRE are to succeed, individuals must be genuinely involved. That means more than empowering districts with the capability to manage resources. Districts must, in turn, involve people in the local communities, or the communities themselves must manage the wildlife. The experience in at least one district shows that sustainable management is feasible given the right incentives. Indeed, the theme of this book is that we must provide incentives for individuals, communities, and nations to look after the natural world.

Notes

1. This has a perverse implication for soil conservation practices upstream that reduce sedimentation rates downstream. Reduced sedimentation can result in degradation of coastal resources since a rise in sea level is not compensated by deposits of sediment. This is thought to be one reason for coastal degradation in Louisiana, for example.

2. Various studies suggest that the costs of control through energy conservation are very low; see Ayres and Walter (1990); United Kingdom, Department of Energy (1989). How far this observation affects the Nordhaus study is not clear, however, since Nordhaus captures energy-saving measures by simulating the effects of a carbon fuel tax.

3. A formal relationship exists between taxes and the price of tradable permits. Both the tax and the permit are aimed at securing a predetermined level of pollution. Under conditions of certainty, the market price of a tradable permit is equal (per unit of emission) to the tax.

4. The minimum cost theorem occurs again here since each country determines its combination of tax and abatement measures according to the rule that the tax rate, which is common to all countries, should equal the marginal cost of abatement. In this way, marginal costs are equated across countries, and this is the requirement for minimizing cost.

5. Unfortunately, it is more complex than this. The assumption here is that the global warming target is set so that global environmental benefits exceed total abatement costs; in other words, a cost-benefit rule is used. Only then is there a global surplus to be redistributed. As we have seen, this may well not be the case. This raises the prospect that some countries will be net payers of tax and their individual avoided damage costs will be less than their net payment. In these circumstances, they are unlikely to cooperate. For this reason, some sort of cost-benefit rule should be used to set global targets.

References

The word "processed" describes informally reproduced works that may not be commonly available through library systems.

Ahmed, Raisuddin, and Mahabub Hossain. 1987. *Infrastructure and Development of a Rural Economy.* Washington, D.C.: International Food Policy Research Institute.

Alfsen, Knut H., Torstein Bye, and Lorents Lorentsen. 1987. *Natural Resource Accounting and Analysis: The Norwegian Experience 1978–1986.* Oslo, Norway: Norway, Central Bureau of Statistics.

Allen, Jennifer, and Douglas Barnes. 1985. "The Causes of Deforestation in Developing Countries." *Annals of the Association of American Geographers* 75 (2): 163–84.

Altaf, M. A., H. Jamal, J. Liu, V. K. Smith, and D. Whittington. 1990. "Prices and Connection Decisions for Public Water Systems in Developing Countries: A Case Study of the Punjab, Pakistan." Applied Economics Research Centre, Karachi, Pakistan. Processed.

Ambio. 1989. Special issue on polar regions. 18 (1).

Anderson, Dennis. 1987. *The Economics of Afforestation: A Case Study in Africa.* Occasional Paper 1. Baltimore, Md.: Johns Hopkins University Press.

———. 1989. "Economic Aspects of Afforestation and Soil Conservation Projects." In Gunter Schramm and Jeremy Warford, eds., *Environmental Management and Economic Development.* Baltimore, Md.: Johns Hopkins University Press.

———. 1990. "Environmental Policy and the Public Revenue in Developing Countries." PRE Working Paper 36. World Bank, Environment Department, Washington, D.C. Processed.

Anderson, Jock R. 1989. "Forecasting, Uncertainty, and Public Project Appraisal." PR Working Paper 154. World Bank, International Economics Department, Washington, D.C. Processed.

Anderson, K. 1992. "The Standard Welfare Economics of Policies Affecting Trade and the Environment." In K. Anderson and R. Blackhurst, eds., *The Greening of World Trade Issues.* London: Harvester-Wheatsheaf.

Archambault, Edith, and J. Bernard. n.d. "Systèmes de compatibilité de l'environnement et problèmes d'évaluation économique." Paris. Processed.

Arden-Clarke, Charles. 1991. "The Cruel Trade-Off." *Guardian* (13 September).

Arnold, J. E. Michael, and J. Gabriel Campbell. 1986. "Collective Management of Hill Forests in Nepal: The Community Forestry Development Project." *Proceedings of the Conference on Common Property Resource Management, April 21–26, 1985.* Washington, D.C.: National Research Council and National Academy Press.

Arntzen, J., and Elmar M. Veenendaal. 1986. *A Profile of Environment and Development in Botswana.* Amsterdam, Netherlands: Free University of Amsterdam, Institute for Environmental Studies.

Arrhenius, Eric, and Carl Lundin. 1990. "Chlorofluorocarbons: The Ozone Layer and Climate Change." World Bank, Environment Department, Washington, D.C. Processed.

Arrow, Kenneth J., and Anthony Fisher. 1974. "Environmental Preservation, Uncertainty, and Irreversibility." *Quarterly Journal of Economics* 88: 312–19.

Ault, David E., and Gilbert L. Rutman. 1979. "The Development of Individual Rights to Property in Tribal Africa." *Journal of Law and Economics* 22 (1): 163–82.

Ayres, Robert U., and Allen V. Kneese. 1969. "Production, Consumption, and Externality." *American Economic Review* 59 (June): 282–98.

Ayres, Robert U., and Jörs Walter. 1990. "Global Warming: Abatement Policies and Costs." International Institute for Applied Systems Analysis, Laxenberg, Austria. Processed.

Barbier, Edward, and others. 1990. *Elephants, Economics, and Ivory.* London: Earthscan Publications.

Barker, Terry, and Roy Lewney. 1990. "Macroeconomic Modelling of Environmental Policies: The Carbon Tax and Regulation of Water Quality." University of Cambridge, Department of Applied Economics, Cambridge. Processed.

Barnett, Harold, and Chandler Morse. 1963. *Scarcity and Growth: The Economics of Natural Resource Availability.* Baltimore, Md.: Johns Hopkins University Press.

Barrett, Scott. 1989. "On the Nature and Significance of International Environmental Agreements." London Business School. Processed.

———. 1990. "Economic Instruments for Global Climate Change Policy." OECD, Environment Directorate, Paris.

Barrett, Scott, and Christopher Heady. 1989. "Agricultural Prices and Natural Resource Management." *The IUCN Sahel Studies 1989.* Gland, Switzerland: International Union for the Conservation of Nature, Sahel Programme.

Bartelmus, Peter. 1986. *Environment and Development.* Boston, Mass.: Allen and Unwin.

Batisse, Michel. 1990. "Probing the Future of the Mediterranean Basin." *Environment* 32 (5): 4–9, 28–34.

Baumol, William J., and Wallace E. Oates. 1988. *The Theory of Environmental Policy.* 2d ed. New York: Cambridge University Press.

Bentjerodt, J. Roberto, and others. 1985. "Domestic Coal Pricing: Suggested Principles and Present Policies in Selected Countries." Working Paper 23. World Bank, Energy Department, Washington, D.C. Processed.

Bentkover, Judith D., and others. 1986. *Benefits Assessment: The State of the Art.* Dordrecht, Netherlands: D. Reidel Publishing Company.

Bernstein, Janice D. 1990. "Alternative Approaches to Pollution Control and Waste Management: Regulatory and Economic Instruments." World Bank, Infrastructure and Urban Development Department, Washington, D.C. Processed.

Bertram, Ian G., Cath C. Wallace, and Robert J. Stephens. 1989. "Economic Instruments and the Greenhouse Effect." Victoria University of Wellington, Economics Department, Wellington, New Zealand. Processed.

Binswanger, Hans P. 1989. "Brazilian Policies That Encourage Deforestation in the Amazon." Working Paper 16. World Bank, Environment Department, Washington, D.C. Processed.

Binswanger, Hans P., and Prabhu Pingali. 1988. "Technological Priorities for Farming Systems in Sub-Saharan Africa." *World Bank Research Observer* 3 (1): 81–98.

Bishop, Joshua. 1990. "The Cost of Soil Erosion in Malawi." World Bank, Country Operations Division, Southern Africa Department, Washington, D.C. Processed.

Bishop, Joshua, and Jennifer Allen. 1989. "The On-Site Costs of Soil Erosion in Mali." Working Paper 21. World Bank, Environment Department, Washington, D.C. Processed.

Bishop, Richard C. 1978. "Endangered Species and Uncertainty: The Economics of a Safe Minimum Standard." *American Journal of Agricultural Economics* 60: 10–13.

———. 1982. "Option Value: An Exposition and Extension." *Land Economics* 58 (1): 1–15.

———. 1988. "Option Value: Reply." *Land Economics* 64: 88–93.

Bishop, Richard C., Kevin J. Boyle, and Michael Walsh. 1987. "Toward Total Economic Valuation of Great Lakes Fishery Resources." *Transactions of the American Fisheries Society* 116: 339–45.

Boadway, Robin, and Neil Bruce. 1984. *Welfare Economics.* Oxford: Blackwell.

Bojo, Jan, Karl-Goran Mäler, and Lena Unemo. 1990. *Environment and Development: An Economic Approach.* Dordrecht, Netherlands, and Boston, Mass.: Kluwer Academic Publishers.

Boserup, Ester. 1965. *The Conditions of Agricultural Growth*. Chicago, Ill.: Aldine.

_____. 1981. *Population and Technological Change: A Study of Long-Term Trends*. Chicago, Ill.: University of Chicago Press.

Boulding, Kenneth E. 1966. "The Economics of the Coming Spaceship Earth." In Henry Jarett, ed., *Environmental Quality in a Growing Economy*. Baltimore, Md.: Johns Hopkins University Press.

Bowker, J. M., and John R. Stoll. 1988. "Use of Dichotomous Choice Non-market Methods to Value the Whooping Crane Resource." *American Journal of Agricultural Economics* 70: 372–81.

Boyd, Roy G., and William F. Hyde. 1989. *Forestry Sector Intervention*. Iowa City: University of Iowa Press.

Boyle, Kevin J., and Richard C. Bishop. 1987. "Valuing Wildlife in Benefit-Cost Analysis: A Case Study Involving Endangered Species." *Water Resources Research* 23: 943–50.

Briones, Nicomedes. 1986. "Estimating Erosion Costs: A Philippine Case Study in the Lower Agno River Watershed." In K. William Easter, John Dixon, and Maynard Hufschmidt, eds., *Watershed Resources Management: An Integrated Framework with Studies from Asia and the Pacific*. Singapore: Institute of Southeast Asian Studies.

Bromley, Daniel W. 1989. "Property Relations and Economic Development: The Other Land Reform." *World Development* 17 (6): 867–77.

Bromley, Daniel W., and Michael M. Cernea. 1989. *The Management of Common Property Natural Resources: Some Conceptual and Operational Fallacies*. World Bank Discussion Paper 57. Washington, D.C.

Bromley, Daniel W., and Devendra P. Chapagain. 1984. "The Village against the Center: Resource Depletion in South Asia." *American Journal of Agricultural Economics* 66 (5): 868–73.

Brookshire, David, Larry Eubanks, and Alan Randall. 1983. "Estimating Option Prices and Existence Values for Wildlife Resources." *Land Economics* 59: 1–15.

Brookshire, David S., Larry Eubanks, and Cindy F. Sorg. 1986. "Existence Values and Normative Economics: Implications for Valuing Water Resources." *Water Resources Research* 22 (11): 1509–18.

Brookshire, David S., William Schulze, and M. Thayer. 1985. "Some Unusual Aspects of Valuing a Unique Natural Resource." University of Wyoming, Department of Economics, Laramie. Processed.

Browder, John O. 1988a. "Public Policy and Deforestation in the Brazilian Amazon." In Robert Repetto and Malcolm Gillis, eds., *Public Policies and the Misuse of Forest Resources*. Cambridge, Eng.: Cambridge University Press.

_____. 1988b. "The Social Costs of Rain Forest Destruction: A Critique and Economic Analysis of the 'Hamburger Debate.'" *Interciencia* 13 (3): 115–20.

Brown, Gardner. 1986. "Preserving Endangered Species and Other Biological Resources." *The Science of the Total Environment* 56: 89–97.

Button, Kenneth, and David W. Pearce. 1989. "Infrastructure Restoration as a Tool for Stimulating Urban Renewal: The Glasgow Canal." *Urban Studies* 26: 559–73.

Bye, Barry, Torstein Bye, and Lorents Lorentsen. 1989. "SIMEN: Studies of Industry, Environment, and Energy toward 2000." Discussion Paper 44. Norway, Central Bureau of Statistics, Oslo, Norway. Processed.

Camacho, R. 1988. "The Implications for Sea Level Rise for the Coastlands of Guyana." Report to the Commonwealth Secretariat, London, Eng.

Capistrano, Aana Doris, and Clyde Kiker. 1990. "Global Economic Influences on Tropical Closed Broadleaved Forest Depletion, 1967–1985." University of Florida, Food and Resource Economics Department, Gainesville, Fla.

Chalamwong, Yongyuth, and Gershon Feder. 1986. "Land Ownership Security and Land Values in Rural Thailand." Working Paper 790. World Bank, Washington, D.C.

Chandler, William U., and Andrew Nicholls. 1990. *Assessing Carbon Emissions Control Strategies: A Carbon Tax or a Gasoline Tax?* ACEEE Policy Paper 3. Washington, D.C.: Battelle Memorial Institute.

Cheung, Steven N. S. 1970. "The Structure of a Contract and the Theory of a Non-Exclusive Resource." *Journal of Law and Economics* 13: 49–70.

Chilton, J. 1989. "Salts in Surface and Groundwater." In Michel Meybeck, Deborah Chapman, and Richard Helmer, eds., *Global Freshwater Quality: A First Assessment*. Oxford: Basil Blackwell.

Ciriancy-Wantrup, Siegfried Von. 1952. *Resource Conservation: Economics and Policies*. Berkeley: University of California Press.

Ciriancy-Wantrup, Siegfried Von, and Richard C. Bishop. 1975. "Common Property: A Concept in Natural Resources Policy." *Natural Resources Journal* 15 (October): 713–30.

Clark, Colin Whitcomb. 1990. *Mathematical Bioeconomics*. 2d ed. New York: Wiley.

Clark, H. L., and others. 1980. "Acid Rain in the Venezuelan Amazon." In Jose I. Furtado, ed., *Tropical Ecology and Development*. Kuala Lumpur, Malaysia: International Society of Tropical Ecology.

Cleaver, Kevin M. 1985. *The Impact of Price and Exchange Rate Policies on Agriculture in Sub-Saharan Africa*. World Bank Staff Working Paper 728. Washington, D.C.

Cline, William. 1989. *Political Economics of the Greenhouse Effect*. Washington, D.C.: Institute for International Economics.

Coase, Ronald H. 1960. "The Problem of Social Cost." *Journal of Law and Economics* 3 (October): 1–44.

Cochrane, Susan Hill. 1985. "Development Consequences of Rapid Population Growth: A Review from the Perspective of Sub-Saharan Africa." PHN Technical Note 85-8. World Bank, Population, Health, and Nutrition Department, Washington, D.C. Processed.

Colander, David C., ed. 1984. *Neoclassical Political Economy: The Analysis of Rent Seeking and DUP Activities*. Cambridge, Mass.: Ballinger Publishing Company.

Conservation International. 1989. *The Debt-for-Nature Exchange*. Washington, D.C.

Conway, Gordon, and Edward Barbier. 1990. *After the Green Revolution: Sustainable Agriculture for Development*. London: Earthscan Publications.

Cook, Cynthia. 1988. "Botswana Land Management and Livestock: A Case Study." World Bank, Environment Divison, Africa Region, Washington, D.C. Processed.

Cornia, Giovanni, Richard Jolly, and Frances Stewart. 1987. *Adjustment with a Human Face*. Vol. 1. *Protecting the Vulnerable and Promoting Growth*. New York: Oxford University Press.

Cropper, Maureen. 1988. "A Note on the Extinction of Renewable Resources." *Journal of Environmental Economics and Management* 15: 64–71.

Crosson, Pierre. n.d. "Climate Change and Mid-Latitudes Agriculture: Perspectives on Consequences and Policy Responses." *Climate Change*.

_____. 1989. "Greenhouse Warming and Climate Change: Why Should We Care?" *Food Policy* 14 (2): 107–18.

Cummings, Barbara J. 1990. *Dam the Rivers, Damn the People*. London: Earthscan Publications.

Cummings, Ronald G., David S. Brookshire, and William Schulze. 1986. *Valuing Environmental Goods*. Totowa, N.J.: Rowman and Allanheld.

Daly, Herman E. 1973. *Toward a Steady State Economy*. San Francisco, Calif.: Freeman.

_____. 1989. "Toward a Measure of Sustainable Social Net National Product." In Yusuf J. Ahmad, Salah El Serafy, and Ernst Lutz, eds., *Environmental Accounting for Sustainable Development*. A UNEP–World Bank Symposium. Washington, D.C.: World Bank.

Daly, Herman, and John B. Cobb. 1989. *For the Common Good: Redirecting the Economy toward Community, the Environment, and a Sustainable Future*. Boston, Mass.: Beacon Press.

Daly, Herman, and George Foy. 1989. "Allocation, Distribution, and Scale as Determinants of Environmental Degradation: Case Studies of Haiti, El Salvador, and Costa Rica." Working Paper 19. World Bank, Environment Department, Washington, D.C. Processed.

Dasgupta, Partha, and Geoffrey Martin Heal. 1979. *Economic Theory and Exhaustible Resources*. Cambridge, Eng.: Cambridge University Press.

Dasgupta, Partha, and Karl-Goran Mäler. 1991. "The Environment and Emerging Development Issues." *Proceedings of the World Bank Annual Conference on Development Economics 1990*. Washington, D.C.: World Bank.

Dasmann, Raymond Fredric. 1975. *The Conservation Alternative*. Chichester, Eng.: Wiley.

Dean, Judith M. 1991. "Trade and the Environment: A Survey of the Literature." Background paper prepared for *World Development Report 1992: Environment*. World Bank, Washington, D.C. Processed.

de Beer, Jenne H., and Melanie J. McDermott. 1989. "The Economic Value of Non-timber Products in South-east Asia." International Union for the Conservation of Nature, Netherlands Committee, Amsterdam, Netherlands. Processed.

Demery, Lionel, and Tony Addison. 1987. *The Alleviation of Poverty under Structural Adjustment*. Washington, D.C.: World Bank.

Demsetz, Harold. 1967. "Toward a Theory of Property Rights." *American Economic Review* 57: 47–59.

Desvousges, William H., V. Kerry Smith, and Anne Fisher. 1987. "Option Price Estimates for Water Quality Improvements: A Contingent Valuation Study for the Monongahela River." *Journal of Environmental Economics and Management* 14: 248–67.

Devarajan, Shantayanan, and Robert J. Weiner. 1988. "Natural Resource Depletion and National Income Accounts." Harvard University, John F. Kennedy School of Government, Cambridge, Mass. Processed.

Dixit, Avinash, and Amy Williamson. 1989. "Risk-Adjusted Rates of Return for Project Appraisal." PR Working Paper 290. World Bank, Agriculture and Rural Development Department, Washington, D.C. Processed.

Dixon, John, and Maynard Hufschmidt, eds. 1986. *Economic Valuation Techniques for the Environment: A Case Study Workbook*. Baltimore, Md.: Johns Hopkins University Press.

Dixon, John, Lee M. Talbot, and Guy Le Moigne. 1989. *Dams and the Environment*. World Bank Technical Paper 110. Washington, D.C.

Dixon, John, and others. 1988. *Economic Analysis of the Environmental Impacts of Development Projects*. London: Earthscan Publications in association with the Asian Development Bank.

Dogse, Peter. 1989. "Sustainable Tropical Rain Forest Management: Some Economic Considerations." Paper prepared for Unesco, Division of Ecological Sciences, Paris. Processed.

Dogse, Peter, and Bernd Von Droste. 1990. "Debt for Nature Exchanges and Biosphere Reserves: Experiences and Potential." *MAB Digest* 6. Paris: Unesco.

Dourojeanni, Marc J. 1985. "Over-Exploited and Under-Used Animals in the Amazon Region." In Ghillean T. Prance and Thomas E. Lovejoy, eds., *Key Environments: Amazonia*. Oxford: Pergamon.

Edmonds, James, and John Reilly. 1983. "Global Energy and CO_2 to the Year 2050." *Energy Journal* 4: 21–47.

Edwards, Steven F. 1988. "Option Prices for Groundwater Protection." *Journal of Environmental Economics and Management* 15: 475–87.

El Serafy, Salah, and Ernst Lutz. 1989. "Environmental and Resource Accounting: An Overview." In Yusuf J. Ahmad, Salah El Serafy, and Ernst Lutz, eds., *Environmental Accounting for Sustainable Development*. A UNEP–World Bank Symposium. Washington, D.C.: World Bank.

"Energy and Global Warming: An Opportunity to Redefine Priorities." 1991. *World Energy Council Journal* (July): 57 (editorial).

Environmental Resources, Ltd. 1984. *Acid Rain: A Review of the Phenomenon in the EEC and Europe*. London: Graham and Trotman.

Farnsworth, Norman R., and R. Morris. 1976. "Higher Plants: The Sleeping Giant of Drug Development." *American Journal of Pharmacy* 147 (2): 46–52.

Farnsworth, Norman R., and Djaja Doel Soejarto. 1985. "Potential Consequence of Plant Extinction in the United States on the Current and Future Availability of Prescription Drugs." *Economic Botany* 39 (3): 231–40.

Faustmann, M. 1849. "On the Determination of the Value Which Forest Land and Immature Stands Pose for Forestry" (English translation). In M. Gane, ed., 1968, *Martin Faustmann and the Evolution of Discounted Cash Flow*. Oxford Institute Paper 42.

Feder, Gershon. 1987. "Land Ownership Security and Farm Productivity: Evidence from Rural Thailand." *Journal of Development Studies* 24 (1): 16–30.

Feder, Gershon, and Raymond Noronha. 1987. "Land Rights Systems and Agricultural Development in Sub-Saharan Africa." *World Bank Research Observer* 2 (2): 143–69.

Feder, Gershon, and others. 1986. "Land Ownership Security and Access to Credit in Rural Thailand." Discussion Paper ARU-53. World Bank, Agriculture and Rural Development Department, Washington, D.C. Processed.

Feenberg, Daniel, and Edwin Mills. 1980. *Measuring the Benefits of Water Pollution Abatement.* New York: Academic Press.

Fisher, Anthony C. 1981. *Resource and Environmental Economics.* Cambridge, Eng.: Cambridge University Press.

Fisher, Anthony C., and W. Michael Hanemann. 1987. "Quasi Option Value: Some Misconceptions Dispelled." *Journal of Environmental Economics and Management* 14: 183–90.

Fones-Sundell, M. 1987. *Role of Price Policy in Stimulating Agricultural Production in Africa.* Issue Paper 2. Uppsala, Sweden: Swedish University of Agricultural Sciences, International Rural Development Centre.

FAO (Food and Agriculture Organization of the United Nations). 1981. *Tropical Forest Resources.* Rome.

———. 1982. "Potential Population Supporting Capacities of Lands in the Developing World." Report FPA/INT/513. Rome.

———. 1984. *Land, Food, and People.* Economic and Social Development Series 30. Rome.

———. 1986. *1986 Yearbook of Forestry Products, 1975–1986.* Rome.

Frederick, Kenneth D. 1986. *Scarce Water and Institutional Change.* Washington, D.C.: Resources for the Future.

———. 1989. "Water Resource Management and the Environment: The Role of Economic Incentives." In OECD, *Renewable Natural Resources: Economic Incentives for Improved Management.* Paris.

Freeman, A. Myrick. 1979. *The Benefits of Environmental Improvement.* Baltimore, Md.: Johns Hopkins University Press.

———. 1982. *Air and Water Pollution Control: A Benefit-Cost Assessment.* New York: Wiley.

———. 1985. "Supply Uncertainty, Option Price, and Option Value in Project Evaluation." *Land Economics* 61: 176–81.

Furtado, Jose I. 1978. "The Status and Future of the Tropical Moist Forest in South East Asia." In Colin MacAndrews and Lin Sien Chia, eds., *Developing Economies in South East Asia and the Environment.* New York: McGraw Hill.

Furtado, Jose I., and Kenneth Ruddle. 1986. "The Future of Tropical Forests." In Nicholas Polunin, ed., *Ecosystem Theory and Application.* New York: Wiley.

Gamba, Julio R., David A. Caplin, and John Mulckhuyse. 1986. *Industrial Energy Rationalization in Developing Countries.* Baltimore, Md.: Johns Hopkins University Press.

Germany, Ministry of the Environment. 1991. *Advantages of Environmental Protection, Costs of Environmental Pollution.* Bonn.

Gillis, Malcolm. 1988. "Indonesia: Public Policies, Resource Management, and the Tropical Forest." In Robert Repetto and Malcolm Gillis, eds., *Public Policies and the Misuse of Forest Resources.* New York: Cambridge University Press.

Goldemberg, José, and others. 1987. *Energy for a Sustainable World.* New York: Wiley.

Goodin, Robert E. 1982. "Discounting Discounting." *Journal of Public Policy* 2: 53–72.

Gordon, H. S. 1954. "Economic Theory of a Common Property Resource: The Fishery." *Journal of Political Economy* 62: 124–43.

Gordon, Robert B., and others. 1987. *Toward a New Iron Age: Quantitative Modeling of Resource Exhaustion.* Cambridge, Mass.: Harvard University Press.

Goulet, Dennis. 1971. *A New Concept on the Theory of Development.* New York: Atheneum Press.

Gradwohl, Judith, and Russell Greenberg. 1988. *Saving the Tropical Forests.* London: Earthscan Publications.

Grais, W., Jaime de Melo, and S. Urata. 1986. "A General Equilibrium Estimation of the Effects of Reduction in Tariffs and Quantitative Restrictions in Turkey in 1978." In T. N. Srinivasan and John Whalley, eds., *General Equilibrium Trade Policy Modelling.* Cambridge, Mass.: MIT Press.

Gray, Lewis Cecil. 1914. "Rent under the Assumption of Exhaustibility." *Quarterly Journal of Economics* 28: 466–90.

Green, Colin H., and S. M. Tunstall. 1991. "The Evaluation of River Water Quality Improvements by the Contingent Valuation Method." *Applied Economics* 23: 1135–46.

Green, Colin H., S. M. Tunstall, A. N'Jai, and A. Rogers. 1988. "Evaluating the Benefits of River Water Quality Improvements." Middlesex Polytechnic Flood Hazard Research Centre, Middlesex, Eng. Processed.

_____. 1989. "Water Quality: The Public Dimension." In David Wheeler and others, eds., *Watershed 89: The Future for Water Quality in Europe.* Oxford: Pergamon.

_____. 1990. "The Economic Evaluation of Environmental Goods." *Project Appraisal* 5(2): 70–82.

Greenaway, David, Michael Bleaney, and Ian Stewart, eds. 1991. *Economics in Perspective.* London: Routledge.

Grenon, Michel, and Michel Batisse. 1989. *The Blue Plan: Futures for the Mediterranean Basin.* New York: Oxford University Press.

Gribbin, John. 1988. *The Hole in the Sky: Man's Threat to the Ozone Layer.* New York: Bantam Books.

Grubb, Michael. 1989. *The Greenhouse Effect: Negotiating Targets.* London: Royal Institute of International Affairs, Energy and Environmental Program.

Hahn, Robert, and Gordon Hester. 1987. "The Market for Bads: EPA's Experience with Emissions Trading." *Regulation* 3 (4): 48–53.

———. 1989. "Marketable Permits: Lessons for Theory and Practice." *Ecology Law Quarterly* 16 (2): 361–406.

Hall, Darwin C., and Jane V. Hall. 1984. "Concepts and Measures of Natural Resource Scarcity, with a Summary of Recent Trends." *Journal of Environmental Economics and Management* 11 (September): 363–79.

Hamilton, Lawrence S., and Peter N. King. 1983. *Tropical Forested Watersheds: Hydrologic and Soils Response to Major Uses or Conversions.* Boulder, Colo.: Westview Press.

Hanley, Nick. 1988. "Using Contingent Valuation to Value Environmental Improvements." *Applied Economics* 20: 541–51.

———. 1989. "Valuing Rural Recreational Benefits: An Empirical Comparison of Two Approaches." *Journal of Agricultural Economics* 40 (Part III, September): 361–74.

Hansen, Stein. 1988. "Structural Adjustment Programs and Sustainable Development." Committee of International Development Institutions on the Environment, Nairobi, Kenya. Processed.

———. 1989. "Debt-for-Nature Swaps: Overview and Discussion of Key Issues." *Ecological Economics* 1: 77–93.

Hardin, Garrett J. 1968. "The Tragedy of the Commons." *Science* 162: 1243–48.

Harley, David C., and Nick Hanley. 1989. "Economic Benefit Estimates for Nature Reserves: Methods and Results." Discussion Paper in Economics 89/6. University of Stirling, Scotland. Processed.

Harrington, Winston. 1988. *Acid Deposition: Science and Policy.* Discussion Paper 88-09. Washington, D.C.: Resources for the Future, Quality of the Environment Division.

Harter, P. 1988. *Acidic Deposition: Ecological Effects.* London: International Energy Agency, Coal Research.

Hartshorn, G., R. Simeone, and J. Tosi. 1987. "Sustained Yield Management of Tropical Forests: A Synopsis of the Palcazú Development Project in the Central Selva of the Peruvian Amazon." Tropical Science Center, San José, Costa Rica. Processed.

Hausman, Jerry A. 1979. "Individual Discount Rates and the Purchase and Utilization of Energy-Using Durables: Comment." *Bell Journal of Economics* 1: 33–54.

Hegenbart, Bärbel, and Michael Windfuhr. 1991. "Systematics of Interdependencies: Trade Instruments and Their Impact on the Environment." In Friedrich Schmidt-Bleek and Heinrich Wohlmeyer, eds., *Trade and Environment.* Laxenberg, Austria: International Institute for Applied Systems Analysis and the Austrian Association for Agricultural Research.

Henry, C. 1974. "Option Values in the Economics of Irreplaceable Resources." *Review of Economic Studies* 41: 88–93.

Herfindahl, Orris C., and Allen V. Kneese. 1965. *Quality of the Environment: An Economic Approach to Some Problems in Using Land, Water, and Air.* Baltimore, Md.: Johns Hopkins University Press.

Herrera, R. 1985. "Nutrient Cycling in Amazonian Forests." In Ghillean Prance and Thomas E. Lovejoy, eds., *Key Environments: Amazonia*. Oxford: Pergamon.

Hicks, John Richard. 1946. *Value and Capital*. 2d ed. Oxford: Clarendon Press.

Ho, Teresa J. 1985. "Population Growth and Agricultural Productivity in Sub-Saharan Africa." In Ted J. Davis, ed., *Population and Food: Proceedings of the Fifth Agriculture Sector Symposium*. Washington, D.C.: World Bank.

Hodgson, Gregor, and John Dixon. 1988. *Logging versus Fisheries and Tourism in Palawan*. Occasional Paper 7. Honolulu, Hawaii: East-West Environment and Policy Institute.

Hoehn, John P., and Alan Randall. 1989. "Too Many Proposals Pass the Benefit-Cost Test." *American Economic Review* 79: 544–51.

Hoel, Michael. 1990. "Efficient International Agreements for Reducing Emissions of CO_2." University of Oslo, Department of Economics, Oslo, Norway. Processed.

Holdgate, Martin W., and others. 1989. *Climate Change: Meeting the Challenge*. London: U.K. Commonwealth Secretariat.

Horowitz, Marvin J., and Hossein Haeri. 1990. "Economic Efficiency v Energy Efficiency: Do Model Conservation Standards Make Good Sense?" *Energy Economics* 12 (2, April): 122–31.

Hosier, R., and M. Bernstein. 1989. "Woodfuel Use and Sustainable Development in Haiti." University of Pennsylvania, Center for Energy and Development, Philadelphia, Penn. Processed.

Hosteland, Jan. 1990. "The Role of Environment in Forest Resource Management." Paper presented at conference on Forest Resource Management. OECD, Paris. Processed.

Hotelling, Harold. 1931. "The Economics of Exhaustible Resources." *Journal of Political Economy* 39: 137–75.

Houghton, R. A. 1989. "Emissions of Greenhouse Gases." In Norman Myers, ed., *Deforestation Rates in Tropical Forests and Their Climatic Implications*. London: Friends of the Earth.

―――. 1990. "The Future Role of Tropical Forests in Affecting the Carbon Dioxide Concentration of the Atmosphere." *Ambio* 19 (4): 204–09.

Houghton, R. A., and others. 1985. "Net Flux of Carbon Dioxide from Tropical Forests in 1980." *Nature* 316 (August): 617–20.

Howarth, David, Paul Nikitopoulos, and Gary Yohe. 1989. "On the Ability of Carbon Taxes to Fend Off Global Warming." Wesleyan University, Department of Economics, Middletown, Conn. Processed.

Hughes, Gordon. 1987. "Impact of Energy Taxes in Thailand." In Maumohan S. Kumar, ed., *Energy Pricing Policies in Developing Countries*. Geneva, Switzerland: International Labour Organisation.

―――. 1990. "Are the Costs of Cleaning Up Eastern Europe Exaggerated? Economic Reform and the Environment." University of Edinburgh, Department of Economics, Edinburgh, Scotland. Processed.

Hultkrans, A. 1988. "Greenbacks for Greenery." *Sierra* (November/December): 43–48.

Ingham, Alan, and Alistair Ulph. 1989. "Carbon Taxes and the UK Manufacturing Sector." University of Southampton, Department of Economics, Southhampton, Eng. Processed.

IEA (International Energy Agency). 1987. *Energy Conservation in IEA Countries.* Paris: OECD.

_____. 1989. *Policy Measures and Their Impact on CO_2 Emissions and Accumulations.* Paris.

_____. n.d. "Newsheet." Paris. Processed.

IIED (International Institute for Economic Development) and World Resources Institute. 1987. *World Resources 1987.* New York: Basic Books.

International Project for Sustainable Energy Paths. 1989. *Energy Policy in the Greenhouse.* El Cerrito, Calif.

International Union for the Conservation of Nature. 1980. *World Conservation Strategy.* Gland, Switzerland.

Irvin, George. 1978. *Modern Cost-Benefit Methods.* London: Macmillan.

Ives, Jack D., and Bruno Messerli. 1989. *The Himalayan Dilemma: Reconciling Development and Conservation.* London: Routledge.

Jaeger, Jill. 1988. "The Development of an Awareness of a Need to Respond to Climate Change." Commonwealth Secretariat, London. Processed.

Jagannathan, N. Vijay. 1987. *Informal Markets in Developing Countries.* New York: Oxford University Press.

_____. 1989. "Poverty, Public Policies, and the Environment." Working Paper 24. World Bank, Environment Department, Washington, D.C. Processed.

_____. 1990. "Poverty-Environment Linkages: Case Study of West Java." Working Paper 1990-8. World Bank, Environment Department, Washington, D.C. Processed.

Jagannathan, N. Vijay, and A. Agunbiade. 1990. "Poverty Environment Linkages in Nigeria: Issues for Research." Working Paper 1990-7. World Bank, Environment Department, Washington, D.C. Processed.

Jagannathan, N. Vijay, Hideki Mori, and H. M. Hassan. 1990. "Applications of Geographical Information Systems in Economic Analysis: A Case Study of Uganda." Working Paper 27. World Bank, Environment Department, Washington, D.C. Processed.

Jansen, Doris. 1990. "Sustainable Wildlife Utilisation in the Zambesi Valley of Zimbabwe: Economics Ecological and Political Tradeoffs." Project Paper 10. World Wildlife Fund Multispecies Project, Harare, Zimbabwe. Processed.

Jansen, Huib, and Johannes Opschoor. 1988. "Debt for Sustainable Development." Report to the Netherlands Ministry of Foreign Affairs. Free University of Amsterdam, Institute for Environmental Studies. Processed.

Jodha, N. S. 1986. "Common Property Resources and Rural Poor in Dry Regions of India." *Economic and Political Weekly* 21 (27).

Johansson, Per-Olov. 1987. *The Economic Theory and Measurement of Environmental Benefits.* New York: Cambridge University Press.

_____. 1988. "On the Properties of Supply-Side Option Value." *Land Economics* 64: 86–87.

Jorgensen, Dale W., and Peter J. Wilcoxen. 1990. "Environmental Regulation and U.S. Economic Growth." *Rand Journal of Economics* 21 (2): 314–40.

Julius, De Anne S., and Adelaida Alicbusan. 1989. "Public Sector Pricing Policies: A Review of Bank Policy and Practice." PPR Working Paper 49. World Bank, Washington, D.C. Processed.

Julius, De Anne S., and Afsaneh Mashayekhi. 1990. *The Economics of Natural Gas: Pricing, Planning, and Policy.* Oxford: Oxford University Press.

Kabala, S. J. 1989a. "The Costs of Environmental Degradation in Poland." Background Paper. World Bank, Land and Energy Operation Division, Washington, D.C. Processed.

_____. 1989b. "Poland: The Environment." Background Paper. World Bank, Industry and Energy Operations Division, Europe, Middle East, and North Africa Region Department, Washington, D.C.

Kapp, K. William. 1950. *The Social Costs of Private Enterprise.* Cambridge, Mass.: Harvard University Press.

Kassenberg, A. 1986. "Zones of Ecological Threat: A New Planning Tool." *Kosmos* 1.

_____. 1989. "Zones of Ecological Threat—A New Planning Tool." *Cosmos* 1/86.

Kneese, Allen V. 1960. "Effluent Charges." RFF, Washington, D.C.

_____. 1964. *The Economics of Regional Water Quality Management.* Baltimore, Md.: Johns Hopkins University Press.

_____. 1984. *Measuring the Benefits of Clean Air and Water.* Washington, D.C.: Resources for the Future.

Komoroski, K. 1988. "The Failure of Governments to Regulate Industry: A Subsidy under GATT?" *Houston Journal of International Law* 10 (2): 89.

Kosmo, Mark Nicholas. 1989a. "Commercial Energy Subsidies in Developing Countries." *Energy Policy* (June): 244–53.

_____. 1989b. "Economic Incentives and Industrial Pollution in Developing Countries." Working Paper 89-2. World Bank, Environment Department, Washington, D.C. Processed.

Kram, T., and P. A. Okken. 1989. "Integrated Assessment of Energy Options for CO_2 Reductions." In P. A. Okken, R. J. Swart, and S. Zwerver, eds., *Climate and Energy: The Feasibility of Controlling CO_2 Emissions.* Boston, Mass.: Kluwer Academic Publishers.

Krautkraemer, Jeffrey A. 1985. "Optimal Growth, Resource Amenities, and the Preservation of Natural Environments." *Review of Economic Studies* 52: 153–70.

Krawczyk, R. n.d. "The Environment in Europe: CMEA versus EEC." Warsaw University, Department of Economics, Warsaw, Poland. Processed.

Kreps, David M. 1990. *A Course in Microeconomic Theory.* London: Harvester-Wheatsheaf.

Krueger, Anne O. 1974. "The Political Economy of the Rent-Seeking Society." *American Economic Review* 64 (3): 291–303.

Krutilla, John V., and Otto Eckstein. 1958. *Multiple Purpose River Development.* Baltimore, Md.: Johns Hopkins University Press.

Krutilla, John V., and Anthony C. Fisher. 1975. "The New Approach to Wilderness Preservation through Benefit-Cost Analysis." *Journal of Environmental Economics and Management* 9: 59–80.

_____. 1985. *The Economics of Natural Environments*. Baltimore, Md.: Johns Hopkins University Press.

Kumar, S. K., and David Hotchkiss. 1988. *Energy and Nutrition Links to Agriculture in a Hill Region of Nepal*. Washington, D.C.: International Food Policy Research Institute.

Lallement, Dominique. 1990. "Burkina Faso: Economic Issues in Renewable Natural Resource Management." World Bank, Agriculture Operations, Sahelian Department, Africa Region, Washington, D.C. Processed.

Laws, R. 1989. *Antarctica: The Last Frontier*. London: Boxtree.

Leach, Gerald. 1988. "Interfuel Substitution." *Proceedings of the ESMAP Eastern and Southern Africa Household Energy Planning Seminar, Harare, Zimbabwe*. New York: United Nations Development Programme.

Ledec, George, and Robert Goodland. 1988. *Wildlands: Their Protection and Management in Economic Development*. Washington, D.C.: World Bank.

Lemel, H. 1988. "Land Titling: Conceptual, Empirical, and Policy Issues." *Land Use Policy* (July): 273–90.

Leonard, H. Jeffrey. 1987. *Natural Resources and Economic Development in Central America: A Regional Environmental Profile*. New Brunswick, Canada: Transaction Books.

_____ 1989a. *Environment and the Poor: Development Strategies for a Common Agenda*. U.S. Third World Policy Perspectives 11. Washington, D.C.: Overseas Development Council.

_____. 1989b. *Pollution and the Struggle for the World Produce*. Cambridge, Eng.: Cambridge University Press.

_____. 1991. "Economic Instruments and the International Location of Industry: Evidence Regarding Whether Industry Will Move to Low-Cost Pollution Havens." Paper presented at the Business Council for Sustainable Development Workshop on Economic Instruments, London. Processed.

Leonard, H. Jeffrey, ed. 1984. *Are Environmental Regulations Driving U.S. Industry Overseas?* Washington, D.C.: The Conservation Foundation.

Leslie, Alan J. 1988. "A Second Look at the Economics of Natural Management Systems in Tropical Mixed Forests." *Unasylva* 39 (155): 46–58.

Lewis, J. 1988. "Sea Level Rise: Tonga, Tuvalu, Kiribati." Report to the Commonwealth Secretariat, London. Processed.

Lidgren, K. 1986. *Economic Instruments for Environmental Protection in Sweden*. Paris: OECD, Environment Committee.

Lind, Robert C. 1982. *Discounting for Time and Risk in Energy Policy*. Baltimore, Md.: Johns Hopkins University Press.

Lone, A. 1988. *Natural Resource Accounting: The Norwegian Experience*. Paris: OECD, Environment Committee, Group on the State of the Environment.

MacRea, Duncan, and Dale Whittington. 1988. "Assessing Preferences in Cost-Benefit Analysis: Reflections on Rural Water Supply Evaluation in Haiti." *Journal of Policy Analysis and Management* 7 (2): 246–63.

Magrath, William B. 1989. "The Challenge of the Commons: The Allocation of Nonexclusive Resources." Working Paper 14. World Bank, Environment Department, Washington, D.C. Processed.

Magrath, William B., and Peter L. Arens. 1989. "The Costs of Soil Erosion on Java: A Natural Resource Accounting Approach." Working Paper 18. World Bank, Environment Department, Washington, D.C.

Mahar, Dennis J. 1989. *Government Policies and Deforestation in Brazil's Amazon Region.* Washington, D.C.: World Bank.

Mäler, Karl-Goran. 1974. *Environmental Economics: A Theoretical Inquiry.* Baltimore, Md.: Johns Hopkins University Press.

_____. 1989a. "The Acid Rain Game." In Henk Folmer and Ekko van Ierland, eds., *Valuation Methods and Policy Making in Environmental Economics.* Amsterdam, Netherlands: Elsevier.

_____. 1989b. "Sustainable Development." Stockholm School of Economics, Stockholm, Sweden. Processed.

_____. 1990. "International Environmental Problems." *Oxford Review of Economic Policy* 6 (1): 80–108.

Manne, Alan S., and Richard G. Richels. 1989. "CO_2 Emission Limits: An Economic Analysis for the USA." Stanford University, Department of Economics, Stanford, Calif. Processed.

_____. 1990. "Global CO_2 Emission Reductions: The Impacts of Rising Energy Costs." Stanford University, Department of Economics, Stanford, Calif. Processed.

Markandya, Anil. 1990. "The Costs to Developing Countries of Joining the Montreal Protocol." London Environmental Economics Centre, London. Processed.

Markandya, Anil, and David W. Pearce. 1988. "Environmental Considerations and the Choice of Discount Rate in Developing Countries." Working Paper 3. World Bank, Environment Department, Washington, D.C. Processed.

_____. 1989. "Marginal Opportunity Cost as a Planning Concept in Natural Resource Management." In Gunter Schramm and Jeremy Warford, eds., *Environmental Management and Economic Development.* Baltimore, Md.: Johns Hopkins University Press.

_____. 1991. "Development, Environment, and the Social Rate of Discount." *World Bank Research Observer* 6 (2): 137–50.

May, John. 1988. *Antarctica: A New View of the Seventh Continent.* London: Dorling Kindersley.

Mazurski, Krzyszof. 1990. "Industrial Pollution: The Threat to Polish Forests." *Ambio* 19 (2): 70–74.

McConnell, Kenneth E. 1983. "An Economic Model of Soil Conservation." *American Journal of Agricultural Economics* 65: 83–89.

McCracken, Jennifer A., and Gordon Conway. 1989. *Pesticide Hazards in the Third World: New Evidence from the Philippines.* London: International Institute for Environment and Development, Sustainable Agriculture Program.

McCracken, Michael C., and Frederick M. Luther, eds. 1986. *Detecting the Climatic Effects of Increasing Carbon Dioxide.* Report DOE/ER-0235. Washington, D.C.: U.S. Department of Energy.

McNeely, Jeffrey A., and others. 1989. *Conserving the World's Biological Diversity*. Washington, D.C.: World Bank, World Resources Institute, International Union for the Conservation of Nature and Natural Resources, Conservation International, and World Wildlife Fund.

Meadows, Donella H., and others. 1972. *Limits to Growth*. London: Earth Island.

Medvedev, Zhores A. 1990. "The Environmental Destruction of the Soviet Union." *The Ecologist* 20 (1): 24–29.

Mellor, John W. 1988. "The Intertwining of Environmental Problems and Poverty." *Environment* 9: 8–30.

Merrick, Thomas W. 1986. "World Population in Transition." *Population Bulletin* 42 (2).

Meybeck, Michel, Deborah V. Chapman, and Richard Helmer. 1990. *Global Freshwater Quality: A First Assessment*. Oxford: Blackwell Reference for the World Health Organization and the United Nations Environment Programme.

Micklin, Philip P. 1988. "Desiccation of the Aral Sea: A Water Management Disaster in the Soviet Union." *Science* 241: 1170–76.

Migot-Adholla, Shem E., and others. 1991. "Indigenous Land Rights Systems in Sub-Saharan Africa: A Constraint on Productivity?" *World Bank Economic Review* 5 (1): 155–75.

Mill, John Stuart. 1900. *Principles of Political Economy*. New York: Collier & Son.

Milliman, John D., James M. Broadus, and Frank Gable. 1989. "Environmental and Economic Implications of Rising Sea Level and Subsiding Deltas: The Nile and Bengal Examples." *Ambio* 18 (6): 340–45.

Mintzer, Irving M. 1989. "Cooling Down a Warming World: Chlorofluorocarbons, the Greenhouse Effect, and the Montreal Protocol." *International Environmental Affairs* 1 (1): 12–25.

Mitchell, Robert Cameron, and Richard T. Carson. 1989. *Using Surveys to Value Public Goods: The Contingent Valuation Method*. Washington, D.C.: Resources for the Future.

Mortimore, Michael. 1989. "The Causes, Nature, and Rate of Soil Degradation in the Northernmost States of Nigeria." Working Paper 17. World Bank, Environment Department, Washington, D.C. Processed.

Mu, Xinming, Dale Whittington, and John Briscoe. 1991. "Modelling Village Water Demand Behaviour: A Discrete Choice Approach." *Water Resources Research* 26 (24): 521–29.

Mutti, John, and David Richardson. 1976. "Industrial Displacement through Environmental Controls: The International Competitive Aspects." In Ingo Walter, ed., *Studies in International Environmental Economics*. New York: Wiley.

Myers, Norman. 1983. "Tropical Moist Forests: Over-Exploited and Under-Utilized?" *Forest Ecology and Management* 6: 59–79.

———. 1986. "Economics and Ecology in the International Arena: The Phenomenon of 'Linked Linkages.'" *Ambio* 15 (5): 296–300.

———. 1988. "Natural Resource Systems and Human Exploitation Systems: Physiobiotic and Ecological Linkages." Working Paper 12. World Bank, Environment Department, Washington, D.C. Processed.

_____. 1990. "The Greenhouse Effect: A Tropical Forestry Response." *Biomass* 18: 73–78.

Naess, Arne. 1973. "The Shallow and the Deep Long-Range Ecology Movement: A Summary." *Inquiry* 16 (1): 95–100.

Nectoux, François, and Yoichi Kuroda. 1989. *Timber from the South Seas: An Analysis of Japan's Tropical Timber Trade and Its Environmental Impact.* Gland, Switzerland: Worldwide Fund International.

Newcombe, Kenneth. 1989. "An Economic Justification for Rural Afforestation: The Case of Ethiopia." In Gunter Schramm and Jeremy Warford, eds., *Environmental Management and Economic Development.* Baltimore, Md.: Johns Hopkins University Press.

New World Dialogue on Environment and Development in the Western Hemisphere. 1991. *Compact for a New World.*

Nordhaus, William D. 1991. "To Slow or Not to Slow: The Economics of the Greenhouse Effect." *Economic Journal* 101 (July).

Nordhaus, William D., and Gary Yohe. 1983. "Future Carbon Dioxide Emissions from Fossil Fuels." In *Changing Climate.* Washington, D.C.: National Academy of Sciences.

Noronha, Raymond. 1988. "The Socio-Cultural and Legal Dynamics of Natural Resource Management." World Bank, Environment Department, Washington, D.C. Processed.

Norway, Central Bureau of Statistics. 1990. *Natural Resources and the Environment 1989.* Oslo.

Olszewski, D., W. Bielanski, and M. Kaminska. 1987. "Economic Pressure on the Environment in the European CMEA Countries: Statistical Tables." Paper 8716. University of Warsaw, Department of Economics, Warsaw, Poland. Processed.

Opschoor, Johannes B. 1986. "A Review of Monetary Estimates of Benefits of Environmental Improvements in the Netherlands." Paper presented at the OECD workshop The Benefits of Environmental Policy and Decisionmaking, Avignon, France.

Opschoor, Johannes B., and Hans B. Vos. 1988. *The Application of Economic Instruments for Environmental Protection in OECD Member Countries.* Paris: OECD.

OECD (Organisation for Economic Co-operation and Development). 1975. *The Polluter Pays Principle.* Paris.

_____. 1985. *The Macroeconomic Impact of Environmental Expenditure.* Paris.

_____. 1988. *Financing and External Debt in Developing Countries, 1987 Survey.* Paris.

_____. 1989. *OECD Environmental Data 1989.* Paris.

_____. 1991. *Environmental Indicators.* Paris.

O'Riordan, Timothy. 1988. "The Politics of Sustainability." In R. Kerry Turner, ed., *Sustainable Environmental Management: Principles and Practice.* London: Belhaven Press.

Ostro, Bart D. 1983. "The Effects of Air Pollution on Work Loss and Morbidity." *Journal of Environmental Economics and Management* 10: 371–82.

Page, Talbot. 1977a. *Conservation and Economic Efficiency.* Baltimore, Md.: Johns Hopkins University Press.

_____. 1977b. "Equitable Use of the Resource Base." *Environment and Planning A* 9: 15–22.

Palo, Matti, G. Mery, and Jyrki Salmi. 1987. "Deforestation in the Tropics: Pilot Scenarios Based on Quantitative Analysis." In Matti Palo and Jyrki Salmi, eds., *Deforestation or Development in the Third World?* Helsinki: Finnish Forest Research Institute.

Parry, Martin L., Timothy R. Carter, and Nicolaas Konijn. 1988. *The Impact of Climatic Variations in Agriculture.* 2 vols. Boston, Mass.: Kluwer Academic Publishers.

Pauly, Daniel, and Chua Thia-Eng. 1988. "The Overfishing of Marine Resources: Socioeconomic Background in Southeast Asia." *Ambio* 17 (3): 200–06.

Pearce, David W. 1980. "The Social Incidence of Environmental Costs and Benefits." In Timothy O'Riordan and R. Kerry Turner, eds., *Progress in Resource Management and Environmental Planning.* Vol. 2. Chichester, Eng.: Wiley.

_____. 1986. *Cost-Benefit Analysis.* London: Macmillan.

_____. 1987. "Forest Policy in Indonesia." World Bank, Indonesia Department, Washington, D.C. Processed.

_____. 1989. "Economic Incentives and Renewable Natural Resource Management." In OECD, *Renewable Natural Resources: Economic Incentives for Improved Management.* Paris.

_____. 1990a. "Assessing the Returns to the Economy and to Society from Investment in Forestry." *Forestry Expansion.* Edinburgh, Scotland: Forestry Commission.

_____. 1990b. "Greenhouse Gas Agreements. Part 1: Internationally Tradeable Greenhouse Gas Permits." London Environmental Economics Centre, London. Processed.

_____. 1990c. "Public Policy and Environment in Mexico." World Bank, Latin America and Caribbean Country Department, Washington, D.C. Processed.

_____. 1991a. "Economics of the Environment." In David Greenaway, Michael Bleaney, and Ian Stewart, eds., *Economics in Perspective.* London: Routledge.

_____. 1991b. "New Environmental Policies: The Recent Experience of OECD Countries and Its Relevance to the Developing World." In Denizhan Erocal, ed., *Environmental Managers in Developing Countries.* Development Centre Series. Paris: OECD.

_____. 1991c. "The Role of Carbon Taxes in Adjusting to Global Warming." *Economic Journal* 101 (407): 938–48.

Pearce, David W., and Edward Barbier. 1990. "Thinking Economically about Climate Change." *Energy Policy* (January/February): 11–18.

Pearce, David W., Edward Barbier, and Anil Markandya. 1990. *Sustainable Development: Economics and Environment in the Third World.* London: Earthscan Publications.

Pearce, David W., and Anil Markandya. 1989. *The Benefits of Environmental Policy: Monetary Valuation.* Paris: OECD.

Pearce, David W., Anil Markandya, and Edward Barbier. 1989. *Blueprint for a Green Economy*. London: Earthscan Publications.

————. 1990. "Environmental Sustainability and Cost-Benefit Analysis." *Environment and Planning* 22: 1259–66.

Pearce, David W., and R. Kerry Turner. 1989. *Economics of Natural Resources and the Environment*. London: Harvester-Wheatsheaf.

Pearce, Fred. 1990. "Bolivian Indians March to Save Their Homeland." *New Scientist* 127 (August): 17.

Pearson, Charles S. 1987. "Environmental Standards, Industrial Relocation, and Pollution Havens." In Charles S. Pearson, ed., *Multinational Corporations, Environment, and the Third World*. Durham, N.C.: Duke University Press.

Perrings, Charles. 1987. *Economy and Environment*. New York: Cambridge University Press.

Peskin, Henry M. 1989. "Accounting for Natural Resource Depletion and Degradation in Developing Countries." Working Paper 13. World Bank, Environment Department, Washington, D.C. Processed.

Peters, Charles M., Alwyn H. Gentry, and Robert O. Mendelsohn. 1989. "Valuation of an Amazonian Rain Forest." *Nature* 339 (June): 655–56.

Pezzey, John. 1989. "Economic Analysis of Sustainable Growth and Sustainable Development." Working Paper 15. World Bank, Environment Department, Washington, D.C. Processed.

Picardi, A., and W. Seifert. 1976. "A Tragedy of the Commons in the Sahel." *Technology Review* (May): 42–51.

Pigou, Arthur. 1932. *The Economics of Welfare*. 4th ed. London: Macmillan.

Pingali, Prabhu L., and Hans Binswanger. 1984. "Population Density and Agricultural Intensification: A Study of the Evolution of Technologies in Tropical Agriculture." Report ARU 22. World Bank, Agriculture and Rural Development Department, Washington, D.C. Processed.

Plummer, Mark L. 1986. "Supply Uncertainty, Option Price, and Option Value." *Land Economics* 62: 313–18.

Plummer, Mark L., and Richard C. Hartman. 1986. "Option Value: A General Approach." *Economic Inquiry* 24: 455–71.

Poore, Duncan. 1989. *No Timber without Trees: Sustainability in the Tropical Forest*. London: Earthscan Publications.

Poore, Duncan, and others. 1988. "Natural Forest Management for Sustainable Timber Production." Report for the International Tropical Timber Organization. International Institute for Environment and Development, London. Processed.

Porter, Richard C. 1982. "The New Approach to Wilderness Preservation through Benefit-Cost Analysis." *Journal of Environmental Economics and Management* 9: 59–80.

Portney, Paul R. 1990. "Air Pollution Policy." *Public Policies for Environmental Protection*. Washington, D.C.: Resources for the Future.

Potvin, Joseph. 1989. *Economic-Environmental Accounts: A Conspectus on Current Developments*. Ottawa: Environment Canada.

Prince, Raymond. 1985. "A Note on Environmental Risk and the Rate of Discount: A Comment." *Journal of Environmental Economics and Management* 12: 179–80.

Principe, Peter. 1987. *The Economic Value of Biological Diversity among Medicinal Plants*. Paris: OECD.

Purseglove, John William. 1968. *Tropical Crops: Dictotyledons*. London: Longman.

Ramsay, W. J. 1986. "Erosion Problems in the Nepal Himalaya: An Overview." In Sharad Chandra Joshi, ed., *Nepal Himalaya: Geoecological Perspectives*. Naini Tal, India: Himalayan Research Group.

Randall, Alan. 1987. "Total Economic Value as a Basis for Policy." *Transactions of the American Fisheries Society* 116: 325–35.

_____. 1990. "Nonuse Benefits." Ohio State University, Columbus. Processed.

Rauscher, Michael. 1991. "Foreign Trade and the Environment." In Horst Siebert, ed., *Environmental Scarcity: The International Dimension*. Tubingen, Germany: J. C. Mohr.

Ray, Anandarup. 1984. *Cost-Benefit Analysis: Issues and Methodologies*. Baltimore, Md.: Johns Hopkins University Press.

Regan, Trevor. 1981. "The Nature and Possibility of an Environmental Ethic." *Environmental Ethics* 3: 19–34.

Reinstein, Robert. 1991. "Trade and Environment." U.S. State Department, Washington, D.C. Processed.

Repetto, Robert. 1985. *Paying the Price: Pesticide Subsidies in Developing Countries*. Washington, D.C.: World Resources Institute.

_____. 1986. *Skimming the Water: Rent Seeking and the Performance of Public Irrigation Systems*. Washington, D.C.: World Resources Institute.

_____. 1987. "Population, Resources, Environment: An Uncertain Future." *Population Bulletin* 42 (2).

_____. 1988a. "Economic Policy Reform for Natural Resource Conservation." Working Paper 4. World Bank, Environment Department, Washington, D.C. Processed.

_____. 1988b. *The Forest for the Trees? Government Policies and the Misuse of Forest Resources*. Washington, D.C.: World Resources Institute.

_____. 1988c. "Overview." In Robert Repetto and Malcolm Gillis, eds., *Public Policies and the Misuse of Forest Resources*. Cambridge, Eng.: Cambridge University Press.

_____. 1989. "Economic Incentives for Sustainable Production." In Gunter Schramm and Jeremy Warford, eds., *Environmental Management and Economic Development*. Baltimore, Md.: Johns Hopkins University Press.

_____. 1990. "Deforestation in the Tropics." *Scientific American* 262 (4): 36–42.

Repetto, Robert, and Malcolm Gillis, eds. 1988. *Public Policies and the Misuse of Forest Resources*. Cambridge, Eng.: Cambridge University Press.

Repetto, Robert, and Thomas Holmes. 1983. "The Role of Population in Resource Depletion in Developing Countries." *Population and Development Review* 9 (4): 609–32.

Repetto, Robert, and others. 1989. *Wasting Assets: Natural Resources in the National Income Accounts*. Washington, D.C.: World Resources Institute.

Ringrose, Susan, and W. Matheson. 1986. "Desertification in Botswana: Progress towards a Viable Monitoring System." *Desertification Control Bulletin* 13: 6–11.

Robinson, H. David. 1988. "Industrial Pollution Abatement: The Impact on the Balance of Trade." *Canadian Journal of Economics* 21 (1): 187–200.

Ruitenbeek, H. Jack. 1989. *Social Cost-Benefit Analysis of the Korup Project, Cameroon.* London: Worldwide Fund for Nature.

Runge, Carlisle Ford. 1981. "Common Property Externalities: Isolation, Assurance, and Resource Depletion in a Traditional Grazing Context." *American Journal of Agricultural Economics* 63: 595–606.

_____. 1982. "Reply." *American Journal of Agricultural Economics* 64: 785–87.

"Russia's Greens." 1989. *The Economist* 313 (7627, November): 27–28, 34.

Ruthenberg, Hans. 1980. *Farming Systems in the Tropics.* 3d ed. Oxford: Clarendon Press.

Salati, Eneas, and others. 1979. "Recycling of Water in the Amazon Basin: An Isotopic Study." *Water Resources Research* 15: 1250–58.

Samples, Karl C., Marcia Gowen, and John Dixon. 1986. "The Validity of the Contingent Valuation Method for Estimating Non-Use Components of Preservation Values for Unique Natural Resources." Paper presented to a meeting of the American Agricultural Economics Association, Reno, Nevada. Processed.

Schelling, Thomas C., ed. 1983. *Incentives for Environmental Protection.* Cambridge, Mass.: MIT Press.

Schneider, Gunther, and others. 1989. *Task Force: Environment and the Internal Market.* Brussels, Belgium: Commission of the European Communities.

Schramm, Gunter, and Jeremy Warford, eds. 1989. *Environmental Management and Economic Development.* Baltimore, Md.: Johns Hopkins University Press.

Schuh, G. E. 1990. "International Economic Policies and Sustainable Development." Paper presented at the United Nations Economic Commission for Europe and U.S. Environmental Protection Agency Workshop on Sustainable Development, Washington, D.C. Processed.

Schulz, Werner. 1986. "A Survey on the Status of Research Concerning the Benefits of Environmental Policy in the Federal Republic of Germany." Paper presented at the workshop The Benefits of Environmental Policy and Decision-making, OECD, Avignon, France. Processed.

Schulze, William D., and others. 1983. "Economic Benefits of Preserving Visibility in the National Parklands of the Southwest." *Natural Resources Journal* 23: 149–73.

Sebastian, Iona, and Adelaida Alicbusan. 1989. "Sustainable Development: Issues in Adjustment Lending Policies." Divisional Paper 1986-9. World Bank, Environment Department, Washington, D.C. Processed.

Sedjo, Roger. 1987a. "The Economics of Natural and Plantation Forests in Indonesia." Resources for the Future, Washington, D.C. Processed.

_____. 1987b. "Incentives and Distortions in Indonesian Forest Policy." Resources for the Future, Washington, D.C. Processed.

_____. 1989. "Forests to Offset the Greenhouse Effect." *Journal of Forestry* 87: 12–14.

Sen, Amartya. 1967. "Isolation, Assurance, and the Social Rate of Discount." *Quarterly Journal of Economics* 81: 112–24.

_____. 1981. *Poverty and Famine: An Essay on Entitlement and Deprivation.* Oxford: Oxford University Press.

_____. 1982. "Approaches to the Choice of Discount Rates for Social Benefit-Cost Analysis." In Robert C. Lind., ed., *Discounting for Time and Risk in Energy Policy.* Washington, D.C.: Resources for the Future.

Shoven, John B., and John Whalley. 1984. "Applied General Equilibrium Models of Taxation and International Trade: An Introduction and Survey." *Journal of Economic Literature* 22: 1007–51.

Shrybman, Steven. 1990. "International Trade and the Environment: An Environmental Assessment of the General Agreement on Tariffs and Trade." *The Ecologist* 20 (1): 30–34.

Siebert, Horst. 1985. "Spatial Aspects of Environmental Economics." In A. Kneese and J. Sweeney, eds., *Handbook of Natural Resource and Energy Economics.* Vol. 1. Amsterdam, Netherlands: North Holland.

Siebert, Horst, and others. 1980. *Trade and the Environment: A Theoretical Enquiry.* Amsterdam, Netherlands: Elsevier.

Simon, Julian Lincoln. 1986. *Theory of Population and Economic Growth.* New York: Blackwell.

Singh, M. M. 1989. "Who Flooded Bangladesh?" UNDP *World Development* 2 (3).

Smith, Kirk R. 1987. *Biofuels, Air Pollution, and Health: A Global Review.* New York: Plenum Publishing Corp.

_____. 1988a. "Air Pollution: Assessing Total Exposure in Developing Countries." *Environment* 30 (10): 16–20, 28–35.

_____. 1988b. "Air Pollution: Assessing Total Exposure in the United States." *Environment* 30 (8): 10–15.

Smith, V. Kerry. 1987. "Nonuse Values in Benefit Cost Analysis." *Southern Economic Journal* 54: 19–26.

Smith, V. Kerry, and William H. Desvousges. 1986. *Measuring Water Quality Benefits.* Boston, Mass.: Kluwer-Nijhof.

Snape, Richard. 1991. "International Regulation of Subsidies." *World Economy* 14 (2): 139–64.

Solow, Robert. 1986. "On the Intergenerational Allocation of Natural Resources." *Scandinavian Journal of Economics* 88 (1): 141–49.

Sorsa, Piritta. 1992. "Environment: A New Challenge for GATT." Background paper prepared for *World Development Report 1992.* World Bank, Washington, D.C. Processed.

Southgate, Douglas Dewitt. 1988. "The Economics of Land Degradation in the Third World." Working Paper 2. World Bank, Environment Department, Washington, D.C. Processed.

_____. 1989. "How to Promote Tropical Deforestation: The Case of Ecuador."

Ohio State University, Department of Agricultural Economics and Rural Sociology, Columbus. Processed.

Southgate, Douglas Dewitt, Rodrigo Sierra, and Lawrence A. Brown. 1989. "The Causes of Tropical Deforestation in Ecuador: A Statistical Analysis." Paper 89-09. London Environmental Economics Centre, London. Processed.

Spence, Andrew Michael. 1973. "Blue Whales and Applied Control Theory." Technical Report 108. Stanford University, Institute for Mathematical Studies in the Social Sciences, Stanford, Calif. Processed.

Squire, Lyn, and Herman G. van der Tak. 1975. *Economic Analysis of Projects.* Baltimore, Md.: Johns Hopkins University Press.

Steeds, David R. 1985. *Desertification in the Sahelian and Sudanian Zones of West Africa.* Washington, D.C.: World Bank.

Steiner, H. 1990. "Markets and Law: The Case of Environmental Conservation." Manchester Polytechnic, Manchester, Eng.

Stewart, John Massey. 1990. "The Great Lake Is in Great Peril." *New Scientist* 126 (1723, June): 58–62.

Stocking, Michael. 1986. *The Cost of Soil Erosion in Zimbabwe in Terms of the Loss of Three Major Nutrients.* Rome: FAO, Soil Conservation Programme, Land and Water Development Division.

Stoll, John R., and L. Johnson. 1984. "Concepts of Value, Non-Market Valuation, and the Case of the Whooping Crane." *Transactions of the North American Wildlife and Natural Resources Conference* 49: 382–93.

Sutherland, Ronald J., and Richard G. Walsh. 1985. "Effects of Distance on the Preservation Value of Water Quality." *Land Economics* 61: 281–91.

Symons, Elizabeth, John Proops, and Philip Gay. 1990. "Carbon Taxes, Consumer Demand, and Carbon Dioxide Emission: A Simulation Analysis for the UK." University of Keele, Department of Economics, Keele, Eng. Processed.

Theys, Jacques. 1989. "Environmental Accounting in Development Policy: The French Experience." In Yusuf Ahmad, Salah El Serafy, and Ernst Lutz, eds., *Environmental Accounting for Sustainable Development.* Washington, D.C.: World Bank.

Thomas, D., F. Ayache, and T. Hollis. 1989. "Use Values and Non-Use Values in the Conservation of Ichkeul National Park, Tunisia." University College London, Department of Geography. Processed.

Thompson, Michael, M. Warburton, and T. Hatley. 1986. *Uncertainty on a Himalayan Scale.* London: Milton Ash Editions.

Tietenberg, Thomas. 1985. *Emissions Trading.* Baltimore, Md.: Johns Hopkins University Press.

——. 1988. *Environmental and Natural Resource Economics.* 2d ed. Glenview, Ill.: Foresman and Company.

——. 1990. "Economic Instruments for Environmental Regulations." *Oxford Review of Economic Policy* 6 (1): 17–34.

Tobey, James A. 1990. "The Effects of Domestic Environmental Policies on Patterns of World Trade: An Empirical Test." *Kyklos* 43 (2): 191–209.

Turner, Jan, and J. Brooke, 1988. "A Cost-Benefit Analysis of the Aldeburgh Sea

Defence Scheme." Environmental Appraisal Group, University of East Anglia. Processed.

United Kingdom, Department of Energy. 1989. *An Evaluation of Energy-Related Greenhouse Gas Emissions and Measures to Ameliorate Them.* Energy Paper 58. London: HMSO.

United Nations Centre for Human Settlements. 1987. *Global Report on Human Settlements, 1986.* New York: Oxford University Press.

United Nations Conference on Trade and Development. 1984. *International Tropical Timber Agreement 1983.* TD/Timber/11/Rev.2. Geneva.

United Nations Environment Programme. 1987. *Environmental Data Report.* Oxford: Blackwell.

———. 1990. *Environmental Data Report.* 2d ed. Cambridge, Mass.: Blackwell.

U.S. Congressional Budget Office. 1989. *Reducing the Deficit: Spending and Revenue Options.* Washington, D.C.

U.S. Department of Energy. 1990. "The Economics of Long-Term Global Climate Change: A Preliminary Assessment." Report of an interagency task force. National Technical Information Service, Springfield, Va. Processed.

van Amstel, A., and others. 1986. *Tapioca from Thailand for the Dutch Livestock Industry.* Amsterdam, Netherlands: Free University of Amsterdam, Institute for Environmental Studies.

Varian, Hal R. 1987. *Intermediate Microeconomics.* New York: W. W. Norton.

Veenendaal, Elmar M., and Johannes B. Opschoor. 1986. *Botswana's Beef Exports to the EEC: Economic Development at the Expense of a Deteriorating Environment.* Amsterdam, Netherlands: Free University of Amsterdam, Institute for Environmental Studies.

Veloz, Alberto, and others. 1985. "The Economics of Erosion Control in a Subtropical Watershed: A Dominican Case." *Land Economics* 61 (2): 145–55.

Viscusi, W. Kip. 1986. "Valuation of Risks to Life and Health: Guidelines for Policy Analysis." In Judith Bentkover and others, eds., *Benefits Assessment: The State of the Art.* Dordrecht, Netherlands: D. Reidel Publishing Company.

Vitousek, Peter, and others. 1986. "Human Appropriation of the Products of Photosynthesis." *Bioscience* 34 (6): 368–73.

Wade, R. 1987. "The Management of Common Property Resources: Finding a Cooperative Solution." *World Bank Research Observer* 2 (2): 219–34.

Walsh, John. 1987. "Bolivia Swaps Debt for Conservation." *Science* 237 (August): 596–97.

Walsh, Julia A., and Kenneth S. Warren. 1979. "Selective Primary Health Care: An Interim Strategy for Disease Control in Developing Countries." *New England Journal of Medicine* 301 (18): 967–74.

Walsh, Richard G., John B. Loomis, and Richard A. Gillman. 1984. "Valuing Option, Existence, and Bequest Demands for Wilderness." *Land Economics* 60: 14–29.

Walter, Ingo. 1973. "The Pollution Content of American Trade." *Western Economic Journal* 11: 61–70.

_____. 1982. "International Economic Repercussions of Environmental Policy: An Economist's Perspective." In Seymour Rubin and Thomas Graham, eds., *Environment and Trade: The Relation of International Trade and Environmental Policy.* Totowa, N.J.: Allanheld, Osmun.

Walter, Jörg, and Robert U. Ayres. 1990. "Global Warming: Damages and Costs." International Institute for Applied Systems Analysis, Laxenberg, Austria. Processed.

Warford, Jeremy. 1987. *Environment, Growth, and Development.* Development Committee Paper 14. Washington, D.C.: World Bank and International Monetary Fund.

Warford, Jeremy, and Zeinab Partow. 1989. *World Bank Support for the Environment: A Progress Report.* Development Committee Paper 22. Washington, D.C.: World Bank and International Monetary Fund.

Weil, Diana E., and others. 1990. *The Impact of Development Policies on Health: A Review of the Literature.* Geneva, Switzerland: WHO.

Weisbrod, Burton. 1964. "Collective Consumption Services of Individual Consumption Goods." *Quarterly Journal of Economics* 78: 471–77.

Whalley, John, and Randall Wigle. 1989. "Cutting CO_2 Emissions: The Effects of Alternative Policy Approaches." University of Western Ontario, Department of Economics, London, Ontario, and Wilfrid Laurier University, Department of Economics, Waterloo, Ontario, Canada. Processed.

_____. 1991. "The International Incidence of Carbon Taxes." In Rudiger Dornbusch and James Poterba, eds., *Economic Policy Responses to Global Warming.* Cambridge, Mass.: MIT Press.

Whitmore, Timothy Charles. 1990. *An Introduction to Tropical Rain Forests.* Oxford: Clarendon Press.

Whittington, Dale, Donald T. Lauria, and Xinming Mu. 1989. "Paying for Urban Services: A Study of Water Vending and Willingness to Pay for Water in Onitsha, Nigeria." World Bank, Infrastructure and Urban Development Department, Washington, D.C. Processed.

Whittington, Dale, Xinming Mu, and Robert Roche. 1990. "Calculating the Value of Time Spent Collecting Water: Some Estimates for Ukundu, Kenya." *World Development* 18 (2): 269–80.

Whittington, Dale, and others. 1989. "Water Vending Activities in Developing Countries." *Water Resources Development* 5 (3): 158–68.

_____. 1990. "Estimating the Willingness to Pay for Water Services in Developing Countries: A Case Study of the Use of Contingent Valuation Surveys in Southern Haiti." *Economic Development and Cultural Change.*

Wilczynski, Piotr. 1990. "Czechoslovakia: Environmental Economics and Finance." World Bank, Infrastructure Operations Division, Europe, Middle East, and North Africa Department, Washington, D.C. Processed.

Wilen, James. 1976. "Common Property Resources and the Dynamics of Overexploitation: The Case of the North Pacific Fur Seal." Resources Paper 3. University of British Columbia, Vancouver, Canada. Processed.

Williams, Robert H. 1989. "Low-Cost Strategies for Coping with CO_2 Emission Limits." Princeton University, Center for Energy and Environmental Studies. Processed.

Willis, Kenneth G., and John Benson. 1988. "Valuation of Wildlife: A Case Study on the Upper Teesdale Site of Special Scientific Interest and Comparison of Methods in Environmental Economics." In R. Kerry Turner, ed., *Sustainable Environmental Management: Principles and Practice*. London: Belhaven Press.

Woodwell, George. 1985. "On the Limits of Nature." In Robert Repetto, ed., *The Global Possible*. New Haven, Conn.: Yale University Press.

World Bank. 1980. *World Development Report 1980*. New York: Oxford University Press.

_____. 1984. *World Development Report 1984*. New York: Oxford University Press.

_____. 1986a. *Commodity Trade and Price Trends*. Baltimore, Md.: Johns Hopkins University Press.

_____. 1986b. *Population Growth and Policies in Sub-Saharan Africa*. Washington, D.C.

_____. 1986c. *Poverty and Hunger: Issues and Options for Food Security in Developing Countries*. Washington, D.C.

_____. 1987. *World Development Report 1987*. New York: Oxford University Press.

_____. 1988. "Madagascar: Environmental Action Plan." Environment Division, Technical Department, Africa Region, Washington, D.C. Processed.

_____. 1989. *Social Indicators of Development 1989*. Baltimore, Md.: Johns Hopkins University Press.

_____. 1990a. "Hungary: Environmental Issues." Environment Division, Technical Department, EMENA, Washington, D.C. Processed.

_____. 1990b. "Toward the Development of an Environmental Action Plan for Nigeria." Washington, D.C. Processed.

_____. 1990c. *World Development Report 1990*. New York: Oxford University Press.

_____. 1991a. "Malawi: Economic Report on Environmental Policy." 2 vols. Washington, D.C. Processed.

_____. 1991b. *World Development Report 1991*. New York: Oxford University Press.

_____. 1992. *World Development Report 1992*. New York: Oxford University Press.

World Bank and European Investment Bank. 1990. *The Environmental Program for the Mediterranean: Preserving a Shared Heritage and Managing a Common Resource*. Washington, D.C.

World Bank and United Nations Development Programme. 1989. "Energy Efficiency Strategy for Developing Countries: The Role of ESMAP." Energy Department, Washington, D.C. Processed.

World Commission on Environment and Development. 1987. *Our Common Future*. Oxford: Oxford University Press.

World Health Organization 1984. *Urban Air Pollution 1973–80*. Geneva.

World Resources Institute. 1985. *Paying the Price: Pesticide Subsidies in Developing Countries*. Washington, D.C.

_____. 1988. *World Resources 1988–89.* New York: Basic Books.

_____. 1990. *World Resources 1990–91.* Oxford: Oxford University Press.

_____. 1991. *Costs of Resource Degradation in Costa Rica.* Washington, D.C.

_____. 1992. *World Resources 1992–93: A Guide to the Global Environment.* New York: Oxford University Press.

World Wildlife Fund. 1988. "WWF Debt-for-Nature Swap." *World Wildlife Fund Letter* 1.

Yezer, Anthony M. J., and A. Philipson. 1974. "Influence of Environmental Considerations on Agriculture and Industrial Decisions to Locate Outside of the Continental U.S." U.S. Council on Environmental Quality, Public Interest Economic Center, Washington, D.C. Processed.

Young, Euan C. 1989. "Ecology and Conservation of the Polar Regions." *Ambio* 18 (1): 23–33.

Credits for photographs

Index

Abatement costs, 312, 341, 348

Accounting rate of interest, 68

Acid rain, 55; composition of, 328–29; international agreements on, 329, 331, 332; international externality and, 328; as production externality, 306–7; side payments and, 332; transfrontier pollution and, 327; transport model and, 331

Adirondack Mountains (New York), 329

Adriatic Sea, 333, 334

Afforestation: discounting and, 66; economic valuation and, 100; in Nigeria, 58; as policy response, 276; for sequestering carbon, 130

Africa: agricultural bias in, 153–54; commodity trade in, 282, 288, 291; consumption rates in, 71; population growth in, 151, 152–54; price discrimination in, 34; resource degradation in, 22–24, 38 n5; role of women in, 154, 270; tourism in, 288–89; traditional tenure rights in, 254. *See also individual countries*

Africa, Sub-Saharan: birth rates in, 171; mortality rates in, 152–53; negative growth in, 263; rate of agricultural growth in, 158–59

Agreement on Technical Barriers to Trade. *See* Standards Code (GATT)

Agricultural subsidies, 319–20

Agricultural systems, 191; and deforestation, 184–85, 187, 286–87; donor agency influence on, 319; in Eastern Europe, 220; fallow periods in, 159, 160, 161, 254; global warming and, 367–68; growth of, 149–150, 158, 165, 184–185; and industrial world's protectionism, 296–97; input taxes in, 208–9; population growth and, 149–50, 159; pricing output of, 189; productivity of, 160, 161, 276; and transition to intensive use, 159

Agroforestry, 287–88

Air pollution: central planning systems and, 220; in Eastern Europe, 221, 222, 224, 226–27; from energy usage, 220–21; forest losses from, 221–22, 329; health damage in U.S. and, 136; in Mediterranean basin, 337; in Mexico,

427

The complete backlist of publications from the World Bank is shown in the annual *Index of Publications*, which contains an alphabetical title list and indexes of subjects, authors, and countries and regions. The latest edition is available free of charge from the Distribution Unit, Office the Publisher, The World Bank, 1818 H Street, N.W., Washington, D.C. 20433, or from Publications, The World Bank, 66, avenue d'Iéna, 75116 Paris, France.